No Child Left Behind
and the Reduction of
the Achievement Gap

No Child Left Behind

and the Reduction of
the Achievement Gap

Sociological Perspectives on Federal Educational Policy

Edited by **Alan R. Sadovnik**
Jennifer A. O'Day
George W. Bohrnstedt
Kathryn M. Borman

Routledge
Taylor & Francis Group
New York   London

Routledge
Taylor & Francis Group
270 Madison Avenue
New York, NY 10016

Routledge
Taylor & Francis Group
2 Park Square
Milton Park, Abingdon
Oxon OX14 4RN

© 2008 by Taylor & Francis Group, LLC
Routledge is an imprint of Taylor & Francis Group, an Informa business

Printed in the United States of America on acid-free paper
10 9 8 7 6 5 4 3 2 1

International Standard Book Number-13: 978-0-415-95531-7 (Softcover) 978-0-415-95530-0 (Hardcover)

Visit the Taylor & Francis Web site at
http://www.taylorandfrancis.com

and the Routledge Web site at
http://www.routledge.com

This book is dedicated to Ruth Sadovnik, Alan R. Sadovnik's mother, whose death on February 26, 2007 prevented her from seeing its completion. Ruth Sadovnik left Berlin in 1939 at the age of 11 on the Kindertransport and lived in England from 1939–1945. She was reunited with her parents and sister in New York City in 1945. For the remainder of her life, she was a civic and community leader dedicated to social justice. Her commitment to education for all children is reflected in the chapters in this book.

Contents

Acknowledgments

The conferences that generated most of the chapters in this book, as well the book's preparation and production, would not have been possible without two generous grants from the American Institutes for Research (AIR).

The editors thank the American Sociological Association's Section on the Sociology of Education for sponsoring these two conferences at the Association's annual meetings in 2005 and 2006.

A number of individuals at Rutgers-Newark provided essential administrative support for the conferences and the production of this book. LaChone McKenzie expertly managed the AIR grants. Ralph Schaefer, an undergraduate summer intern from Princeton University, read and commented on all the chapters. A number of graduate assistants in the Urban Educational Policy Ph.D. Program, including Tara Davidson, Paula Gordon, Elizabeth Morrison and Yanique Taylor provided administrative and proofreading assistance.

At Routledge, our editor Catherine Bernard provided substantive advice that enabled us to successfully edit the manuscript down to an acceptable length. Heather Jarrow, the editorial assistant in education, provided important administrative support. Lynn Goeller supervised the production process effectively and efficiently.

Preface

This book presents a sociological analysis of federal educational policy, focusing especially on No Child Left Behind (NCLB), and whether it can or will accomplish its major goal: to eliminate the achievement gap by 2014. Based on theoretical and empirical research, the chapters examine the history of federal educational policy and place NCLB in a larger sociological and historical context, as well as a number of policy areas affected by the law, including accountability and assessment, curriculum and instruction, teacher quality, parental involvement, and school choice. The book concludes with a discussion of the important contributions of sociological research and sociological analysis to understanding the limits and possibilities of the law to reduce the achievement gap by 2014.

Given the importance of NCLB, it is imperative that legislators, policymakers, educators, and parents have objective, data-driven, theoretical, and nonideological information and analyses to guide decision making and policy debates. Unfortunately, the discussion of NCLB has too often been ideological, rhetorical, and lacking in data about the law and its effect.

As a discipline, sociology has much to say about key concerns of No Child Left Behind: accountability and assessment, instructional improvement, teacher quality, recruitment and professional development, parental involvement, and school choice. However, the discourse on NCLB has been dominated by educational psychology and economics, with insufficient regard to the issues of stratification processes, organizational dynamics, and institutional structure that our discipline would illuminate.

Much of the public debate about NCLB has been political and ideological with little light shed on the effects of the law on the organizational contexts of schools. Within these contexts, sociological analyses examine the effects of NCLB on different groups of students and schools and the ways in which school organization and structure affect achievement. Further, sociologists of education provide much needed data-driven analyses of the law's components and their effects on children, teachers, parents, and schools. Finally, sociological analysis provides an understanding of how the organizational and interactional processes within schools may change to respond to the specific mandates of the law.

There were two conferences on No Child Left Behind at the 2004 and 2005 American Sociological Association Annual Meetings, sponsored by the Sociology of Education Section of ASA and supported by grants from the American Institutes for Research, thus continuing the section's long and rich tradition of holding conferences on important policy issues and then publishing a book on the subjects discussed.

These conferences on NCLB and this book would not be possible without the generous financial support of the American Institutes for Research and the support of Kevin Dougherty and James Rosenbaum, the chairs of the section in 2004 and 2005 and Laura Salganik of AIR. The idea for the first mini-conference was Kevin Dougherty's, and James Rosenbaum supported the idea of a second conference. The organizers of both conferences included Alan R. Sadovnik, Kathryn M. Borman, Kevin Dougherty, James Rosenbaum, and Laura Salganik.

The presenters at one or both conferences included Christopher Cross, Russlynn Ali, Robert Copeland, James Nevels, Alan R. Sadovnik, Kathryn Borman, Kevin Dougherty, Tamela McNulty Eitle, Douglas B. Downey, Paul T. von Hippel and Melanie Hughes, Christopher B. Swanson, Barbara Schneider, John Robert Warren, Eric S. Grodsky, Jennifer C. Lee, University of Minnesota, and Rachael B. Kulick, Kathryn Schiller, and Chandra Muller, Laura Salganik, Jennifer Booher-Jennings and Andrew Beveridge, Gary Dworkin and John Lorence, Katie Weitz White and James Rosenbaum, Thomas Smith Joyce L. Epstein, Steven B. Sheldon, Timothy Madigan, Maureen Hallinan, Richard Ingersoll, Joan Talbert, Janelle Scott, Kimberly Scott, Jamie Lew, Douglas Lauen, Roslyn Mickelson and Stephanie Southworth, David Karen, Elizabeth Useem, Jeanne Powers and Carl Hermanns, Adam Gamoran, David Armor, Mary Metz, Rachel Pereira, David Levinson, and Susan Semel.

The first conference was held in San Francisco on Tuesday, August 17, 2004 on the last day of the ASA meetings and it attracted over 90 participants.

The presentations provided the basis for a "Perspective" section of the journal *Sociology of Education,* which was published in April 2005. The essays were:

1. "Overview Essay: Sociological Analysis of Federal Involvement and NCLB," David Karen, Bryn Mawr College
2. "Accountability and Assessment," Gary Dworkin, University of Houston
3. "High Quality Teachers," Richard Ingersoll, University of Pennsylvania
4. "Parental Involvement," Joyce Epstein, Johns Hopkins University

The second Sociology of Education/NCLB conference was held in Philadelphia on August 12, 2005 on the day before the ASA meetings, and it was attended by 125 sociologists. This book includes substantive revisions of a number of papers and discussions presented at the 2005 conference. All of the papers have benefited greatly from the discussions at both conferences.

As editors, we were fortunate to have such high quality papers from which to choose. The chapters in this book demonstrate the importance of sociological analysis for understanding educational policy, and we hope they will provide evidence for the upcoming debates on the reauthorization of the law.

Introduction

George W. Bohrnstedt and Jennifer A. O'Day

The year is 2007—five years since the landmark No Child Left Behind Act (NCLB) became law and the year when reauthorization talks begin in earnest. The purpose of this volume is to contribute to those discussions, as well as to ongoing implementation efforts in the field, by bringing the insights of sociological theory and research to bear on the design and implementation of the Elementary and Secondary Education Act (ESEA), of which NCLB is but the latest iteration.

HISTORY AND BACKGROUND OF NCLB

Since Lyndon Johnson signed the first Elementary and Secondary Education Act in 1965, the lion's share of federal funding for K–12 education has been directed toward improving educational opportunities for poor and low-achieving students in the nation's schools. From its inception, aspirations for ESEA have been high, as exemplified by Johnson's promise that "...every one of the billion dollars that we spend on this program, will come back tenfold as school dropouts change to school graduates." Although Johnson's promise has not been realized, federal efforts have persisted. ESEA has been reauthorized six times, each iteration attempting to rectify the shortcomings of its predecessors.

Under the first four reauthorizations, ESEA primarily provided supplementary services to poor and low-achieving children under Title I/Chapter 1 of the law. With Improving America's Schools Act of 1994 (IASA), however, the scope of ESEA broadened. Following on the heels of the Goals 2000 Act, which provided funds for the voluntary creation of state content and performance standards, IASA *required* such standards and aligned assessments for students served by the act. Because the standards for Title I students had to be the same as for all other students in the state, the 1994 reauthorized ESEA was essentially leveraging

1

the federal government's seven percent contribution to K–12 spending to spark standards-based reform throughout the states.

By the time NCLB came along in late 2001, standards-based reform had become a bulwark of state education policy. NCLB incorporated many of the standards-based principles in the 1994 reauthorization, but propelled the law's reach further into the classroom by instituting a specified timeline for improvement and by ratcheting up accountability criteria and consequences. Under NCLB, not only do schools need to demonstrate progress in student achievement, but states, districts, and schools are required to ensure that *all* students in their charge are proficient in reading and mathematics by the end of the 2013–14 school year.

The linchpin of NCLB's accountability component, called annual yearly progress (AYP) is based primarily on annual state assessments in grades 3 through 8 and on high-school tests and graduation rates. Virtually all students are expected to participate in these assessments, and jurisdictions and schools must demonstrate AYP for all subgroups of sufficient size to allow for reliable test score disaggregation. Schools and districts that do not make their AYP targets for two years running will be "identified for improvement" and face increasingly severe consequences if that improvement is not forthcoming. NCLB also required that by 2006 all children should be taught by "highly qualified" teachers in their core subjects and that children in schools identified for improvement be provided with supplemental educational services or the option to attend another, higher performing school in the district.

To ensure compliance, NCLB couples these requirements with real teeth—that is, with the threat of removal of Title I funds, on which many high-need jurisdictions have become dependent.

SOCIOLOGY AND NCLB

The provisions of this five-year-old federal law provide fertile ground for sociological inquiry and comment, as demonstrated by the chapters in this volume. While some of the chapters tackle technical issues, such as strategies for defining and measuring graduation rates or advantages of growth models to assess AYP, others address more macroconcerns related to the historic and current promise of ESEA to redress social inequalities and foster universal attainment of high academic standards.

In particular, the 12-year timeline to 100 percent proficiency (2002–14), coupled with the high stakes placed on schools and districts for meeting this timeline, has rekindled long-standing sociological debate over schools' comparative contribution to student achievement and attainment. This debate has raged in varying forms since James Coleman and his associates (Coleman et al. 1966) showed that services for children in poverty—including the quality of teachers, facilities, and other resources—had only small effects on student achievement.

Other factors such as the child's socioeconomic status (SES) and especially the average SES of children in the school have been shown to have larger effects on student performance. These findings called into question just how much schools, in and of themselves, can be expected to do in the improvement of student achievement. While none of the authors in this volume suggests that states and districts not be expected to provide effective schools for all their children, sociological analyses remind us of the importance of addressing structural and cultural factors as well, including both those inside and those outside schools. Indeed, if such factors are not addressed, some authors question whether NCLB in the long run might not perpetuate rather than relieve persistent inequalities and achievement gaps among groups of students.

While some authors focus on technical questions and others on macro patterns of social inequality, several authors use case studies and other methodologies to delve further into the conditions under which NCLB or similar accountability policies might produce measurable and sustainable progress in schools. Indeed, a central thesis of this volume is that sociological theory and analyses can provide important understandings of how the implementation of NCLB plays out in real schools and can suggest strategies to help meet the lofty goals of the law. Examples include:

- Understanding how schools operate as formal organizations and the interplay of policy, normative structures, and organizational and individual capacities
- Understanding how districts operate as social systems and the ways in which they facilitate or hinder progress at the school level
- Understanding the role of teaching as a profession and examining the potential contribution of professional forms of accountability and of communities of practice to the goal of ensuring high quality teachers and teaching
- Understanding the effects of labeling on the ability of schools to attract and retain administrators, teachers, and students
- Understanding how supposedly rational incentives built into the law can lead to unintended consequences

The reauthorization debate provides an opportunity for sociologists, using evidence-based approaches, to suggest changes that can help NCLB meet the laudable goal of ensuring that all children perform at high levels of achievement.

The chapters in this volume, which grew out of a series of meetings held at the American Sociological Association in 2004 and 2005, explore these and related issues. At the time of these meetings, NCLB was in its infancy and little research had yet been completed on its implementation or effects. Yet sociologists had long been studying issues of educational equity, accountability, teacher quality, and choice, all of which lay at the core of NCLB's provisions. In addition, a number of states and districts had already instituted policies that closely resembled the recently reauthorized ESEA, and there were ample lessons and evidence on which to draw.

ORGANIZATION AND OVERVIEW OF THE CHAPTERS

This book is organized into five sections: "Federal and State Education Policy and NCLB"; "Accountability and Assessment"; "Teaching and Teacher Quality"; "School Choice and Parental Involvement"; and "Federal Involvement, NCLB, and the Reduction of the Achievement Gap."

Federal and State Educational Policy

In the first chapter in the volume, David Karen lays out the history leading up to NCLB, the current version of ESEA, and the provisions in the law itself. He then expands on the macroconcerns discussed above, arguing that the law has ignored some fundamental understandings that sociologists have about the influence of inequality and discrimination on academic achievement. He concludes by suggesting ways in which the work of sociologists can help the law as it comes up for reauthorization.

Accountability and Assessment

The second section of the book, "Accountability and Assessment," gets into the heart of NCLB.

In the first chapter, Jennifer A. O'Day addresses the conditions under which school-based accountability policies such as NCLB are likely to contribute to significant and sustainable school improvement. Drawing on sociological theories of organizational complexity and organizational learning, she explores the utility and limitation of external, bureaucratically based approaches to accountability. Using examples from her research in Chicago public schools, she argues that while policies such as NCLB are successful in drawing attention to low performing schools and possibly in allocating resources for improvement, they are inadequate for helping educators discern the causes of low performance, for motivating movement away from the dysfunctional normative structures common in low performing schools, or for building the capacity needed to sustain improvement. She goes on to argue for a combination of administrative (bureaucratic) accountability with professional accountability; that is, with accountability that focuses on a model of expertise brought by professionals to the workplace, and on standards of practice that are defined and enforced by those in the profession.

In the second chapter in this section, Christopher Swanson moves the focus to a key feature of high school accountability under NCLB—graduation rates. The chapter begins with a discussion of what he calls the nation's best kept secret—the crisis in high school graduation rates, including their variation from state to state and the fact that some states are graduating fewer than 60 percent of their students. He argues that the NCLB definition of graduation rates is so vague that it provides little guidance to states as to how to measure graduation or how to show progress in raising it. He then reviews various ways in which graduation rates can be computed and shows how this variation in methodology can lead to substantially different conclusions about how a state is doing. Under NCLB, states retain the right to choose the method they use to compute graduation rates, whether to establish target levels of graduation rates or to use a growth criterion, and whether or not to break out results by relevant subgroups. Using national school and district data to simulate results for the various states and assuming the use of target rates on the one hand and desegregation of results into relevant subgroups on the other, Swanson demonstrates that these choices produce dramatic differences in calculated rates. He concludes with a set of principles that Congress might draw upon as it considers "midcourse corrections" when NCLB is reauthorized.

While NCLB requires virtually all students to be tested in grades 3 through 8, the law does allow certain testing exemptions for some students with disabilities and some English language learners. In the third chapter in this section, Jennifer Booher-Jenkins and Andrew Beveridge examine the effects of these exemptions on whether schools make AYP or not and whether schools or districts might "game" the accountability systems by deciding who gets tested and who does not. The data for their chapter come from Houston, Texas, and are especially relevant for NCLB because the Texas Accountability System (TAS) was in many ways a prototype for the federal law. The chapter shows how the decision to exempt or test certain students can have substantial effects on whether schools are classified as having made AYP or not. The authors conclude with a discussion of the importance of these issues for NCLB especially in terms of the amount of flexibility schools and districts are given for deciding who should or should not be tested.

The final accountability chapter moves into the classroom, examining teachers' classroom behavior in the context of high stakes accountability. Using classroom observational data from a Chicago school with a high proportion of disadvantaged students, Katie Weitz White and James Rosenbaum explore three important questions related to high stakes accountability: (1) how students are labeled and responded to as a result of the accountability provisions; (2) whether being in an identified school changes how and what teachers teach; and (3) how teachers in such circumstances view themselves as teachers. Based on the data from this school, the authors conclude that NCLB is likely having substantial negative effects in all three of these areas.

Teaching and Teacher Quality

Along with accountability for performance, NCLB's emphasis on ensuring that all students are taught by a highly qualified teacher is a central feature of the law and a dramatic expansion of the reach of federal legislation. Even without the highly qualified teacher provisions, however, teacher response to NCLB is critical as teachers are the core actors in the law's implementation.

Leading off, Kerstin LeFloch reviews two of the major accountability provisions of NCLB, those dealing with AYP and those concerning the requirement for highly qualified teachers. She describes various ways that states have chosen to meet a key feature of the law, viz., the need for all relevant subgroups of students to make adequate yearly progress if a school is to be seen as making AYP. She then moves to the requirement that every child be taught by a highly qualified teacher, noting that this is the first time that federal legislation has laid out official guidelines for what constitutes teacher quality. She reviews how states have responded to the option of instituting a High Objective Uniform State Standards of Evaluation (HOUSSE) process for assessing whether a currently practicing teacher is highly qualified in his or her assigned subjects. She then points out how states have pushed back on aspects of the law that they view as untenable and discusses how the federal government has in turn responded. The chapter concludes with an analysis of three policy features that appear to mediate states' responses to the AYP and highly qualified teacher components of *NCLB*—the perceived efficacy of the policy, the salience of its consequences, and the novelty versus maturity of the policy.

In the second chapter of this section, Steven Brint and Sue Teele examine what teachers themselves have to say about No Child Left Behind, using a sample of roughly 300 teachers from Southern California drawn from five school districts with quite different demographic profiles. The chapter's quantitative data are enriched by a set of set of in-depth interviews with 28 of the respondents. The results suggest that these teachers, overall, have a very unfavorable attitude toward NCLB, with large percentages of the teachers reporting that because of NCLB they are teaching to the test and their classes are less creative than they otherwise would be. Only a small percentage of the teachers saw positive outcomes in their classrooms and schools because of the law.

The third chapter in this section, by Richard Ingersoll, examines teacher quality in the context of NCLB. The central theme of the chapter is that there is not a shortage of qualified teachers; instead the problem is in how schools organize teacher assignments, especially in schools with large numbers and percentages of disadvantaged students. As a result, even schools with an adequate supply of credentialed teachers still have substantial numbers of students being taught by teachers who are teaching outside of their fields of expertise and training.

In the fourth chapter, Joan Talbert and Milbrey McLaughlin posit that the NCLB strategy of mandating that all schools have highly qualified teachers, even when supplemented with professional development, will not be sufficient to meet the law's achievement goals. Good instruction, they argue, depends upon schools building teacher learning communities. After presenting data showing the positive effects of teacher learning communities on instruction and achievement outcomes, they discuss the challenges schools face in trying to "reculture" themselves in order to be able to build effective teacher learning communities, followed by suggestions as to how to overcome some of these challenges. The authors also point out how some of the features of NCLB designed to improve instruction, achievement outcomes, and teacher quality, may impede the ability of schools to build coherent and effective teacher learning communities.

School Choice and Parental Involvement

The fourth section of the book deals with two key issues of the law, school choice and parental involvement. In the first of the chapters, Douglas Lauen lays out the various forms of school choice (e.g., intradistrict, charter schools, vouchers, etc.) and then discusses the theoretical rationales and research base behind choice as a mechanism for school improvement. He points out that, thus far, very few parents who have children in schools identified for improvement are exercising their transfer option, and he uses the Chicago Public School District as a case study to examine why this might be the case. The chapter concludes with a call for more research on the reasons why parents aren't using the choice option and what the effects are when they do.

The second chapter in this section, by Roslyn Mickelson and Stephanie Southworth, uses the history and experience of the Charlotte-Mecklenburg school district to examine the school choice option of NCLB. Beginning in 1996, North Carolina, as part of its statewide school reform efforts, put in place a plan that in many ways foreshadowed NCLB. Like NCLB, parents were allowed to transfer their students to other schools, if those schools failed to meet the state's growth standards for two years in a row. The chapter reviews the percentage of families that availed themselves of the transfer option, the kinds of schools parents chose for their children, and the overall impact of these choices on educational equity, student performance, and opportunity to learn. The authors conclude by pointing out that race, socioeconomic status, school quality, and school choice intersect in ways that do not always advantage the children whom programs such as NCLB were designed to most serve.

As mentioned above, in many respects, the Texas accountability system put in place in the middle 1990s was a prototype for NCLB and therefore might foreshadow how NCLB's choice option could operate nationwide. In the third chapter in this section, using three cohorts of data from Texas Education Agency, Gary Dworkin and Jon Lorence examine the achievement effects for students moving from schools not meeting AYP to schools meeting them, as well as the performance levels of both the sending and receiving schools. While the data do not allow the authors to pinpoint why students transferred, the results nonetheless are suggestive of some of the outcomes that might be realized and the challenges faced as the NCLB choice option continues to roll out.

The next two chapters in this section examine the issue of how school districts and schools themselves are addressing NCLB's requirements for parental involvement. The law requires that districts provide professional development on creating partnerships between schools, parents, and the community to ensure that parents understand the law's requirements for testing, AYP for schools, and parents' right to information about the qualifications of their children's teachers and the existence of choice options. Districts must create parent resource centers for this purpose and ensure that all parents, even those with language barriers, have access to this information. Joyce Epstein uses longitudinal data from a sample of school districts from across the United States to examine the degree to which districts are fulfilling this provision of the law. She documents the degree to which implementation of this provision occurs and looks at the effects of a set of predictor variables (e.g., the district's demographic characteristics, the development of written plans, the breadth of support for the plan, etc.) on implementation. The chapter concludes with a discussion of the importance of district leadership on the creation of partnerships required by NCLB.

A companion chapter by Steven Sheldon examines the degree to which schools themselves are following the law's requirements for the establishment of family involvement programs as well as other activities that inform parents about their children's education as provided for by NCLB. Using a sample of schools drawn from the district data used by Epstein, Sheldon studies the implementation of school level partnerships by examining the types of groups put together at the school, the frequency of group meetings, and the factors (e.g., type of school, stability of leadership, coordination of organizational efforts, and district support) that contribute to why some schools had greater or less success with their partnership efforts.

Federal Involvement and the Achievement Gap

The fifth section of the book, "Federal Involvement, NCLB, and the Reduction of the Achievement Gap" is comprised of four chapters. In the first, Elizabeth Useem discusses how NCLB has reinforced the reform effort already in progress in Philadelphia. In light of the continuing poor performance of its schools, Philadelphia was taken over by the state, replacing the superintendent with a school reform commission. The commission used a variety of tools including top-down pressure, capacity building through hiring and professional development, choice, and contracting with education management organizations (including private management firms) to run some of its schools. Combining quantitative and qualitative data, Useem examines the experience of having a diverse provider model of school management, discusses what has worked and what has not, and considers the effect of the reform on teacher quality, parental and community involvement, and student performance. She concludes by noting that NCLB pressure and funding probably caused the reform in Philadelphia to move quickly and with less contentiousness than might otherwise have been the case.

While strongly supporting the goals and ideas behind NCLB to close the persistent gaps in achievement that exist in the United States, in his chapter, David Armor is pessimistic about NCLB's ability to reach its lofty goals. Noting that reformers often point to schools as the problem in student achievement gaps, Armor uses extant data from national studies to show that it is not schools that create the gaps, but instead they are caused by family and social factors that are well in place by the time children arrive at school. He doesn't disagree that schools should be pressured to reduce or even eliminate the gaps, but he argues that at the present time we do not have the technical know-how for accomplishing this task. In his conclusion, he suggests some changes in the way AYP is defined and argues that the reauthorized law should measure AYP by examining actual growth in school achievement rather than the attainment of uniform state cut points as currently required.

In her contribution to this section, Metz discusses the importance of examining how NCLB is interpreted in states, districts, schools, and classrooms. She cites evidence that it will be impossible to reach the law's requirement of 100 percent proficiency by 2014 and notes that increasing numbers of schools will be labeled as failing ("in need of improvement") as a result. Metz fears that as the numbers of identified schools rise, the public will eventually judge the entire public school system to be failing and will turn their support to private schools instead. Indeed, she sees such an outcome as what some supporters of the law had in mind when they voted for it. Finally, Metz notes that private schools currently do not fall under the purview of NCLB and therefore escape the sanctions leveled at public schools when they fail to make adequate yearly progress.

In the concluding chapter of the book, Alan Sadovnik, Gary Dworkin, Adam Gamoran, Maureen Hallinan, and Janelle Scott bring together the key sociological messages from the various chapters that comprise the volume and make recommendations for the reauthorization of the law. In doing so, they underscore the usefulness of sociological perspectives in examining the effectiveness and potential of NCLB for reducing achievement gaps. Because of the power of these analyses, they express the hope that legislators will use them when NCLB comes up for reauthorization in 2007. While Sadovnik et al. believe that programs such as NCLB are critically important to reducing the achievement gap between majority and historically disadvantaged students, they argue that such programs are not enough. For significant reductions in achievement gaps to occur, educational reforms need to be paired with efforts to reduce society-wide poverty and discrimination. Only when we recognize that achievement deficits are more than simply a problem with our schools, do we have a chance to eliminate them.

Reference

Coleman, James S., Ernest Q. Campbell, Carol F. Hobson, James M. McPartland, Alexander M. Mood, Frederic D. Weinfeld, and Robert L. York. 1966. *Equality of educational opportunity.* Washington, D.C.: U.S. Government Printing Office.

Part I

Federal and State Educational Policy and NCLB

1
No Child Left Behind?
Sociology Ignored!
David Karen

Too many American children are segregated into schools without standards, shuffled from grade-to-grade because of their age, regardless of their knowledge. This is discrimination, pure and simple—the soft bigotry of low expectations. And our nation should treat it like other forms of discrimination. We should end it. One size does not fit all when it comes to educating children, so local people should control local schools. Those who spend tax dollars must be held accountable. When a school district receives federal funds to teach poor children, those children should learn. If they don't, parents should get money to make a different choice. (Bush 2000)

Except for his inability to include vouchers in the No Child Left Behind Act (NCLB) of 2001, President George W. Bush got Congress to pass legislation that included most of the educational platform that he proposed when he was nominated in August 2000. Decrying the "soft bigotry of low expectations," Bush replaced it with the hard bigotries of inadequate funding,[1] poor understanding of the nature of educational and social inequality, and an even worse implementation plan. Despite the president's view that educational problems stem from discrimination, his plans for reforming education have ignored sociological research on the role of schools and communities in challenging or reinforcing discrimination and inequality. The goal of this essay is to provide sociologists with a number of ways to enter the debate on NCLB and its central focus: gaps in achievement among students from different backgrounds. Toward that end, I briefly review the history of NCLB and lay out its basic provisions. Then I discuss the research and public-engagement opportunities for sociologists that have been provided by the passage, implementation, and evaluations of NCLB.

Federal involvement in elementary and secondary education in the United States is relatively new and, until recently, has been laissez-faire. Although Washington contributes only $1 out of every $14 that is spent on K–12 education, NCLB insinuates the federal government into every state, school district, school, and even classroom. NCLB is a reauthorization of Public Law 89-10, the Elementary and Secondary Education Act (ESEA), which was signed by President Lyndon B. Johnson in 1965. In thanking Congress for passing the ESEA, Johnson said:

> By passing this bill, we bridge the gap between helplessness and hope for more than 5 million educationally deprived children. We put into the hands of our youth more than 30 million new books, and into many of our schools their first libraries. We reduce the terrible time lag in bringing new teaching techniques into the Nation's classrooms. We strengthen State and local agencies which bear the burden and the challenge of better education. And we rekindle the revolution—the revolution of the spirit against the tyranny of ignorance. (Johnson 1965)

Section 201 of P.L. 89-10 specifically recognized the "special educational needs of children of low-income families and the impact that concentrations of low-income families have on the ability of local educational agencies to support adequate educational programs." What was most remarkable about the passage of this legislation was its *national* focus in an arena that even now is dominated by local and state control (the U.S. Constitution does not mention "education" as a governmental function; education is left to the states). Since its original passage, the ESEA has been reauthorized in various guises approximately every five to seven years. Since 1965, the United States has established a cabinet-level Department of Education and increased federal expenditures on elementary and secondary education by a factor of 14.[2] Despite the changes, the goals of our new ESEA are similar to those mentioned by LBJ. Though it is framed as a program for increasing the nation's human capital to compete more successfully in the global economy,[3] NCLB is also centrally aimed at educational inequality: "We have a genuine national crisis. More and more, we are divided into two nations. One that reads, one that doesn't. One that dreams, one that doesn't" (Bush 2001, 1). President Bush's version of the ESEA tiptoes around the state and local control issues and focuses on bringing new teaching techniques and new technology (computers rather than books) into the classroom. Yet from the perspective of goals, degree of financial involvement, and even strategies, the country has not come far in these decades: *plus ça change, plus c'est la même chose.* At the same time, just as the original ESEA represented a sea-change in federal involvement in a state function, NCLB truly kicks it up a notch. Though I cannot, in this short piece, review the complete history of the ESEA's reauthorizations, I will highlight some of the key moments of federal redirection between LBJ's ESEA and Bush's NCLB.

During the Reagan administration, we were warned that the educational foundations of the United States were "being eroded by a rising tide of mediocrity." The report began:

> Our Nation is at risk. Our once unchallenged preeminence in commerce, industry, science, and technological innovation is being overtaken by competitors throughout the world.

With a martial tone throughout, the report led us toward a back-to-basics approach in education. Along with a spate of reports from foundations and business groups,[4] it appeared that A Nation at Risk was pushing educational reform to be a top agenda item of Reagan's second term. In the context of the fiscal crisis created by tax cuts and defense spending, however, funding for educational reform was given short shrift. Terrell Bell, Reagan's Secretary of Education, resigned when it became clear that the President was cutting educational spending more than he was cutting most other programs (Cross 2004, 82).

George W. Bush's immediate predecessors also proposed major educational initiatives: America 2000 (George H. W. Bush), and, with some revision and elaboration, Goals 2000 (Bill Clinton). To gain both support and publicity for America 2000, G. H. W. Bush met with the nation's governors for a two-day education summit at the symbolically important University of Virginia, Thomas Jefferson's public university. The "Charlottesville 51," with Governor Clinton of Arkansas as the Chair of the National Governors Association, hammered out six educational goals for the United States to meet by 2000, including having every child "ready to learn" when they enter school, a 90 percent high-school graduation rate, and the United States in the lead in international tests of science and mathematics. Though America 2000 was never passed as legislation, its nonvoucher components were key parts of Clinton's Goals 2000, which was passed in 1994.

There were a number of major reorientations of federal educational involvement associated with Goals 2000. For the first time, Washington dictated that states were required to set academic standards and districts would be responsible for implementing curricula that met those state standards. Teachers would be provided with professional development so that they could teach the new material. "Finally, new tests [would] be developed that are carefully aligned to the standards, which in turn must be reflected in the curriculum, and adults (and students) [would] be held accountable for learning the material" (Cross 2004, 113). Desperately trying to walk the fine line between providing support and avoiding federal meddling, it appeared that Clinton's Goals 2000 had found a proper balance. In theory, perhaps; in practice, by the end of 2000, only one-third of the states had complied with its requirements (Cross, 2004, 119, 124). Even with considerable autonomy to set their own standards and assessments and with federal monies at stake, states balked at implementing the new federal requirements.

NCLB continues, in different ways, many educational initiatives of Goals 2000. The primary difference is that NCLB's requirements have more bite and explicitly tie the performance of schools and districts, measured by many more standardized tests, to the receipt of federal funds. It is interesting that NCLB has seemingly left laissez-faire behind. By raising the stakes in these ways, it has the potential for producing radical change in U.S. schools. The key questions, ultimately, are these: what kinds of change will occur, and will they actually decrease the gaps in achievement?

Having overseen the supposed "Texas miracle" of increased achievement on annual tests in Texas,[5] Bush pushed for annual testing for accountability to be central to his educational plan. NCLB demands that we attend not only to the *average* test performance in schools, which can mask underperforming groups, but to *all* groups of students in the school. "In order to hold schools accountable for improving the performance of all students, … results must … be reported to the public disaggregated by race, gender,[6] English language proficiency, disability, and socioeconomic status" (Bush 2001, 8). In addition, NCLB promises funding for "effective, research-based programs and practices" and increasing teacher quality. NCLB also assures parents that they will have more information about their children's schools and provides them with choice if the school is not performing up to par. Finally, according to the NCLB Overview, there will be less bureaucracy and more flexibility in funding both to states and to school districts.[7]

The key components of NCLB are as follows:

1. Requires annual testing of students in grades 3–8 in reading and math, plus at least one test in grades 10–12; science testing to follow. Graduation rates are used as a secondary indicator of success for high schools.
2. Requires states and districts to report school-by-school data on students' test performance, broken down by whether the students are African American, Latino, Native American, Asian American, white non-Hispanic, special education, limited English proficiency (LEP), and/or low income.
3. Requires states to set "adequate yearly progress" (AYP) goals for each school. To meet AYP goals, not only must each subgroup make progress in each year in each grade in each subject, but 95 percent of each subgroup

must participate in testing. AYP goals must be constructed so that 100 percent of the students reach proficiency by 2014.

4. Labels schools that fail to meet AYP goals for two years "in need of improvement" (INOI). Initially, this requirement meant that schools must offer students opportunities to attend other public schools or to receive federally funded tutoring. Funds would also be provided for teachers' professional development. A school that fails to meet future AYP targets will be subject to "restructuring" (firing of the teachers and the principal, the takeover of the school by the state or a private company, and so forth).

5. Requires schools to have "highly qualified" teachers for the "core academic subjects" (English, reading or language arts, math, science, foreign languages, civics and government, economics, arts, history and geography) by 2005–6.

One might wonder how Bush was able to bring such overwhelming majorities in Congress (381–41 in the House and 87–10 in the Senate) to support a bill that infringed on the prerogatives of so many, often cross-cutting, constituencies. States, districts, schools, and teachers have lost autonomy. Supporters of vouchers for private schools did not get what they wanted. Supporters of a national curriculum failed as well. Ultimately, it appears, Bush promised enough money to placate the liberals and Democrats and enough accountability and choice to placate the conservatives and Republicans.

A key consideration in the bill was how to keep the 800-pound federal gorilla from inflicting too many constraints on state and local autonomy. Without a national curriculum or national annual tests, the United States cannot compare schools across states and districts. Thus, NCLB allows each state to oversee its districts, with state plans reviewed by the U.S. Department of Education (USDOE). Each state can develop or buy tests that are needed to meet the accountability provisions. Local districts can negotiate with states about how they will abide by the approved state version of NCLB. Experience to date has shown that local districts regularly plead their cases for exceptions, exemptions, and modifications to state departments of education, which, in turn, negotiate with the USDOE about how particular pieces of NCLB are being implemented in ways that do not make sense. Examples include grouping *very* needy special education students with students who have mild disorders; having LEP students take the same tests as non-LEP students; and encouraging low scorers to drop out, thereby raising a school's and category's proficiency (see Meier and Wood 2004 for an overview of these issues).

President Bush's claim about "the soft bigotry of low expectations" connects with sociologists' concerns with the ways in which students' aspirations and the opportunity structure are mutually reinforcing in students' pursuit of academic and socioeconomic success. Sociologists of education are particularly interested in how these relationships may vary for groups of different racial/ethnic backgrounds or social classes. If we try to unpack all the factors that affect the lack of proficiency throughout the population, as well as the achievement gaps among the groups under study, we move well beyond the focus of NCLB. That is as it should be, and that is where sociologists can help.

Sociologists of education examine social forces that affect how students learn by examining schools in their many contexts. We study the production of teachers (schools of education) as well as their practices within the classroom. We look at how individual schools organize instruction for different subpopulations. We investigate the sources of inequalities in funding among states, districts within states, schools within districts, classrooms within schools, and students within classrooms (Rothstein 2000). We also study the implementation and effects of social policies. From Coleman et al.'s landmark study in 1966 to the present, sociologists have grappled with identifying key factors—inside and outside schools—that affect student outcomes.

Sociologists of education can contribute to the NCLB conversation by using the natural experiment that has been handed to us and analyzing the consequences of its 50 different implementation plans. Not only may we learn something concrete about the effects of a given plan on educational outcomes, but we may better understand how federal policies are translated at the state level. As in the past, sociologists will try to understand how states that varied along many dimensions—urbanicity, size, number, and size of school districts and schools, K–12 or P–16 educational systems, racial and national-origin diversity, and the like—differed in their educational outcomes. States, districts, and schools with large immigrant populations, much racial/ethnic diversity, and many LEP students have been (and will be) more likely to be labeled "INOI" than will others (Kane and Staiger 2003). We are particularly interested in how INOI schools and districts vary in their approaches to return to the AYP track. What instructional or organizational changes do schools use to raise test scores or participation rates for specific groups? Do they increase tracking? What happens to class sizes in better-performing schools if students from INOI schools transfer in? Some teachers may change their instruction and narrow the curriculum in response to high-stakes tests (Hamilton 2004). What then happens to trust and tradition in classrooms and schools (Bryk, Lee, and Holland 1993), especially if student mobility increases as well? What happens to opportunities to learn in heterogeneous classrooms (Gamoran 1986)? Finally, what happens to the state standards that represent a broader and deeper knowledge across many subjects—are they simply ignored? Through all the federal government's focus on schools' and districts' accountability, how does *children's* achievement ever come into view?

Following Wilson (1998) and Tilly (1998), I suggest that we think about the issues surrounding the outcomes of individual students in terms of the *social structure of inequality*. Rather than focus on an individual's attributes (such as race and class), we should think about the larger social contexts wherein individuals move through organizations to positions of different rewards and privilege. When we think about what cultural factors are important in affecting test performance or educational achievement, we should be thinking about how these operate in the context of given social relations. In other words, *our* unique contribution as *sociologists* is in demonstrating how social structure affects educational outcomes.

To understand the achievement gaps among students of different racial/ethnic groups and social classes, we should pay attention to how and why the groups' lived experiences differ from one another. Lee and Burkam (2002) documented the strong association between race/ethnicity and test scores before children enter kindergarten, but they also documented sharp reductions in differences when socioeconomic status is taken into account. In thinking about why children perform differentially, we need to examine the larger patterns of resource distribution in the society: unequal access to medical and dental care; unequal access to housing; unequal access to labor markets and adequate incomes;[8] unequal access to vibrant communities with high levels of social capital; and, yes, unequal access to educational (preschool, too!) resources. The proponents of NCLB (even the often-liberal Education Trust) have suggested that any attempt to distract attention from students' learning by moving away from a focus on tests, classrooms, and schools is tantamount to the "soft bigotry" of Bush's campaign. Forty years of sociological research on the contextual factors that shape students' learning suggest otherwise, however.

Given this social structure of inequality, how can sociologists of education illuminate the gaps in achievement that the NCLB seeks to address? Previous research has found that factors, such as access to medical care, residential stability, community integration, and community resources, to name just a few, influence gaps in achievement. If these elements of social structure matter, then our goal should be to provide: universal access to medical care, housing vouchers (Rothstein 2000), community-based economic development, and economically and racially integrated schools (Orfield, Eaton, and the Harvard Project 1996). Such changes will not only reduce differences in educational performance, but will ultimately be a part of a society in which the social structure of inequality and its many effects will have radically changed.

ACKNOWLEDGMENTS

The author thanks Katherine Conner, Linda Grant, Katherine McClelland, and Suet-Ling Pong for their useful comments on previous versions of this article. Alan Sadovnik provided useful comments and strong encouragement throughout.

Notes

1. Thanks to Katherine Conner for suggesting this apt phrase.
2. The year before Bush came into office federal expenditures on elementary and secondary education were over $27 billion, compared to just under $2 billion in 1965–66. Interestingly, this represented a decrease in percentage terms from 7.9 to 7.3.
3. In the Foreword to the overview of NCLB (Bush 2001), President George W. Bush states the underlying reason for his interest in fundamental educational reform: "In a constantly changing world that is demanding increasingly complex skills from its workforce, children are literally being left behind." The original ESEA, even though crafted in the context of the Cold War, did not highlight worldwide political or economic competition as its raison d'etre; it was unswervingly focused on its contribution to LBJ's War on Poverty and Great Society programs.
4. Among others, reports were issues by the Task Force on Education for Economic Growth, the Twentieth Century Fund, and the Business-Higher Education Forum.
5. According to various observers, the "Texas miracle" was not miraculous at all. Increased achievement levels and declining gaps between races were a function of teaching to the tests. Texas students' performances on non-Texas tests (e.g. NAEP, SAT, etc.) were stagnant or declined (see Haney 2000; Klein et al. 2000)
6. Gender has been dropped from reporting requirements.
7. It is interesting and quite ironic that a bill that demands massive increases in testing and reporting claims to reduce bureaucracy. It is perhaps worth noting in this context that the original 1965 version of ESEA was 31 pages long compared to the current 670 page version.
8. NCLB attends to achievement differences between low-income and other students. LBJ's original ESEA was part of a larger set of programs that attempted not only to educate those from low-income households but to make the low-income category smaller.

References

Bryk, Anthony, Valerie Lee, and Peter Holland. 1993. *Catholic schools and the common good.* Cambridge, MA: Harvard University Press.

Bush, George W. 2000, August 3. Acceptance speech at the Republican Convention. Available online at http://www.2000gop.com/convention/speech/speechbush.html

———. 2001. No child left behind. The White House. Available online at https://www.whitehouse.gov/news/reports/no-child-left-behind.pdf

Coleman, James S., Ernest Q. Campbell, Carol F. Hobson, James M. McPartland, Alexander M. Mood, Frederic D. Weinfeld, and Robert L. York. 1966. *Equality of educational opportunity.* Washington, D.C.: U.S. Government Printing Office.

Cross, Christopher T. 2004. *Political education: National policy comes of age.* New York: Teachers College Press.

Gamoran, Adam. 1986. Instructional and institutional effects of ability grouping. *Sociology of Education* 59:185–98.

Hamilton, Laura. 2004. Assessment as a policy tool. *Review of Research in Education* (2003) 27: 25–68.

Haney, Walt. 2000. The myth of the Texas miracle in education. *Education Policy Analysis Archives* 8 (41), August 19. Available online at http://epaa.asu.edu/epaa/v8n41/

Johnson, L.B. 1965. President Lyndon B. Johnson's remarks in Johnson City, Texas, upon signing the Elementary and Secondary Education Bill April 11, 1965. Available online at http://www.lbjlib.utexas.edu/johnson/archives.hom/speeches.hom/650411.asp

Kane, Thomas J., and Douglas O. Staiger. 2003. Unintended consequences of racial subgroup rules. In *No child left behind? The politics and practice of accountability,* ed. Paul E. Peterson and Martin R. West, 152–76. Washington, D.C.: Brookings Institution Press.

Klein, Stephen P., Laura S. Hamilton, Daniel F. McCaffrey, and Brian M. Stecher. 2000. *What do test scores in Texas tell us?* Available online at http://www.rand.org/publications/IP/IP202

Lee, Valerie E., and David Burkam. 2002. *Inequality at the starting gate: Social background differences in achievement as children begin school.* Washington, D.C.: Economic Policy Institute.

Meier, Deborah, and George Wood, eds. 2004. *Many children left behind: How the No Child Left Behind Act is damaging our children and our schools*. Boston: Beacon Press.

Orfield, Gary, Susan Eaton, and the Harvard Project on School Desegregation. 1996. *Dismantling desegregation*. New York: New Press.

Rothstein, Richard. 2000. Equalizing education resources on behalf of disadvantaged children. In *A notion at risk: Preserving public education as an engine for social mobility*, ed. Richard D. Kahlenberg, 31–92. New York: Century Foundation Press.

Tilly, Charles. 1998. *Durable inequality*. Berkeley: University of California Press.

Wilson, William Julius. 1998. The role of the environment in the black–white test score gap. In *The black–white test score gap*, ed. Christopher Jencks and Meredith Phillips, 501–10. Washington, D.C.: Brookings Institution Press.

Part II

Accountability and Assessment

2

NCLB and the Complexity
of School Improvement[1]

Jennifer A. O'Day

INTRODUCTION

School accountability for student performance lies at the very heart of the No Child Left Behind Act of 2001, and consequently at the heart of much of the controversy surrounding it. While NCLB supporters tout it as landmark legislation demonstrating the government's commitment to educating underserved students and closing the achievement gap(s), others see it as unprecedented federal intrusion into arenas more appropriately left to the purview of states and local districts. Some focus on the unfairness of holding schools accountable for outcomes over which they have limited control. Others believe the "no excuses" approach is the only way to push the system to fulfill its promise to large numbers of students traditionally "left behind" in American schools.

This chapter steps back from these bigger questions about fairness and governance and considers NCLB and similar performance-based accountability policies more at face value. Most educators and observers, whether they agree or disagree with the particularities of NCLB, would argue that the goal of such accountability measures is or should be the improvement of instruction and student learning. The assumption is that to improve outcomes for students, we must improve the schools those students attend. The question then becomes whether and under what conditions performance-based school accountability policies, like NCLB, actually contribute to meaningful and sustained school improvement, particularly in the low performing schools that they target.

To address that question, this chapter applies theoretical perspectives on organizational complexity and system learning to analyses of performance-based accountability policies in Chicago and other jurisdictions prior to the institution of NCLB.[2] The use of pre-NCLB experience is warranted for two reasons. First, while some particularities of the policies differ, NCLB reflects the same underlying theory of action of prior state and district manifestations of performance-based accountability—particularly those implemented in Chicago in the late 1990s. Labeled the "new accountability" by researchers at the Consortium for Policy Research in Education (CPRE)[3] because of its departure from traditional input-based models, this approach to accountability is distinguished by several core features. These include an emphasis on student outcomes as the measure of adult and system performance, a focus on the school as the basic unit of accountability, public reporting of student achievement, and the attachment of consequences to performance levels (Elmore, Abelmann, and Fuhrman 1996; Fuhrman 1999). Another reason for examining pre-NCLB experience is that it enables us to consider the longer-term effects of such policies on the functioning of targeted schools, something which is not yet possible from the more recently implemented NCLB. Lessons from such an examination may help to foreshadow or explain patterns that emerge under NCLB and to suggest areas in which policies might be modified for more productive impact.

I begin the chapter with an abbreviated discussion of improvement in schools as complex systems,[4] focusing on the role of information and interaction in system change and on critical mechanisms of, and barriers to, the use of information for improvement. This focus on information derives in part from its centrality in theories of organizational development and learning but also from the accountability goal to promote evidence-based practice (also called data driven decision making) in NCLB and similar policies. Based on this review of complexity in school organizations, I argue that accountability systems will foster improvement to the extent that they generate and focus attention on information relevant to teaching and learning, motivate individuals and schools to use that information and expend effort to improve practice, build the knowledge base necessary for interpreting and applying the new information to improve practice, and allocate resources for all of the above.

I then turn to an examination of how this theory applies in practice. Using the Chicago experience[5] as an example, I consider both the promise and limitations of an NCLB-like approach to school accountability in light of the theory-based framework. Noting the shortcomings of an outcomes-based bureaucratic model like that of Chicago and NCLB, I consider professional accountability as a potential alternative. I conclude that the combination of administrative and professional accountability is the most promising approach for fostering organizational learning and improvement in schools. In the final section I draw out several implications of the discussion for the refinement of NCLB and other accountability policies.[6]

SCHOOL-BASED ACCOUNTABILITY: TENSIONS AND PROBLEMS

School accountability mechanisms seek to increase student performance by improving the functioning of the school organization. Despite variation with respect to targets and consequences for performance, policies that take the school as the basic unit of accountability must contend with several inherent problems if they are to effect organizational change. Three such problems are these:

1. *The school is the unit of intervention, yet the individual is the unit of action.* While NCLB defines the school as the unit for monitoring, intervention, and change, it is individual teachers, administrators, and parents who must change their actions in order to increase student learning. School-level accountability approaches bank on school members' identification with their organizational environment to motivate and direct individual action. How will school accountability mechanisms mobilize changes among individuals?

2. *External control seeks to influence internal operations.* Performance accountability policies seek to influence from outside what happens inside schools. The limitations of such externally initiated change efforts have generated a vast literature on policy implementation in education.[7] In short, this literature finds that rules decreed from on high often have little impact on the core technology of teaching and learning (Elmore 1996; Marion 1999). Normative structures inside schools, such as the privacy of classroom practice, are often the determining factors not only in policy implementation but the school's overall effectiveness.[8] This raises several questions: What is the appropriate and most effective balance between external and internal control? What are the mechanisms for achieving this balance? Can external accountability measures influence the development of internal norms that are more conducive to improving student learning?

3. *Information is both problematic in schools and essential to school improvement.* Current school accountability policies, such as public reporting of student test scores, assume that, armed with accurate information about the achievement of students in the school, stakeholders and participants in the instructional process will take whatever action is necessary to improve learning outcomes.[9] But again, this simple assumption raises a host of questions, the answers to which are anything but straightforward. What are the most effective forms and uses of information in the school improvement process? What is the potential for the external accountability system to generate and disseminate the information needed to accomplish the accountability goals? What are the motivational and learning links between information on the one hand and individual and collective action on the other?

These three problems—collective accountability versus individual action, internal versus external sources of control, and the nature and uses of information for school improvement—undergird this discussion of school accountability. To illuminate their interrelationships, I turn to theories of organizational complexity and adaptation, focusing on the central role of information in both accountability and school improvement processes.

COMPLEX ADAPTIVE SYSTEMS AND CHANGE: A FRAMEWORK FOR UNDERSTANDING SCHOOL ACCOUNTABILITY

Complexity theorists[10] use the term *complex adaptive systems* (CAS) to describe "a world in which many players are all adapting to each other and where the emerging future is very hard to predict" (Axelrod and Cohen 1999, xi).

Complexity Theory and Organizations

A few central concepts from complexity theory as applied to organizations aid understanding of the potential and the limitations of current approaches to school accountability.

Interaction and Interdependence in Complex Adaptive Systems A central characteristic of complex adaptive systems (CAS) is the interdependence of individual and collective behavior. CAS are defined as populations of interacting "agents," each of which pursues a limited set of strategies in response to its surroundings and in pursuit of its goals. In a school, for example, teachers interact with students, with other teachers, with administrators, with parents, and so forth. In each of these interactions, the individual actor follows his or her own goals and strategies, which differ from those of other actors to varying degrees. This variation among individual actors and their strategies is central to the notion of complexity and adaptation. Equally central, however, are the constraints placed on that variation by the interaction of actors within the organization and between them and the larger environment. The more frequent and powerful those interactions are, the more influence they are likely to have on the behavior of individual actors (Axelrod and Cohen 1999; Marion 1999).

Learning and Organizational Change In complex systems, the strategies that individual agents and organizations pursue reflect both stability and change over time—with both these characteristics being manifestations of learning. As new members come in to the organization, they become socialized into (i.e., learn) its "code" —the languages, beliefs, and routines that make up the dominant behaviors of the organization and define it as an interactive system (March 1991); hence, the stability of the system. But organizational codes and practices also change. Such change occurs through the selection, recombination, and adaptation of strategies, based on information derived from the interactions of system members with one another and with their environment, a process that is also dependent on learning.

At the heart of the learning process in any complex system is the movement of information among agents and subunits through patterns of interaction and the interpretation of information by individuals and groups based on prior experience. Interpretation is critical here because it is through interpretation that information is given its meaning (Daft and Weick 1984, 294). Interpretation depends on "a person's prior cognitive map (or belief structure or mental representation or frame of reference)," is socially constructed, and varies across organizational units having different responsibilities (Huber 1991, 102–3). One implication of this is that the meaningfulness of the information generated by the system will vary in relation to the knowledge and skills of the users. To the extent that such knowledge and skills are weak or are unequally distributed, so too will be the meaning and usefulness of the accountability information.

Learning and Improvement It is important to note that even when learning and change occur, they do not necessarily lead to improvement. Complexity theorists Robert Axelrod and Michael Cohen (1999) use the term *adaptation* to indicate when learning and change produce "improvement along some measure of success" (7). This concept of adaptation is highly consistent with the goals of school accountability systems, which seek improvement in terms of specific assessments of student performance.

Unfortunately, in complex systems interaction and interpretation of information make learning unreliable. Agents and organizations may misinterpret feedback from their environment, causing "superstitious learning" (Levitt and March 1988).[11] If individuals and organizations act on that superstitious learning, using it to select a strategy, the results may be maladaptive rather than adaptive; that is, they may lead to a decline rather than an improvement in relevant measures of success. In addition, learning at one point in an individual's or system's experience may inhibit learning and change at another point. As individuals and organizations gain competence in certain activities through learning, they may actually decrease their range of potential strategies (Levinthal 1991). By repeatedly selecting strategies that have led to success in the past and interacting with other entities based on those strategies, an organization reduces variation, thus potentially reducing future learning and adaptation. The end result is that individuals and mature organizations over time may get caught in "competency traps," becoming prisoners of their own past success (Levitt and March 1988) even when continuation of those strategies no longer produces the desired result.[12] One might argue that the general inertia of the educational system is a reflection of such competency traps.

BARRIERS TO IMPROVEMENT IN SCHOOLS

Too much or too little information, faulty incentive and resource allocation structures, and the problem of attribution in schools as complex systems are some of the organizational barriers to improvement that occur.

Too Much or Too Little Information

Teachers and schools are constantly bombarded by information and by demands to do something about that information. In many schools, teachers' and students' work is subject to continual interruption as others try to thrust new information upon them. Much of the information is irrelevant to the improvement of instruction and learning. It merely distracts attention and resources from what is supposed to be the main work of school personnel and students. Sifting through the morass to find that which is likely to lead to improvement requires time, resources, and knowledge that school personnel may not possess. Unable to make productive choices, some teachers and schools move chaotically from one demand or source of information to another, with insufficient focus and time to learn.

Alternatively, teachers and schools may metaphorically and literally close the door on new information, shutting out the noise. This is a coping strategy that potentially allows them to focus, but it also leads to isolation. Such isolation prevents their having sufficient opportunity to encounter variation and the information it engenders, and thus little opportunity for learning. Norms of private practice in education and loose coupling[13] throughout the system reinforce this isolation.

This situation creates a paradox. On the one hand, external sources thrust an overload of information on schools and school personnel, while on the other hand, isolation creates a lack of information sharing among teachers. What seems to be needed is some middle ground. Teachers given the right amount of information will be able to attend to it, interpret it, and use it for learning and adaptation. The question is, how will the accountability system ensure that school personnel receive an adequate amount of information, can interpret the information, and have the ability to focus on what is most appropriate for improving teaching and learning?

Complexity and the Problem of Attribution in Schools

The amount of information is only one part of the problem. Also of concern are the kinds of information available, how that information is interpreted, and whether the interpretations will lead to learning.

Theorists (e.g., Levitt and March 1988) tell us that organizations are oriented toward targets and adapt based on feedback (information) about those targets.

Discrepancies between observed outcomes and aspirations for those outcomes can provide motivation for change (Simon 1986). Such is certainly the assumption of NCLB and similar outcomes-based accountability. But agents within schools vary in their definition of a target (sometimes it is just getting through the day!), and schools also have multiple and changing targets. Moving a school community from an emphasis on discipline and order to a focus on student learning, for example, is difficult and represents this sort of change. Even taking a single generally agreed upon goal, such as independent reading by the third grade, does not remove the ambiguity. Other targets remain, agents have differing views about what independent reading entails, and measurement is difficult.

Perhaps most important, even in an ideal situation where the goals and measures are clear, the complexity of interaction patterns inside and outside the organization and of the learning process itself makes attribution of cause and effect difficult and unreliable. Consider the following hypothetical example: Only 15 percent of third graders in Bryant Elementary are reading independently by the spring assessment. Do we conclude that the third-grade teachers are not teaching appropriately? And if so, in what particular ways is the instruction inadequate? Are the textbooks too difficult? Are they too easy? Are they boring? Perhaps the low performance is due to constant interruptions during reading time or lack of order in the school. Maybe the problem is that the students do not see any reason for reading, or perhaps they speak a language other than English and do not have the requisite English vocabulary. Perhaps the real problem lies in first- or second-grade instruction, in the fear induced by violence in the neighborhood, or in the low expectations of the adults. Perhaps it is all or some combination of the above. Alternatively, if the majority of students at Bryant are doing well, we are not necessarily any closer to understanding the cause of their performance. Is it class background? School selection processes? Motivated teachers? Effective instruction? All of the above? Indeed, it is often more difficult to pinpoint the cause of success than it is of failure.

The tendency toward faulty attribution in education is commonplace, exacerbated both by the lack of valid and appropriately detailed information on outcomes and by the lack of opportunity and knowledge to reflect on and explore alternative interpretations of what might have contributed to producing those outcomes. Actions based on faulty attribution are unlikely to result in improved performance.

Faulty Incentive and Resource Allocation Structures

Adaptation in schools is also inhibited by incentive and resource structures that undermine motivation and the opportunity for organizational learning and the adoption of more productive strategies. These inhibitors include such things as incentives that pull attention and effort to goals other than student learning,[14] insufficient time or other resources for collaboration and sharing information about instruction, and human resource systems that reward mediocrity and concentrate the most knowledgeable teachers where they are least needed. Thus, we might ask whether the school has an effective strategy for allocating resources to foster student learning. Does the district? As with other aspects of the system, resource allocation is dependent on accurate and reliable information. Again, the goal of the accountability system should be to supply that information.

SCHOOL ACCOUNTABILITY FRAMEWORK

This discussion suggests a framework for analyzing the potential impact of NCLB and other accountability-based interventions on school improvement. School accountability mechanisms will be successful in improving the functioning of school organizations to the extent that those interventions are able to:

- *Generate and focus attention on information relevant to teaching and learning.* Note that in order to alter what happens in classrooms, this focus must occur not only at the school level, but at the level of individual teachers as well. Interaction patterns are likely to be very important in the generation and spread of such information.
- *Motivate educators and others to attend to relevant information and to expend the effort necessary to augment or change strategies in response to this information.* Central here is the problematic relationship of collective accountability and individual action. Motivation must ultimately occur at the individual level, but it is likely to be dependent in part on the normative structures of the school as well as on individual characteristics of educators and students.
- *Develop the knowledge and skills to promote valid interpretation of information and appropriate attribution of causality at both the individual and system levels.* As discussed above, learning takes place through the interpretation of information, whether that information is data from a student assessment, research on reading instruction, or observation of a colleague's lesson. Interpretation is dependent on prior learning and is constrained and informed by such. Data often remain unused because educators lack the knowledge base for interpretation and incorporation of the new information. If accountability systems are to be successful, they will need not only to build knowledge and skills for interpretation in the short run, but also to establish mechanisms for continued learning.
- *Allocate resources where they are most needed.* Information at all levels can promote the allocation of human and material resources to where they are most needed. A classroom teacher might reallocate resources by spending more of her time and attention on a student she sees is having trouble

understanding a new concept. Similarly, district administrators might move additional resources to a low-performing school or one taking on a new challenge. To what extent does the accountability system encourage allocation (or reallocation) of resources to foster student learning based on information generated?

BUREAUCRATIC ACCOUNTABILITY AND SCHOOL IMPROVEMENT

How do NCLB-like school accountability policies fare with respect to the framework outlined above? That is, to what extent do they generate and focus attention on relevant information, motivate the use of that information for individual and collective change, contribute to the knowledge base needed for appropriate interpretation of that information, and use information to provide adequate resources where needed? To answer this question, I turn to analyses of the new accountability in education (Elmore, Ableman, and Fuhrman 1996), as well as to more expansive typologies of educational accountability (Adams and Kirst 1999; Darling-Hammond and Ascher 1991; O'Reilly 1996).

Accountability systems, according to these and other observers, differ in large part by the way they respond to four central questions: *Who* is accountable? *To whom* are they accountable? *For what* are they accountable? And *what are the consequences of accountability*? Elmore et al. (1996) note that one of the distinguishing characteristics of the new accountability in standards-based reform is that the "who" is generally the school unit[15] while, the "to whom" designation almost universally refers to the district or state agencies.[16] That is, schools as collective entities are accountable to the higher levels of the educational system. Certainly this is the case in NCLB, in which the federal government sets the parameters but it is states that actually hold schools (and districts) accountable. In this respect, such policies represent a form of administrative (O'Day and Smith 1993) or bureaucratic accountability (Adams and Kirst 1999; Darling-Hammond and Ascher 1991). They differ from traditional forms of bureaucratic accountability in one very important respect, however: schools and school personnel are accountable not for delivering designated educational inputs and processes but for producing specific results in student learning. Thus, NCLB, like many of its precursors, is an example of what might best be termed "outcome-based bureaucratic accountability."[17] In this section, I examine Chicago school probation policy as an exemplar of this form of school accountability.[18]

ADDRESSING THE FRAMEWORK: OUTCOME-BASED ACCOUNTABILITY, CHICAGO STYLE

The Chicago Public Schools (CPS) provide a particularly useful model to illustrate this framework and to suggest lessons of potential relevance to NCLB.

When the Illinois legislature amended the Chicago School Reform Act in 1995 to include specific provisions for school accountability, the Chicago School Board designated school-level targets for student performance and instituted sanctions (probation and reconstitution) for schools falling below those targets. At the time when the analyses reported here were completed, the district had accumulated six years of experience with school accountability, during which time several colleagues and I had the opportunity to follow the policy's design, practice, and results. Our investigation included in-depth interviews with business, political, education, and community stakeholders; analyses of school improvement plans and the planning process; interviews and shadowing of support providers; school case studies; and multilevel analyses of survey and achievement data on all CPS elementary schools since 1994 (two years prior to the implementation of sanctions). Our data are thus both rich and varied. They provide an inroad into understanding the links between outcomes-based school accountability and school improvement.

At first glance, CPS and similar school accountability systems seem to address well the criteria laid out in the framework above. Below I discuss how the four components of the school accountability framework are reflected in the CPS accountability system.

Attention

On the most basic level, these accountability systems call attention to information on student outcomes by designating a particular indicator (or indicators) of those outcomes and by defining specific performance targets. In Chicago's case, the focus was sharpened by the district's use of a single indicator—the Iowa Test of Basic Skills (ITBS)[19]—in only two subject areas, reading and mathematics. Moreover, the targeted performance benchmark was simple, measurable, and clear: schools had to have at least 15 (then 20, then 25) percent of their students in grades 3–8 or 9–11 reading at or above national grade-level norms in the spring administration of the ITBS, or be declared "on probation." Attention to the outcomes was further enhanced through school planning and reporting mechanisms that singled out reading and math scores and required all schools to provide information on how they would increase student performance in these areas. In theory, such mechanisms establish priorities in the organization and thus should help school personnel sift through the usual information overload to focus on that most directly related to student achievement and improvement strategies.

Motivation

Chicago's policy, like outcome-based policies in other jurisdictions, provided motivation for this sifting process and related improvement efforts by attaching consequences to the outcome targets. For all schools, these consequences came in the form of public and administrative scrutiny of reported school outcome data. For schools falling below the target, sanctions included the stigma of the "probation" label; decreased autonomy as local school councils lose authority to select their principals; additional requirements for planning, monitoring, and assistance; and potentially even reconstitution or reengineering, both of which entail involuntary changes in personnel.[20] Policy designers believed that even the threat of such sanctions would increase educator motivation and efforts to improve student learning.

Knowledge Development

It is of little value for school personnel to attend to outcome information if they do not know how to interpret it, and motivation to act will produce nothing if educators do not know what actions they should take. Recognizing the need for site-based knowledge and skill development, CPS administrators instituted an elaborate program of assistance for schools, including mentoring for principals, help with business and school improvement plans, and professional and organizational development provided by external partners. A particularly interesting feature of the CPS design of external assistance was the district's response to the tension between internal and external sources of control discussed earlier. In an effort to balance these sources of control and enhance normative buy-in among school personnel, CPS allowed probation schools to select their own partners from an approved list. The policy designers hoped that this selection process would both enhance motivation and ensure that support providers pay attention to the particular conditions in each school.

Resource Allocation

Finally, funding for this assistance demonstrates a major way in which the district used information generated by the accountability system to allocate resources. Low test scores triggered the targeting of discretionary monies—initially from the district surplus and then from federal programs, including the Comprehensive School Reform Demonstration (CSRD) program[21] and class-size reduction—to probation schools. The district covered 100 percent of the cost of the first year of assistance, 50 percent of the second year, and the school bore the full cost in subsequent years. In the first two years of the probation policy, CPS spent $29 million for external support alone.[22]

The similarities between CPS probation policies and NCLB accountability provisions should be readily apparent, providing a rationale for using the CPS experience to illuminate expected patterns for the federal program. Similarities include the reliance on annual standardized test scores in grades 3–8 (for elementary schools), the establishment of specified targets (percent of students at or above the threshold score in reading and mathematics) that increase over time, the identification of schools not meeting performance targets and application of specified consequences (in CPS a decrease in the authority of the local school councils and mandatory assistance from "external partners"); and finally, a last resort measure (reconstitution in CPS, restructuring in NCLB) for schools that continued to fail despite intervention. Differences also exist between the two sets of policies; CPS neither disaggregated accountability for subgroups nor included choice provisions. Nonetheless, despite variations in details, the general school accountability model in CPS, NCLB, and in multiple jurisdictions nationally has been the same: define certain expected levels of performance, designate schools as high or low performing based on student assessments, require planning to focus attention and coordinate action in the school, provide assistance in some form, and administer sanctions for continued failure to improve.

Impact of School-Based Accountability

Although experience with and research on school accountability were still in the early stages at the time of our Chicago study, some evidence of its impact was already beginning to accumulate. Our data from Chicago (Finnigan and Gross 2001) and CPRE research in Kentucky and Charlotte-Mecklenburg, North Carolina (Kelley et al. 2000) indicated that teachers were working harder in response to the accountability measures and were more focused on externally set student learning goals. In addition, many systems (e.g., Boston, San Diego, Tennessee, and California) were using school level data on student outcomes to allocate additional discretionary resources where they appeared to be most needed. Some jurisdictions, such as New York City and Baltimore, even put in place special monetary incentives to attract and retain highly skilled teachers and principals for the lowest performing schools (Westat 2002).

There was also evidence of an impact on achievement, as measured by standardized tests. In each of the first four years after instituting its school ac- countability policy, Chicago schools posted increased scores in both reading and mathematics, though reading scores began to level off after 2000 (Chicago Public Schools 2002). Similarly, Kentucky, California, Texas, Tennessee, and other jurisdictions claimed that their accountability policies had resulted in higher student achievement.[23]

However, schools respond unevenly to outcome-based accountability policies; this unevenness may be directly tied to internal conditions in schools that make them more or less able to use the information generated by the accountability systems. The CPRE research team led by Richard Elmore and Leslie Siskin, for example, found that schools that are better positioned in terms of their socioeco- nomic composition responded more positively to external performance-based accountability systems than did schools less well positioned (DeBray et al. 2001; Elmore 2001). Their research suggests that lower performing schools actually lose ground relative to the well-positioned schools once an external accountability system is instituted.

Our research on the lowest performing schools in Chicago extends the CPRE analysis, identifying variations in responses among schools that might all be considered less well positioned; that is, among those at similarly low socioeconomic and achievement levels.[24] The first indication of this variation is a rapid bifurcation in the achievement trends for all elementary schools placed on probation in 1996, despite comparable initial achievement. More specifically, one group of schools—those that came off the probation list by spring of 1998—posted a significantly sharper increase in scores than those schools that remained on probation after 1998. Multilevel analysis of survey data for this rapidly improving group suggests that they differed significantly from other probation schools along several dimensions of initial school capacity: peer collaboration, teacher–teacher trust, and collective responsibility for student learning (Gwynne and Easton 2001). Applying the earlier discussion of complexity, we might surmise that the first two of these dimensions indicate stronger patterns of interaction while they and the third together indicate normative structures already directed toward the common goal of improving student learning.

Limitations of Bureaucratic, Outcome-Based School Accountability

Our data from Chicago indicate several ways in which bureaucratic outcome-based accountability may inhibit—or at least fail to promote— widespread organizational adaptation.

Inadequate Information A central limitation of outcome-based school accountability in Chicago and elsewhere is that the nature and quality of the information produced and dispensed by the system are simply inadequate for effective organizational change. Three aspects of this inadequacy stand out.

The first limitation of the information dispensed in such a system concerns the validity of the outcome measure on which improvement is to be based. Much of the criticism of Chicago's model of school accountability has centered on the use of a norm-referenced basic skills test that is not fully aligned with either the district or the state standards, that emphasizes fragmented and discrete skill acquisition, and that lacks validation for the types of decisions (e.g., probation and grade retention) made on the basis of its results. Validity with respect to measurement of the goals (e.g., standards) is a critical aspect of an assessment's quality: if the assessment does not measure what it purports to measure, it could actually draw attention away from the goals of the system rather than toward them. This potential problem is compounded in a situation like that in Chicago, where the use of a single measure and the attachment of consequences to that measure (see below) intensify attention to the measure rather than to the larger goal of increased student learning. In this regard, it is important to note that the Iowa Test of Basic Skills has not been validated for the purpose of either school or student accountability.[25]

A second limitation of Chicago's and most other school accountability systems concerns the periodicity and specificity (grain size) of the information provided by the outcome measure.[26] On the one hand, a test given once a year that reports a general indication of the content and skills that students have and have not mastered can be extremely valuable for identifying schools and subjects areas that may need additional attention, resources, or, possibly, changes in strategies. An important contribution of school accountability systems in places like Chicago and Maryland, for example, is that they have directed the spotlight at failing parts of the system that can then be given additional assistance.[27] A similar argument could be made for some states under NCLB (see LeFloch, this volume). However, while such information is useful at these higher levels of aggregation, its potential for directly improving strategies in the classroom is limited. Such assessments are usually administered in the spring to measure student learning during the academic year, but the results are not available in time for the relevant teacher to alter instruction in response to the test. Even if the scores were available earlier in the year, the infrequency and lack of specificity of results is still a problem.

A third limitation of the quality of the information is an extension of the second, and concerns the appropriate balance of information about outcomes and information about processes. The implication is that the actor—whether that actor is an individual or an organization—must have valid and reliable information on both outcomes and processes. Yet, school accountability systems focus almost exclusively on outcomes, producing little in the way of reliable information on instruction or organizational practices. Some authors have argued that the production of such process-based information at aggregated levels would introduce further measurement problems and unduly constrain practice.[28] That the external accountability system does not generate information on practice might not be a problem if such information were available at the school level. Substantial research suggests that when teachers share information about instruction as well as student learning, they are better able to adapt their practice to the needs and progress of their students.[29] However, the egg-crate structure of U.S. schools impedes such adaptation; information on instructional strategies and processes is held privately by teachers and only rarely shared across the school as the basis for future learning (Lortie 1975; McLaughlin and Talbert 2001). Our research in Chicago suggests that bureaucratic school accountability policies are insufficient to establish the patterns of interaction that might foster more effective information sharing in low capacity schools.

Patterns of Interaction Instead, our data reveal a fairly unidirectional (top-down) flow of information throughout the system. For example, rather than being opportunities for collective sharing of information and knowledge, meetings between assistance providers and central office staff and between principals and district liaison personnel were reportedly occasions in which schools and those working with them were simply the recipients of information and mandates rather than sources of valuable information in their own right. When information did flow the other way (from schools and those working with them up into the system), it focused on whether people were carrying out prescribed tasks; that is, whether external partners were providing agreed upon services, whether schools were implementing specifics of school plans, and whether teachers were understanding and using the tools and techniques disseminated by the external partners (Finnigan, O'Day, and Wakelyn 2001).

Even those instances in which one might expect more collective problem solving—such as in the school improvement planning process—more often than not became symbolic exercises in responding to formulaic requirements of the district office rather than thoughtful and inclusive learning experiences for the staff.[30] The planning template was handed down from the Office of Accountability and schools complied, with emphasis on compliance over self-reflection being noticeably stronger in the least improving, lowest capacity schools.[31] What was perhaps most distressing was that this transmission model of information flow also characterized the professional development provided by the external partners, the bulk of which consisted of traditional short workshops rather than intensive inquiry-based explorations of either content or instructional practice (Finnigan et al. 2001).

The end result is that much of the response we saw in schools involved their reacting to directions imposed from above and outside the school rather than reflecting on internal practices. This response is perhaps unsurprising. Hierarchical control and information dissemination are characteristic of large bureaucracies like CPS, and well-established, internalized organizational codes are difficult to change (March 1991). Moreover, the "get tough" approach and the urban politics underlying the school probation policy could be expected to exacerbate these tendencies. By defining the problem as low expectations and a lack of effort on the part of school staff, the forces that come from higher in the system and outside the schools seek to push those inside to work harder. The accompanying incentives only reinforce control and enforcement over system learning.

Maladaptive Incentive Structures While much of the benefit of current school accountability schemes is supposed to be that they provide incentives to motivate improvement, we found the incentive structures in Chicago actually exacerbated the problem of motivation in some low-performing, low-capacity schools.

The emphasis on negative incentives (stigma of probation, threat of reconstitution) tied to a single measure (ITBS) appears to have resulted in two tendencies that work against long-term improvement. First, attention in these schools became focused not so much on student learning per se, but on getting off or staying off probation. This goal essentially places adult desires (to remove the professional stigma and avoid administrative scrutiny) over the needs of students (Evans and Wei 2001). Second, to achieve this goal, probation schools exhibited an emphasis on strategies to produce immediate increases in test scores, often to the neglect of longer-term success. The combination of these tendencies produced a number of dysfunctional practices.

Most common was the emphasis on test preparation in the form of intensive drill and practice to raise student scores. Some schools even redesigned their curriculum not only to reflect the general skills on the ITBS but to align the proportion of time allotted in the curriculum to a given discrete skill with the proportion of test items measuring that skill. In such cases, the test specifications became the curriculum specifications as well. Another common practice was to triage assistance (mostly test preparation) to students scoring near grade-level cutoffs in the hope that, by raising these students' scores slightly, the school could escape probation. These and similar practices suggest the allocation of resources to achieve adult ends (e.g., getting off probation) rather than to meet the greatest student needs.

Such patterns, which have been noted in prior research on high-stakes testing in education,[32] are not uncommon in organizations in crisis. A focused search for short-term strategies to satisfy a specific target is typical when an organization's performance falls below its aspirations or goals (March 1994; Simon 1986). Low performance combined with negative incentives, including a threat to the organization's position or survival (as is the case of school probation), increases the potential for maladaptive response.

A comprehensive review of research on organizational response to threat (Staw, Sanderlands, and Dutton 1981) uncovered two dominant and often maladaptive patterns, both of which are relevant to the earlier discussion of organizational learning. First, rather than expanding their use of information to find solutions to the problem, threatened organizations and individuals actually restrict their information processing, relying instead on previously held internal hypotheses and expectations. Exacerbated by stress, this reliance produces a rigidity of action rather than an expansion of strategies and adaptation. A second pattern associated with the presence of threat is centralization of authority, which in the case of schools serves to further enhance the bureaucratic, control-oriented patterns of interaction mentioned earlier (Staw et al. 1981). Both patterns were observed in low-performing schools in Chicago. We can expect individual and system learning to be constrained under these conditions, as well as innovation and examination of existing practice and assumptions.[33]

A second limitation of the incentive structures is the unbalanced reliance on collective incentives. This relates to a problem raised at the beginning of this chapter regarding the relationship between individual action and collective accountability. With a focus on schoolwide consequences, the policy offers few incentives for individuals to improve their practice. Individual teacher evaluation is not well aligned with either outcome measures or standards of practice likely to produce those outcomes. In many schools there is little accountability for individual teachers at all, and in others, teachers receive little recognition for improving their practice. One revealing example occurred at one of our case study schools in which a teacher who was working hard to improve practice was repeatedly told by her principal that she could not get an "excellent" rating because "if we had excellent teachers, this school would not be on probation." In other words, until the school as a whole was removed from probation, this teacher could not expect any reward for her individual efforts, no matter what the actual quality of her work. The effect of this proclamation was a sharp decrease in this teacher's motivation and commitment to the school. While we could attribute this result to the actions of a single principal, what becomes clear is that the policy relies on the ability of the principal (or others in the school community) to motivate the individuals on the school's staff. Where the principal is unable to provide such motivation (often the case in low-performing schools), the effect of the policy on individual teachers is likely to be weak, or even negative. Alternatively, where the principal is an effective motivator or where the connections among individuals are mutually reinforcing, the lack of individual incentives may be mitigated by the strong identification of individuals with the group. This may help to explain why probation schools with higher levels of teacher–teacher trust, peer collaboration, and collective responsibility improved more rapidly than others in our Chicago study (Gwynne and Easton 2001). Perhaps other incentives are at work in these schools to motivate individual behavior.[34]

Weak Resource Allocation and Knowledge Development Strategies   One of the most promising aspects of outcomes-based school accountability is the use of information to direct attention and resources where they are most needed. In Chicago, this reallocation mainly took the form of external assistance to low-performing schools. Our data indicate, however, how the potential effect of this substantial reallocation of resources was mitigated by the low intensity and lack of focus of most of the support actually provided to schools. For example, External Partners[35] on average spent only one or two person-days per week in the schools and with few exceptions their work provided neither a consistent and coherent focus on literacy instruction (the target of the policy) nor a clear strategy for organizational change (Finnigan et al. 2001). The limitations of the assistance may be attributed in part to problems of implementation, such as the weak quality control in the selection of the external partner candidates. In addition, however, the weak specification of the policy with regard to the content or goals of the assistance gave little guidance to either the schools or the support providers themselves about where to concentrate their energies. Such weak specification is common in school accountability policies in other jurisdictions as well. It derives on the one hand from a desire to respond to internal school context and on the other from the policy's emphasis on student outcomes to the neglect of information—or a theory of action—about instruction. The resulting diffuseness of the assistance, however, does little to highlight or solve problems of attribution discussed earlier. Moreover, the policy neglect of other inputs—such as reallocation of human or other resources—also weakens the potential impact.

Summary of Chicago Probation

What does this discussion of the CPS experience add up to in light of the framework and central problems of school accountability outlined earlier? On the one hand, school accountability policies like those in Chicago or NCLB have clearly helped focus attention throughout the system on student outcomes and have provided data that can be used for targeting resources and assistance where they are most needed, particularly in low-performing schools. On the other hand, this outcome-based school accountability approach suffers from a number of inherent weaknesses that make it, as it is currently construed, unlikely to effect the deep changes necessary for long-term improvement, particularly in low-performing, low-capacity schools. Four such weaknesses stand out:

1. The problems of validity, periodicity, and specificity in the outcome measures, coupled with inattention to information on instructional practice, make attribution and thus learning at the school or individual teacher level difficult.[36]

2. Most school accountability systems, including those under NCLB, still operate from a bureaucratic control model and thus fail to create the interaction patterns and normative structures within schools that encourage sustained learning and adaptation. Most low-performing schools lack such patterns and structures.

3. Reliance on negative incentives undermines innovation and risk-taking in threatened schools and diverts attention to organizational survival rather than student learning. Moreover, most current incentive structures fail to foster individual motivation or to reward adult learning and changes in practice that might lead to sustained improvement.

4. Finally, the reallocation of assistance and resources for increasing the capacity of low-performing schools is generally inadequate and weakly specified. Unfocused assistance based on transmission models of learning

does little to build the knowledge base needed for valid interpretation of information produced by the system.

While some of these shortcomings are exacerbated by poor implementation, they derive from fundamental assumptions inherent in the design of current school accountability systems, including NCLB. Current approaches have not solved any of the three problems outlined at the beginning of this chapter: the relationship between collective accountability and individual action; the tension between external and internal sources of control; and the production, spread, and use of information that can help solve problems of attribution caused by the complexity of school organizations. Thus, reliance on bureaucratic forms of accountability, even with better implementation, is unlikely to lead to the kind of improvement desired.

Is there an alternative?

PROFESSIONAL ACCOUNTABILITY: ALTERNATIVE OR ADDITION?

Perhaps the most commonly posed alternative to bureaucratic or administrative accountability in education is that of professional accountability (Adams and Kirst 1999; Darling-Hammond and Ascher 1991; O'Reilly 1996). Professional accountability is rooted in the assumption that teaching is too complex an activity to be governed by bureaucratically defined rules and routines. Rather, like other professions, effective teaching rests on professionals acquiring specialized knowledge and skills and being able to apply such knowledge and skills to the specific contexts in which they work. In mature professions, the requisite knowledge is articulated in professionally determined standards of practice, and professional accountability involves members of those professions assuming responsibility for the definition and enforcement of those standards.

In education, the focus of professional accountability might be described as threefold. First, it is centered on the process of instruction; that is, on the work of teachers as they interact with students around instructional content (Cohen and Ball 1999; McLaughlin and Talbert 2001). Professional accountability thus concerns the performance of adults in the system at least as much as the performance of students.[37] Second, much of the focus of professional accountability involves ensuring that educators acquire and apply the knowledge and skills needed for effective practice. Knowledge development is front and center. Third, professional accountability involves the norms of professional interchange. These norms include placing the needs of the client (students) at the center of professional work, collaborating with other professionals to address those needs and ensure the maintenance of standards of practice, and committing to the improvement of practice as part and parcel of professional responsibility (Darling-Hammond 1990).

At the system level, mechanisms of professional accountability center on teacher preparation, teacher licensure, and peer review. At the school level, professional accountability rests both on individual educators assuming responsibility for following standards of practice and on their professional interaction with colleagues and clients. Mentoring, collaboration, and collective problem solving in response to student needs, and some form of peer review to ensure quality of practice are all aspects of school-site professional accountability. Advocates for professionally based forms of accountability argue that this approach holds the most promise for the improvement of teaching and, by extension, for the improvement of student learning.

Beyond the theoretical appeal of professional accountability, a growing body of empirical evidence points to aspects of professionalism as important components of school improvement. Lee and Smith (1996), for example, find a significant positive relationship between student achievement gains and teachers' collective responsibility for students' academic success in high school.[38] Meanwhile, various researchers have pointed to the positive impact on instruction and student achievement of teacher interaction and collaboration in school-based professional communities (Little 1990; McLaughlin and Talbert 2001; Newmann and Wehlage 1995; Talbert and McLaughlin, chapter 9 this volume). Community School District 2 in New York City provides proof of the deep impact professional culture and professional development can have as a strategy for improvement and system management (Elmore 1997).

Combining the Bureaucratic and the Professional

Elsewhere (O'Day 2002), I have argued that despite its appeal, professionalism is as yet too weak in the United States to provide the sole impetus for school improvement. In addition, certain tools associated with bureaucratic accountability at higher levels of the system provide much-needed mechanisms for managing and allocating resources effectively and in ways that professional accountability alone cannot. I concluded that a combination of administrative and bureaucratic accountability may be most useful to create an environment that would foster long-term improvement. Such combinations are common in other professions.

Using the CEO District in Baltimore City Schools as an example, I examined how a combination of administrative and professional accountability allows for a more thorough and balanced incorporation of all aspects of the accountability framework outlined earlier. In doing so, such a combination also addresses the three underlying problems of accountability described at the beginning of this chapter. Recall that the first of these problems concerned the interplay between collective accountability for the school unit and the requisite change in behavior of the individuals within that unit. The addition of professional accountability at the school site strengthens the linkages between individual teachers and their schools by fostering interaction around common work, a sense of shared purpose, and identity as members of the school community. These ties increase individual motivation to act in accordance with the community's collectively defined endeavor. Regarding the second problem—that of influencing the internal workings of the school—the strong professional norms generated by the infusion of professional accountability, especially collective responsibility for student learning, become potential resources and mechanisms for orienting the entire school community toward the higher levels of student performance sought by reformers and the general public. Finally, specific information generated through ongoing professional examination of student performance and adult practice and the sharing of this information in professional communities of practice help to solve the information problems that have been so much the focus of this chapter.

CONCLUDING THOUGHTS: IMPLICATIONS FOR NCLB

A thoughtful combination of outcome-based school accountability and professional accountability can provide the means of addressing all these information needs and thus for fostering the evidence-based improvement sought by many system reformers and policy makers. Whether such a thoughtful combination is likely to come about, however, particularly in light of the highly prescriptive and stringent testing and accountability provisions of the No Child Left Behind Act, is another matter. Indeed this analysis suggests that the legislation will need substantial revision if it is to have any hope of stimulating real and sustained school improvement. Here I suggest just three broad areas to consider. More specific recommendations would need to address the details of a broad range of NCLB's accountability-relevant provisions.

Increase Flexibility

There is a need for greater flexibility in nearly all aspects of the law but especially in the identification and intervention processes. Evidence suggests that NCLB's one-size fits all timeframe and delineation of consequences have resulted in considerable activity at the state and local levels to comply with the requirements of the law (Center on Education Policy 2006; LeFloch et al. 2006). But compliance and improvement can be at odds, as the example of Chicago's probation policy demonstrates. This is particularly true when there is little room for risk taking and creative solutions to difficult problems of practice, which is often the case when sanctions are tied so closely to such narrow outcome indicators.

An alternative would be to use test scores as a trigger for professional review and assistance, employing multiple measures of both outcomes and processes to determine actual consequences.

Expand Incentive Structures

There is also a need for more varied incentive structures to motivate improvement. Indeed the incentive structures under NCLB have the same or even greater punitive character as those in CPS probation. With the exception of a few states which have applied for flexibility to use value-added models in their identification systems, NCLB does little to recognize improvement. Schools either make the target or they don't; there is no credit for getting closer. As a result, the only incentives are negative ones. Moreover, with the multiple independent indicators and overlapping subgroups, NCLB has exponentially more ways for a school or district to fail to reach targets, and the likelihood of failure will only increase as the performance objectives approach the 2014 goal of 100 percent of students at proficiency. If prior experience is any indication, the threats associated with failure are likely to decrease rather than increase professional interaction and creative problem solving in the most threatened schools. My earlier admonition about the importance of state and federal accountability structures not getting in the way of professional community and professional accountability is relevant here.

Increase Capacity Building

Finally, there is a clear need for greater resources and attention to capacity building, particularly in the lowest performing schools. As more and more schools become identified, the already limited resources for capacity building and professional development will become scarcer and be spread so thinly across schools as to be negligible against the need. Without the knowledge to interpret data on performance and link it with information on instructional practices, teachers and school leaders are likely to fall into attribution errors and knee-jerk responses to missed targets. Since low performing schools are often also low in initial capacity, it is essential that the assistance provided be of sufficient intensity, duration, and quality to build the foundation for success. This is an expensive proposition. It means that states need not only *more resources* for capacity building, but also *greater flexibility* to decide the best means and places for targeting these resources where they are likely to have the greatest impact.

In the months following publication of this volume, debate over reauthorization of the Elementary and Secondary Education Act will heat up, with many and varied proposals for revising or eliminating multiple provisions of the 2001 version of the law, the NCLB Act. The political process surrounding such legislative events is notorious for attempts to reduce complex problems to easily understood sound bites and then to construct (or sell) simple policy solutions to these reframed problems. While simple actions can indeed have far-reaching effects in complex systems, the result is not always the one predicted by the straightforward logic of the policy framers. And even if the outcome seems to be consistent in the short term—that is, even if test scores go up—processes may be put in place that undermine the longer term objectives. Congress and its staff would thus do well to consider carefully the impact of accountability measures not only on test scores but also on the functioning of the educational entities—classrooms, schools, and districts—responsible for producing these and other student outcomes over the long haul.

Notes

1. Work for this paper was supported in part by Office of Educational Research and Improvement (Grant #R308A60003 to the Consortium for Policy Research in Education and by two grants from the Spencer Foundation (one to the Wisconsin Center for Educational Research for the study of school probation in Chicago elementary schools and the other to Marshall S. Smith to explore implementation issues in standards-based reform). All findings, opinions, and conclusions expressed in this paper are those of the author and do not necessarily reflect the views of any of the funders. This chapter draws heavily on an earlier paper published in the *Harvard Educational Review* (O'Day, 2002). Reprinted by permission of the *Harvard Educational Review*.

2. Note: Much of this chapter is reprinted from an earlier version published in the *Harvard Educational Review* (O'Day, 2002). The editors of this volume requested its inclusion because of the relevance of the policies and analysis to sociological perspectives on NCLB.

3. The Consortium for Policy Research in Education unites five leading research institutions: the University of Pennsylvania, Harvard University, Stanford University, the University of Michigan, and the University of Wisconsin-Madison, in collaborative efforts to improve educational systems and student learning through research on educational reform, policy, and finance.

4. See O'Day (2002) for a more extended discussion of complexity theory and school improvement.

5. Chicago's school accountability policy is explained in greater detail in the section on bureaucratic accountability and in note 22. In brief, the Chicago system identifies low performing schools for "probation" based on student test results and metes out both assistance and sanctions to spur improvement in those schools. This chapter draws on data from a three-year study of school probation policies and practices in Chicago elementary schools.

6. While this chapter focuses on the explicit organizational improvement goals of school accountability, these policies have symbolic and political purposes as well. For a fuller discussion of some of the politics underlying Chicago's school probation policies, see Bennett (2001).

7. For a range of implementation discussions over the past three decades, see, for example, Berman and McLaughlin (1974), Goertz, Floden, and O'Day (1995), McLaughlin (1987), Spillane (2000), and Weatherly and Lipsky (1977).

8. See, for example, McLaughlin and Talbert (1993), Newmann and Wehlage (1995), DeBray et al. (2001), or Elmore (2001) for a discussion of the power of internal norms.

9. Reliance on the power of such information is central not only to the school accountability policies of NCLB but also to the choice provisions and to processes for ensuring that teachers are "highly qualified" in the subjects they teach.

10. For popular accounts of complexity theory in the natural and social sciences, see Kauffman (1995), Lewin (1992), and Waldrop (1992).

11. "Superstitious learning occurs when the subjective experience of learning is compelling but the connections between actions and outcomes are misspecified" (Levitt and March 1988, 325).

12. It is important to note that organizational inertia is enhanced as the web of supporting relationships grows, creating codependencies among units of the organization and between it and external systems. For a discussion of how initial advantage and increasing returns serve to lock in certain solutions and strategies, see Arthur (1989) or Marion (1999).

13. Coupling, in organizations literature, refers to the connections and interdependence of elements of a system. . . . According to Weick (1976), loosely "coupled events are responsive [to one another], *but* each event also preserves its own identity and some evidence of its physical or logical separateness…and their attachment may be circumscribed, infrequent, weak in its mutual effects, unimportant, and/or slow to respond…. Loose coupling also carries connotations of impermanence, dissolvability, and tacitness all of which are potentially crucial properties of the 'glue' that holds organizations together" (p.3).

14. An example of such incentives would be salary increases given to teachers for taking additional course credits whether or not such coursework has any bearing on school improvement plans and strategies, any effect on teachers' actual instructional knowledge, or any impact on student performance.

15. In addition to school accountability, student accountability—in which consequences for individual students such as graduation or grade promotion are based on standardized measures of academic performance—has become an increasingly prevalent aspect of standards-based reform in the past several years. School accountability remains the lynchpin in most jurisdictions, however, as well as in NCLB.

16. In the case of federal policies (e.g., Title I) *to whom* may also refer indirectly to the federal government, but still by way of the state and local education agencies (SEAs and LEAs). Similarly, where authority for a given policy derives from state law (legal accountability) and the courts are the ultimate arbiter, administration remains the responsibility of the superordinate levels of the educational bureaucracy to whom the schools are most directly accountable. From the perspective of the schools, then, these cases are almost indistinguishable from other examples of bureaucratic accountability.

17. Note: In this chapter, the terms *bureaucratic accountability, outcome-based accountability,* and *outcome-based bureaucratic accountability* will be used interchangeably with school accountability. This discussion excludes choice systems in which schools are held accountable directly to parents through the market.

18. It may be important here to note that the designation "outcome-based bureaucratic accountability" differs somewhat from the terms used in prior typologies—in large part because it incorporates two somewhat different approaches to categorizing accountability systems. For a fuller explication of these typologies and their relationship to the designation used here, please see note 20 in O'Day (2002).

19. The ITBS is an example of the type of commercially produced, norm-referenced, multiple-choice, timed assessment used in many jurisdictions for accountability, monitoring, and placement purposes.

20. All probation schools were required to develop a corrective action/school improvement plan and literacy plan to organize their improvement efforts. These plans were reviewed at the central office, and their implementation is monitored by the probation manager assigned to the school. Assistance came in the form of additional resources for external support providers called External Partners. If the necessary improvement in test scores is not manifest at the end of a vaguely specified number of years, school personnel may be replaced en masse (reconstitution) or individually through a more extended peer review process (reengineering). Such consequences, however, have rarely been administered.

21. The Comprehensive School Reform Demonstration (CSRD) Program was a federal effort to encourage the adoption of research-based, whole school reform models, especially in Title I schools identified as being in need of improvement.

22. This does not include the resources allocated for remedial summer or after school classes or for practice and testing materials. See Finnigan, O'Day, and Wakelyn (2003) for a fuller discussion of the assistance program.

23. For varying prespectives on the impact of these accountability systems, see Grissmer, Flanagan, Kawata, and Williamson (2000), Haney (2000), Klein, Hamilton, McCaffrey, and Stecher (2000), and Koretz and Barron (1998).

24. This research was conducted by a team of researchers from the University of Wisconsin-Madison and the Consortium on Chicago School Research and was sponsored by the Spencer Foundation and the Office of Educational Research and Improvement.
25. Similarly, although assessments used for NCLB accountability are required to be aligned with the state's content standards, many such assessments have not actually been validated for accountability purposes.
26. By periodicity I mean the frequency and regularity of information on student learning generated by the system. Specificity refers to the degree of detail of the information. For example, information on student knowledge regarding particular decoding skills (like facility with beginning or ending consonants) is more specific than would be a single test score covering all aspects of decoding, let alone a single score for reading.
27. The No Child Left Behind Act of 2001 has substantially altered the specifics of many existing school accountability systems—for example, the nature of the assessments or the timeframe for improvement—but the general intent (to implement a system that identifies lower performing units for intervention) remains.
28. See, for example, *The Debate on Opportunity to Learn Standards: Supporting Works* (National Governors' Association 1993) or the Report of the National Academy of Education Panel on Standards-Based Education (McLaughlin, Shepard, and O'Day 1995).
29. See, for example, the literature on the role of professional community (e.g., McLaughlin and Talbert 1993, 2001; Newmann and Wehlage 1995) and on information sharing in high-performing schools (Darling-Hammond 1996; Mohrman and Lawler 1996).
30. This conclusion derives primarily from our observations and interviews regarding the planning process in our 10 case study schools but is augmented by additional analysis of the planning documents and processes in a slightly larger and more diverse group of schools. See Gross, Wei, and O'Day (2002) for further discussion of this pattern.
31. Some exceptions exist, of course, with the more self-reflective school communities generally showing the greater gains in performance (Gross et al. 2002).
32. See, for example, Firestone and Mayrowetz (2001), McNeil and Valenzuela (2000), Nolen, Haladaya, and Haas (1992), and Smith and Rottenberg (1991).
33. These tendencies might be mitigated if a policy included positive incentives (rewards) for learning and for improvements in instructional practice. While some systems do include rewards, these are tied to improvements in outcomes, not practice or learning. Observers often note the need for interim indicators of organizational practice and capacity to be included in the accountability structures, but they rarely are.
34. For a discussion of these other incentives, see, for example, Mohrman and Lawler (1996) and Darling-Hammond (1996).
35. External partners are the official external support providers approved and funded through the school probation policy. See note 20.
36. The use of standards-based assessments in NCLB accountability could help to alleviate the validity problem, but only if such assessments have been validated for this purpose. The periodicity and specificity shortcomings remain. Indeed, even the heightened attention to low performing schools—the most successful result of outcomes-based accountability—may be mitigated under NCLB as more and more schools become identified for improvement, thus watering down the attention any can receive and potentially undermining the legitimacy of the identification system.
37. See Campbell, McCloy, Oppler, and Sager (1993) for the importance of the distinction between performance and outcomes.
38. See also Porter and Brophy (1988).

REFERENCES

Adams, J. E. and M. Kirst. 1999. New demands for educational accountability: Striving for results in an era of excellence. In *Handbook of research in educational administration*, 2nd ed., ed. J. Murphey and K. S. Louis, 463–89. San Francisco: Jossey-Bass.
Arthur, W. B. 1989. The economy and complexity. In *Lectures in the sciences of complexity*, ed. D. L. Stein, 713–40. Redwood City, CA: Addison-Wesley.

Axelrod, R. and M. D. Cohen.1999. *Harnessing complexity: Organizational implications of a scientific frontier*. New York: Free Press.

Bennett, A. 2001. The history, politics and theory of action of the Chicago probation policy. Paper presented at the annual meeting of the American Educational Research Association, April, Seattle, WA.

Berman, P. and M. McLaughlin. 1978. *Factors affecting implementation and continuation*. Vol. 7 of *Federal programs supporting educational change*. Santa Monica, CA: RAND.

Campbell, J. P., R. A. McCloy, S. H. Oppler, and C. E. Sager. 1993. A theory of performance. In *Personnel selection in organizations*, ed. N. Schmitt, W. C. Borman, and Associates, 35–70. San Francisco: Jossey-Bass.

Enter on Education Policy. 2002. *From the capital to the classroom: Year 4 of the No Child Left Behind Act*. Washington, D.C.: Center on Education Policy.

Center on Education Policy, March 2006. *From the Capital to the Classroom: Year 4 of the No Child Left Behind Act*. Washington, DC: Center on Education Policy

Chicago Public Schools.2002. *Iowa test of basic skills: Citywide results over time, 1997–2002* (Report: ITOT-CW-white). Chicago: Author. Available: http://research.cps.k12.il.us/resweb/pdf/itbs_over_read_a.pdf

Cohen, D. K. and D. L. Ball. 1999. *Instruction, capacity, and improvement*. Philadelphia, PA: Consortium for Policy Research in Education.

Daft, R. L. and K. E. Weick. 1984. Toward a model of organizations as interpretation systems. *Academy of Management Review* 9:284–95.

Darling-Hammond, L. 1990. Teacher professionalism: Why and how? In *Schools as collaborative cultures: Creating the future now*, ed. A. Lieberman, 25–50. Bristol, PA: Falmer Press.

———. 1996. Restructuring schools for high performance. In *Rewards and reform: Creating educational incentives that work*, ed. S. Fuhrman and J. A. O'Day, 144–92. San Francisco: Jossey-Bass.

———. 1997. *The right to learn: A blueprint for creating schools that work*. San Francisco: Jossey-Bass.

——— and C. Ascher. 1991. *Creating accountability in big city school systems*. Urban Diversity Series No. 102. New York: ERIC Clearinghouse on Urban Education.

DeBray, E., G. Parson, and K.Woodworth. 2001. Patterns of response in four high schools under state accountability policies in Vermont and New York. In *From the capitol to the classroom: Standards-based reform in the states*, ed. S. Fuhrman, 170–92. Chicago: University of Chicago Press.

Elmore, R. F. 1996. Getting to scale with successful educational practices. In *Rewards and reform: Creating educational incentives that work*, ed. S. Fuhrman and J. A. O'Day, 294–329. San Francisco: Jossey-Bass.

———.1997. *Investing in teacher learning: Staff development and instructional improvement in Community District 2.* Philadelphia: Consortium for Policy Research in Education and the National Commission on Teaching and America's Future.

———. 2001. Psychiatrists and light bulbs: Educational accountability and the problem of capacity. Paper presented at the annual meeting of the American Educational Research Association, Seattle, WA.

———, C. H Abelmann, and S. H. Fuhrman. 1996. The new accountability in state education reform: From process to performance. In *Holding schools accountable: Performance-based reform in education*, ed. H. F. Ladd, 65–98. Washington, D.C.: Brookings Institution Press.

Evans, L. E. and H. H. Wei. 2001. Focusing the work of teachers and schools: The Chicago public schools probation policy. Paper prepared for the annual meeting of the American Educational Research Association, Seattle.

Finnigan, K. S. and B. M. Gross. 2001. Teacher motivation and the Chicago probation policy. Paper presented at the annual meeting of the American Educational Research Association, Seattle.

Finnigan, K., J. O'Day, and D. Wakelyn. Forthcoming. *External support to schools on probation: Getting a leg up?* Philadelphia: Consortium for Policy Research in Education and Consortium on Chicago School Research.

Firestone, W. A. and D. Mayrowetz. 2000. Rethinking "high stakes": Lessons from the United States and England and Wales. *Teachers College Record* 102:724–49.

Fuhrman, S. H. 1999. *The new accountability*. (CPRE Policy Brief No. RB 27). Philadelphia: Consortium on Policy Research in Education.

Goertz, M., R. Floden, and J. O'Day. 1995. *Findings and conclusions,* Vol. 1 of *Studies of education reform: Systemic reform.* New Brunswick, NJ: Consortium for Policy Research in Education.

Grissmer, D., A. Flanagan, J. Kawata, and S. Williamson. 2000. *Improving student achievement: What state NAEP test scores tell us* (MR-924-EDU). Santa Monica, CA: RAND.

Gross, B., H. Wei, and J. A. O'Day.2002. *Planning for improvement in Chicago schools on probation.* Unpublished Report, University of Wisconsin-Madison.

Gwynne, J. and J. Q. Easton. 2001. Probation, organizational capacity, and student achievement in Chicago elementary schools. Paper presented at the Annual Meeting of the American Educational Research Association, Seattle, WA.

Haney, W. 2000. The myth of the Texas miracle in education. *Education Policy Analysis Archives* 8: 41.

Huber, G. P. 1991. Organizational learning: The contributing processes and the literatures. *Organizational Science* 2 (1):88–115.

Kaufmann, S. 1995. *At home in the universe: The search for the laws of self-organization and complexity.* New York: Oxford University Press.

Kelley, C., A. Odden, A. Milanowski, and H. Heneman. 2000. *The motivational effects of school-based performance awards* (CPRE Policy Brief **No.** RB-29). Philadelphia: University of Pennsylvania, Consortium for Policy Research in Education.

Klein, S. P., L. S. Hamilton , D. F. McCaffrey, and B. M. Stecher. *What do test scores in Texas tell us?* Washington, D.C.: RAND.

Koretz, D., and S. Barron. 1998. *The validity of gains on the Kentucky instructional results information system* (MR-1014-EDU). Santa Monica, CA: RAND.

LeFloch, K. C., F. Martinez, J. O'Day, B. Stecher, and J. Taylor. 2006. *Increasing accountability for all students:Early implementation of the No Child Left Behind Act.* Washington D.C.: U.S. Department of Education.

Lee, V. and J. Smith. 1996. Collective responsibility for learning and its effects on gains in achievement for early secondary school students. *American Journal of Education* 104:103–47.

Levinthal, D. A. 1991. Organizational adaptation and environmental selection: Interrelated processes of change. *Organizational Science* 2 (1): 140–45**.**

Levitt, B., and J. G. March. 1988. Organizational learning. *Annual Review of Sociology* 14:319–40.

Lewin, R. 1992. *Complexity: Life at the edge of chaos.* New York: Macmillan.

Linn, R. L. 1997. Evaluating the Validity of Assessments: The consequences of use. *Educational Measurement: Issues and Practice* 16(2):14–16.

———. 2001. *The design and evaluation of educational assessment and accountability systems.* CSE Technical Report. Los Angeles, CA: Center for Research on Evaluation, Standards, and Student Testing, University of California, Los Angeles.

Little, J. W. 1990. The persistence of privacy: Autonomy and initiative in teachers' professional relations. *Teachers College Record* 91:509–36.

Lortie, D. C. 1975. *Schoolteacher: A sociological study.* Chicago: University of Chicago Press.

March, J. G. 1991. Exploration and exploitation in organizational learning. *Organizational Science* 2(1):71–87.

———. 1994. *A primer on decision making: How decisions happen.* New York: Free Press.

Marion, R. 1999. *The edge of organization: Chaos and complexity theories of formal social systems.* Thousand Oaks, CA: Sage.

McLaughlin, M. 1987. Learning from experience: Lessons from policy implementation. *Educational Evaluation and Policy Analysis* 9(2):171–78.

McLaughlin, M. W. and L. A. Shepard, with J. A. O'Day. 1995. *Improving education through standards-based reform: A report by the National Academy of Education Panel on Standards-Based Reform.* Stanford, CA: National Academy of Education.

McLaughlin, M. W. and J. E. Talbert. 1993. *Contexts that matter for teaching and learning.* Stanford, CA: Stanford University, School of Education, Center for Research on the Context of Teaching.

———. 2001. *Professional communities and the work of high school teaching.* Chicago: University of Chicago Press.

McNeil, L. and Valenzuela, A. (2000). The harmful impact of the TASS system of testing inTexas: Beneath the accountability rhetoric. In G. Orfield & M. Kornhaber (Eds.), *Raising standards or raising barriers: Inequality and high-stakes testing in public education* (pp. 127–150). Cambridge, MA: Harvard Civil Rights Project.

Mohrman, S. A. and E. E. Lawler. 1996. Motivation for school reform. In *Rewards and reform:*

Creating educational incentives that work, ed. S. H. Fuhrman and J. A. O'Day, 115–43. San Francisco, Jossey-Bass.

National Governors' Association. 1993. *The debate on opportunity-to-learn standards: Supporting works.* Washington, D.C.: Author.

Newmann, F. M. and G. G. Wehlage. 1995. *Successful school restructuring: A report to the public and educators by the Center on Organization and Restructuring of Schools.* Madison, WI: Center on Organization and Restructuring of Schools.

News in Brief. (2001). *Education Week*, November 14. http://www.edweek.org/ew/newstory. cfm?slug=11briefs.h21.

Nolen, S. B., T. M. Haladyna, and N. Haas. 1992. Uses and abuses of achievement test scores. *Educational Measurement: Issues and Practice* 11(2): 9–15.

O'Day, J. A. 1996. Incentives and school improvement. In *Rewards and reform: Creating educational incentives that work*, ed. S. Fuhrman & J. A. O'Day, 1–16. San Francisco: Jossey-Bass.

———. 2002. Complexity, accountability, and school improvement. *Harvard Educational Review* 72 (3): 293–329.

———. M. S. Smith. 1993. Systemic school reform and educational opportunity. In *Designing coherent education policy: Improving the system,* ed. S. H. Fuhrman, 250–312. San Francisco: Jossey Bass.

O'Reilly, F. E. 1996. *Educational accountability: Current practices and theories in use.* Cambridge, MA: Harvard University, Consortium for Policy Research in Education.

Porter, A. and J. Brophy. 1988. Good teaching: Insights from the work of the Institute for Research on Teaching. *Educational leadership* 45:75–84.

Scott, W. R. 1998. *Organizations: Rational, natural, and open systems,* 4th ed. Upper Saddle River, NJ: Prentice Hall.

Simon, H. A. 1986. Theories of bounded rationality. In *Decision and organization.* Vol. 2, ed. C. B. McGuire and R. Radner, 161–76. Minneapolis: University of Minnesota Press.

Siskin, L. S. 2004. The challenge of the high schools. In S. H. Fuhrman and R. F. Elmore (Eds.) *Redesigning accountability systems for education.* New York: Teachers College Press.

Sitkin, S. B. 1992. Learning through failure: The strategy of small losses. *Research in Organizational Behavior* 14:231–66.

Smith, M. L. and C. Rottenberg. 1991. Unintended consequences of external testing in elementary schools. *Educational Measurement: Issues and Practice,* 10(4):7–11.

Spillane, J. 2000. Cognition and policy implementation: District policy-makers and the reform of mathematics education. *Cognition and Instruction* 18:141–79.

Staw, B. M., L. E. Sanderlands, and J. E. Dutton. 1981. Threat-rigidity effects in organizational behavior: A multilevel analysis. *Administration Science Quarterly* 26:501–24.

Waldrop, M. M. 1992. *Complexity: The emerging science at the edge of order and chaos.* New York: Simon and Schuster.

Weatherly, R. and M. Lipsky. 1977. Street-level bureaucrats and institutional innovation: Implementing special-education reform. *Harvard Educational Review* 47: 171–97.

Weick, K. 1976. Educational organizations as loosely coupled systems. *Administrative Science Quarterly* 21: 1–19.

Westat 2001. *Report on the final evaluation of the city-state partnership.* Rockville, MD: Author.

3

Double Standards for Graduation Rate Accountability?

Or None?

Christopher B. Swanson

INTRODUCTION

The No Child Left Behind Act (NCLB), requires that the nation's public schools be held accountable for achieving high levels of educational proficiency for all students. The considerable public attention directed toward the state accountability systems mandated by NCLB has focused largely on the expansive student assessments required under the federal law and on the high-stakes sanctions applied to schools that consistently fail to meet established performance benchmarks. Often overlooked in these debates has been the fact that, in addition to test scores, state accountability systems must also incorporate at least one other indicator of academic performance. At the secondary education level this additional measure must be the high-school graduation rate.

Holding schools and districts accountable for improving both test scores and graduation rates is intended to serve as a critical safeguard against gaming strategies that may be abetted by high-stakes accountability systems. Suppose, for example, that an educational accountability system attached stakes only to test scores. One way to boost test scores would be to push the lowest performing students out of school. This kind of gaming strategy would result in higher achievement scores and would, therefore, help schools to avoid sanctions. But these apparent gains would be artificial, obtained only at the high cost of creating more dropouts. Requiring accountability for graduation rates is intended to counteract such perverse incentives that could undermine the spirit of the law.

The federal regulatory process has given states a tremendous amount of flexibility when implementing the accountability provisions related to graduation rates, latitude that does not exist for test scores. Some degree of state autonomy could be beneficial when enacting a complex law like NCLB and tailoring its provisions to better meet local needs. However, as this chapter will demonstrate, there is ample evidence that most states have constructed key aspects of their accountability systems in ways that systematically undermine the weight attached to graduation rates. This study attempts to move the debate over graduation rates and accountability forward by addressing a subsequent and more complicated question. Namely, what happens when an accountability system takes a low road on high-school graduation and how does this affect the number of school systems identified for assistance and corrective action?

We start by briefly sketching the nature of the nation's crisis in high-school graduation. We then review the status of state efforts to implement accountability over graduation rates under No Child Left Behind. This examination identifies several key aspects of these accountability systems over which states exert considerable control, provisions that could be manipulated in order to affect (presumably raise) the number of schools identified as making adequate progress under the law. The main portion of this study conducts a series of simulation analyses that gauge the extent to which two major choices states face—whether to impose a firm performance threshold and whether to disaggregate performance for specific subgroups—might skew the results that these accountability systems produce.

PUBLIC EDUCATION'S BEST-KEPT SECRET—
THE GRADUATION CRISIS

In an age of data-driven accountability, it is hard to imagine being surprised by a statistic, especially a basic piece of information that we think we already know about. Since 2002, as states have gone about the business of implementing the federal No Child Left Behind Act, the performance of the nation's public schools in a fundamental, albeit largely neglected area has been brought into a penetrating and unflattering light. As it turns out, graduation rates are lower than previously thought, probably much lower.

If asked to guess the graduation rate in the nation's public schools, the conventional wisdom would suggest a figure in the neighborhood of 85 percent. For decades, in fact, commonly reported statistics from sources like the Current Population Survey (CPS) would have pointed to an answer in that range. Databases like the CPS or Census are readily available and well-known, which have made them attractive sources of information. But at the same time, it is also important to note that statistics derived from these sources typically capture eventual level of educational attainment in the adult population rather than attempting to gauge the percent of public schools students earning diplomas with their expected graduating class. In addition, estimates from population-based surveys often are not able produce reliable annual estimates below the regional level; cannot readily distinguish between public and private school students; and reflect the educational attainment of adults who no longer live in the place where they attended, graduated from, or dropped out of high school. Ultimately, population statistics from sources like the CPS are ill-suited for measuring the performance of public education systems, which has become a primary concern with the advent of No Child Left Behind.

A much more sanguine perspective on graduation rates emerges from a recent wave of research examining data from the actual public school systems being held accountable under No Child Left Behind. To take an example from this growing body of research, a 2006 study by Editorial Projects in Education found that just under 70 percent of public high-school students nationwide graduate from high school with a diploma. Graduation rates also differ dramatically from state to state. In the highest performing states, about 80 percent of all students complete high- school with a diploma. New Jersey, North Dakota, Iowa, Vermont, and Wisconsin each have graduation rates around this level. At the opposite end of the spectrum, some states graduate little more than half of their students. Graduation rates in six states fall below 60 percent, with South Carolina last in the nation at 53 percent. This constitutes a gap of about 30 percentage points between the highest and lowest performing states.

Further cause for concern can be found in the extremely large disparities found among racial and ethnic groups, which can exceed 25 percentage points at the national level. American Indian and black students have around a 50-50 chance of graduating from high-school, with Hispanic students graduating at around 56 percent. This compares to over three-quarters of white and Asian students earning diplomas. Similar disparities exist within many states. The situation appears to be even more dire for students in the nation's urban and high-poverty districts. About 60 percent of *all* students graduate in urban districts, with similar rates found in racially segregated and high-poverty school systems.

NCLB ACCOUNTABILITY AND GRADUATION RATES

The two stated goals of NCLB are to raise overall performance levels and to close gaps between high- and low-performing groups. Perhaps the most visible means through which the federal law attempts to accomplish these goals is by mandating that all states must enact rigorous performance-based accountability systems. Schools that consistently fail to meet established standards are subject to a series of escalating sanctions. The law requires that these systems must focus on test scores as the primary outcome but must also include another academic indicator—graduation rates for high schools and another outcome of the state's choosing for the lower grades. In theory, the principles of high-stakes account-ability should apply to both test scores and graduation rates. In practice, however, federal regulations issued for the implementation of Title I (which includes requirements for designing these accountability systems) have permitted the states to exercise considerable autonomy when deciding on the standards and stakes for graduation rates.

Indeed, reviews of approved accountability plans reveal that states are tak-ing full advantage of the flexibility that the federal regulations grant them over graduation rates, with two main consequences. First, a double standard has es-sentially developed within the world of NCLB accountability—high standards for test scores and very weak standards for graduation (Table 3.1). Second, as a result of this effective lack of uniform federal standards, both the rules govern-ing graduation accountability and the standards are much different and highly variable from state to state.[1]

There are no commonly accepted methodological standards for calculating graduation rates. NCLB outlines a general definition for a graduation rate, which must be the "percentage of students who graduate from secondary school with a regular diploma in the standard number of years." However, neither the law nor federal regulations offer recommendations or guidance regarding specific methods for operationalizing this definition in a more concrete way. This has left states in the position of choosing their own statistical indicators for measuring the graduation rate. Studies by Editorial Projects in Education and the Urban Institute have reviewed the state plans that document the accountability systems being implemented under NCLB, in an effort to document the various methods being used to calculate graduation rates.[2] An examination of these approaches reveals a veritable patchwork quilt, with numerous distinctive methodologies currently in use across the nation. In fact, several states have actually adopted dropout rates or persistence rates (i.e., the percent of students not dropping out of school). While use of these latter measures has been approved by the

Table 3.1 Accountability standards under NCLB for tested achievement and graduation

Element of NCLB Accountability	Academic Achievement	High School Graduation
Accepted methodological standards for measuring outcomes	✓	✗
High and uniform goal for final performance levels	✓	✗
States must set annual measurable objectives (AMOs) for performance	✓	✗
To make AYP in the "first instance" goals must be meet 1. overall and 2. for each individual subgroup	✓	✗

U.S. Department of Education, neither indicator actually counts high-school graduates nor could either be reasonably construed as a "graduation" rate as stipulated under the law.

Of greater concern, however, is the fact that different formulas for computing a graduation rate can generate much different results. How large are these discrepancies? A study by the Urban Institute calculated graduation rates for a large number of school districts employing four different formulas similar to those states are using under NCLB. The results reveal average differences of as much as 14 percentage points between the results produced by the various formulas.[3] This research found a clear distinction between formulas based primarily on enrollment data and those that incorporate data on dropouts. Comparatively speaking, the latter systematically overestimate the graduation rate. It is worth noting that this is what would be expected if large numbers of dropouts were going uncounted, as researchers have long suspected. Since the majority of states use such dropout-dependent graduation rate formulas, many publicly reported statistics may present school performance in a distorted, rose-colored light.

The regulations issued by the Department of Education have also allowed states the discretion to establish their own performance targets for graduation rates. Whereas NCLB mandates an unequivocal 100 percent proficiency target for test scores, final states goals for graduation range anywhere from 50 to 100 percent of students finishing high school with a diploma.[4] In practice, however, the absence of a high and uniform goal for graduation may carry less of an impact than one might expect. This reality follows from another twist in the federal regulatory provisions. Namely, states are not required to establish annual measurable objectives setting out incremental performance targets for graduation rates, as they must do for test scores. In fact for most states, any amount of improvement is considered "adequate progress" when it comes to graduation rates. This would hold true even if gains are vanishingly small and even if the graduation rate itself does not meet a reasonable minimum threshold for satisfactory performance. Under these conditions, a school could make AYP if its graduation rate creeps up from an abysmal 25.1 percent to a nearly as abysmal 25.2 percent.

Finally, graduation accountability breaks with a fundamental principle underpinning NCLB's mission to close achievement gaps. State accountability systems are not required to examine subgroup graduation rates when making their primary determinations for whether a school or district is making adequate yearly progress. In the absence of a firm federal mandate, states need only consider the graduation rates of specific subgroups (i.e., historically low-performing groups such as racial–ethnic minorities or students living in poverty) when invoking the second-chance "safe harbor" provision of NCLB accountability. Under safe harbor, schools or districts that fail to meet annual benchmarks for a particular student group may nonetheless make AYP if they: (1) demonstrate a specified amount of progress on test scores, and (2) meet performance expectations for the other academic indicator, which would be high-school graduation rates. When exercising the safe harbor provision for subgroups at the high-school level, the disaggregated graduation rates must be considered.

It should be noted that the states are required to calculate graduation rates for these subgroups and to publicly report these statistics as part of school report cards, even if those results do not factor into actual accountability decisions. But in light of the sometimes striking racial gaps in graduation levels cited earlier, the lack of disaggregated accountability for graduation rates represents a significant weakening of NCLB's commitment to addressing the performance deficits of historically disadvantaged groups.

To date, there has been little attempt to quantify the consequences of the alternative graduation accountability rules states may establish under NCLB or similar accountability regimes. Using simulation analyses that draw data from a national census of schools and districts, we will explore the consequences of two fundamental state choices in depth: whether to set a firm performance objective for graduation rates and whether to disaggregate results for specific subgroups.

DATA AND METHODS

Although researchers, educators, and policymakers all recognize the benefits of having accurate graduation rates, we have yet to arrive at a consensus regarding the best way to generate national, state, and local estimates given the data at hand. Fortunately, it will not be necessary to decide on the optimal solution for our present purposes. The way in which we calculate graduation rates (provided this is done in a uniform manner) is actually a secondary concern. Our primary interest lies in understanding the implications of state decisions for attaching stakes to these rates, regardless of how they are calculated.

In this study, graduation rates are computed in the same way for all school districts nationwide. A single, publicly accessible data source is used in these analyses—the U.S. Department of Education's Common Core of Data (CCD). A national census of public schools and districts, the CCD provides the most comprehensive source of data on student enrollment and graduation currently available. This study aims to investigate key features of educational account-ability systems in general. It is not intended to be a referendum on No Child Left Behind in particular. As such, we will examine data on high-school gradu-ates from the 1999–2000 and 2000–2001 school years, a period predating the federal law.

To measure public high-school graduation rates this study employs the Cu-mulative Promotion Index (CPI), a widely cited statistic developed by the author. The CPI indicator estimates the probability that a student in the 9th grade will complete high school on time with a regular diploma. This approach represents graduating from high school as a process rather than a single event. Specifically, the CPI captures the four key steps a student must take in order to graduate: making three grade-to-grade promotions (9 to 10, 10 to 11, and 11 to 12) and ultimately earning a diploma (grade 12 to graduation).

The CPI measure is composed of four subcomponents, each of which corresponds to a grade-specific promotion rate. By multiplying these promotion ratios together, the CPI estimates the likelihood that a 9th grader from a particular school system will complete high school with a regular diploma in four years, *given the conditions prevailing in that school system during the 2000–2001 school year*. Graduation rates are first calculated at the district, with data aggregated upward to generate state-level and national statistics.

It should be noted that for the CPI indicator graduates are defined as students receiving regular high-school diplomas. Although some researchers or government agencies may consider individuals who receive other high-school credentials to be "graduates" for certain purposes, the definition used for the present study is consistent with the provisions of the No Child Left Behind Act. The federal law clearly stipulates that for purposes of federal accountability, the recipients of a regular standards-based state diploma are counted as graduates while those who obtain other state-issued credentials (e.g., certificates of attendance) or the GED are not to be considered graduates.

In the second major stage of the analysis, the CPI graduation rate results are incorporated into a series of simulations that examine alternative accountability regimes. Each of these regimes imposes a different set of "rules" for graduation rates. Specifically, we consider two key decisions states face with respect to conditions under which a school or district is considered to make adequate yearly progress under NCLB: (1) States may establish a firm performance goal for graduation rates versus allowing any improvement to count as making AYP; and (2) states may require the disaggregation of results for student subgroups versus considering only the overall aggregate graduation rate for AYP.

Because of the complex nature of the accountability systems being implemented under NCLB, the study could also have explored other decisions that states make with regard to graduation rates. For example, we might have considered various statistical indicators that could be used to measure the graduation rate or the amount of improvement required to make AYP if the annual target is not attained. The rules being examined in the current study, however, correspond to more fundamental aspects of the accountability schemes.

DESIGNING A (SIMULATED) ACCOUNTABILITY SYSTEM

The first step in assessing the impact of alternative accountability rules is to construct a reasonable, uniform system similar to those the states are required to implement under NCLB. An essential property of such a system should be its ability to support valid comparisons across schools, districts, or other account-able units. As noted earlier, we cannot make meaningful direct comparisons of graduation-rate information from actual state accountability systems. Important sources of state-to-state variation in their accountability schemes include the different methods used to calculate graduation rates, widely varying levels at which performance targets are set, and the amount of improvement (if any) considered to be "adequate" progress.

As a result of these real-world complications, this study must rely on simu-lations in order to isolate the contribution of particular accountability rules to the outcomes of the determination process (e.g., the number districts placed in to various accountability categories). It should be noted that, rather than using purely abstract simulations, this study employs analyses based on real-world graduation data that reflect naturally existing variation in performance across districts and states. The same sets of AYP determination rules described below will be applied across all of the states. The AYP outcomes generated by these simulations will not necessarily align with the results of actual accountability systems. However, our analytic approach does offer a significant benefit. Because graduation rates are calculated in the same way for all states (using the CPI in-dicator) and because the same accountability rules are applied to all states, the study's results will support valid state-to-state comparisons.

The flow charts presented in Figures 3.1a and 3.1b illustrate the accountability models employed in our AYP analyses. In most respects, these models capture the same decision-making points that schools and districts must progress through when determining a school system's accountability status under NCLB. One notable exception here, of course, is that we are considering only performance on graduation rates, whereas in practice states must consider both achievement test scores and graduation rates. Naturally, some of the districts meeting performance standards for graduation rates might fail to do so for academic assessments. This study, therefore, will serve to approximate an upper limit for the number of districts that would make AYP under a more complete NCLB-like accountability regime that accounts for multiple performance indicators.

The General AYP Determination Framework

Our basic accountability scheme contains five steps by which districts eligible for graduation rate accountability are identified and their performance is evaluated. The main focus of this analysis is on the AYP status of districts for the 2000–2001 school year. Accordingly, the primary determinant of a district's accountability status will be its graduation rate for 2001. Under NCLB, the imposition of sanc-tions is triggered by the failure to meet standards for two consecutive years. So in keeping with this principle, the final disposition of districts in our simulations will also take into account the district's AYP status during the previous year.

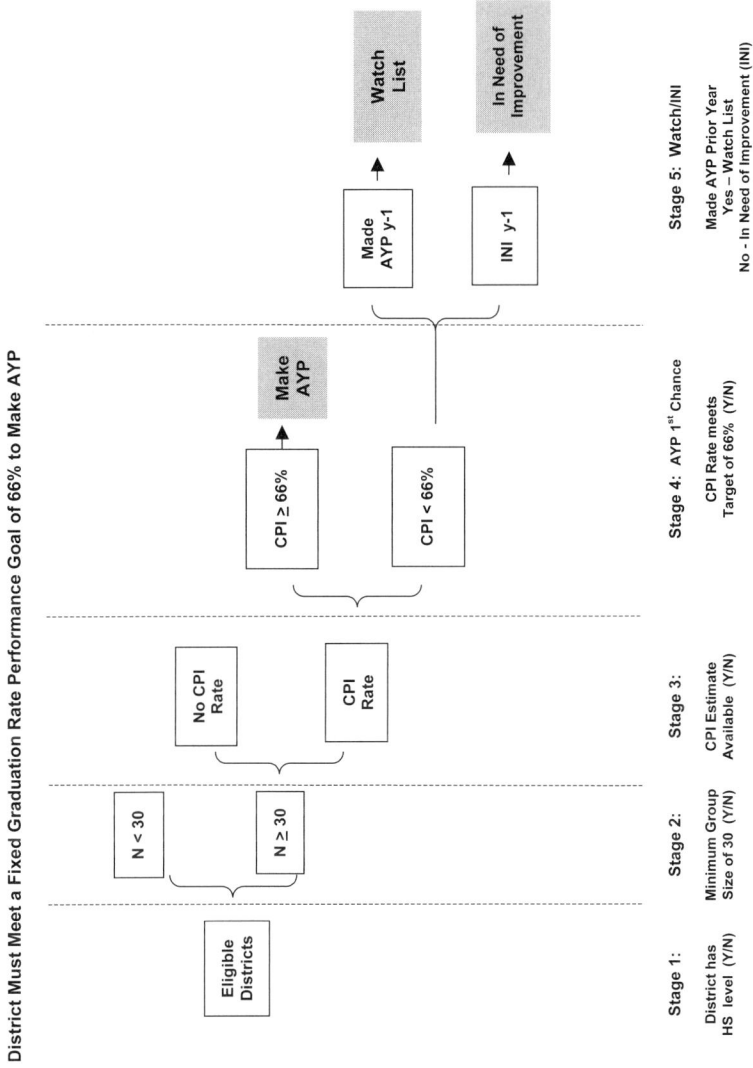

Figure 3.1a AYP determination flow charts—alternative models.

District has a Second Chance to Make AYP by Showing a Gain in the Graduation Rate

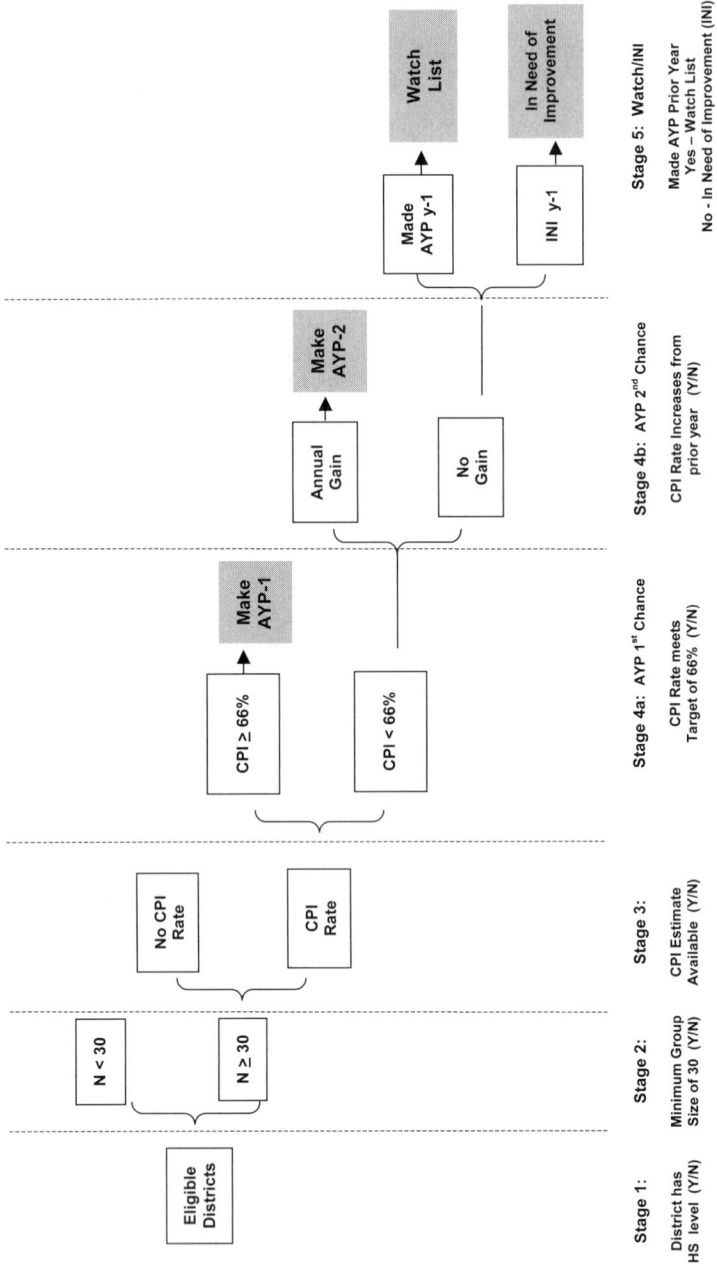

Stage 1:	Stage 2:	Stage 3:	Stage 4a: AYP 1ˢᵗ Chance	Stage 4b: AYP 2ⁿᵈ Chance	Stage 5: Watch/INI
District has HS level (Y/N)	Minimum Group Size of 30 (Y/N)	CPI Estimate Available (Y/N)	CPI Rate meets Target of 66% (Y/N)	CPI Rate Increases from prior year (Y/N)	Made AYP Prior Year Yes – Watch List No - In Need of Improvement (INI)

Figure 3.1b AYP determination flow charts—alternative models.

Stage 1 We start the AYP determination process by identifying the set of school districts that could legitimately be held accountable for graduation rates. At a minimum, for instance, in order to produce graduates a district must enroll students at the high-school level. The issue of which grades count as high school is a salient one; in particular, NCLB's definition of a high-school graduation rate deals with on-time completion, which implies that a starting point for high school must be defined. Federal Title I regulations acknowledge the normative definition of secondary schooling as spanning grades 9 through 12. In keeping with this convention, throughout the current AYP investigation, our point of reference will be regular school districts with enrollment in grades 9, 10, 11, and 12.

Stage 2 Under NCLB, a state may exclude a group from the AYP determination process if it does not meet a minimum size threshold, on the grounds that statistically reliable estimates of performance would not be produced. A group here may refer to students in the aggregate, to specific subgroups defined on the basis of race-ethnicity and other criteria, or to organizational units. Under the law, states may decide where to set this minimum group size threshold for AYP. Higher group-size thresholds effectively exclude a larger number of students from the accountability system, while lower ones allow more students to be represented. Our AYP simulations will employ a minimum group size of 30 9th graders for a school district. Smaller districts will not be included in the AYP analysis. This criterion is comparable to those employed by many states in their NCLB accountability plans.

Stage 3 An evaluation of a district's graduation performance cannot be made, of course, if an estimate of the graduation rate itself cannot be calculated. The CCD database nominally contains the information necessary to calculate aggregate graduation rates and disaggregated rates for the five major racial–ethnic groups for every school district in the nation. However, the CCD does contain missing data holes. There are two reasons a CPI estimate may not be available for this study. In a small number of cases, statewide data collections may not include a key piece of information (e.g., counts of graduates for specific subgroups). In other situations, data may be missing for less systematic reasons, such as unreported or unreliable data for a particular school or district. As the analyses below show, the amount of missing data on graduation rates for accountability-eligible districts in general appears to be quite modest and unlikely to affect the substantive results of the simulations.

Stage 4 In the fourth stage of this accountability process, we evaluate graduation rate performance for eligible districts. To standardize our simulated AYP determination process, we establish a uniform graduation rate target of 66 percent. In our simulated accountability system, districts with a graduation rate of 66 percent or higher are considered to "make AYP." On the whole, a goal of two-thirds of students graduating might seem to be a rather unambitious performance benchmark, particularly when viewed against NCLB's required achievement target of 100 percent proficiency. However, even this arguably modest goal may pose significant challenges for districts in low performing states or for historically disadvantaged minority groups.

Stage 5 Both under NCLB and in the present simulations, the ultimate accountability status or classification of a district will depend on its performance over time. Specifically, districts will only be identified as "Meeting Standards" in our simulation if they meet the specified performance expectations for two consecutive years. Districts will be placed on a "Watch List" if they miss the graduation target in 2001 but make it for 2000 (or vice versa). Finally, districts that fail to reach the target for these two consecutive years would be identified as "In Need of Improvement" (INI).[5] Under NCLB, districts falling into this latter category become subject to a combination of technical assistance and corrective action.

Allowing a Second Chance to Make AYP

This study's accountability analysis explores two major variations in the basic AYP determination rules described above. The first of these decision variants or points of divergence arises within the fourth stage of the determination process, where we add an alternative route to making AYP (see bottom panel of Figure 3.1). Specifically, if a district fails to meet the 66 percent performance *goal* described above, it will receive a second chance to make AYP by demonstrating a *gain* over the previous year. Districts where graduation rates are below 66 percent and not on a rising trajectory do not make AYP.

In some situations, a second-chance provision of this type offers a reasonable accommodation for districts that are making real progress toward established performance goals, but fall a little short in the final analysis. For example, suppose that a district has a graduation rate of 58 percent in 2000 and 64 percent in 2001. Marked progress has been made during this period and the district is approaching the goal of 66 percent. However, it would not make AYP under a system that maintains a strict performance target. But this district would make AYP if a second chance was allowed to demonstrate improvement.

It is also worth nothing that under this second-chance accountability regime a low-performing district that makes a marginal annual improvement in its graduation rate from (e.g., 30 to 31%) would also make AYP. The fact that two districts with such disparate levels of performance could both be considered to make AYP is arguably indicative of an accountability system that lacks a meaningful standard of performance. Nevertheless, the inclusion of an "any improvement" route to AYP mirrors NCLB's graduation rate provisions as they have been implemented in the majority of states.

Adding Subgroup Accountability

The AYP determination schemes outlined above deal with accountability for graduation rates in the aggregate. The study's simulations introduce a final variation to the basic AYP model by stipulating that performance-based accountability must be applied in the aggregate and also for students from each major racial–ethnic category.[6] In this disaggregated scheme, students from each category are separately evaluated using the same accountability determination process. The minimum group size and data availability criteria, for instance, are applied independently to each subgroup. Each racial–ethnic group will likewise be subject in the final two simulations, respectively, to a firm graduation rate target of 66 percent or to the second-chance system with an "any improvement" provision. Here, determining a district's accountability status will require synthesizing results across up to six separate AYP determination analyses—one for students in the aggregate and five for the racial–ethnic subgroups.

Our disaggregation simulations follow the guidelines used where subgroup accountability is required by NCLB (e.g., test scores). A district will be considered to be meeting standards only when performance targets are achieved separately for each and every subgroup meeting the minimum group-size threshold. Accordingly, the entire district would be classified as in need of improvement (INI) if at least one subgroup fails to meet standards during both years of the simulation. It should be noted that a district would be considered INI even if different subgroups fell short of the target in different years (e.g., Hispanics in 2001 and whites in 2000). Districts will appear on the watch list if a subgroup misses AYP during one year of the simulation (but all subgroups meet the target in the other year).

Four Variations on a Theme— Alternative AYP Models

The outcome of the accountability systems required under NCLB, that is, whether a district makes AYP or not, will depend on critical decisions that are under the discretion of the states. Two major issues were discussed above: whether districts must meet a fixed performance goal to make AYP versus showing a gain over past performance levels; and whether subgroup accountability is required. To briefly summarize, the analyses below will investigate these provisions in the context of four specific variations on a basic AYP determination model.

Model 1   AYP defined as meeting a *fixed goal*, accountability in the *aggregate* only

Model 2   AYP defined as meeting a *fixed goal*, accountability with *disaggregation* for racial–ethnic subgroups

Model 3   AYP defined as meeting a *fixed goal* or making a *gain*, accountability in the *aggregate* only

Model 4   AYP defined as meeting a *fixed goal* or making a *gain*, accountability with *disaggregation* for racial–ethnic subgroups

We can anticipate the general pattern of our results based on the nature of these accountability rules. More districts would be expected to make AYP when accountability is only required in the aggregate compared to situations where disaggregation is mandated for individual subgroups. Likewise, allowing a second-chance provision where any improvement in graduation rates also counts as meeting standards will result in a greater number of districts making AYP. What is less clear, of course, is how large these differences will be across the simulated variations and also how the disaggregation and goal versus gain provisions will interact with each other.

THE AYP DETERMINATION ANALYSES

The first stages of the AYP determination process are common across the model variations we examine. The top panel of Table 3.2 reports the percent of districts and proportion of the student population nationwide meeting the mINImum group size threshold of 30 9th graders in the 2000–2001 school year. Results are presented for the student population as a whole and for individual racial–ethnic groups. The starting point for this analysis is the set of 11,110 school districts with students at the secondary level.

Inclusiveness of the Accountability Process

On the whole, about 86 percent of districts serving high-school students nationwide meet the minimum size threshold, with at least 30 9th graders enrolled. These districts educate the vast majority (99%) of all students across the nation. Conversely, this indicates that the districts not meeting this size threshold collectively enroll very few students. When results are disaggregated for specific racial–ethnic groups, we find that the large majority of districts in the nation do not enroll sufficient numbers of minority students to be included in the AYP determination process. For instance, only 3 percent of districts in the nation

Table 3.2 Inclusion of districts and student population in AYP determination system, minimum group size criterion and availability of CPI graduation rate

Inclusion Criteria	All students	Disaggregated racial–ethnic subgroups				
		Native American	Asian	Hispanic	Black	White
Minimum Group Size (at least 30 9th graders)						
Districts meeting threshold (%)	85.7	2.9	6.1	14.1	17.9	79.9
Students in included districts (%)	99.0	58.1	84.6	93.8	95.2	98.2
if group size criterion is met…						
CPI Estimate Available						
Districts with estimate (%)	90.5	63.6	61.7	64.9	71.9	88.9
Students in included districts (%)	93.7	65.7	84.9	81.0	84.5	91.4

Source: Common Core of Data Local Educational Agency and School Surveys, National Center for Education Statistics.

have 30 or more American Indian freshmen, while 18 percent meet this threshold for blacks. By comparison, 80 percent of school districts meet the group size requirement for white students, the largest nationally of the individual racial–ethnic category. This finding has implications beyond the current study because a similar pattern would likely be replicated for other NCLB outcomes as well (e.g., test scores).

Despite the considerable number of *districts* excluded from AYP determination for subgroups, we find that most of the students in these racial–ethnic groups attend school systems that would be part of the accountability process. With the exception of American Indians, at least 85 percent of all students from each racial–ethnic group will be represented. The disparity between the district and student inclusion rates underscores the fact that racial–ethnic minorities tend to live and attend school in highly segregated environments.

The lower panel of Table 3.2 reports the percent of eligible districts (those meeting the minimum group size criterion) for which CPI graduation rate estimates are available. We are able to calculate a valid graduation rate estimate for over 90 percent of the districts meeting our size requirement. These districts enroll about 94 percent of all students nationwide. Results for individual racial–ethnic groups similarly show that the majority of districts and an even larger share of the student population will be captured in the formal AYP determination process, having met both the minimum group size and data availability criteria.

Results of AYP Determinations

Table 3.3 summarizes the findings obtained when our four NCLB-inspired models for AYP determination are applied to the set of eligible districts nationwide. The four columns of results report the percent of districts that meet standards under the conditions of the four respective accountability models. Values are reported for the nation as a whole and for each state (including the District of Columbia). Figure 3.2 presents more detailed results for the nation and selected states, illustrating the percent of districts falling into each of the final accountability categories—Meeting Standards, Watch List, or In Need of Improvement.[7]

National AYP Results In our first hypothetical graduation rate accountability regime (Model 1), performance is evaluated in the aggregate only and districts can make AYP only by reaching or exceeding an absolute performance goal of 66 percent. Under this system, we classify 73 percent of all school districts in the nation as meeting standards. Figure 3.2 shows that 10 percent of districts appear on the watch list, while the remaining 17 percent are identified as in need of improvement for failing to make AYP for two consecutive academic years.

As would be expected, fewer districts make AYP if accountability for the performance of racial–ethnic subgroups is also required (Model 2). Here about 66 percent of districts meet standards by achieving a graduation rate of 66 percent or higher in the aggregate and for each eligible subgroup for two consecutive years. About 12 percent of districts appear on the watch list and 22 percent are labeled INI. In short, introducing subgroup accountability results in an increase of almost 8 percentage points in the districts placed in the watch list or INI categories. The relative share of districts in these latter two categories, however, does not change noticeably when subgroup accountability is introduced.

Our second pair of models introduces the more lenient any-improvement provision to the simulation. In this case, AYP can be made by either reaching a graduation rate of 66 percent or by making some amount of improvement over the previous year (even if the graduation rate falls below the target level). Under these conditions, about 83 percent of districts would meet standards if accountability were required in the aggregate only (Model 3). This is 10 percentage points higher than under an accountability regime that adheres to a strict performance goal criterion (Model 1). Allowing a second chance to make AYP by showing some level of improvement in graduation rates also produces a substantial shift in the distribution of districts between the watch list and INI categories. For example, with the fixed performance target of Model 1, the majority of districts that fail to meet standards appear in the INI category rather than on the watch list. The opposite pattern holds when the any-improvement provision is allowed in Model 3.

Model 4 adds subgroup accountability to the second-chance AYP regime. This more stringent requirement reduces the share of districts meeting standards to

Table 3.3 Results of AYP analyses for the nation and states

	Percent of Districts "Meeting Standards" for the 2000-01 School Year, According to Alternative AYP Models			
	Model 1	**Model 2**	**Model 3**	**Model 4**
	Goal of 66% = AYP	Goal of 66% = AYP	Goal or Gain = AYP	Goal or Gain = AYP
	AYP in Aggregate	Disaggregation by Race-Ethnicity	AYP in Aggregate	Disaggregation by Race-Ethnicity
NATION	73.0	65.5	83.2	75.1
Alabama	32.5	20.3	69.9	51.2
Alaska	30.8	22.2	69.2	63.0
Arizona	36.8	36.8	36.8	36.8
Arkansas	73.9	68.3	82.4	74.8
California	73.7	49.2	81.9	58.6
Colorado	73.8	56.2	77.7	60.0
Connecticut	87.9	79.7	92.2	85.6
Delaware	55.6	38.9	66.7	55.6
Dist. of Columbia	0.0	0.0	100.0	100.0
Florida	10.6	6.0	74.2	41.8
Georgia	15.3	7.6	57.6	42.7
Hawaii	0.0	0.0	100.0	100.0
Idaho	84.7	84.7	87.5	87.5
Illinois	88.5	80.5	92.0	85.2
Indiana	83.0	79.9	89.5	86.0
Iowa	90.6	88.9	91.0	89.3
Kansas	84.1	81.2	89.1	85.0
Kentucky	61.5	56.2	75.8	71.6
Louisiana	43.1	29.0	84.5	69.4
Maine	75.3	73.2	79.4	77.3
Maryland	82.6	56.5	91.3	69.6
Massachusetts	79.7	72.0	85.5	75.4
Michigan	73.9	68.6	81.0	74.6
Minnesota	90.1	86.0	91.7	88.7
Mississippi	23.4	15.9	56.0	40.0
Missouri	78.1	72.9	84.2	78.6
Montana	81.7	71.6	87.3	77.0
Nebraska	90.9	86.7	92.0	86.7
Nevada	46.2	15.4	61.5	30.8
New Hampshire	77.3	77.3	80.3	80.3
New Jersey	92.9	81.9	93.4	82.9

(Continued)

Table 3.3 Continued

	Percent of Districts "Meeting Standards" for the 2000-01 School Year, According to Alternative AYP Models			
	Model 1	Model 2	Model 3	Model 4
	Goal of 66% = AYP	Goal of 66% = AYP	Goal or Gain = AYP	Goal or Gain = AYP
	AYP in Aggregate	Disaggregation by Race-Ethnicity	AYP in Aggregate	Disaggregation by Race-Ethnicity
New Mexico	39.7	27.1	63.8	50.8
New York	74.7	69.5	81.6	76.2
North Carolina	30.1	14.8	69.0	44.3
North Dakota	87.3	83.6	96.4	94.5
Ohio	84.2	82.3	89.7	87.4
Oklahoma	73.0	59.0	81.3	65.9
Oregon	70.4	58.1	81.7	68.5
Pennsylvania	91.6	86.5	94.1	90.9
Rhode Island	80.6	71.0	90.3	77.4
South Carolina	10.0	10.0	62.9	62.9
South Dakota	87.7	84.8	90.8	86.4
Tennessee	31.3	31.3	84.8	84.8
Texas	65.1	50.8	78.6	64.4
Utah	97.3	78.9	97.3	81.6
Vermont	83.3	83.3	89.6	89.6
Virginia	66.4	51.2	73.1	61.8
Washington	55.8	55.8	73.8	73.8
West Virginia	76.4	65.5	87.3	72.7
Wisconsin	93.0	89.4	93.6	90.9
Wyoming	74.4	66.7	79.5	69.2

about 75 percent, with about 18 percent of districts on the watch list and the remaining 7 percent labeled INI. The 8 percentage point reduction in the share of districts meeting standards between Models 3 and 4 is comparable to the results observed above when subgroup accountability was added to a system with a fixed goal for graduation rates (cf., Models 1 and 2). However, the much larger share number of districts appearing on the watch list compared to the INI category in Model 4 more closely mirrors the pattern found for the other second-chance simulation, which examined performance in the aggregate (i.e., Model 3).

Decisions made when designing accountability systems for graduation rates, therefore, can matter a great deal both in terms of the outcomes they report and the equity of their results. In fact, the percent of districts considered to be meeting

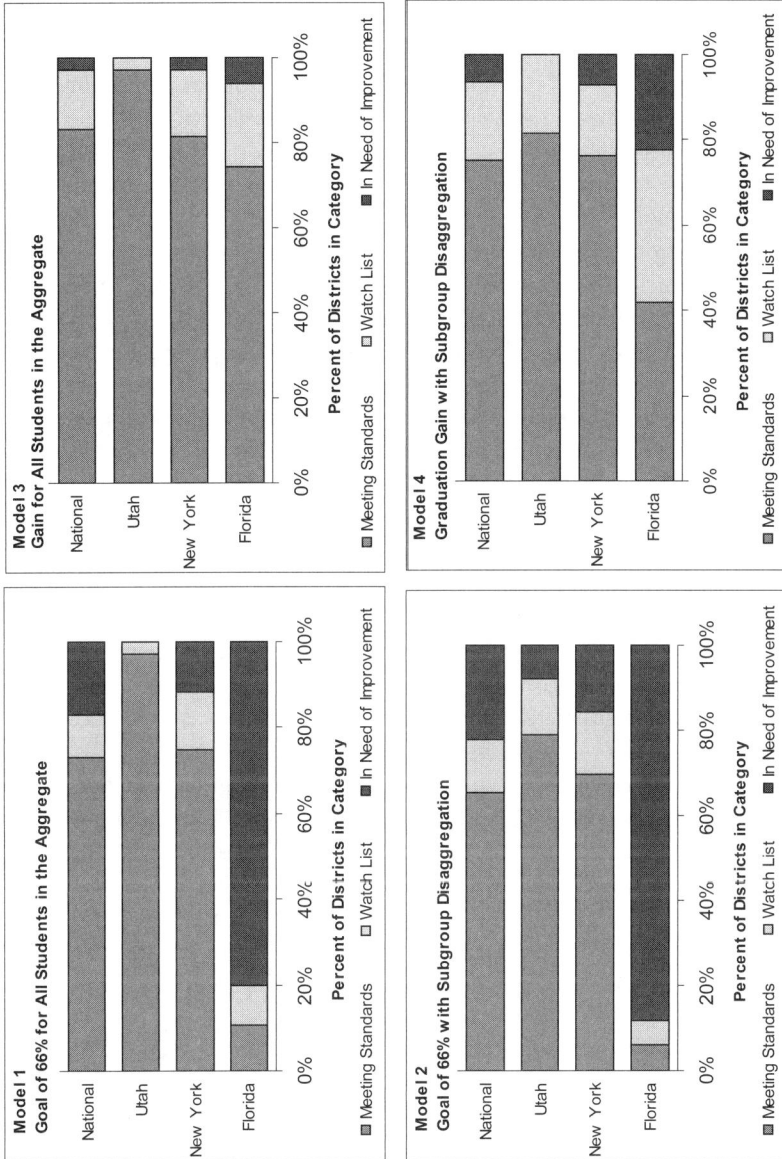

Figure 3.2 Selected results for alternative AYP simulations

standards varies considerably (by as much as 18%), depending on which of the four accountability models examined in this study is actually applied. Summarizing the results across these four variations on our basic AYP determination model, we can draw two important conclusions.

First, systems requiring accountability for subgroups impose a higher standard of performance. This is no surprise given the fact that accountability for multiple subgroups allows more opportunities for a district making AYP in the aggregate to fall short for a particular group. More importantly, however, these simulations provide an estimate for the overall magnitude of this impact. Based on our results, holding all else equal, we expect that the share of districts failing to meet standards will increase by 8 percentage points if targets must also be met for individual racial–ethnic subgroups. In other words, when accountability systems evaluate performance in the aggregate only, they effectively overlook the existence of underperforming, at-risk racial and ethnic groups in 8 percent of all districts. It should be emphasized that because our data can only provide disaggregated rates by race-ethnicity, these finding offer a minimum estimate for the impact of subgroup accountability under the kinds of regimes mandated by NCLB. The differences across the simulated models would become even more pronounced if we could also disaggregate graduation rates by socioeconomic, limited English proficiency, and special education statuses.

Second, permitting an alternative route to meet standards through an any-improvement allowance has a dual effect on the accountability process. To start with, the second-chance provision increases the number of school systems making AYP by about 10 percentage points on the whole. This second chance allowance has a somewhat larger practical impact than does the racial subgroup accountability. One reason for this finding may be that while the majority of districts nationwide do not enroll enough minority students for subgroup accountability to apply, all districts would be given an opportunity to demonstrate gains in their high-school graduation rates. The other consequence of the any-improvement provision can be observed among the set of districts failing to make AYP. Specifically, we find that a large proportion of districts that would have been labeled in need of improvement under a fixed-goal system are effectively shifted onto the watch list when a second chance for making AYP is permitted.

State AYP Results In addition to the national analysis discussed above, we also replicated the four alternative accountability models for each state and the District of Columbia. These state analyses confirm the broader patterns discovered when accountability is viewed from a national perspective. As would be expected, however, we also find substantial state-to-state variability in the consequences that would follow from introducing either subgroup accountability or a second chance to meet AYP by showing some improvement in graduation rates. These differences should not be surprising considering, for example, that the effect of mandating subgroup accountability will depend on factors like the number of districts with sizable minority enrollments, the graduation rates among those subgroups, and the performance gaps between subgroups and the student population as a whole. Each of these factors will vary somewhat, perhaps considerably, across the states.

Space does not permit a comprehensive exposition of the findings for all states. However, for the sake of illustrating state-level accountability patterns, we will select a set of three states that display high, moderate, and low levels of performance in Model 1. These states are, respectively: Utah, New York, and Florida. The results for each state will then be compared across the four simulated AYP models in order to consider the effects of requiring subgroup accountability and allowing a second chance to meet standards by demonstrating improvement.

Utah is among the highest performing states nationwide, with an average graduation rate of 78 percent in the focal 2000–2001 school year. Nearly every district in the state (97%) would meet standards under the terms of Model 1—accountability in the aggregate with a firm graduation rate goal of 66 percent. The remaining districts appear on the watch list, for making AYP only in one of the two years included in the analysis. Utah ranks first among the states in performance under this model. When subgroup accountability is introduced (Model 2), the percent of districts meeting standards drops by almost 20 points (to 79%). About 8 percent of districts are identified as in need of improvement. Utah's ranking drops considerably to 16th under this accountability regime. Similar patterns are also found under accountability schemes that allow for a second change to make AYP through annual improvement. For example, 97 percent of Utah school districts would meet standards by achieving a 66 percent graduation rate in the aggregate or by posting a gain between the 2000 and 2001 school years (Model 3). But when more stringent subgroup accountability is added, 82 percent of districts meet standards, a 15-point decline. In Utah's case, subgroup accountability shows a much larger impact on AYP determinations than does the second chance allowance.

New York State has a graduation rate of 61 percent, placing it somewhat below the national average. However, under the accountability requirements of Model 1 almost 75 percent of districts in the state would meet standard, with 12 percent labeled INI. This compares to 73 percent of districts meeting standards nationwide. This pattern—an above-average proportion of districts meeting standards in a state that generally performs below average—suggests highly disparate graduation rates among the districts in the state. In particular, the low state average is driven to a considerable extent by the very poor performance of the state's largest school systems.[8] When subgroup accountability is required, 70 percent of New York school districts meet standards (Model 2). This raises the state's rank slightly, suggesting that within-district differences in graduation rates among racial–ethnic groups may be slightly less pronounced here than in most other states. Allowing for a second chance to make AYP through annual improvement, 82 percent of districts would meet standards in the aggregate and 76 percent would do so if subgroup accountability were also required (Models 3 and 4 respectively). Again New York ranks around the middle of the nation, but improves its standing relative to other states (although not in absolute terms) when subgroup accountability is introduced. In New York the subgroup and second chance accountability provisions exert equivalent effects on the proportion of districts performing to standards, in the range of 5 to 6 percentage points.

In our final example, Florida ranks as the second lowest performing state in the nation with an average graduation rate of 53 percent in 2000–2001. Accordingly, the state also has among the lowest proportion of districts meeting standards under the provisions of Model 1—just over 10 percent. A large majority of districts in Florida (80 %) are identified as in need of improvement for failing to achieve a 66 percent graduation rate in two consecutive years. Given the almost uniformly low performance of districts in the state, requiring subgroup accountability has little effect on Florida's standing. Under these terms (Model 2), the share of districts meeting standards drops further (to 6%) and the state's ranking remains essentially unchanged. Florida fares much better under an accountability system that allows districts to make AYP by showing some improvement (Model 3). Here the proportion of districts making standards would skyrocket to 75 percent, raising the state's relative ranking considerably. This suggests that while the large majority of Florida districts are low performing (relative to a 66% graduation rate standard), many are making movement in a positive direction. Of course, this does not indicate the amount of improvement these districts are making. When subgroup accountability is added to the second-chance model, however, Florida once again drops toward to bottom of the nation, with only 42 percent of districts meeting standards. The implication here is that, while many districts may be making improvements in their overall graduation rates, the performance of at least some racial–ethnic groups is lagging considerably behind.

IMPLICATIONS FOR POLICY: MAKING GRADUATION RATE ACCOUNTABILITY "SMARTER"

This study has shown that the rules governing accountability systems for graduation rates have the potential to exert dramatic influences on the AYP determination process mandated under NCLB. Further, if accountability proves to be an effective policy tool, then the judicial use of such systems might also have the potential to boost the educational attainment levels of public school students. That is, this could take place if the stakes attached to graduation rates under state accountability systems were reasonably uniform and rigorous. While such conditions can be applied hypothetically in this study's simulations, at present they cannot typically be found in the actual accountability systems being implemented by the states.

Prospects for the future, however, are not as bleak as they appear at first or actually may be at present. The accountability systems mandated under No Child Left Behind are very much a work in progress, with states continuing to refine their approaches in both large and small ways. As a result, the federal government may yet have another chance to reassess its priorities and take a more aggressive stance toward graduation rate accountability. Likewise, states will have ample opportunity to take the initiative and raise the bar on their own. Changes made in an attempt to adhere more faithfully to the spirit of the law would require midcourse corrections, which could prove unpopular among local actors who would rather remain on their current, and perhaps smoother, course, and only time will tell whether federal and state authorities will show the desire and political will to take such steps.

In the end, if accountability systems are to function properly, they must involve all affected parties in a meaningful way and establish clear expectations and responsibilities for each respective agent. Buy-in can be as critical a factor for building an accountability system as it is for carrying out a potentially unpopular school reform or intervention. Thoughtful accountability must be about more than just sanctions and rewards—it must be about providing students with the opportunities they need to achieve to their fullest potential. There are five principles of smart accountability that policymakers should keep in mind when it comes to high-school graduation.

1. States should calculate graduation rates in comparable ways and use methods that research indicates are valid and reliable. The work of independent analysts and initiatives like the Data Quality Campaign and the National Governors Association's graduation rate compact represent steps in the right direction.
2. There should be meaningful and (eventually) attainable goals for graduation rates. States should map out a year-by-year improvement schedule and persistent failure to make progress should carry real consequences.
3. If we are serious about closing the high-school completion gap, principles of smart accountability and social justice demand that real stakes must be attached to the graduation rates of individual student subgroups. Otherwise, it will be all too easy to lose sight of our most disadvantaged students, as has happened so often in the past.
4. Accountability for graduation must also go hand-in-hand with high standards for academic achievement. A diploma without the knowledge and skills to back it up is little more than an empty scrap of paper.
5. Accountability must evolve beyond its current punitive spirit, to become relentlessly and constructively focused on providing children with the

0

supports and services they need to succeed. Only when educational accountability becomes a true partnership among federal, state, and local stakeholders will it be able to serve its intended purpose, improving the education and lives of our nation's youth.

This will not be easy work. In fact, it will be exceedingly difficult. However, smarter forms of accountability may be a key ingredient to finding solutions for the nation's struggling high schools.

Notes

1. There has been some debate over the extent to which states may also be manipulating the accountability provisions related to test scores under NCLB. See, *No Child Left Behind Act: Improvements Needed in Education's Process for Tracking States' Implementation of Key Provisions* (Washington, D.C.: Government Accountability Office, 2004).
2. See, *Diplomas Count: An Essential Guide to Graduation Policy and Rates* (Bethesda, MD: Editorial Projects in Education, 2006) and *High-School Graduation, Completion, and Dropout (GCD) Indicators: A Primer and Catalog* (Washington, D.C.: The Urban Institute, 2004).
3. *Who Graduates? Who Doesn't?* (Washington, D.C.: The Urban Institute, 2004).
4. For more information, see *Diplomas Count*.
5. In Stage 5, districts missing information necessary to determine prior AYP status (for 2000) are assigned to the watch list category by default. This category constitutes a very small fraction of districts nationwide. The only notable exception is Arizona, which did not report graduation data to the CCD for the class of 2000.
6. This study will focus on the racial–ethnic groups identified in the CCD database (American Indian, Asian/Pacific Islander, Hispanic, black, and white). The CCD does not contain the information necessary to calculate disaggregated graduation rates for the other subgroups identified under NCLB.
7. Full 50-state results are available upon request.
8. The 1 million student New York City school district, for instance, has an overall graduation rate of 38 percent.

4

Who Counts for Accountability?

High-Stakes Test Exemptions in a Large Urban School District[1]

Jennifer Booher-Jennings and Andrew A. Beveridge

Should NCLB hold schools accountable for all students, including special education students, English Language Learners (ELL), and students new to the school? Two competing goals of accountability systems—to improve the performance of all students and to fairly measure the performance of schools—collide uncomfortably in this question.

Proponents of holding all students to the same standard—in other words, testing all students on the same grade-level tests—contend that exemptions or alternate assessments for these students perpetuate the educational neglect that NCLB is intended to correct. If students are exempted or held to a different standard, they argue, schools will have little incentive to focus time and attention on these students. As a result, they are unlikely to ever reach proficiency. Moreover, excluding the scores of students new to the school[2] will lead educators to divert attention away from these students. The consequence of excluding some students, then, is their loss of access to scarce educational resources. Avoiding such negative consequences would entail testing and holding schools accountable for all students, though measurement accuracy would be sacrificed and schools serving the most vulnerable students would be unfairly penalized.

Opponents of NCLB's current participation requirements hold that grade-level English-only tests are inappropriate measures for some special education and ELL students. Requiring students to take these tests, it is argued, is detrimental to the students themselves and punishes schools serving large numbers of these students. If accuracy of measurement is privileged, these students should be excluded from accountability calculations. Furthermore, in order to best measure the performance of the school, a school should not be responsible for students attending the school for a short period of time. In sum, adherents to this view believe that there are valid reasons, from both an educational and a measurement perspective, for excluding categories of students from schools' scores.

Until this point, the participation debate has been grounded in rhetorical rather than empirical claims. In this chapter, we address this question empirically. First, we establish how schools would be likely to use exemptions if the exemption provisions in NCLB were extended. Second, we demonstrate the collective impact of both elective and mobility exemptions on schools' test scores and the perceived size of the achievement gap. Finally, we use our findings to inform a discussion of NCLB's potential impact on its target population: poor and minority students.

INCENTIVE SYSTEMS AND GAMING

Test-based accountability systems aim to direct the behavior of educators to the improvement of student achievement. By threatening sanctions and sometimes instituting rewards, educational accountability systems assume that educators will respond to systemic incentives. The No Child Left Behind Act (NCLB) codified this theory of action, requiring schools to incrementally increase test scores so that all students are proficient in reading and math by 2014. Despite the stated intent of NCLB—to improve outcomes for all students, particularly those who have been historically neglected—educational actors may adopt a series of gaming practices in order to artificially inflate schools' passing rates. Such practices include excluding students from high-stakes tests by classifying students as special education (Cullen and Reback 2002; Figlio and Getzler 2002; Jacob 2002); retaining students to forestall test-taking (Haney 2000; McNeil 2000, 2005); focusing resources on students scoring close to the passing mark or on students counted toward a school's accountability rating (Booher-Jennings 2005); diverting attention away from subjects not evaluated on high-stakes tests (McNeil and Valenzuela 2001; Sloan 2005); and cheating (Jacob and Levitt 2003).

Though the "elective" or discretionary exemption of students from taking tests used for accountability calculations has been fiercely debated, it has received much less scholarly attention. Initially, NCLB allowed only 1 percent of students to take an alternate assessment while being counted as a participant. Much of the burgeoning resistance to NCLB grew from this 1 percent cap on proficient scores from an alternate test that can be counted toward adequate yearly progress (AYP) calculations. In response to mounting pressure, the U.S. Department of Education amended this rule in March 2005, inviting states to apply for a variance from the 1 percent cap (U.S. Department of Education 2005). The regulations now allow schools to test up to 3 percent of students on an alternate assessment and count these scores toward AYP.

Yet, schools are not the sole actor implicated in gaming NCLB. Schools only respond to the structure of the accountability system created by the state. Because NCLB required each state to design its own implementation plan, many states have interpreted the law loosely in order to minimize the number of schools deemed "in need of improvement." States exercise discretion in defining which students are "accountable," or count toward each school's accountability rating. States also define the minimum number of students required for a subgroup to be separately evaluated. As a result of NCLB's loopholes, as well as states' interpretations of NCLB, some students face de facto exemption. In the case of mobile students, students may be tested, but their scores do not count toward their schools' scores. Furthermore, if states define subgroup size expediently, the scores of various subgroups will continue to be buried in schoolwide averages. Because of the manifold ways that states can game NCLB, which in turn influence schools' behaviors, this chapter will also address states' roles in responding to NCLB.

In this chapter, we examine the state of Texas as an adjudicative case regarding schools' use of student exemptions, and an instructive case in evaluating states' roles in the gaming process. Because the 13-year-old Texas Accountability System served as the prototype for NCLB, Texas schools' responses to the opportunity to exempt students offer insight into schools' probable responses to NCLB's exemption provisions. Moreover, a unique feature of the Texas system makes it particularly relevant to current policy debates. Texas has maintained a more lenient exemption policy than that allowed by NCLB. As a result, understanding Texas schools' use of exemptions provides a window into the likely outcome of extending the exemption provisions in NCLB.

Drawing on a unique student-level data set from the Houston Independent School District, this paper will address the following questions:

- When schools have an opportunity to exempt students, what types of students are more likely to be exempted?
- How would schools' passing rates be affected if all students were tested and counted in passing rates?

DATA AND METHODS

Our analyses for this study make use of a longitudinal data set of all students tested in the Houston Independent School District for the six school years ending in 2003–4. What makes this data set particularly useful is its inclusion of two measures of student achievement, a high-stakes test (the Texas Assessment of Knowledge and Skills) and a low-stakes test (the Stanford 10). These data represent a significant improvement upon previously available student-level administrative data.[3]

HISD is the seventh largest school district in the country and the largest in the state of Texas. Fifty-six percent of HISD students are Hispanic, while 31 percent are African American. Seventy-four percent of students qualify for free or reduced-price lunch. Twenty-four percent of students are classified as Limited English Proficient (LEP), and 11 percent are classified as special education. The composition of this district makes it a useful test case in evaluating NCLB's potential impact on poor students, students of color, and students with special needs.

How would we know if schools used exemption to "game the system?" After all, many educators feel that they are acting in the best interests of the students themselves when they exempt students from taking a test that is inappropriate for them. In order to rule out this alternate explanation for educators' behavior, we exclude from our analyses those students who *did not* also take the Stanford 10 exam (1.5% of students in Houston).[4] The Stanford 10 is an on-grade level test. Students who are able to take this on-grade level test should, from an educational standpoint, also be able to take the high-stakes test. If low-scoring students are more likely to be exempted, this would suggest that exemption is used strategically.

RESULTS

Who Takes High-Stakes Tests? Gaming at the School Level

Tables 4.1 and 4.2 present the percent of students taking the reading and math TAKS by demographic group and by grade. Overall, 87.6 percent of students who took the Stanford test also take the TAKS reading test, while the figure for math is 88.0 percent.

Table 4.1 HISD students taking TAKS by subgroup

Subgroup	Reading % (count)	Math% (count)
White	92.79 (11,768)	92.88 (11,780)
Asian	91.96 (3,695)	92.19 (3,704)
Hispanic	87.63 (64,239)	87.83 (64,381)
Poor	86.22 (82,395)	86.73 (82,874)
African American	85.37 (34,067)	86.25 (34,418)
LEP	79.47 (24,709)	79.76 (24,798)
Special Education	31.25 (4,626)	36.85 (5,455)
Total	87.58 (113,845)	87.97 (114,357)

Table 4.2 HISD students taking TAKS by grade

Grade	Reading % (count)	Math % (count)
3	91.36 (15,568)	91.94 (17,040)
4	88.71 (15,183)	90.00 (17,115)
5	87.93 (14,205)	89.13 (16,154)
6	87.50 (13,052)	88.28 (13,168)
7	86.46 (12,803)	87.17 (12,908)
8	86.90 (11,485)	87.26 (11,533)
9	84.21 (13,979)	83.02 (13,782)
10	88.12 (10,099)	87.55 (10,034)
11	86.11 (7,471)	86.02 (7,463)
Total	**87.58 (113,845)**	**87.97 (114,357)**

Test-taking, however, varies significantly by demographic group and by grade. Among racial and ethnic groups, white students are the most likely to take the TAKS (reading = 92.8%, math = 92.9%), while African-American students are the least likely (reading = 85.4%, math = 86.3%). LEP and special education students are much less likely to take the TAKS than their general education counterparts. Only 31.3 and 36.9 percent of special education students take the reading and math tests, respectively. In addition, students in the upper grades are less likely to take the TAKS. While 91.4 percent of 3rd graders take the reading test, 86.1 percent of 11th graders do.

TAKS test-taking is strongly associated with students' academic performance. Figure 4.1 presents the percentage of students taking the TAKS test by their national percentile on the Stanford 10 test. Students with low scores on the Stanford are much less likely to take the TAKS, suggesting that exemption is used strategically in Houston.

The previous results examine test-taking by demographics, grade level, and Stanford percentile independently. In Table 4.3, we show how the odds of taking the TAKS vary when we take all of these variables into consideration. (Please see the methodological appendix for a full description of these models.) Table 4.3 demonstrates that students' Stanford percentile is strongly and positively associated with taking the TAKS. Special education and LEP students have much lower odds of taking the TAKS, but higher scoring students in these categories have higher odds of taking the TAKS. This effect is particularly strong for special education students.

Our main finding is that exemption is used strategically in Houston. Educators do not blindly exempt students; rather, they take students' likelihood of passing into account when they make this decision.

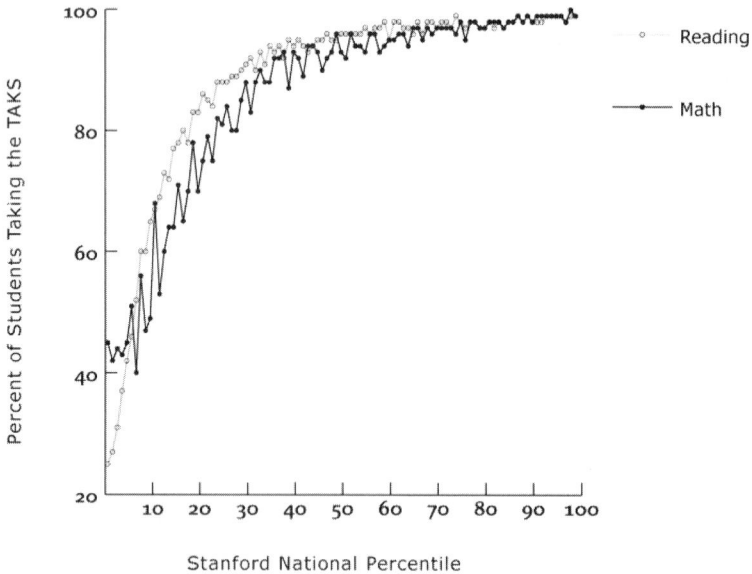

Figure 4.1 The relationship between TAKS Test-Taking and Stanford National Percentile

Who Counts? Gaming at the State Level

The previous section substantiated that test exemptions are not randomly distributed across students or across schools. In this section, we ask how schools' scores would have changed under two different conditions: first, if all tested students' scores were included in accountability calculations, and, second, if all students' scores counted and all students were tested. Addressing the first condition necessitates reviewing the structure of the NCLB implementation plan in the state of Texas.

The State of Texas: Response to NCLB NCLB required each state to submit an implementation plan that described how the state's accountability system would align with the requirements of the law. In response to NCLB's provision that students attend a school for a full academic year before their scores are counted, Texas altered its definition of the "accountability subset." Since the inception of the Texas accountability system, each school has only been measured by its "accountability subset"—those students who "count" in a school's accountability rating. The composition of the accountability subset has changed over time. In 2003, mobile students who moved within a district after a state-determined date at the end of October still counted toward a school's accountability rating. In response to NCLB, Texas amended this definition. Since 2004, the school accountability subset excludes students who move within the district or into the district after the October cutoff date, in addition to students who do not take the state test.[5]

Table 4.3 Hierarchical logistic regression of taking the TAKS on selected student and school characteristics

Variables	Reading			Math		
	1	2	3	1	2	3
Intercept	7.708***	10.596***	8.300***	8.336***	13.315***	12.739***
	(0.060)	(0.114)	(0.318)	(0.061)	(0.117)	(0.318)
Individual (Level 1)						
Stanford National Percentile (NPR)		37.822***	37.984***		16.126***	16.095***
		(0.173)	(0.173)		(0.157)	(0.157)
Poverty		1.033	1.036		0.921	0.925
		(0.059)	(0.059)		(0.061)	(0.061)
NPR*Poverty		1.112	1.107		1.150	1.154
		(0.157)	(0.157)		(0.142)	(0.142)
African American		1.189^	1.198^		1.232*	1.247*
		(0.093)	(0.093)		(0.098)	(0.099)
NPR*African American		1.268	1.254		1.109	1.099
		(0.211)	(0.211)		(0.191)	(0.192)
Hispanic		2.125***	2.111***		1.364**	1.360**
		(0.086)	(0.087)		(0.097)	(0.097)
NPR*Hispanic		0.475***	0.473***		1.714**	1.709**
		(0.201)	(0.201)		(0.186)	(0.186)
LEP		0.229***	0.229***		0.270***	0.270***
		(0.057)	(0.057)		(0.059)	(0.059)
NPR*LEP		1.155	1.159		0.428***	0.428***
		(0.159)	(0.159)		(0.136)	(0.136)
Special Education		0.017***	0.017***		0.020***	0.020***
		(0.050)	(0.050)		(0.051)	(0.052)
NPR*Special Education		8.150***	8.219***		9.97***	9.984***
		(0.142)	(0.142)		(0.131)	(0.131)
Grade 4		0.689***	0.687***		0.751***	0.749***
		(0.054)	(0.054)		(0.052)	(0.052)
Grade 5		0.604***	0.602***		0.622***	0.621***
		(0.054)	(0.054)		(0.052)	(0.052)
Grade 6		0.558***	0.521***		0.589***	0.545***
		(0.110)	(0.114)		(0.110)	(0.114)
Grade 7		0.388***	0.361***		0.407***	0.378***
		(0.114)	(0.118)		(0.114)	(0.118)
Grade 8		0.363***	0.337***		0.383***	0.355***
		(0.115)	(0.119)		(0.114)	(0.118)
Grade 9		0.309***	0.247***		0.203***	0.160***
		(0.148)	(0.174)		(0.146)	(0.172)
Grade 10		0.429***	0.344***		0.369***	0.291***
		(0.151)	(0.177)		(0.149)	(0.174)
Grade 11		0.191***	0.153***		0.229***	0.181***
		(0.152)	(0.178)		(0.150)	(0.175)

(*Continued*)

Table 4.3 Continued

Variables	Reading			Math		
	1	2	3	1	2	3
School (Level 2)						
% Poverty			0.259* (0.665)			0.196* (0.659)
% African American			6.464* (0.748)			6.361* (0.741)
% Hispanic			10.507** (0.810)			10.781** (0.803)
% LEP			0.674 (0.413)			0.727 (0.412)
% Special Education			0.021*** (0.711)			0.019*** (0.695)
n	127,202			127, 229		
Residual Level 2 Variance	0.982 (0.097)	0.701 (0.072)	0.611 (0.064)	1.033 (0.102)	0.709 (0.073)	0.604 (0.063)

^ $p \leq .10$; * $p \leq .05$; ** $p \leq .01$; *** $p \leq .001$

Such a definition is logical in the sense that it attempts to isolate the impact of schools on students. Including students who have not attended the school for a reasonable period of time might downwardly bias estimates of the school's quality and unfairly penalize schools serving more mobile students. By shifting this definition, however, the average percentage of mobile, unaccountable students has almost doubled, as displayed in Table 4.4. In 2003, the average HISD school had 4.2 percent of its students' scores excluded from its accountability subset because of student mobility. After the definition changed, the average HISD school had 8.1 percent of students excluded from its accountability subset. Altering the definition did not impact all schools equally, however. Under the 2003 definition, only 2.4 percent of schools (seven schools) excluded more than 10 percent of their students from their scores. Under the new definition, 31.2 percent of schools (91 schools) exclude more than 10 percent of their students.

Moreover, because mobility is not uniformly distributed across the population, some demographic groups have much higher numbers of mobile, unaccountable students. Figure 4.2 reveals that, across HISD schools, an average of 16.3 percent of special education, 12.7 percent of whites, and 11.3 percent of African-American students are not counted in schools' accountability subsets. Examining the range of mobile unaccountable students across racial groups is also useful in demonstrating the variable impact of this provision across schools and across populations. The minimum and maximum percentages of African-American students that are unaccountable because of mobility are 0 and 100, while they are 0 and 61.5 for special education students.

Table 4.4 Mobile, unaccountable students in HISD, 2002–4

Year	% Mobile unaccountable	SD	Range
2004	8.10	4.59	0–26.10
2003	4.18	3.25	0–33.3
2002	3.95	2.83	0–24.1

Data source: Texas Academic Excellence Indicator System

A second way in which Texas's NCLB implementation plan strayed from the structure of its state accountability system is its definition of subgroup size required for disaggregation. Under the state system, subgroups must include at least 30 students and comprise at least 10 percent of all students, or include 50 or more students, to be evaluated. Under the Texas NCLB implementation plan,

Table 4.5 Mobile, unaccountable students in HISD by subgroup

Subgroup	Mean	SD	Range	N
All	8.10	4.59	0–26.1	292
African American	11.30	10.50	0–100	264
Hispanic	6.81	4.96	0–37.5	284
White	12.70	13.80	0–80	156
Asian	4.50	6.17	0–25	102
Poor	7.93	4.67	0–28.6	292
Special Education	16.30	10.80	0–61.5	278
LEP	6.04	4.64	0–25	259

Data source: Texas Academic Excellence Indicator System.

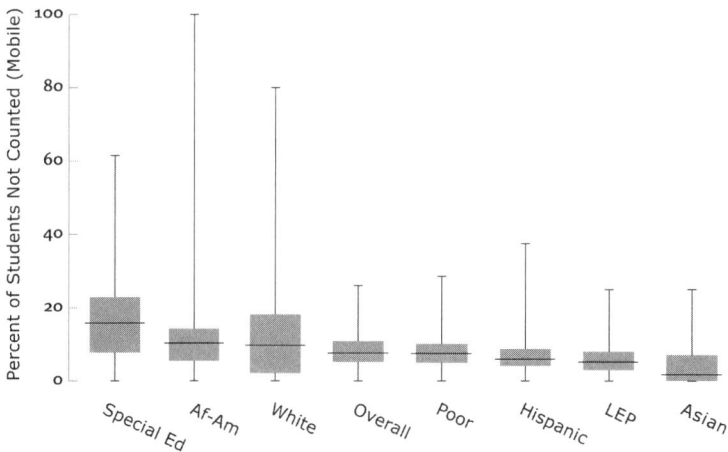

Figure 4.2 Mobile students whose scores are not counted at the school level by demographic group. Data source: Texas Academic Excellance Indicator System.

Table 4.6 HISD schools disaggregating subgroups under state and federal minimum subgroup size definitions

Subgroup	State system (30&10 %/>50)	NCLB (50&10 %/>200)	N
African American	82.11 (179)	65.60 (143)	218
Hispanic	90.48 (228)	84.13 (212)	252
White	56.34 (40)	46.48 (33)	71
Poor	97.45 (268)	94.91 (261)	275
Special Education	54.73 (133)	23.46 (57)	243

Data source: Texas Academic Excellence Indicator System.

subgroups must include at least 50 students and comprise at least 10 percent of all students, or include 200 or more students, to be evaluated (Texas Education Agency [TEA] 2004). Under the state system, 82.1 percent of HISD schools with any African-American test-takers disaggregate scores for African-American students, while 90.5 percent disaggregate for Hispanic students, and 97.5 percent disaggregate for poor students (see Table 4.6). However, for the purposes of NCLB, only 65.6 percent of HISD schools disaggregate scores for African-American students, while 84.1 percent disaggregate for Hispanic students, and 94.9 percent disaggregate for poor students. Though Texas does not include a special education subgroup in its state system, the impact of using the 50 and 10 percent/greater than 200 definition rather than the lower threshold is significant. Shifting the definition reduces the percentage of schools disaggregating scores for special education from 54.7 to 23.5. Based on the data displayed in Table 4.6, we conclude that some groups are disproportionately affected by this definitional shift. In Houston, African-American and special education students bear the brunt of this change.

How Would Schools' Test Scores Change if All Students Were Tested and Counted? Because our dataset includes Stanford 10 data for students who did not take the TAKS, we were able to estimate the scores that exempted students would have received had they taken the TAKS. As discussed previously, these students took an on-grade level Stanford 10 test; thus, according to both Texas and NCLB guidelines, these students should have taken the TAKS as well.

Table 4.7 provides descriptive statistics for three different ways of measuring schools' performance. First, we display the official passing rates released by the Texas Education Agency. Using this measure, an average of 71.5 and 80.2 percent of students in HISD schools passed the math and reading tests, respectively. Second, we calculate the percent passing if schools were held accountable for all of the students who were tested on the TAKS. In this case, the mean school pass rate falls to 70.0 and 78.7 percent for math and reading.

Table 4.7 The impact of the NCLB mobility provision and TAKS exemption on HISD schools' math and reading pass rates

Methods of calculating pass rates	Mean	SD	Median	Range	N
Official math pass rate	71.47	19.71	76.00	8.00–99	282
Math pass rate if mobile students were counted	70.02	19.84	73.91	7.69–100	287
Math pass rate if all students were tested and counted	63.94	21.00	68.42	0–100	295
Official reading pass rate	80.23	11.57	81.00	27.00–99	281
Reading pass rate if mobile students were counted	78.72	11.84	78.51	34.29–100	289
Reading pass rate if all students were tested and counted	71.78	15.80	72.87	0–100	295

The impact of this mobility provision is not uniform across schools. The graphs in the left panel of Figure 4.3a and 4.3b plot the official passing rate against the passing rate if all tested students are counted. A school with no difference in the two passing rates would fall on the 45 degree line; data points above this line indicate that schools had a higher percentage of students passing because of this provision.

Finally, based on students' Stanford scores, we impute the scores of students who were not tested. This new passing rate assumes that all students are tested *and* that all students are counted. In this scenario, the mean school passing rate falls to 63.9 for math and 73.8 for reading. The right panel of Figure 4.3a and 4.3b visually displays the difference in these two rates. Almost all schools fall above the 45 degree line, and some fall substantially above this line. This amounts to

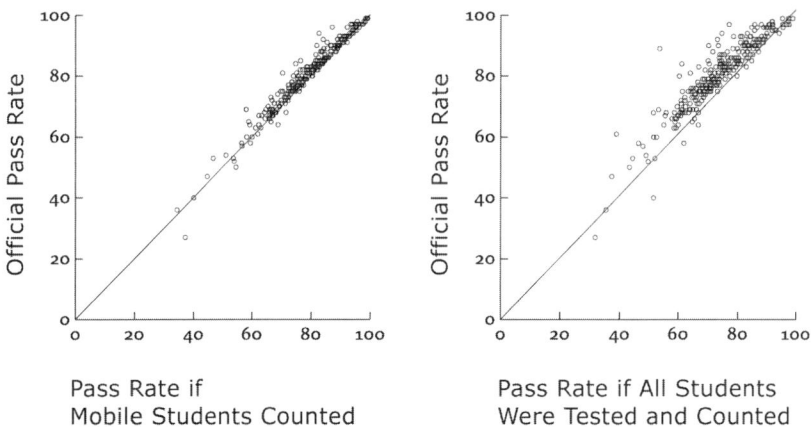

Figure 4.3a The impact of mobility and elective test exemption on schools' reading pass rates

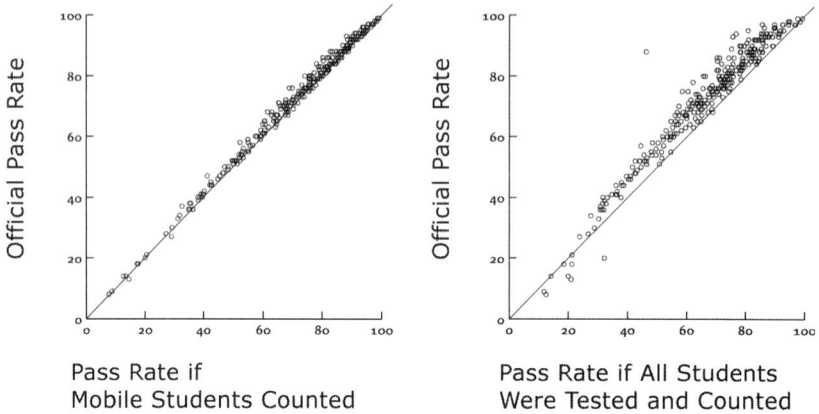

Figure 4.3b The impact of mobility and elective test exemption on schools' reading pass rates

an average increase of 6 to 7 percentage points in the passing rate for both math and reading.

Table 4.8 displays the new passing rates by subgroup, and again corroborates that exemptions are not uniformly distributed across subgroups. Because of the way in which Texas releases subgroup data, we present the official and imputed pass rate at the district rather than the school level. The difference between the official pass rate for reading and the pass rate if all students were tested and counted is greatest for special education and LEP students. For math, the official

Table 4.8 The impact of the NCLB mobility provision and TAKS exemption on HISD's district-level math and reading pass rates by subgroup

	All students	African American	Hispanic	White	Poor	Limited English Proficient	Special Education
Official math pass rate	67.0	59.0	65.0	89.0	63.0	61.0	43.0
Math pass rate if all students were tested and counted	57.5	50.4	55.8	81.9	53.7	47.2	14.3
Official reading pass rate	80.0	79.0	77.0	94.0	77.0	63.0	59.0
Reading pass rate if all students were tested and counted	69.0	66.5	66.6	86.5	65.3	49.8	17.0

special education pass rate is 28.7 percent higher than our imputed rate, while it is 13.8 percent higher for LEP, 9.3 percent higher for poor students, and 8.6 percent higher for African-American students. For reading, the official special education pass rate is 42 percent higher than our imputed rate, while it is 13.2 percent higher for LEP, 12.5 percent higher for African-Americans, and 11.7 percent higher for poor students. Because of elective and mobility test exemptions, the size of the achievement gap is significantly underestimated.

Another way of thinking about the impact of these differences in passing rates is to consider what accountability rating Texas would assign each school if all students had been tested and counted. We calculate new ratings only for reading and math, and do so separately. In other words, while multiple subjects are used together to calculate ratings, we consider the rating parameter into which a school falls based on its reading or math scores alone. Schools in Texas can earn one of four ratings: Exemplary, Recognized, Acceptable, or Academically Unacceptable. To earn an exemplary rating, 90 percent of students must pass all subjects; to earn a recognized rating, 70 percent of students must pass all subjects, and to earn an acceptable rating, 70 percent of students must passing the reading test and 35 percent of students must pass the math test. Table 4.9 illustrates how schools' ratings would change if all students were tested and counted, while Table 4.10 disaggregates the various trajectories that schools would follow. The downward mobility that would result is striking:

- For reading, 106 schools, or 37.7 percent of all Houston schools, would fall into a lower rating category if all students were accountable and all students were tested on the TAKS.
- For math, 78 schools, or 27.7 percent of Houston schools, would fall into a lower rating category.
- For reading, 36.8 percent of Exemplary schools would decline to Recognized status. For math, 39.2 percent of Exemplary schools would decline to Recognized status.
- 15.2 percent of Recognized schools would decline to acceptable status for reading, while 29.4 percent of Recognized schools would do so for math. One Recognized school would decline to Academically Unacceptable status.
- 13.3 percent of Acceptable schools would decline to Academically Unacceptable status for reading, while 9.9 percent of Acceptable schools would do so for math.

In short, the performance of HISD schools would be dramatically lower if all students took the TAKS and were counted toward schools' scores.

Table 4.9 Official accountability ratings and ratings if all students were tested and counted

	Official reading accountability rating	Rating if all students tested and counted	Official math accountability rating	Rating if all students tested and counted
Exemplary	24.20% (68)	8.90% (25)	18.09% (51)	7.09% (20)
Recognized	58.36% (164)	53.38% (150)	44.68% (126)	42.20% (119)
Acceptable	16.01% (45)	34.16% (96)	32.27% (91)	42.20% (119)
Academically unacceptable	1.42% (4)	3.20% (9)	4.96% (14)	8.51% (24)

DISCUSSION AND IMPLICATIONS

This study was motivated by a desire to understand how HISD schools were using elective test exemptions, which students were more likely to be exempted, and how schools' passing rates were affected as a result. We also examined how the structure of states' accountability systems results in mobility exemption for some students. We found that HISD schools took advantage of the exemption opportunities provided by the state, and, in doing so, increased their passing rates. The data presented in this paper suggest that HISD schools utilize exemptions strategically, while also benefiting from mobility exemptions. Taken together, elective and mobility student exemptions substantially increased schools' passing rates. Thirty-eight percent of schools would drop to a lower rating category for reading in the absence of these exemptions, while 28 percent would do so for math.

The findings presented in this paper raise a series of questions about the potential unintended consequences of NCLB. If some students are excluded from counting, either at schools' discretion or by the structure of the system, are schools less likely to direct scarce resources toward these students? If so, how large

TABLE 4.10 School trajectories: Official accountability ratings and ratings if all students were tested and counted

Trajectory	Reading % (count)	Math % (count)
Exemplary to exemplary	36.76 (25)	39.22 (20)
Exemplary to recognized	63.24 (43)	60.78 (31)
Recognized to recognized	65.24 (107)	69.84 (88)
Recognized to acceptable	34.76 (57)	29.37 (37)
Recognized to unacceptable	0	0.79 (1)
Acceptable to acceptable	86.67 (39)	90.11 (82)
Acceptable to unacceptable	13.33 (6)	9.89 (9)
Unacceptable to unacceptable	75.00 (3)	100.00 (14)
Unacceptable to acceptable	25.00 (1)	0

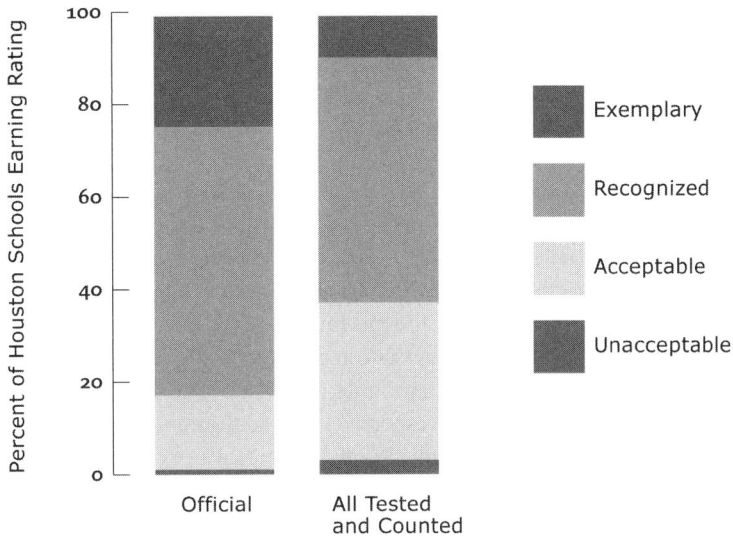

Figure 4.4 HISD school's accountability ratings before and after all students are tested and counted.

is the effect of the denial of resources on students' outcomes? These questions are beyond the scope of this paper. Nonetheless, this paper has demonstrated that the students that NCLB aims to serve are often not counted toward schools' scores, or are not counted in a way that will require schools to address poor and minority students' needs. Ironically, the very students NCLB was designed to target are often the least likely to be counted.

What is likely to happen if schools are given increased flexibility? Because the schools that serve historically neglected students face the most difficulty in making AYP, they are most likely to exclude students who are low-performing from high-stakes tests. High-stakes accountability may thus make it increasingly difficult for parents and citizens to know how ELL, minority, and special education students are performing. Schools' difficulty in meeting the standards will only increase as the standards rise over time. As these pressures bear down on schools, we fear they will shift resources only to the students who "count," especially those close to passing the test. Such a strategy will not result in truly addressing the needs of those students for which NCLB was designed.

NCLB could, of course, mandate that all students are tested and all scores are reported, regardless of subgroup size, students' special education or LEP status, or students' tenure at the school. At the very least, we believe that both sets of scores should be reported. Even if these scores are not used to determine accountability ratings, the public would have a more accurate portrait of student performance. Such a policy is unlikely to be attractive to the federal government or to states, since it would painfully reveal that NCLB is overlooking the very students it was meant to reach.

METHODOLOGICAL APPENDIX

Description of Data

Our dataset includes test score data (both state tests and the Stanford Achievement Test, a nationally norm-referenced exam) for students in grades 1 to 11, demographic data, and classification status data for approximately 160,000 students per year for 1999–2004. Students must have taken the Stanford Achievement Test and be enrolled in a TAKS-tested grade (grades 3–11) in 2004 to be included in our analysis, which amounts to 127,229 and 127,202 of 129,989 students for math and reading, respectively. In addition, using data from the Texas Education Agency's Academic Excellence Indicator System, we integrated additional school-level achievement data. In this chapter, we limit our analyses to the 2003–2004 school year.

Analytic Strategy

We present two sets of analyses to address our questions of interest: what are the characteristics of students who are excluded, how do these exclusions vary by school, and how does excluding these students impact schools' pass rates? First, because students are nested within schools, we fit a series of hierarchical logit models. In this case, using conventional logit models would downwardly bias our standard errors (Bryk and Raudenbush 1992).

Second, we estimate the impact of excluding these students on schools' scores. Because our data include a second measure of achievement, the Stanford 10, we use multiple imputation to estimate scores for each of the students excluded from the test. To impute TAKS scores, we employed the Markov-Chain Monte Carlo method using the SAS MI (multiple imputation) procedure. Students' Stanford scores, in addition to student demographics, program status, and grade level were used. Five imputations were performed, and the differences between the imputations were not statistically significant. We then reestimated schools' passing rates and simulated how schools would have performed if all students were tested and counted in schools' passing rates.

Dependent Variable for Hierarchical Logistic Regression Models

The dependent variable in this analysis is whether the student took the TAKS test in math or reading. Taking either the English- or Spanish-language test[6] is coded as having taken the TAKS. As discussed previously, an off-grade level test, the SDAA, is also offered for special education students, and Texas counts these students as passing if they meet the criteria set by their special education committee. The state mandates that special education students, whose IEPs specify instruction in grade-level state standards, should take the TAKS. Accordingly, we include in our analysis only those students who also took the Stanford test, which is an on-grade level test. Based on the state's regulations, any student sitting for the Stanford exam should also sit for the TAKS exam. Because previous research has argued that channeling students to the SDAA is one mechanism through which schools game the system, we wanted to model taking the TAKS, rather than taking either assessment.

Student and School-Level Covariates

Student and school-level covariates included in our analysis are listed in Table 4.A. To test our hypotheses regarding the exclusion of students unlikely to pass the TAKS test, we include students' national percentile rank on the Stanford test. To address schools' responses to the opportunity structure of the Texas system, we include dummy variables for being classified as special education[7] or as LEP, as well as a series of terms that interact Stanford national percentile with special education and LEP. Demographic dummy variables indicating whether a student is African American or Hispanic (reference group is white) or poor (measured as qualifying for free or reduced-price lunch) are also included. We also interact race, ethnicity, and poverty with the Stanford percentile. To examine the relationship between grade level and test-taking, we include dummy variables for grade level. The reference grade is grade 3.

The school-level covariates include a series of composition variables, including the proportion of the school that is LEP, poor, African American, Hispanic, and special education students.

Notes

1. We would like to thank Diana Schemo and the *New York Times* for providing access to the data, which were obtained through an open records request to the Houston Independent School District. The authors are solely responsible for the opinions expressed herein. We are also grateful to Chris Weiss and Aaron Pallas for their thoughtful comments and suggestions.
2. NCLB requires that students are enrolled for a full academic year before their scores are attributed to the school. However, students who move within a district within a given school year do count towards the district's scores.
3. All tables and figures, except where otherwise noted, are based on analyses of these data.
4. Since 2001, Texas has maintained a parallel, off-grade level assessment (the State-Developed Alternate Assessment, or SDAA). Special education students may take this alternate test in lieu of the TAKS if a student's Individual Education Plan (IEP) specifies *off-grade level* instruction. A student's IEP committee sets the passing rate required of the student, and a student's scores are counted as proficient if she or he performs at this level (TEA 2004). If a student's special education committee rules that neither test is appropriate for a given student, the student can be exempted from both tests. Students of Limited English Proficiency face a

Table 4.A Descriptive statistics for variables used in the analysis

Variable	Mean	SD	Range	N
Individual level				
Stanford Reading National Percentile	0.48	0.28	0.01–0.99	127,202
Stanford Math National Percentile	0.54	0.27	0.01–0.99	127,229
Poor (qualifies for free/reduced lunch)	0.74	0.44	0–1	129,989
African-American	0.31	0.46	0–1	129,989
Hispanic	0.56	0.50	0–1	129,989
LEP	0.24	0.43	0–1	129,989
Special education	0.11	0.32	0–1	129,989
Grade 3	0.13	0.34	0–1	129,989
Grade 4	0.13	0.34	0–1	129,989
Grade 5	0.12	0.33	0–1	129,989
Grade 6	0.11	0.32	0–1	129,989
Grade 7	0.11	0.32	0–1	129,989
Grade 8	0.10	0.30	0–1	129,989
Grade 9	0.13	0.33	0–1	129,989
Grade 10	0.09	0.28	0–1	129,989
Grade 11	0.07	0.25	0–1	129,989
School level				
% Poor	0.79	0.22	0.04–1	295
% African-American	0.35	0.31	0–1	295
% Hispanic	0.55	0.32	0–1	295
% LEP	0.27	0.23	0–1	295
% Special Education	0.13	0.11	0–1	295
African-American Subgroup	0.61	0.49	0–1	293
Hispanic Subgroup	0.80	0.40	0–1	293
Poverty Subgroup	0.92	0.27	0–1	293
Percent Passing Reading TAKS, 2003	76.96	13.89	14.10–100	283
Percent Passing Math TAKS, 2003	73.28	19.35	3.80–100	283
Charter School	0.06	0.25	0–1	295

similar exemption structure. A student's language proficiency committee can decide that the TAKS is an inappropriate measure for the student.
5. Again, students who move within the district after the October cutoff date are counted at the district-level, however.
6. A Spanish language TAKS test is only offered in grades 3–6.
7. In this paper, we do not examine change in special education populations, though classifying additional students as special education is another way of gaming the system.

References

Bingenheimer, J. B. and Raudenbush, S. W. 2004. Statistical and substantive inferences in public health: Issues in the application of multilevel models. *Annual Review of Public Health* 25:53–77.

Booher-Jennings, J. 2005. Below the bubble: "educational triage" and the Texas accountability system. *American Educational Research Journal* 42 (2):231–68.

Bryk, A. S. and S. W. Raudenbush. 1992). *Hierarchical linear models: Applications and data analysis methods*. Newbury Park, CA: Sage.

Cullen, J. B. and R. Rebeck. 2002. Tinkering towards accolades: School gaming under a performance accountability system. University of Michigan (unpublished draft).

Figlio, D. N. and L. S. Getzler. 2002. Accountability, ability and disability: Gaming the system. National Bureau of Economic Research Working Paper 9307. http://www.nber.org/papers/w9307 (accessed July 7, 2004).

Haney, W. 2000. The myth of the Texas miracle in education. *Education Policy Analysis Archives* 8 (41): http://epaa.asu.edu/epaa/v8n41 (accessed January 9, 2003).

Jacob, B. A. 2002. Accountability, incentives, and behavior: The impact of high-stakes testing in the Chicago public schools. National Bureau of Economic Research Working Paper 8969. http://www.nber.org/papers/w8968. (accessed July 7, 2004).

———. S. Levitt. 2003. Rotten apples: An investigation of the prevalence and predictors of teacher cheating. *Quarterly Journal of Economics* 118 (3):843–77.

McNeil, L. M. 2000. *Contradictions of school reform: The educational costs of standardized testing*. London: Routledge.

———. 2005. Faking equity: High-stakes testing and the education of Latino youth. In *Leaving children behind: How "Texas-style" accountability fails Latino youth*, ed. A. Valenzuela , 57–112. Albany: SUNY Press.

———. A. Valenzuela. 2001. The harmful impact of TAAS testing in Texas: Beneath the accountability rhetoric. In *Raising standards or raising barriers? Inequality and high-stakes testing in public education,* ed. G. Orfield and M. L. Kornhaber, 127–50. New York: Century Foundation.

Sloan, K. 2005. Playing to the logic of the Texas accountability system: How focusing on "ratings"—not children—undermines quality and equity. In *Leaving children behind: How "Texas-style" accountability fails Latino youth*, ed. A. Valenzuela, 153–78. Albany: SUNY Press.

Snijders, T. A. and R. J. Bosker. 1994. Modeled variance in two-level models. *Sociological Methods and Research* 22:342–63

Texas Education Agency. 2004. *2004 accountability manual*. http://www.tea.state.tx.us/perfreport/account/2004/manual (accessed September 1, 2004).

U.S. Department of Education. (2005). Spellings announces new special education guidelines, details workable, "common-sense" policy to help states implement *No Child Left Behind*. http://www.ed.gov/news/pressreleases/2005/05/05102005.html (accessed July 15, 2005).

5

Inside the Black Box of Accountability

How High-Stakes Accountability Alters School Culture and the Classification and Treatment of Students and Teachers

Katie Weitz White and James E. Rosenbaum

Accountability is the latest approach in the perennial battle to get public schools to meet society's high aspirations for academic efficiency and excellence. No Child Left Behind (NCLB) has also made accountability the centerpiece of recent federal education policy. Like all new programs, NCLB is still working out implementation details that interfere with the operation of the central idea, so it may be too early to assess this policy. However, older accountability programs, such as the one in the Chicago public schools, can suggest the potential consequences of the basic model.

The Chicago public schools (CPS) pioneered accountability in 1996 and its model is similar to current NCLB legislation. Every year, each school was expected to increase students' test scores by a prescribed amount on a standardized exam in reading (and later in math). This is similar to NCLB's annual yearly progress (AYP) requirement, although CPS did not require subgroup breakdowns of scores. Schools in Chicago that did not meet the targeted increase in scores were subject to sanctions similar to those of NCLB, namely probation and closure. However, since additional resources, training, and curriculum materials are provided in CPS, but not in NCLB, the disturbing features we observe in Chicago may be even more problematic under NCLB.

While policy analysts often focus on whether a policy achieves its goals, sociologists ask about underlying processes. This sociological inquiry asks what behaviors, social classifications, and cultural values are created by Chicago's accountability policy. The literature is vague about the underlying mechanisms by which accountability works inside schools. This paper uses symbolic interaction theory to examine underlying processes. We find that high-stakes accountability creates a powerful incentive system that dramatically alters behaviors. However, we find that these strong incentives create many unintended processes and consequences: they alter how school personnel define, interpret, evaluate, and treat students and teachers, they encourage and reward unintended behaviors, and they alter the ways decisions are made and resources are deployed. Building on prior quantitative studies of CPS's accountability policy, this paper uses qualitative analyses to examine how high-stakes accountability alters the ways schools operate. In particular, we examine the following three questions:

1. Does high-stakes accountability encourage new ways of labeling, treating, and responding to *students*?
2. Does high-stakes accountability encourage new ways of labeling, treating, and responding to *teachers' activities*?
3. Does high-stakes accountability encourage new ways of labeling, treating, and responding to *teachers themselves*?

While quantitative methods have assessed input–output analyses of easily measured outcomes, they have difficulty seeing changes in individuals' behaviors, labels, and values that alter the meaning of schooling. Yet such intervening processes are crucial for seeing hard-to-measure outcomes and for knowing what kinds of schools we are creating. We use qualitative methods to explore the ways school staff react to high-stakes accountability, and the ways their reactions lead to new intervention processes which have unanticipated consequences for students, teachers' activities, and teachers themselves.

Although this is a study of a single school, the underlying logic of the observed responses suggests that these responses are reasonable and may be generalizable. Indeed, school staff members see these departures as the most reasonable actions they can take to accomplish the stated goals given available resources and deadlines. Accountability advocates are correct that school staff will behave rationally in response to incentives, yet they fail to anticipate *which rational responses* will be chosen. Although the rosy picture offered by accountability advocates may sometimes occur, it is not the only rational response, nor the most likely one, particularly in high-poverty schools. We find that strong incentives succeed in getting teachers to depart from customary practices, but many innovations have dramatically changed schools' purposes in unanticipated ways. Moreover, these behaviors are perfectly logical responses to the particular incentives being posed. If we are disturbed by what we see, we must rethink the design of high-stakes accountability, and in the conclusion we suggest another approach.

THEORETICAL FRAMEWORK

We examine here how school staff understand and respond to high-stakes accountability. Symbolic interaction theory provides a framework for examining such processes. This theory contends that actions, objects, and people acquire meaning through the interpretations conferred by interactions and contexts. Individuals make decisions and take actions based on how they interpret and understand the meanings of their social interactions, which in turn are influenced by larger social structures, statuses, and incentives (Rubington and Weinberg 1968). People's shared meaning of a label affects their response to the labeled person and leads them to interpret their actions accordingly (Becker 1968; Rosenbaum, Deil-Amen, and Person 2006, 66–93). Similarly, research in the workplace suggests that in the face of a challenge or important event, there is a cycle of socialization, interpretation, and redefinition of self and others (Katz 1980). In an organization, workers assume they know what the organization is about, but if they find others do not share these assumptions, or rewards do not arise from their actions, they will reorient themselves (Van Maanen 1977). Organizational theorists suggest that this process of "labeling" and revising reactions to the "label" are central to understanding professionals' identities and behavior.

Symbolic interaction theory generally assumes that labels arise from strong social norms and rewards. The ways in which school staff label and evaluate students is influenced by the perceived rewards from working with different students, which are associated with race, ethnicity, socioeconomic status (SES), gender, and academic performance (Rist 1970). The ways in which schools label and evaluate different teaching activities and teachers are influenced by their consequences for desirable outcomes for the school, which are traditionally defined by professional standards. Symbolic interaction theory suggests that given powerful new incentives and threats, labels may be created that may distort behaviors in new ways. In addition to the intended achievement benefits for students, high-stakes accountability may alter the ways in which different *students are labeled and treated.* High-stakes accountability also provides new incentives for teachers that may alter the way *teacher activities and teachers themselves are labeled and treated.* While high-stakes accountability gains its power from focusing incentives on certain outcomes (Wiener and Hall, 2004), an increased focus on one group and certain goals inevitably leads to altering the focus on others, and to changing the labels, evaluation, treatment, and behaviors of teachers and other students in unintended ways.

This study examines the way in which a single school responds to high-stakes accountability. Although such a study can never prove generalizability, it can prove that unexamined assumptions are sometimes wrong and anticipated responses are not inevitable. Moreover, this study shows that school staff members are responding rationally to policy incentives, so one may infer that other rational actors might engage in the same behaviors. The burden is now to demonstrate if teachers in high-poverty schools facing threats to their employment would ever act differently from the ways we observed, and if so, under what circumstances. Indeed, at a minimum, this study may challenge readers to imagine what alternative actions teachers could take in response to these circumstances.

PRESENT STUDY: DATA AND METHODS

Prior studies of CPS accountability have analyzed test score and survey data outcomes over many schools (Jacob 2005; Roderick et al. 1999), but they could not see what behaviors were occurring inside schools. For instance, Jacob notes that it is unclear whether the "modest increases in special education placements and grade retention" are only small distortions at the margin or whether they are important concerns (791). While many of our observations are supported by large-scale research, our observations also give a picture of the ways in which accountability is profoundly transforming teachers' behaviors, school culture, the meaning of education, and the profession of teaching. This study examines intervening processes that are hard to detect in large-scale studies and which may affect outcomes that are rarely measured.

Building on the prior quantitative studies, this study uses ethnographic methods to understand what behaviors occur inside a school, mechanisms invisible to survey research: the ways teachers adapt to policy levers. We selected a school serving a low-income neighborhood. CPS had given this school probation status for poor performance (just as current NCLB policy would do). If student scores did not reach "proficiency level" in reading and math by the end of the school year, the school would be closed. This study examines how the school staff responded to this challenge.

The first author conducted observations in this school, observing every week of the school year. Through close observation, this study identifies the social processes that occur within the black box of accountability. The study describes school-level policies and practices, the principal's decisions, and teachers' behaviors that may explain prior quantitative results and identify social processes not noted by prior research.

To avoid the risk of subjective distortions, our observations emphasize changes that were highly visible in the school, though not easily measured (nor accurately reported) in surveys. These include changes in the allocation of space, student and staff time, resources, and school programming made explicitly to serve accountability goals. Although some aspects were subtle, many were not. It was hard to miss the equipment piled up in the back of a science classroom, the closing of the library, or many other observations reported below. Other findings are based on the researcher's field notes listing the principal's informal decisions, reported and observed (nonpublic) directives to individual faculty, and informal allocations of resources to particular faculty. In addition, informal interviews were conducted with all 32 teachers, who reported on their own strategies, behaviors, and use of time. We followed up with eight of these teachers using taped, semistructured interviews. Few of our reports are based on secondhand descriptions of conversations, and where they happen, they are noted.

FINDINGS

Our findings are divided into three sections, addressing the changes related to students, teachers' behaviors, and teachers themselves.

Does High-Stakes Accountability Encourage New Ways of Labeling, Evaluating, and Treating Students?

Advocates contend that accountability will make schools more businesslike. If so, then businesslike schools may segment their markets, and treat different kinds of students in different ways. Just as health insurance companies consider unhealthy clients too expensive to cover, a businesslike school might regard students far below pass levels as poor investments that probably won't help the school's bottom line (over the next nine months, when it counts). Accountability makes students far below the "passing test score" more threatening to the school's "bottom line," its survival. While public schools cannot avoid covering such students, school classifications can accomplish something similar.

Just as health insurers regard healthy clients as resources whose low costs pay for expensive illnesses in others, a businesslike school may regard faster students as resources. A school can pay for extra services for students just below the pass level if they have enough students who already meet standards and require few costs.

Ordinarily, although some teachers give equal attention to all students, most teachers devote more attention to students with higher motivation or achievement (Gamoran et al. 1995; Rist 1970; Rosenbaum 1976, 1999). This may be understandable because teachers are likely to feel more effective with students who pay attention and exert effort (Jencks 1985). Although teachers' preference for high-achieving students is a persistent finding of research, accountability succeeds in altering these behaviors in three ways.

Resources Focused on Students Who Can Most Affect the School's Bottom Line CPS hired experts to provide advice in schools performing below goals. These experts advised teachers to target instruction to children near the pass level. Booher-Jennings (2005) noted the same strategy. For 6th-grade students for whom 5th-grade level achievement was required, teachers should target children in stanines 3 and 4—scores near the pass level. Many children were below these levels, and the hired experts told teachers that those students should be deemphasized.

CPS also developed the Lighthouse program to provide one-hour after-school sessions three days a week. While ostensibly helping all students, this school's program targets only students in stanines 3 and 4. The program provides curriculum and workbooks targeted just to these students. The program is carefully designed and it is highly structured. It is often scripted, includes extensive practice tests and drilling, and is targeted at 3rd, 6th, and 8th grade students, the three years of the accountability tests.

While the curriculum's focus is only targeted at third and fourth stanine students in these three grades, after-school sessions are offered to all students because older children in this program may be responsible for younger siblings after school hours. For other grades and other achievement levels, the school offers rooms and supervision, but no academic program. Higher achieving students, much above pass level, were given a space to do their homework (which many had already completed during the day), and the school offered a gym program for younger and slower students. The program also provided dinner at 4:30. In effect, although the after-school program is offered to all students, the school system efficiently deploys resources to develop curricula and offer instruction only for students near pass level in the years tested.

Resources Diverted Away from Students Far Below Pass Levels Sociologists of education have long been interested in the process of classification and how it affects the way students are treated (Rosenbaum 1976; Hallinan 1994; Gamoran et al. 1995). However, research rarely has the opportunity to study the ways in which school reform policies may alter the operation of classifications. Special education incidence has skyrocketed in CPS since the imposition of standards. For example, "[T]he timing of the increases in the percent of elementary students eligible for special education services suggests a systematic response to Chicago's promotion policy—there was a large jump in the identification of students with disabilities after the policy was introduced in 1996–1997" (Miller and Gladden 2002, 9). Roderick et al. (1999) estimate that there are three times as many 3rd graders and six times as many 6th graders classified as special education since the accountability policy was put in place. It seems possible that accountability is encouraging special education, but these statistical analyses cannot prove causality nor discern how the process takes place.

Our observations provide a very clear example of the process used by one teacher, who became a model for others. The teacher with one of the best test score gains openly talked about his strategy for success in raising test scores:

A teacher can tell which students are not going to improve…I make a list of these kids, and keep a detailed log for 90 days listing their problems in learning, their problems in paying attention, and their behavior problems…. After 90 days, I can get them reclassified into special education so they won't count against my test scores.

This strategy had an additional benefit. This teacher was able to claim the school special education teacher for his classes for half of the school day. He explained, "After all, I have more special education students than other teachers." For reasons noted later, he also was held up as a model, and given the special education teacher as a reward for the high performance of his other students, the ones whose test scores counted toward the school's goal.

However, while this teacher was clearly devising a strategy to increase special education reclassifications, he did not regard this as cynical. In a statement that seemed very sincere, he described his actions as "taking accountability seriously" and taking such actions that would "assist his school in meeting the systemwide goals." He stated that students far from the pass level clearly need "extra attention and special instruction," which special education is intended to provide. He saw his actions as honest efforts to help the students and the school. He made no effort to conceal his actions. Moreover, his obvious success at meeting school achievement goals led to esteem and status, reinforcing his belief that he was doing what was intended. Accountability intends to encourage innovation to achieve stated goals. This teacher believed that's what he was doing.

Jacob (2005) finds preemptive retention increases in the grade before high-stakes tests were given, which may imply cynical manipulation. However, some teachers openly state that they retain slower students; but they explained that they believed it was good for students to get an extra year to learn the material, particularly in the year before they would be tested. Getting a failing grade on a test would not help these students' efforts.

Some teachers also reported strategies for getting poor performing students to be absent, suspended, or otherwise unqualified. One teacher justified these practices because she felt it would not be fair to the students, to her, or to the school to assess students on standards that had never been within their reach. Students two to four years behind grade level when they entered 6th grade never really had a chance to attain the goals in one school year, so it was inappropriate to count their scores in evaluating their learning or to use these scores to disrupt the schooling of other students. While advising students not to take the test may not be in the students' interests, high-stakes accountability creates conflicts of interest among individual students, other students, and the schools. Teachers must revise their perceptions of students and react to these children as a threat to the school, their jobs, and the education of other students in the school.

Students possess a variety of attributes, and culture translates students' attributes into classifications (formal or informal) that influence how students are treated. "Learning disability" (LD) is one such category that became redefined by the new accountability culture. Traditionally, this category is the result of a complex assessment process relating to student needs. Although often correlated with test scores, LD is traditionally diagnosed by a large number of factors besides test scores. Accountability seems to have changed that.

LD acquired a new operational definition: Students are LD if they have such low test scores that they seem unlikely to meet the pass level by the time of the next test. In the new accountability system, this classification acquires a new meaning: LD is those students who represent a threat to the school's survival. These students have acquired a new urgent importance, they are a threat, and as such, these students become less threatening if they are classified as learning disabled, or some other special education category. Although this classification originally served the purpose of diagnosing students' needs for special treatment, now this classification has a new purpose that is concerned with the school's survival.

Low-stakes accountability does not require such reclassifications. In Texas schools, teachers label many of the lower students "foundation" or "remedial kids." These students are also referred to as "DNQs" or "does not qualify," meaning "does not qualify for special education but is too low to spend time on" with efforts to get them to pass (Booher-Jennings, 2005). However, high stakes made these classifications more urgent, and led to systematic techniques which were justified and even honored as aiding the school's survival. The business approach would be to charge extra for such students or to exclude them, as private schools do. Since public schools cannot do that, reclassification and other strategies are used.

Resources Diverted Away From Students Safely Above Pass Levels   Although it may be more gratifying to work with motivated and capable students, teachers report that accountability provides no reason to work with such students, since they already meet standards. In contrast, accountability will close their school and end their jobs if the teacher doesn't work with the students just below pass level. Even in the Texas school observed by Booher-Jennings, teachers focused efforts on students "on the bubble," rather than those labeled a "passer." When the Chicago school offered additional programs after school hours, the students above pass level were put in study halls, where they received no instruction. Similarly, the Texas school had special weekend and after-school classes for the "bubble kids." With only one month before the exam in Texas, the school gave the bubble kids an additional 90-minute session with a reduced class size, while children who were safely at passing levels were largely ignored.

However, we noted additional procedures that resulted from high-stakes accountability. Challenging faster students through enriched curricula was precluded by the demands of accountability. Teachers who wished to provide extra challenge to more advanced students were discouraged from doing so, and even stigmatized if they tried, as we detail later.

Moreover, double promotions were prevented. A few high-achieving students could have been promoted to a higher grade where they would get more challenge. Although such promotions would improve students' achievement, the promotions would deprive the school of students who would achieve pass levels with certainty.

If these students were middle-class or very high achievers, one might worry less about this strategy. However, in this school, these "faster" students safely above pass level are often only at the 50th percentile nationally, and they come from lower income homes. Compared to other students in the school, these students have the most potential to attend college, but high-stakes accountability creates strong incentives to ignore them and retain them in their current grade.

In effect, high-stakes accountability creates a conflict of interest between the school's survival and these students' academic achievement. Under ordinary circumstances, teachers would promote and challenge these students. However, high-stakes accountability has succeeded in focusing teachers' attention solely on the narrow test goals, the survival of their school, and the continuation of their jobs, a focus away from these students.

Just as the accountability model supposes, principals and teachers responded in highly innovative ways to improve the bottom line. While the school cannot exclude or charge more for "more costly" students, this school figured out innovative ways to accomplish equivalent processes. Under accountability in this school, only students near the pass line were targeted. High-stakes accountability creates strong incentives to ignore students far below or safely above pass level.

Does High-Stakes Accountability Encourage New Ways of Labeling and Evaluating Teachers' Activities?

Public schools have had a very broad mission: educate all children to prepare them for a life in society. Obviously, such diffuse goals are ambiguous and hard to operationalize. High-stakes accountability provides much clearer goals, radically changes the school's mission, and directs teachers to very different activities. Before accountability, teachers were encouraged to develop innovative programs to help all students. Even schools in low-income areas like this one had innovative programs, often created by donations and by teacher efforts. High-stakes accountability changed that approach, introduced a focus, and encouraged other goals to be sacrificed.

Programs Sacrificed that Broaden and Motivate Students In this school, accountability led to some changes that entailed clear sacrifices. To improve test scores, the school added time for instruction in tested subjects. This required cutting some activities. The principal of this school, Mr. E (names and identifying details removed), abolished art classes and recess, and curtailed music and gym. The music teacher who had worked hard to get a grant for a wired keyboarding classroom went from seeing the students three times a week, to one 40-minute period a week. This freed her to do small-group tutoring in reading and math for targeted kids in the mornings. Gym classes were cut from twice to once a week in the first year of probation, and in the second year, the physical education teacher's position was cut to half-time, and each class had gym only once every two weeks for 40 minutes. These actions are similar to those observed in other research (Booher-Jennings, 2005).

While these may seem logical ways to address achievement goals, they may be counterproductive. In Japan, where achievement levels are much higher than the United States, recess is much more frequent than it is in the United States, and art and music are taught, on the assumption that these activities improve concentration and learning (Stevenson and Stigler 1992).

Time Sacrificed in Other Academic Subjects: Excellence Cut to Teach Basic Skills Jacob (2005) found that scores in science and social studies (untested subjects) had significantly smaller gains across all schools than scores in reading and math (tested subjects). These findings suggest differential emphasis, but they do not necessarily raise concerns.

However, the observations in this school suggest cause for concern. The principal cut staff and shifted faculty duties out of untested subject areas to devote more time to reading and math, the two areas tested. The principal cut out the librarian resource teacher entirely. The school had recently received special funding to establish a Spanish course, but that was cut so students could focus on reading and math. Just a few years before, the school was honored for developing an African culture course, but that was now cut. These teachers' time was diverted to teaching reading and math.

While Jacob suggested subtle incremental changes, the changes in this school were not subtle. They involved terminating courses that were widely perceived as highly valuable to students. Even mainstream courses taught by excellent teachers were virtually terminated. One of the best teachers in the school taught history. This teacher had taught for many years and developed an excellent curriculum integrating history with geography and culture. Students had produced large impressive projects and museumlike displays in prior years, and some remained in the school. Moreover, for the first time in memory, the school had just hired a science teacher whose college major was biology. Yet all history and science courses were terminated.

This school made extensive cuts in academic subjects. The principal explicitly demanded an end to science and history. Both the science and history teachers reported that the principal told them not to teach their subjects. As one teacher reported, the principal explicitly said, "I don't want to see social studies or science taught in your classes. I want you to focus on teaching reading and math skills." Although the science teacher had recently received lab equipment and science curriculum materials from a local university, this equipment and the lab tables were stacked in the back of the room, to make space for single desks, placed in rows where students could do drills in reading and math. The science teacher was new to the school and had no choice but to comply. The social studies teacher had tenure and seniority, but she also felt compelled to comply, although she began quietly talking about leaving for a suburban school.

The idea of stressing reading and math skills for students who lack these skills may seem reasonable. However, high stakes shifted priorities so that science and history courses were not taught to *any* students in this school. Moreover, teachers did not object. They saw these changes as legitimate under the conditions of perceived threats to the school's existence

Sacrificing Content to Teach Test-Taking Methods: "Testing Through the Curriculum" Jacob (2005) found that improvement largely took place with very simple skills, and he inferred that teaching may have been aimed at basic skills. Our observations confirm that speculation, and they also indicate an additional aspect: enormous efforts to teach test-taking skills.

Accountability assumes that the policy will put pressures on schools to solicit and benefit from expert opinion. It is assumed that university-based experts possess advanced specialized knowledge about how schools can accomplish accountability goals. Indeed, in Chicago, schools on probation were required to work with a university partner who would provide expert advice about how to meet standards.

The university experts devised a strategy for how teachers could improve test scores: they proposed instruction on test-taking strategies for multiple-choice tests. For instance, middle grade students would write multiple-choice items themselves and then answer each other's questions. The strategy of eliminating two answers and choosing between the remaining ones was reinforced daily.

Teachers were told to practice on very clear material. They were advised to give multiple-choice tests on what had been said over the intercom after the morning announcements. This was seen as a good way to learn because these announcements contained very clear factual material, although the content was of dubious value. Teachers were told to use multiple-choice tests for every assessment, even spelling. In a school with too few funds to purchase recent textbooks, money was used to buy an additional scan-tron.

In a strange parody of "writing across the curriculum," the school practiced "testing across the curriculum." All learning and teaching were presented in the context of multiple-choice tests. These strategies are like the decontextualized type of teaching to the test criticized by researchers (Firestone et al. 2004). Unlike Texas, where practice tests were done at meaningful intervals, based on meaningful curricula, and scores were broken down to convey useful skill information and distributed to teachers for curriculum planning and targeting students (Booher-Jennings 2005), Chicago's weekly practice sessions used haphazard materials, scores were not distributed to teachers or students, and testing was an exercise in the mechanics of testing irrelevant content.

Most of these actions were largely invisible to the world outside of school. However, they were not concealed. When representatives from the local university that donated laboratory equipment and science resources visited and saw the lab equipment and lab tables stacked in the back of the room, they requested the return of their equipment so another school could use it. The principal complied with their request, and he reported to the observer that it was without regret, since this equipment was irrelevant to the school's goals; it didn't help the school meet accountability goals.

The school also eliminated the African culture program and the Spanish language program. The principal told the observer that these were not appropriate priorities for a school facing extinction.

One could see the relabeling of teachers' activities when the principal revised his definition of appropriate teacher activities. While the music teacher is still understood as having an expertise in music education, her primary value now is as a certified instructor with a flexible schedule, who can now be redeployed to work on accountability goals. The principal labeled resource teachers differently as a result of having to meet the challenge of accountability. Amid the concern about out-of-field teaching, accountability led to a change in how specialist teachers were used: everyone focused on the two tested subjects: math and reading. In middle-class neighborhoods, some parents might complain, but in this disadvantaged neighborhood, no one did. If they had, they would have been told that accountability goals had priority.

Does High-Stakes Accountability Encourage New Ways of Labeling and Evaluating Teachers Themselves?

Changing the context where professionals interact influences how professionals interpret behavior and react to certain activities. While prior sections described individual actions and strategies, reforms will only persist or become institutionalized if they change school culture. Since traditional school culture often resists school reforms, the success of accountability policies may depend on whether the school can change its culture. We saw indications that accountability was having some successes in changing school culture.

Culture is the shared values and norms that guide the behavior of a group of people. Although culture itself is often invisible, it can be seen in prestigious awards, teacher status, and teacher stigma. As high-stakes accountability succeeded at changing these aspects of school culture, we must ask if these cultural changes are the ones the policy intended.

Systemwide Teaching Awards The Golden Apple teaching award was created to praise exemplary teachers, and shine attention on model teachers for others to emulate. Not surprisingly, the criteria are abstract and changing because good teaching is hard to define. Accountability changed that—now good teaching can be measured.

In this school, the Golden Apple award finalist was the teacher who excelled in strategies for meeting the accountability goals, and who had the top pass rate in the school. It is testament to the power of accountability that accountability measures came to be used in selecting the teacher who was nominated for the award in this school. Accountability creates a clear, easily measured definition of quality teaching—improving the percentage of one's students above pass level. Pass level is no longer merely an organizational or systemwide goal but the definition of quality teaching. Although pass level was not very high and emphasizes basic skills rather than higher-order thinking skills, pass level has become the standard of quality even for nominations to this prestigious award.

Organizational Status and Control of Resources—Teachers Who Meet Targets Another indication of culture is status. Teachers with privileged status in the school receive deference and resources. The teacher noted above, who was effective at reclassifying students into special education, and had one of the top pass levels in the school, carried favor with the principal as a result. As Ingersoll (2003) notes, principals control many resources, which affect teachers' workload and signal teachers' status.

This teacher was the recipient of many privileges. If status is signaled by the control of school resources, this teacher clearly had high status. He was allowed to choose the topics for in-service sessions, he could use school equipment (e.g., digital cameras) at his convenience, he was allowed to distribute art supplies at his discretion, he got the special education teacher for half a day, and he was exempted from participation on two school committees—considered a "requirement" for all teachers.

Only a few teachers have taken systematic actions to reclassify students into special education or get them otherwise excluded from their numbers. What is important is how the school and the school system responded to these few individuals. One possible response is censure. After all, these actions were likely to harm the students, to create extra costs for the school system (because of the greater expense of special education), and to distort the meaning of their test score outcomes. There is no indication that the school, other teachers, or the system criticized these actions. On the contrary, the teacher who excelled at these actions got rewards from the principal and prestigious recognition from the school system.

Organizational Stigma and Withdrawal of Resources—Teachers Who Don't Help School Targets Culture defines value, both positive and negative, and shared culture leads to shared feelings of disdain and even stigma toward individuals who violate cultural norms. Because accountability made the school's survival and jobs depend upon increasing pass levels, these pass levels became strongly valued, and the school culture created a clear stigma against teachers whose efforts were not working toward that goal. This stigma was widely shared and led to vocal criticism by other teachers.

Efforts that did not contribute to the school's survival were seen as disloyal. When one teacher requested funds for the Junior Great Books program, the principal explicitly stated that no resources would be provided because this program did not contribute to pass levels, it "wasted" resources on students safely above pass level. When a teacher spent time developing a challenging inquiry-based curriculum for an after-school program (for students who otherwise would sit in a study hall they didn't need), other teachers criticized this teacher's efforts. Teachers disparaged these activities, and regarded these teachers as traitors who were not contributing to the school's test score goals. By making stakes high enough, accountability got teachers to stigmatize teachers who "waste time" on already adequately performing students whose improved achievement would do nothing to help the school's survival.

Teachers themselves are rewarded or punished based on how willing and able they are to achieve the goals of accountability. Interactions between the principal and these teachers in the forms of directives and resource allocation clearly indicate this, but it is even more telling that teachers themselves began to alter how they perceived one another.

CONCLUSION

Sociologists often find that in any reform, the poor suffer. The reform mandated under No Child Left Behind was intended to help the poor, but it has imposed the most severe sacrifices on the schools serving low-income students. While accountability succeeded in getting schools to focus on helping the portion of students near the pass level in reading and math, our observations suggest many sacrifices. This school sacrificed instruction for students far below and safely above pass level, the teaching of science and history for *all* students, double promotions for faster students, and good programs in science, history, geography, music, and arts. These reactions to accountability demands are hard to see with available quantitative data. It is hard to see promotions that should have happened or to monitor history, science, music, and art when they are not tested. Students just below pass level had significant gains on the accountability goals, and all students experienced significant deprivations in everything else.

These sacrifices are not an accident. As noted, high-stakes accountability seeks to induce teachers to depart from traditional behaviors that do not maximize stated goals. It assumes that high stakes can persuade teachers to overcome factors that previously prevented them from taking actions to accomplish stated goals. Under ordinary circumstances, teachers would not choose to make the above sacrifices, which some teachers might consider unprofessional. Accountability has been highly successful in inducing teachers to change their behavior and ignore these concerns.

We found that accountability is not merely changing individuals' behavior; it changes a school's culture, which may have long-lasting effects. Teachers acquire new behaviors and new attitudes about what is good teaching. In this new culture, the school norms stigmatize higher-level instruction, intrinsically interesting lessons, and attention to students who are safely above pass level (even though they are only at the 50th percentile nationally).

Ironically, while high-stakes accountability based on threats has few upfront costs, it may increase long-term costs. As teachers reclassify students into special education to avoid high-stakes punishments, special education budgets will skyrocket. Given that special education costs three to five times more than regular programs, high-stakes accountability will lead to exploding financial costs. However, faced with the threat of losing their school and their jobs, the principal and the school's model teacher encouraged practices to increase classifying students as special education.

Accountability's strength is to pose clear priorities. But priorities require sacrifices, although they are rarely mentioned. While advocates sometimes state a willingness to sacrifice other subjects until students acquire basic math and reading skills, our observations suggest that the sacrifice is much broader than that. This school is sacrificing important academic areas (science and history), excellent programs, and content for *all* students in order to help the subset of students near the pass level in reading and math. When the school system committed itself to high-stakes accountability, no one mentioned these sacrifices. Are these sacrifices really what policymakers want?

These findings are likely to generalize to other schools. Although the reactions to high-stakes accountability may be stronger in the school we studied, whose existence was immediately threatened because it was below threshold, schools just above the threshold cannot be complacent, and they may take similar actions to avoid becoming at risk.

These findings are not likely to apply to affluent schools. While inner-city schools whose existence is in peril because of accountability are forced into many sacrifices, affluent schools with few students below threshold will require few sacrifices of other educational goals. Although high-stakes accountability aims to reduce inequalities by social class background, it merely changes the nature of the inequalities.

Policy Recommendations

Symbolic interaction theory helps us think about policy solutions. Strong incentives can encourage new ways to label, evaluate, and respond to students, teachers' activities, and teachers themselves. When high-stakes policies pose goals without providing means for attaining them, teachers will pursue these goals in nontraditional ways, or they will leave the schools. In an attempt to avoid some of the pitfalls unanticipated by accountability policies, we suggest the following:

Collect Information for a Broader Range of Subjects and Cut-Points We would not abandon the use of tests to monitor student performance. This information can be useful to teachers. However, if there were multiple tested subjects and multiple pass lines in each subject, teachers could see the benefits of working with students at every level in multiple arenas.

Instead of High-Stakes Punishments, Pose Low-Stakes Rewards, and Make Rewards Apply to Both Students and Teachers High stakes are neither warranted nor effective. High stakes are warranted when actors are lazy and when the organization only has a few narrow goals. However, none of the teachers in the school were lazy, and no one ever asserted that teachers were not following prescribed procedures that would have accomplished the desired goals. Moreover, prior to accountability, the school's goals were broader than those that can be posed in any accountability scheme.

As we have seen, high-stakes accountability distorts behaviors in unprofessional ways. In contrast, Booher-Jennings and others have shown that merely providing low-stakes outcome data is sufficient to motivate teachers' actions.

View Shortcomings as Shared Problems and Devise Systematic Strategies Blaming teachers and making them accountable makes sense only if there is a clear set of behaviors that teachers can take that have a high probability of improving outcomes. When it comes to teaching in schools with many low-income students, no one has sure-fire strategies that have been proven to work consistently over long periods of time. Even the university experts hired to assist this school mostly advocated strategies for gaming the tests. Holding people accountable for outcomes they don't believe they control is unfair and leads to cynical gaming and unprofessional behavior.

Invest in Improving Organizational Capability to Accomplish Goals School capacity is a crucial prerequisite for effective accountability (Carnoy, Loeb, and Smith 2003), and research finds that teachers want to improve outcomes (Sunderman et al. 2004). CPS has increasingly focused on improving school capability with additional programs, and teachers have welcomed many of these new programs.

However, this strategy has been ignored by NCLB, and NCLB may even be undermining effective reforms. In the late 1990s, Louisiana devised procedures to enhance capacity, provide new teaching techniques, new curriculum, consultants to assist teacher training, and additional resources for after-school and summer programs. Unfortunately, in Louisiana, most of the resources for these effective reforms have had to be redirected into purchasing tests for NCLB.

In sum, we find that high-stakes accountability is highly successful at getting teachers to focus on clear goals, to interpret student potential and teacher behaviors in new ways, and to take actions they would not otherwise undertake. Unfortunately, we find that high stakes can get teachers to sacrifice their professional standards and judgment, and even get them to reward cynical scheming and to stigmatize and relabel teachers who try to remain committed to their professional standards. High stakes works to make changes, but do we really want these changes?

References

Becker, Howard. (1968). On labeling outsiders. In *Deviance: The interactionist perspective*, ed. E. Rubington and M. S. Weinberg, 13–17. London: Macmillan.

Booher-Jennings, Jennifer. (2005). Below the bubble: "Educational triage" and the Texas Accountability System. *American Educational Research Journal* 42:231–68.

Carnoy, M., S. Loeb, and T. L. Smith. (2003). The impact of accountability policies in Texas high schools. In *The new accountability*, ed. M. Carnoy, R. Elmore, and L. S. Siskin, 147–73. New York: RoutledgeFalmer.

Firestone, William A., Lora Frances Monfils, and Roberta Y. Schorr. (2004). *The ambiguity of teaching to the test : standards, assessment, and educational reform*. Mahwah, NJ: Erlbaum.

Gamoran, Adam, Martin Nystrand, Mark Berends, and Paul C. LePore. (1995). An organizational analysis of the effects of ability grouping. *American Educational Research Journal* 32:687–715.

Hallinan, M. T. (1994). Tracking: From theory to practice. *Sociology of Education* 65:79–84.

Ingersoll, Richard. (2003). *Who controls teachers' work? Power and accountability in America's schools*. Cambridge, MA: Harvard University Press.

Jacob, B. A. (2005). Accountability, incentives and behavior: the impact of high- stakes testing in the Chicago Public Schools. *Journal of Public Economics* 89 (5–6):761–96.

Jencks, Christopher. (1985). How much do high school students learn? *Sociology of Education* 58:128.

Katz, Ralph. (1980). Time and work: Toward an integrative perspective. In *Research in organizational behavior*, Vol. 2, ed. B. M. Staw and L. L. Cummings, 81–128. Greenwich, CT: JAI Press.

Miller, S. R. and R. M. Gladden. (2002). *Changing special education enrollments: Causes and distribution among schools*. Chicago: Consortium on Chicago School Research.

Rist, R. (1970). Student social class and teacher expectations. *Harvard Educational Review* 40 (3):411–51.

Roderick, M., A. S. Bryk, , B. A. Jacob, J. Q. Easton, and E. Allensworth. (1999). *Ending social promotion: Results from the first two years*. Chicago: Consortium of Chicago School Research.

Rosenbaum, James E. (1976). *Making inequality: The hidden curriculum of high-school tracking*. New York: Wiley.

———. (1999). If tracking is bad, is detracking better? *American Educator* 28–47.

———. Regina Deil-Amen, and Ann Person. (2006). *After admission: From college access to college success*. New York: Russell Sage Foundation Press.

Rubington, Earl, and Martin S. Weinberg. (1968). *Deviance: The interactionist perspective*. Toronto: Macmillan.

Stevenson, H. W. and J. W. Stigler. (1992). *The learning gap: Why our schools are failing and what we can learn from Japanese and Chinese education*. New York: Summit Books.

Sunderman, G. L., C. A. Tracey, J.Kim, and G. Orfield. (2004). *Listening to teachers: Classroom realities and no child left behind*. Cambridge, MA: The Civil Rights Project.

Van Maanen, John. (1977). Experiencing organization: Notes on the meaning of careers and socialization. In *Organizational careers: Some new perspectives*, ed. J. Van Maanen, 15–48. London: Wiley.

Wiener, R. and D. Hall. (2004). Accountability under No Child Left Behind. *Clearing House*, 78 (1):17–21.

Part III
Teaching and Teacher Quality

6

State Policy Activity under NCLB

Adequate Yearly Progress and Highly Qualified Teachers

Kerstin Carlson Le Floch

The passage of the No Child Left Behind Act (NCLB) signaled an augmented role for the federal government in public education; likewise, state education agencies (SEA) were laden with more policy responsibilities than they had previously assumed. Under NCLB, states are required to establish content standards; administer aligned assessments in grades 3 through 8 and once in high school; determine state academic achievement standards; develop definitions of adequate yearly progress for all schools; identify schools for improvement; approve supplemental educational service providers; administer targeted school improvement funds; determine which teachers are "highly qualified" in core academic subjects; outline state equity plans for the equitable distribution of "highly qualified teachers"; develop standards for English language proficiency and aligned assessments; and calculate annual measurable achievement objectives for Title III districts—to name but a few of the state-level responsibilities. Although these are all important obligations, this chapter will focus primarily on the activities of state officials in two key policy areas: (1) the development of state definitions of adequate yearly progress (AYP), and (2) state approaches to defining what it means to be a highly qualified teacher[1] under NCLB.

In the years since NCLB became a law, state officials have worked diligently to ensure that their states are in compliance with the core requirements of NCLB. In doing so, state officials have demonstrated that they are active policy actors who have worked to shape policies that they perceive to best suit the needs of their states, and to improve educational process in their schools. Indeed, NCLB is not a static policy, nor are state officials passive recipients of the law. Some have suggested that the result of this state activity is 50 different accountability models, reflective of the flexibility that lawmakers incorporated into the act. Nonetheless, some of NCLB's legal requirements have been perceived as overly stringent, contradictory, or poorly designed, prompting state officials to push back against federal requirements, seeking further flexibility.

State policy officials have been somewhat more active in their efforts to push back against the federal statute and the U.S. Department of Education with regard to certain policies. Specifically, states have been creative in the ways in which they have progressively modified their definitions of adequate yearly progress. Although state officials have chafed against some statutory requirements for highly qualified teachers, they have been somewhat less active in their pressure to seek modifications to these policies.

What are some possible reasons for which state officials may be more or less active in seeking to mold NCLB policy? First, we will provide an overview of NCLB provisions for school-level adequate yearly progress (AYP) and requirements for highly qualified teachers (HQT), then we will discuss features of these policies that may stimulate more active policy implementation and manipulation on the part of state officials.

OVERVIEW OF AYP AND HQT REQUIREMENTS OF NCLB

Although AYP has received a great deal of attention since the passage of NCLB, it is not a new policy mechanism. Indeed, AYP was a relatively prominent, if more flexible feature of the Improving America's Schools Act (IASA), the previous reauthorization of the Elementary and Secondary Education Act, or the precursor to NCLB. Under IASA, states were expected to develop challenging content and performance standards and tests aligned with these standards. States were also required to determine if Title I schools made adequate yearly progress, based on state assessments in specific grade spans, including grades 3 through 5, 6 through 9, and 10 through 12. Overall, the law extended considerable flexibility to states in the manner in which they chose to define what constituted adequate progress.

AYP: Policy Summary

As of the 1999–2000 school year, there were three main strategies that characterized the ways in which states defined AYP (Goertz and Duffy 2001). First, some states held schools to an *absolute target*; that is, the average level of proficiency within a school was expected to be at a specific level, in which case the school was considered to have made AYP. The second category of states considered the *relative growth* of each school toward a state-defined target. In such cases, the state identified a required level of proficiency, for example, 80 percent of students, and determined the appropriate number of years by which each school would have attained this target. To do so, each school would divide their current level of proficiency by the number of years required to reach the target, and the result would be a school-specific annual growth target. The third approach to AYP under IASA was to *narrow the achievement gap*. In states with this approach to AYP, schools were expected to improve the performance of students at the lowest achievement levels. In general, few states accounted for subgroup performance under IASA accountability systems.

Under NCLB, however, subgroup accountability is a prominent feature. Indeed, states must disaggregate AYP indicators by all subgroups, including race/ethnicity, socioeconomic status, English language proficiency, and disabilities. The key AYP indicators under NCLB include:

- Achievement level in mathematics (disaggregated by subgroup)
- Achievement level in reading/language arts (disaggregated by subgroup)
- Participation rates in mathematics assessments (disaggregated by subgroup)
- Participation rates in reading/language arts assessments (disaggregated by subgroup)
- An "other academic indicator" (most often attendance rate in elementary schools or graduation rate in high schools)

State approaches to AYP under IASA generally focused on a school's average performance, but under NCLB, a school must ensure that all subgroups meet AYP expectations. Indeed, if a school misses AYP targets for a single subgroup, such as the participation rate for Asian students in the reading/language arts assessment, then the entire school is considered to have failed AYP for that academic year.

Another key distinction under NCLB is that states must measure AYP for all schools, not only Title I schools. Moreover, 34 states have opted to identify non-Title I schools for improvement, which takes effect when schools fail to meet AYP targets for two consecutive years. The most serious NCLB sanctions are still levied against Title I schools—few states impose the school transfer and supplemental educational services requirements on non-Title I schools—but the scope and visibility of AYP is much broader under NCLB than under IASA.

Despite the apparent stringency of the federal AYP requirements, states have devised a wide range of approaches to AYP. For example, under NCLB, states are required to determine the minimum number of students to constitute a subgroup for AYP purposes; this component of AYP is known as the "minimum n." The range of subgroup sizes among states varies from five students in Maryland, to 50 students in Virginia and West Virginia. In another example of state variation, states are required to define how they will determine AYP for schools with special circumstances—very small schools, or schools that do not include tested grades. For example, for Arizona schools that do not have enough students to meet the minimum n size, the state will aggregate data by subject and grade level over the past three years until there is adequate data to determine AYP. If a Colorado school does not have enough students to calculate AYP, the district AYP status is attributed to the school. A third strategy was adopted by Montana, which conducts a qualitative review of student performance data to determine the AYP of small schools.

In addition, states were required to set annual measurable objectives (AMOs) that chart progress from the state's "starting point" in 2001–2 to the NCLB target of 100 percent proficiency by 2013–14. These state trajectories towards 100 percent proficiency fall into three primary categories: first, 6 states simply charted a linear path from the starting point to 100 percent proficiency. In the second set of 17 states, the trajectory appears like a set of "stair steps"; that is, a plateau for two or three consecutive years, followed by a jump in the expected level of proficiency. Finally, 29 states[2] have combined these approaches, starting with small "stair steps" followed by rapid, linear growth around 2008. Perhaps prudently, these states have delayed most of the academic growth required under NCLB. Overall, each state has assembled a unique configuration of AYP components, resulting in a different calculus for the status of public schools in every state.

In the years since NCLB went into effect, states' approaches to AYP have evolved as they borrow from the initiatives of other states. Indeed, it appears that states learn from each other: when the U.S. Department of Education approves a new policy modification through the annual amendments to state accountability plans, additional states follow suit one year later (Erpenbach and Forte 2005). One aspect of AYP definitions to which states frequently asked for changes was the "minimum n." States either asked to raise the minimum n size for the "all-student" subgroup, to increase the minimum n size for a specific subgroup, or to introduce a proportional minimum n model, in which AYP is calculated for a minimum number of students *or* a required percent of the student population of a school, whichever is greater. In 2003, Ohio and Wisconsin were among the first states to set higher minimum n sizes for the students with disabilities subgroup; in the same year Oklahoma received approval for a minimum n of 30 for the all students group, and 52 for all other subgroups (Erpenbach, Forte Fast, and Potts 2003). One year later, six states requested changes to the minimum n for specific student subgroups (Forte Fast and Erpenbach 2004). For the spring 2005 accountability amendments, 10 states had requested changes to the way in which they determined the minimum number of students in an AYP subgroup (Erpenbach and Forte 2005).

These modifications to state AYP policies have enabled states to push back against components of the law that were perceived as untenable—for example, the testing requirements for students with disabilities. They have also enabled states to better manage the number of schools that fail AYP and are identified for improvement, thus facilitating the longer-term viability of the accountability system. If the public perceived the number of schools identified for improvement to be excessive, the legitimacy of the accountability designations might be questioned. Moreover, states' capacity to provide appropriate support to schools identified for improvement would be strained. By tinkering with AYP policies, states are in fact helping to avoid the implosion of NCLB accountability.

HQT: Policy Summary

Although issues related to teacher quality were not ignored under IASA, improving the qualifications of teachers has received greater prominence and vigor under NCLB. In earlier federal education laws, targeted grants was the primary mechanism through which lawmakers sought to improve teacher quality, complemented by increased reporting requirements for collegiate schools of education. In contrast, NCLB establishes the first set of federal guidelines through which teachers are determined to be highly qualified. As with the requirements for AYP, the teacher quality requirements of NCLB apply to all teachers of core academic subjects, regardless of Title I status. (Under NCLB, core academic subjects include English, reading or language arts, mathematics, science, foreign languages, civics and government, economics, history, geography, and arts.) Under the law, all teachers of these subjects were required to be highly qualified by the 2005–6 school year, although states received extensions to this deadline. To be considered highly qualified, teachers much fulfill three requirements. Each teacher must:

1. Have a bachelor's degree
2. Be fully certified
3. Demonstrate appropriate content knowledge for every subject taught.

To demonstrate content knowledge, most teachers have several different options, with the exception of new elementary teachers, who may only do so by passing a rigorous, state-approved test. New secondary school teachers have the additional possibilities of fulfilling the content knowledge requirement if they have completed a college major, coursework equivalent to a major, advanced certification (such as that of the National Board of Professional Teaching Standards), or a graduate degree in the subject taught.

Experienced teachers at both the elementary and secondary school levels may choose to pass their state's High Objective Uniform State Standard of Evaluation (HOUSSE), a policy designed to acknowledge the teaching experience of veteran teachers. As of the spring of 2005, 47 states had established HOUSSE procedures to enable these experienced teachers to demonstrate content knowledge. Of these 47 states, 29 had developed HOUSSE policies that credited teachers with a certain number of points for activities related to subject matter knowledge, such as professional development hours, graduate coursework, improved student test scores, or participation in the development on content standards or related assessments. (However, some states allocate points for activities which may not necessarily enhance content knowledge, such as acting as a mentor teacher.) In seven other states, HOUSSE procedures consisted of teacher performance evaluations, often a required component of maintaining certification. In eight states, HOUSSE was essentially congruent with existing certification requirements (Stullich, Eisner, McCrary, and Roney 2006).

As with AYP, states have been somewhat resistant to components of the NCLB requirements for highly qualified teachers, and in some cases, the U.S. Department of Education has issued regulatory statements that extended flexibility to states. For example, in the earliest years of NCLB implementation, the Department of Education established the Teacher Assistance Corps, comprised of Department staff and leaders in the field of teacher quality. The Teacher Assistance Corps visited nearly every state to discuss the challenges of implementing the HQT requirements of NCLB. As a result of these visits, the Department of Education addressed a letter to Chief State School Officers on May 31, 2004, extending special flexibility for multiple subject teachers in rural schools. Such teachers in qualified school districts were allowed one extra year to demonstrate content knowledge in each subject taught. In the same letter, the U.S. Department of Education also allowed states to "streamline their HOUSSE procedures by developing a process for current, multidisciplinary teachers to demonstrate subject matter mastery in each of their subjects through a single set of procedures" (U.S. Department of Education, 2004). This flexibility benefited all multisubject teachers, regardless of the rural status of their school district.

In the fall of 2005, the U.S. Department of Education acknowledged that many states were likely to fall short of the target of ensuring that all teachers were highly qualified by 2005–6. In response, states that adequately demonstrated a "good faith effort" to implement the teacher quality requirements of NCLB were extended an extra year in meeting the statutory deadlines. In the spring of 2006, the Department of Education further specified how they would determine which states were indeed making a "good faith effort," and addressed decision letters to states on May 12, 2006.

Of the 40 states for which the U.S. Department of Education had released decision letters by late May 2006, 29 were determined to have made a "good faith effort" to implement HQT policies. However, national data suggest that many states have simply set the bar rather low. For example, many states have chosen one of the Praxis II exams to determine if teachers are highly qualified under NCLB. Of the 35 states that use the Praxis II Mathematics Content Knowledge exam, 29 have set their minimum passing score below the national median, and nine states set their scores below the 25th percentile. Only four states opted to set their cut scores above the national median (Stullich et al. 2006). In addition, some have argued that HOUSSE policies, in general, do not set a high standard of evaluation, as the name would suggest (Education Trust 2003; Walsh and Snyder 2004). Notably, of the 29 states that have established a HOUSSE system based on an accumulation of points, 15 states allow teachers to accrue up to half of the total required points for prior teaching experience—an activity which does not ensure increased content knowledge (Stullich et al. 2006). Finally, reports of U.S. Department of Education monitoring noted that 11 states had inadequate requirements for elementary school teachers; in many cases elementary teachers were simply considered highly qualified by virtue of holding state certification (see Highly Qualified Teachers and Improving Teacher Quality State Grants Monitoring Reports, available at: http://www.ed.gov/programs/teacherqual/hqt.html).

Although the Department of Education has made incremental movement in clarifying, specifying, and adding flexibility to the HQT requirements established by law, state officials have proven somewhat less active in this policy arena than with regard to accountability. Through the annual amendments to accountability policies, states have engaged in an obvious give-and-take process with the Department of Education. Although states have revised their teacher quality plans, there are few examples of comparable push back with regard to teacher quality. Rather, with regard to teacher quality, some states have simply opted to set the bar rather low. What policy features may stimulate more or less activity on the part of state officials?

Policy Features that Mediate the Behavior of State Policy Actors

Although the accountability and teacher quality components of NCLB are both of relatively high profile, until 2006, the reaction of state policy officials had been somewhat less vigorous with regard to the teacher quality requirements. Drawing primarily from literature on accountability systems, we point to three features of these policies that may be associated with the reactions of state policy actors: (1) the perceived efficacy of the policy; (2) the salience of consequences associated with the policy; and (3) the maturity of the policy.

Perceived Efficacy

First, policy actors' perceptions of the potential efficacy of the policy will mediate their efforts toward implementation. Based on the probability of attaining goals and the perceived value of the associated outcomes, state policy makers will be more or less active in implementing policy and tailoring the policy to the needs of their states. Fuhrman and her colleagues at CPRE developed a model of responses to accountability mechanisms based on Expectancy Theory and Goal-Setting Theory (Fuhrman 1999; Kelley, Odden, Milanowski, and Heneman 2000). As Fuhrman explains,

> this model suggests that a teacher will be motivated to try to reach the school's student achievement goals to the extent that she (a) perceives a high probability that teacher effort will lead to students' reaching achievement goals (expectancy perception); (b) perceives a high probability that the goal attainment will lead to certain consequences or outcomes such as a bonus award (instrumentality perception); and (c) places value, either positive or negative, on these outcomes. (1999, 9)

Although this framework is articulated with regard to teachers, the same motivational mechanisms may shape the behavior of state policymakers with regard to the implementation of NCLB policies.

When implementing key NCLB policies, state officials weigh their expectancy perception (that their actions will lead to the attainment of policy goals) with the instrumentality perception and the value associated with the policy objective. In other words, they try to determine if the activities required to implement the policy are likely to be successful, given the scope of the challenges associated with the mandate, and whether state actions are worth the expended effort. If one side of the implied cost-benefit analysis is lacking, there is a lower likelihood of energetic implementation. For example, if state officials doubt they have the capacity to attain the policy objectives, even the most laudable goal will fail to stimulate a vigorous response. For a policy to be effective there should be an appropriate balance between the pressure to improve, and the capacity of stakeholders to achieve the goals of the policy

Implicit in the discussion above is the assumption that state capacity is a limited resource and that state officials must determine the extent to which their organization can address policy demands, given the constraints associated with their state context. In the case of AYP, state officials needed to determine the approximate number of schools identified for improvement that the state could support—that is, an implicit tipping point, after which the accountability system would become unstable. If too many schools were identified for improvement, a state would not be able to develop a viable system of support for identified schools (as required under NCLB), nor would districts be able to ensure that appropriate sanctions were meted out. Hence, the concerns about capacity were likely to have played a role in the ways in which state officials established and subsequently modified AYP definitions.

The challenges for state capacity were even greater with regard to highly qualified teachers. Most notably, state officials had to ensure that they did not create HQT policies that were so restrictive that they pushed more teachers out of the classroom than were available in the pool of new teachers. Although states were working to develop strategies to recruit and train greater numbers of new, highly qualified teachers, they were nonetheless limited in their capacity to effect rapid changes in the supply of teachers. Thus, the availability of new teachers likely acted as a disincentive for states to set very high standards for highly qualified teachers under NCLB.

Aspects of the law that are perceived as unreasonable (and intractable) will result in an imbalance between the pressure to improve and state capacity and will diminish effectiveness. An example of this are the timelines associated with the student accountability and teacher quality components of NCLB. AYP is intended to stimulate improved student achievement such that 100 percent of students are proficient by the year 2013–14. This deadline, which at the time of NCLB passage seemed distant, created incentives for states to set sensible—yet challenging—goals and to keep the numbers of schools identified for improvement at a manageable level. The HQT provisions of NCLB are designed to ensure that all teachers of core academic subjects have adequate content knowledge by 2005–6—a target that was just a few short years after NCLB went into effect. The quick timeline associated with the HQT requirements created incentives for states to set low standards, enabling them to demonstrate that (nearly) all teachers were highly qualified.

To be sure, scholars have criticized the timeline associated with the student accountability components of NCLB as being entirely unrealistic. But when compared to the HQT requirements, the accountability schedule appeared, at least, more manageable. Indeed, in setting AMO trajectories that delayed most growth until the years following the projected reauthorization, states devised a policy response that enabled them to balance the statutory demands with their own capacity. However, the notion that a state could weed out all the truly unqualified teachers and replace them with better qualified teachers in only three years seemed implausible. So in the case of the HQT requirements, NCLB created a system in which all states were obliged to comply with the letter of the law, but most were hard-pressed to address the spirit of the law.

Salience of Consequences

The consequences associated with a given policy are also critical to implementation. The role of sanctions has been described by Porter (1994; see also Porter and Brophy 1988; Porter, Kirst, Osthoff, Smithson, and Schneider 1993) in terms of the "power" of a policy—policies that have stronger sanctions (as well as other key attributes) are more likely to be fully implemented. O'Day and Bitter (2003) also describe the motivational role of sanctions in an accountability system, specifically, the degree to which the sanctions are perceived as salient and realistic. When stakeholders believe that the rewards or sanctions are likely to take effect—and they attach importance to these rewards or sanctions—then they are more likely to stimulate a change in behavior consistent with the intent of the policy.

In the case of the teacher quality requirements of NCLB, the consequences of failing to meet the established targets seemed relatively remote. While states were expected to ensure that 100 percent of teachers were highly qualified by the 2005–6 school year, the U.S. Department of Education did not clearly articulate what sanctions (if any) would be levied against states that could not do so. Moreover, the announcement extending this deadline for an additional year further suggested that severe sanctions would not be forthcoming. Indeed, a former official with the U.S. Department of Education's Office of Elementary and Secondary Education admitted, "ED's primary and first focus was getting that accountability system in place. States followed our lead. We were doing work on HQT, but it was not nearly with the same level of intensity as accountability," (Sawchuk, 2007, 7).

While potential consequences of failing to meet goals for highly qualified teachers seemed remote, a more pressing challenge also served to diminish incentives to implement the HQT requirements: a shortage of teachers. Some school districts have more than enough applicants for each teaching position, but other hard-to-staff schools (often rural, central urban, or low-income) are not so fortunate (Prince 2002). If states set high standards for highly qualified teachers, such schools would have little choice but to hire teachers who were not highly qualified or to adopt other undesirable strategies. The threat of classrooms without teachers served to further diminish incentives to enact strong policies for highly qualified teachers.

In contrast, the U.S. Department of Education vigorously pushed states to submit their state accountability plans by the statutory deadline, characterizing accountability as "the most fundamental aspect" of No Child Left Behind (see: http://www.ed.gov/policy/elsec/guid/secletter/020724.html). Moreover, the local sanctions associated with failing to meet AYP targets (and hence being identified for improvement) were both salient and meaningful. There seemed little way to avoid providing Title I transfer options and supplemental educational services for students in identified Title I schools (although more subtle tactics could dampen student uptake rates). Moreover, the increasingly serious sanctions would require even more active intervention on the part of states. Faced with these sanctions, but obliged to work within the guidelines established by law, states officials had incentives to gradually push against the federal AYP requirements that they perceived as most problematic.

Policy Maturity/Novelty

Finally, AYP is not a new policy mechanism under NCLB. Between the 1994 passage of IASA, and the passage of NCLB in late 2001, state officials had ample opportunity to experiment with different approaches to AYP. Although NCLB did enact some substantial changes to AYP, state policymakers were able to become fluent in the details of AYP rather quickly. Hence, the policy discussion was rapidly elevated to a sophisticated level: state officials began to tinker with AYP definitions at the earliest opportunity to do so. In contrast, the requirements for highly qualified teachers were a novelty, as encoded in federal law. Most notably, the HOUSSE policy option was entirely new, and state officials were faced with the unusual challenge of drafting policy with no prior precedent. The capacity of state officials to resist components of NCLB, through the development of creative policy strategies, was more limited in the case of highly qualified teachers.

Moreover, the presence of AYP as a component of ESEA had another policy consequence: AYP was established as a policy mechanism with staying power. The stability of a policy is among the attributes that Porter (1994) suggests will lead to stronger policy implementation. Because AYP appeared likely to remain a stable part of the state education policy landscape for several years, state policy makers were motivated to ensure that the numbers of schools that failed AYP (and were later identified for improvement) did not become unwieldy. Hence, they had incentives to manipulate definitions of AYP and to thus manage the number of schools that missed AYP targets. In contrast, the NCLB requirements for highly qualified teachers were not yet established as stable policy mechanisms. Just as teachers who are initially wary of new reform strategies may be inclined to "wait out" such reforms, state policymakers may have been less motivated to approach the NCLB teacher requirements with much vigor.

CONCLUSION

As we have seen, state officials are not passive recipients of the NCLB, nor is the law a static policy. In the case of accountability, state officials were engaged in an active process of fine-tuning aspects of the law with the U.S. Department of Education. This process served two important purposes. First, it bolstered the viability of the accountability systems, by enabling states to balance policy demands with capacity constraints. Second, by incorporating successive changes to state AYP definitions, state officials buffered their constituents from some of the components of the law that were perceived as most problematic.

However, not all components of NCLB stimulated a similar level of activity. With regard to the HQT provisions of the law, most states were less vigorous in pushing back, and more inclined to adopt standards that enabled them to demonstrate that the large majority of teachers were highly qualified. The possibility of achieving the true intent of these NCLB provisions—namely, to ensure that all teachers have strong content knowledge, and to erase inequities in the distribution of well-qualified teachers—was tempered by the realities of the supply of teachers, as well as characteristics of the policy itself.

Attaining the appropriate balance is difficult to achieve. In the case of both AYP and HQT policies, the NCLB statute did not achieve an ideal balance. However, the stability, sanctions, and schedule associated with accountability goals enabled state officials to manage AYP implementation in a way that resulted in a viable policy—at least in the short term. Sustaining the long-term viability of the NCLB accountability system, however, will depend on the degree to which stakeholders—among them, state officials—are engaged in a meaningful and reflective debate that fuels the reauthorization of ESEA.

Notes

1. In all cases the chapter refers to the components of NCLB that establish policies for highly qualified teachers, but this is not a description of a highly qualified teacher in any broader sense.
2. These numbers include the 50 states, plus the District of Columbia and Puerto Rico.

References

Education Trust. 2003. *Telling the whole truth (or not) about highly qualified teachers.* Washington, D.C.: Education Trust.

Erpenbach, W. J., E. Forte Fast, and A. Potts. 2003. *Statewide educational accountability under NCLB: Central issues arising from an examination of state accountability workbooks and U.S. Department of Education reviews under the No Child Left Behind Act of 2001.* Washington, D.C.: The Council of Chief State School Officers.

Erpenbach, W.J. and Forte, E., 2005. *Statewide educational accountability under the No Child Left Behind Act: A report on 2005 amendments to state plans.* Washington, D.C.: Council of Chief State School Officers.

Forte Fast, E. and W. J. Erpenbach. 2004. *Revisiting statewide educational accountability under NCLB: A summary of state requests in 2003–2004 for amendments to state accountability plans.* Washington, D.C.: Council of Chief State School Officers.

Fuhrman, S. 1999. *The new accountability* (RB-27-January-1999). Philadelphia: University of Pennsylvania, Graduate School of Education, Consortium for Policy Research in Education.

Goertz, M. E., and M. Duffy. 2001. *Assessment and accountability systems across the 50 states: 1999–2000.* Philadelphia: University of Pennsylvania, Graduate School of Education, Consortium for Policy Research in Education.

Highly Qualified Teachers and Improving Teacher Quality State Grants Monitoring Reports. http://www.ed.gov/programs/teacherqual/hqt.html).

Kelley, C., A. Odden, A. Milanowski, and H. Heneman III. 2000. The motivational effects of school-based performance awards. CPRE Policy Brief (RB-29) . Philadelphia: University of Pennsylvania, Graduate School of Education, Consortium for Policy Research in Education

O'Day, J., and C. Bitter. 2003. *Evaluation study of the immediate intervention/underperforming schools program and the high achieving/improving schools program of the Public Schools Accountability Act of 1999.* Washington, D.C.: American Institutes for Research.

Porter, A. C. 1994. National standards and school improvement in the 1990s: Issues and promise. *American Journal of Education* 102:421–49.

———. J. E. Brophy. 1988. Good teaching: Insights from the work of the Institute for Research on Teaching. *Educational Leadership* 45 (8):75–84.

———. M. W. Kirst, E. J. Osthoff, J. L. Smithson, and S. A. Schneider. 1993. *Reform up close: An analysis of high school mathematics and science classrooms.* Madison, WI: University of Wisconsin-Madison.

Prince, C. 2002. *The challenge of attracting good teachers and principals to struggling schools.* Arlington, VA: American Association of School Administrators.

Sawchuk, S. 2007. *HQT mandate produced greater data, transparency.* Education Daily. Vol. 40, No. 21, February 1, 2007, pp. 6-8.

Stullich, S., E. Eisner, J. McCrary, and C. Roney. 2006. *Implementation.* Vol. 1 of *National assessment of Title I: Interim report.* Washington, D.C.: U.S. Department of Education, Institute of Education Sciences.

U.S. Department of Education. 2004. *Key policy letters signed by the education secretary or deputy secretary.*
http://www.ed.gov/policy/elsec/guid/secletter/040331.html

———. 2006. *Letters to chief state school officers regarding states' good-faith efforts in meeting the highly qualified teachers goal.* http://www.ed.gov/programs/teacherqual/hqtltr/index.html.

Walsh, K., and E. Snyder.2004. *Searching the attic: How states are responding to the nation's goal of placing a highly qualified teacher in every classroom.* Washington D.C.: National Council on Teacher Quality.

7

Professionalism under Siege

Teachers' Views of NCLB[1]

Steven Brint and Sue Teele

One important set of voices has been all but completely left out of public debate and discussion on NCLB—that of the teachers themselves. This is particularly unfortunate because teachers are on the front lines of change. Their everyday experiences with NCLB provide a window onto key issues: how the legislation is influencing teachers' work and the organization of schools; how teachers feel about the strong and weak points of the legislation; and whether NCLB has had unintended consequences.

In this paper, we draw on survey responses from 300 Southern California teachers and in-depth interviews with 28 of these teachers to bring the experiences of educators themselves into an assessment of the strengths and weaknesses of NCLB.

Thus far, only one large-scale study has been conducted of teachers' views of NCLB. Sunderman et al. (2004) found that nearly half of 580 elementary school teachers surveyed in Richmond, VA said that the overall effect of NCLB was negative. Nearly two-fifths of the teachers said the effect was positive, and the remainder said that it had no effect. Answers did not vary significantly between teachers whose schools were making adequate yearly progress and those whose schools were in program improvement status. In this study, teachers criticized NCLB most often for creating pressures that contributed to poor performance in the classroom and lower morale. Teachers said the most important unintended consequence of NCLB had been a narrowing of the curriculum so that subject areas not tested were deemphasized or neglected. This view was held somewhat more often among teachers in schools identified as making adequate yearly progress. A pilot study of 160 teachers in Southern California, also conducted in 2004, also showed about half of teachers favoring NCLB and half opposing (Valencia et al. 2005).

One other study, by the Center on Educational Policy (CEP; 2006), surveyed district and school officials and collected information on the characteristics of program improvement schools. This study showed that officials in several of the 38 case study districts believed the law had increased pressure on teachers to a stressful level and had a negative effect on morale. More than 70 percent of survey respondents reported that instructional time in their schools had been reduced in at least one subject to add time for reading and mathematics, the two core subjects tested for NCLB purposes. Findings of increased teacher stress due to NCLB were reported also by Kauffman et al. (2002) for a small sample of new teachers.[2]

Sunderman et al. (2004) and Valencia et al. (2005) collected data in spring 2004, just two-and-one-half years after passage of the legislation. Our data, from early 2006, indicate that teachers' views of NCLB may have become significantly more negative over the last two years. Only one out of every five teachers in our sample reported a favorable assessment of NCLB. The primary criticisms of the Act may also have changed from the years immediately following passage of NCLB. Teachers continue to think that NCLB sets unrealistic goals, but the teachers in our sample also expressed particular concern about a loss of creativity in the classroom and the failure of NCLB to take advantage of teachers' skills and experiences. Teachers said they ware afraid that "scripted learning" approaches following the designs of powerful textbook companies will lead teaching to become a technician's job rather than a profession. They believe this will lead to lower quality in public education, as schools ignore the social and emotional development of children, cut out important untested subjects (such as art, music, and physical education), and fail to develop critical thinking skills and the capacity for depth in children who are taught exclusively to multiple choice tests.

In addition to the advantage of a longer elapse of time between the passage of NCLB and our work in the field, our study is distinguished from previous research by the wider range of questions in our survey instrument, by the inclusion of middle- and high-school teachers in the sample, and by the incorporation of interview data as a complement to the survey data. At the same time, it is important to note that our sample is smaller than that of Sunderman et al. (2004), and the data is limited to teachers working in one region of the country.

In California, content standards exist for virtually every subject taught in school, including music and art, but testing focuses on language arts, mathematics, and science. California accountability testing measures school performance based on an Academic Performance Index (API). Each school's API is based on a composite of students' test results in the major subjects tested. The API for every school is posted on the state education website and school comparisons are also published every year in local newspapers. API scores are consequently of great interest, because the community's reputation for quality education (and therefore, at least indirectly, also its property values) are connected to each year's test results. The tests used to construct API are also used to measure adequate yearly progress for NCLB purposes.[3]

DATA AND METHODS

The study is based on cluster sampling of teachers in five school districts. The school districts vary in student composition from two predominantly low-income and minority districts to one relatively affluent and predominantly white district. The two other districts have sizable low-income populations, but also have significant middle-income populations. We asked superintendents in the five districts to allow us to conduct surveys in three elementary schools, one middle school, and one high school. We were able to obtain the cooperation of all districts, but high schools in one district declined to participate. We substituted a high school from a nearby area, one whose sociodemographic profile closely paralleled the high schools in the target district.

We requested that at least two of the elementary schools and the middle school closely parallel the overall socioeconomic and racial–ethnic composition of the district. (Most of the districts had only one high school.) In consultation with designated officials of the school district, we chose schools that fit our criteria. Some principals from selected schools declined to participate, and these schools were replaced by comparable schools whose principals were willing to participate. We were able to obtain samples from schools varying considerably in both socioeconomic and racial–ethnic composition. As Table 7.1 indicates, schools in our sample ranged from under 33 percent to more than 90 percent minority. They ranged from under 12 percent to over 85 percent of children on free or reduced lunch. Eleven of the 20 elementary and middle schools were "program improvement" schools.

We randomly chose respondents from lists provided by the principals or school districts. Each respondent was assigned a unique identifier. We sampled 18 teachers from each elementary and middle school, and 36 teachers from each high school. We replaced teachers who we discovered were on leave or had left the school. In high schools, we sampled only teachers in core subjects, excluding physical education, vocational education, and other areas falling outside the purview of state accountability testing. We set a target of a two-thirds response rate from each school: 12 responses from each elementary and middle school and 24 responses from each high school. Our final response rate, after an initial distribution and two follow-ups, was 56 percent. The responses ranged between 6 and 15 from the elementary and middle schools and between 12 and 24 from the high schools. In all, we received responses from 301 teachers. Teachers from

Table 7.1 Community and school context variables

Sample N			301	
City size				
City (over 200,000)			12%	
Small city (50,000–200,000)			52%	
Town (under 50,000)			36%	
School type				
Elementary			53%	
Middle school			21%	
High-school			26%	
AYP status (Elementary and middle schools only)				
Achieving AYP			47%	
Program improvement school			53%	
Percent free/reduced lunch				
Min.	Max.	Mean	S.D.	
11.6%	87.1%	51.3%	25.7%	
Percent racial/ethnic minority				
Min.	Max.	Mean	S.D.	
33.5%	97.5%	73.3%	19.3%	

12 of the 25 schools met our two-thirds response goal. Teachers from three of the 25 schools returned eight or fewer surveys.

The survey instrument asked teachers to describe ways that teaching at their schools had changed due to NCLB; how their own teaching had changed; and what their schools were doing to meet AYP. The survey also asked teachers for their assessments of the strong and weak points of NCLB; the unintended consequences of NCLB; and whether after-school tutoring programs were working. It asked teachers for their views of the ways in which NCLB would change the teaching profession. We also asked for their overall assessment of NCLB. We collected basic demographic information (years of experience, grades taught, subjects taught, gender, and ethnicity). We subsequently coded school site information (percent of students on free or reduced lunch, percent minority students, and program improvement status). We coded city size from census data. Frequencies for community and school context variables are reported in Table 7.1.

All questions were close-ended, though we offered an open-ended "other" option for those unsatisfied with the close-ended choices. In multiple response questions, teachers were asked to limit their responses to five items only. For example, our question on the strong points of NCLB included 15 possible answers, from which teachers were asked to choose no more than five.[4] We balanced all multiple response questions with an equal number of positive affect and negative affect options.

Teachers were asked at the end of the survey if they wished to volunteer for a longer interview. The interviews explored a wider range of issues surrounding NCLB. These issues included: changes in the teachers' preparation time; changes in the teachers' ability to individualize instruction; changes in student behavior due to accountability testing; and teachers' views of the types of students most and least affected by NCLB. We conducted these longer interviews with 28 teachers. The interviews lasted between 45 and 90 minutes.

RESULTS

We will first report frequency distributions on key dependent variables and statistics on selected bivariate associations. The main part of the analysis is based on logistic regression of overall favorability scores with fixed effects for school sites. We also use logistic regression to look into the causes of school context effects. We use quotes from the interviews to illustrate themes from the survey analysis and to introduce important themes that the survey questionnaire did not fully capture.

Univariate Statistics

Perhaps the most important finding of our research is the high level of dissatisfaction teachers in our sample reported with NCLB. Four out of five of the teachers expressed an overall unfavorable attitude toward NCLB. This level of dissatisfaction is much higher than that reported by Sunderman et al. (2004) or Valencia et al. (2005) , based on surveys two and one-half years after enactment.

NCLB has led to four major changes in teachers' practices, according to our respondents: First it has led to more teaching to the test. Fully 91 percent of teachers mentioned this change when asked to select no more than five choices from 15 options. Other changes frequently mentioned by teachers included less creativity in the classroom (79% mentioning), more scripted learning (61%), and a more single-minded focus on core subjects (53%). Teachers were less likely to say that NCLB had led to changes in their *own* practices. Nevertheless, three-quarters of the teachers said they personally taught more to tests, and two-thirds said their classrooms were less creative because of NCLB. Smaller proportions said that NCLB had introduced more scripting into their own classrooms (46%), that they now required students to work more intensively (43%), and that they focused more on core subjects than they had in the past (39%).

More than 50 percent of teachers cited three weak points of NCLB: that it sets unrealistic goals (76% mentioning), that it leads to diminished creativity in the classroom (60%), and that it is based on an overly narrow concept of education (53%). Sizable proportions of teachers also mentioned increased stress either for themselves (44%) or for their students (28%). Teachers found fewer strong points in NCLB than weak points. However, substantial minorities of teachers mentioned three strong points of NCLB: the intent to bring greater accountability to public schools (37% mentioning), the effort to bring more qualified teachers into the profession (23%), and the clear performance focus for teachers (21%). One-quarter of the teachers surveyed found no strong points in NCLB, compared to just 1 percent of teachers who found no weak points in the law.

Many of the positive changes legislators hoped would result from NCLB have not been realized, according to the teachers in our sample. Only very small minorities of our respondents mentioned such changes as improved student performance (8% mentioning), more help for disadvantaged students (6%), more equality in educational achievement (4%), and more parental involvement in the schools (2%).

The two most frequently mentioned unintended consequences of NCLB were less creativity in the classroom (78% mentioning) and increased time demands on teachers (75%). Nearly half of the teachers said that students lose interest in education because of NCLB (46%) and that textbook companies have increased influence because they design materials closely aligned to state standards and manuals about how to teach these materials successfully (44%). Two out of five teachers cited as unintended consequences an exodus of teachers from the profession (39%) and the treatment of students "as numbers" (38%). These responses suggest that many teachers feel threatened by the prospect of a system of formal education under the control of state bureaucrats and textbook publishers, and insufficiently engaging to retain either teacher or student interest.

The same concerns about the consequences of an externally controlled form of education were apparent in teachers' responses to our question about how NCLB would change the teaching profession. Four out of five said that teachers would focus on tests to the detriment of other aspects of education (81% mentioning). Nearly half said that scripted learning would replace teaching (46%) and another 30% said teaching would become a less skilled occupation. Only about one-fifth (22%) said that teachers would develop more effective techniques for teaching because of NCLB, and fewer still said that teachers would focus on tests to the benefit of education (13%) and that teaching would become a more skilled occupation (6%).

Our last set of questions asked teachers what their schools were doing to achieve adequate yearly progress. Most said their schools were engaging in collaborative planning (75% mentioning), after-school tutoring programs (66%),[5] and targeting particular students for improvement (59%). The latter approach typically means focusing not on low performing students, but on students that are close to reaching the levels of proficiency mandated by the state. Other approaches included providing coaches for teachers (33%), group discussions about pedagogy (32%), training students for testing (18%), small-group activities (17%), new grouping patterns (11%), and material incentives to motivate teachers (11%). Although scripted learning emerged as a major concern of teachers, only 17 percent of the teachers said that their own schools had adopted scripted learning programs as an approach to meeting AYP.

Bivariate Associations

It is clear from the bivariate associations that teachers' overall assessment of NCLB is influenced by their school context. At four of our schools, all responding teachers were opposed to NCLB. At two of the schools, more than 50 percent of teachers were in favor of NCLB. Some other schools showed substantial minorities in favor of NCLB or very large majorities opposed. School context captures everything about a school that can lead teachers to have more similar positions than we would expect on the basis of their individual demographic characteristics or their individual attitudes alone. Different sources of staff similarity may be at play in different schools: the recruitment of like-minded teachers by principals; the development of a group culture even among philosophically dissimilar teachers; the force of the principals' leadership as a proponent or opponent of NCLB; or resistance among teachers to the principals' leadership.

One of the most important findings of the study is that teachers who said that their schools were not making adequate yearly progress were *more likely* to be favorable toward NCLB than teachers who said their schools were making adequate yearly progress. This result is surprising; we expected that teachers in low-performing schools, who are frequently under intense pressure to perform, would be less likely than others to embrace the Act. Some teachers at program improvement schools may find the clear focus, narrowed curriculum, and repetition encouraged by NCLB well suited to the epistemic level of their students. They may also feel pressure to identify with the goals of NCLB, if they wish to hold onto their jobs. By contrast, teachers who say their schools are making adequate yearly progress may feel both more confidence in their students' abilities and less pressured to identify with the goals of NCLB.[6]

Demographic characteristics of teachers were also associated with variation in assessments of NCLB. Less experienced teachers (less than 8 years of teaching) and minority teachers were more favorable toward NCLB, as were high-school teachers who taught core subjects tested by NCLB at lower levels of education. Less experienced teachers have been socialized under the assumptions of the accountability era and trained for teaching to standards during their credentialing. Unlike new teachers who have been trained for a culture based on high-stakes testing, experienced teachers can compare schooling before and after accountability legislation like NCLB. Teachers say they are more critical because they experienced the possibilities of schooling during a different era. The greater support of minority teachers for NCLB may be due to the law's explicit goal to equalize achievement across all groups, and its explicit attention to social class and ethnicity in test reporting. Rod Paige, the Houston schools superintendent who later became Secretary of Education, often spoke of the need for improvement in minority schools, and the intent of NCLB to ensure that improvement.

Many other demographic and context variables showed insignificant bivariate associations with overall favorability. Neither gender nor grades taught showed significant bivariate associations with overall favorability. Nor did the schools' free and reduced lunch quartile, the ethnic composition of the school, or the size of the city in which the school was located.

Specific attitudes of teachers were, however, significantly and strongly related to opposition to NCLB. Attitudes consistent with the tenets of progressive pedagogy were evident in these responses; so too were responses to reduced workplace autonomy. The strongest bivariate relationships were between negative views of NCLB and teachers who said NCLB leads to a focus on tests to the detriment of other aspects of education (phi = .26); that NCLB is based on unrealistic goals (phi = .25); that NCLB leads to less creativity in the classroom (phi = .25); that NCLB fails to take advantage of teachers' skills and experience (phi = .22); that students lose interest in education because of NCLB (phi = .19); that teaching will become a deskilled occupation (phi=.16) and that NCLB increases the influence of textbook companies (phi = .15).

Specific teachers' attitudes were also significantly and strongly related to more favorable attitudes toward NCLB. Attitudes consistent with the tenets of traditional pedagogy were evident in these favorable responses. The strongest bivariate relationships were between positive views of NCLB and teachers who said NCLB brings more accountability to schools (phi = −.34); that NCLB leads to improved student performance (phi = −.30); that NCLB brings a clear focus for schools (phi = −.20); that teachers focus on tests to the benefit of education (phi = −.16); and that NCLB leads to more qualified teachers in the profession (phi = −.16).

Multivariate Models

Multivariate analysis is necessary to determine which factors most strongly influence teachers' overall assessment of NCLB: teachers' demographic characteristics; their school context; their community context; their commitments to the tenets of traditional or progressive pedagogy; or their concerns about the erosion of workplace autonomy due to NCLB.

Table 7.2 provides information on the variables used in our multivariate analyses.

Table 7.2 Variables in the multivariate analyses

I. Dependent variable	
Overall favorability	
Favorable	21%
Unfavorable	79%
II. Independent variables	
Teaching experience	
Less than 8 years	33%
8 years or more	67%
Racial–ethnic identity	
Minority[a]	21%
White	79%
Attitudes	
Weak points of NCLB: It sets unrealistic goals	
Yes	76%
No	24%
Weak points of NCLB: It fails to make use of teachers' professional skills/experience	
Yes	33%
No	67%
Unintended consequences of NCLB: It has led to less creativity in schools	
Yes:	78%
No:	22%
Unintended consequences of NCLB: It has led students to lose interest in learning	
Yes	46%
No	54%
Strong points of NCLB: It leads to more accountability in the schools	
Yes	37%
No	63%
Strong points of NCLB: It leads to improvement in students' academic performance	
Yes	8%
No	92%

Note: [a]Minority includes: African-American, Latino/a, Asian-American/Pacific Islander, and Native American.

We built a model based first on teachers' demographic characteristics only. We then added school context.[7] We modeled school context using fixed effects for each of the 25 schools in the sample. We next built models based on positive and negative attitudes only, and added teacher demographics and school context to these models. We then developed a final model that included school context, and both positive and negative attitudes. (Demographic variables were insignificant in models including both school context and teacher attitudes.) As a last step in the analysis, we investigated the sources of differences in school sites that were more and less opposed to NCLB.

Teachers' Overall Assessment of NCLB

The results of our regression analysis are summarized in Table 7.3. In each case, overall favorability is the dependent variable. The measure is dichotomized as "favorable/unfavorable." Favorable includes "very favorable" (1% of respondents) and "somewhat favorable" (20%). Unfavorable includes "somewhat unfavorable" (39%) and "very unfavorable" (40%).

As Model 1 shows, demographic variables alone were weak predictors of teachers' overall assessments of NCLB. In so far as demography matters, teachers' experience and ethnicity were the most important influences. As the bivariate associations suggest, less experienced teachers and minority teachers were more supportive of NCLB.

Model 2 shows that school site was a stronger predictor of teachers' attitudes toward NCLB than demographic characteristics. Coefficients for the 25 schools are not reported because, by definition, they sum to 0. (Confidentiality guarantees do not permit us to name the schools.) In Model 3, which includes both fixed school effects and teacher demographics, teacher demographics were statistically insignificant. Teacher demographics remain insignificant in all other tests, and we consequently do not report teacher demographics for other models.

Four criticisms of NCLB were strong and significant predictors of unfavorable attitudes toward NCLB. These criticisms are: (1) NCLB has unrealistic goals; (2) it fails to take advantage of teachers' professional skills and experience; (3) it leads to less creativity in the classroom; and (4) it leads students lose interest in learning.

The criticism that NCLB sets unrealistic goals has received widespread attention in the press and on NCLB websites. In a widely reported analogy, the educational psychologist Robert Linn observed that bringing all students to proficiency in math and reading by 2014 would be equivalent to requiring the big automobile manufacturers to produce engines averaging 288 miles per gallon by 2014 (Linn, quoted in Bracey 2003). Teachers in our interviews developed similar analogies. One said that bringing all students to proficiency by 2014 would be equivalent to the police eliminating all crime over the next eight years. Another said it would be like requiring all students to run five-minute miles by 2014.

One of the most important findings of this study is the conflict we have discovered between teacher professionalism and the "deskilled" character of teaching work under NCLB. The other major criticisms are related to tenets of progressive pedagogy that teachers find unsupported by NCLB: the importance of creativity in the classroom and the importance of maintaining student interest.

Table 7.3 Logistic regressions on overall attitude toward NCLB: Unfavorable

Variable	Model 1 B (S.E.)	Model 2 B (S.E.)	Model 3 B (S.E.)	Model 4 B (S.E.)	Model 5 B (S.E.)
School site (fixed effects)	No	Yes	Yes	No	Yes
8 yrs. + Experience	.76* (.32)	.32 (.38)			
White/Euro-American	.66* (.35)	.44 (.43)			
Unrealistic goals				1.36** (.50)	
Unused professional skills/experience				1.79** (.62)	1.77* (.82)
Less creativity in classrooms				1.06* (.48)	3.68*** (.1.04)
Students lose interest				1.14* (.48)	1.83** (.71)
More accountability in classrooms					
Improved student performance					
N	260	289	260	169	180
Cox-Snell R^2	.040	.175	.215	.165	.358
Nagelkerke R^2	.063	.274	.337	.275	.597

Variable	Model 6 B (S.E.)	Model 7 B (S.E.)	Model 8 B (S.E.)
School site (fixed effects)	No	Yes	Yes
8 yrs. + experience			
White/Euro-American			
Unrealistic goals			
Unused professional skills/experience		1.70* (.84)	
Less creativity in classrooms		3.63*** (1.07)	
Students lose interest			
More accountability in classrooms	−1.91*** (.51)	−1.67** (.63)	−2.39*** (.66)
Improved student performance	−1.60*** (.33)	−2.06*** (.40)	
N	286	286	179
Cox-Snell R^2	.150	.293	.391
Nagelkerke R^2	.234	.457	.649

* $p < .05$, ** $p < .01$, *** $p < .001$

Model 4 shows that teacher criticisms and school site context are approximately equivalent predictors of overall favorability. When school context is added to teacher criticisms (in Model 5), the power of the prediction increases dramatically—from under 30 percent of the variance explained to nearly 60 percent of the variance explained. As indicated in Model 6, two features of NCLB are particularly important for those teachers who had favorable attitudes: the capacity of standardized subject-matter tests to improve accountability and student performance. Two other variables approached statistical significance in regressions controlling for accountability and performance: the clear focus provided by NCLB and the capacity of NCLB to use standardized testing to the benefit of education. Taken together, these findings reinforce our view that tenets of traditional pedagogy—structure, focus, repetition, testing, and feedback—are strongly associated with support for NCLB. Again, the addition of school context to these positive features of NCLB improved the prediction substantially.

Our best prediction, Model 8, included one perceived strong point of NCLB (greater accountability), two criticisms of NCLB (failure to draw on teachers' professional skills and experience and lower creativity in the classroom), plus the school context variable. This model explained nearly two-thirds of the variance in overall favorability. Teacher attitudes were somewhat more important in this prediction than school context. Of the 65 percent of the variance we can explain, slightly less than two-fifths (38%) was due to teacher attitudes and slightly more than one-quarter (27%) was due to school context. The results show clearly that teachers' views of NCLB reflect a culture clash in education, between partisans of traditional and progressive pedagogy, as well as the influence of school context.

School Context Effects

Our ability to explain school context effects is limited by the variety of factors that may be at work in any given school setting. However, it is clear from our data that better-performing schools employing more experienced teachers are more likely to develop a climate that is critical of NCLB, while low-performing schools employing less experienced teachers who are coached on how to improve test results are more likely to develop a climate that is relatively supportive of NCLB. This counterintuitive finding suggests that fear of the erosion of privilege is a potent force in opposition to NCLB, while inexperience and institutional pressures to raise scores may strengthen the identification of teachers with NCLB.

Table 7.4 divides schools into polar types: those in which 100 percent of responding teachers opposed NCLB and those in which 50 percent or more of responding teachers favored NCLB. The differences among these schools are clear. The schools in which teachers were unified against NCLB had significantly more experienced teachers. Teachers in these schools were more likely to say they

Table 7.4 Characteristics of polarized schools (+=100% favorable)

Variable	B (S.E.)
8 yrs. + Experience	2.85*
	(1.22)
School is described as	−2.55*
failing to meet AYP	(1.10)
School provides coaching to	−3.17**
improve test performance	(1.20)
N	64
Cox-Snell R²	.567
Nagelkerke R²	.787

* p<.05   ** p<.01   *** p<.001

were meeting their AYP goals. They also said they were not receiving coaching on how to improve student test performance.

The schools in which teachers were more favorable toward NCLB had the opposite characteristics: more inexperienced teachers, teachers who said they were not meeting their AYP goals or were in program improvement status, and teachers who said their schools provided coaching on how to improve student test performance. We were able to explain 80 percent of the variance of school location using these three variables. Teachers' race was nearly significant in this analysis as well; favorable schools had more minority teachers, while oppositional schools had more white teachers. This finding, too, lends support to our interpretation that teachers who oppose NCLB may be unified by the fear of erosion of privileges related to professionalism.

Interview Themes

Frequently voiced sentiments in the interviews provide a window into teachers' thinking that the survey questions cannot fully capture. In this section, we will discuss interview themes that are directly related to the quantitative analysis and provide texture and more specific content to the quantitative findings.

Like the surveys, the interviews yielded some positive assessments of NCLB. Many teachers endorsed the idea of accountability and said they wanted to be held accountable for their work in the classroom. (Some qualified this support by saying they should be most accountable to teachers in the higher grades.) Several teachers said they liked the uniform content and pacing introduced by NCLB: "The standards are good in that everybody is on the same page. It's uniform across the board" (kindergarten teacher). Some teachers said that NCLB had encouraged more staff discussion, because teachers are working on the same lessons. "The sharing between teachers is the most positive thing that has come out of it" (4th grade teacher). One teacher said that she was getting to know her students better because of NCLB. "The students that are quiet and tend to get lost—now I'm getting to know those students (better), as well as my (more vocal) students" (8th grade teacher). Another teacher said that students at her school were becoming more comfortable with testing situations. "(Because of practice testing), it seems that we had a better response this year…. They were a little less agitated…" (middle school teacher).

However, as in the surveys, the majority of teachers we interviewed were critical of NCLB. The interviews provided specific, targeted criticisms of NCLB. In particular, teachers we interviewed said the state had included too many curriculum standards to cover well. They said that some state standards were developmentally inappropriate for the grade level of the students being tested. They also emphasized that important features of a well-rounded and engaging education were being sacrificed to the regimen of high-stakes testing.

Perhaps the most frequent sentiment expressed in the interviews was frustration with the number of standards—and the pace required of teachers to cover these standards. One teacher spoke of having the equivalent of three-quarters of a year to cover a full year's worth of work. "You do fall behind, because it's practically impossible to teach all of (the standards) in the amount of time that you have" (kindergarten teacher). The number of standards affects how well they are covered. "The fact that there are so many standards to be covered, we're not reaching mastery because our goal is just to get through things and get them tested" (middle school teacher). Another teacher spoke of sacrificing hands-on projects because of time constraints: "(I have) less time for labs, because labs usually take a little bit longer…. Instead of making sure that everyone gets the concept, it's more like, okay, let's cover this now because in a few weeks it's going to be testing time…" (middle school teacher).

Several teachers stated flatly that some content standards were "developmentally inappropriate." "What students are expected to know at each level is too high. In second grade, my students are already learning division, word problems with division, and how to calculate fractions" (2nd grade teacher). Another said, "There are things that I was expected to teach my students in third grade that, when I was in school, I didn't learn until 4h or 5th grade, or sometimes even 6th grade" (3rd grade teacher). "When we look at Piaget and his developmental stages, some of the 5th grade math standards (are not appropriate)…. Their brains aren't…ready for this" (middle school teacher). "The expectation for understanding is grade levels beyond what it used to be 10 years ago. Many of the materials introduced at a higher grade are being introduced to kids too quickly at the lower grade levels. You must introduce it to them (at the right age) so that they are not afraid to try" (2nd grade teacher).

The pace required to keep up with standards leads to fewer "creative detours" that can enhance understanding: "I used to take creative detours and explore more. Since implementation of NCLB, school districts want a tight adherence to the guides the publishers have laid out. There are a lot of things I cannot go into very deeply" (2nd grade teacher). Another said, "In order to raise our test scores, we really need to drill, and so a lot of my teaching has changed into drilling" (8th grade teacher). The interviews also underlined previous findings that nontested subjects are crowded out of the curriculum so that teachers can concentrate on standards in tested subjects: "You start cutting other things, you start cutting the other things that make well-rounded kids. You start cutting the social studies project that we were going to work on in small groups this afternoon, so that we can get through the language arts things we didn't get through. You find yourself cutting music or poetry, or, you know, PE" (3rd grade teacher). Some teachers fear that even recess is on the chopping block. "Someone said to me that (in one district) they were thinking of doing away with recess. And I said, 'Isn't that legally mandated?'" (kindergarten teacher).

According to the teachers we interviewed, the pace required to keep up with state standards—combined with the absence of "fun" activities and "creative detours"—may lead some children to become alienated from schooling at an early age. "The kids get…frustrated. They can't keep up and have no passion…They have so many tests, they don't care anymore" (Middle school teacher). Teachers see the loss of untested subjects as influencing students' interest in learning. "I miss the direction and excitement that science and the arts put toward learning. Students are less likely to want to learn" (2nd grade teacher). Another added, "Students are just tired of testing, testing, testing! Some even refuse to take the tests or don't show up to school on test day" (8th grade teacher). "You do see the number of absences increase (during testing)…. (Y)ou can tell the kids (are thinking), 'Well, if I'm not there…you can't tell me I failed'" (middle school teacher).

The long-term goal of NCLB to bring all students to the level of "proficiency" by 2014 was dismissed by teachers who said that not all students have the home support or the intellectual interest to reach this level of achievement. "On the surface, the idea that all children will perform (at the level of) 80% and above is shocking and absurd" (2nd grade teacher). "If I could get one (message) to George Bush, (it would be) that schools are a mirror of society. If you have kids whose minds are damaged because their mothers took drugs or drank too much alcohol, or kids who were raised by a television, you aren't going to be able to produce the same level of proficiency as you can for kids who had two loving parents who graduated from college and read to their kids from an early age" (1st grade teacher).

DISCUSSION

In this section, we will discuss the implications of our finding in relation to three important organizational changes in American public education related to

NCLB and the accountability movement generally: (1) the centrality of a culture of standardized testing; (2) the erosion of teacher professionalism; and (3) the "reindustrialization" of schooling. In discussing these themes, we will draw on both the quantitative and qualitative data from our study.

The Centrality of a Culture of Testing

High-stakes testing and preparation for high-stakes testing have taken up increasing amounts of time during the school year. Nearly every teacher in our sample said that teachers now "teach more to the test." In addition to time devoted to district, state, and (in some cases) national tests, many schools spend time preparing students for testing through orientations and regular practice tests. "We did practice tests almost weekly and then we had our quarterly tests that we give them" (5th grade teacher). "A big chunk of our time is taken up with test prep, and it begins in September" (1st grade teacher). In some schools, testing has spread into dailiy classroom activities through the introduction of "openers" —tests that are given to open the school day as a way of preparing students for testing situations.

This test-based system of schooling has many consequences. One outcome, according to teachers, is the creation an atmosphere of anxiety as students approach test time. In some teachers' minds, state tests loom over their classrooms like a menacing force: "There's this ever-present…monster, lurking" (multigrade elementary school teacher). Furthermore, the mobilized energy of "gearing up" for testing encourages a let down after the test: "The day after the test, going into a math lesson, a student said, 'The test is over. Do we really have to do this?'" (multigrade elementary school teacher).

Teachers' relationships with students are impacted by test results and the strategies schools have adopted for improving test results. Some teachers begin to see their students in terms of their test numbers. "A lot of times a student can have a bad day, wasn't comfortable with the test on that day, didn't score well, and then a teacher has a negative view of that student, of where they're at" (7th grade teacher). High scoring students can also suffer, because they have already reached the "proficiency" level the state wants, and nothing more is required of them. "In expecting every child to be 'average' we frustrate those who are not and hold back those who have more potential." (kindergarten teacher)

State testing builds a particular conception of the world of knowledge as divided into "information bits" arranged in a multiple choice format with one right answer. "We have no open-ended questions anymore. Everything is factoids." (1st grade teacher).: The techniques used to help students acquire knowledge have also been affected by the format: "Being able to transfer it to paper and pencil has become much more important than it ever used to be. So now, to a large degree, we bypass the hands-on to go straight to the paper and pencil to be sure that when the test comes, that's the format that they're used to. The process-project part has largely gone by the wayside" (3rd grade teacher). Hands-on and visually-based activities that helped some students understand materials are now given lower priority. "'Read and draws' are great for my students who need to learn how to visualize a scene in a story to understand and analyze the narrative. But it's not going to help them on a test, so if I get behind I get rid of them" (middle school teacher).

The Erosion of Teacher Professionalism

NCLB was introduced, in part, as an effort to improve teacher professionalism. It is therefore important to consider whether teacher resistance to NCLB represents simply a desire to escape professional accountability. Teachers themselves have adopted a broader view of the meaning of professionalism. Accountability is one element of professionalism in this view, but it also includes the capacity to employ effectively a range of judgments and pedagogical skills.

Indeed, a widespread sense exists among the teachers we surveyed that teachers' professionalism is under attack from state educational bureaucrats and textbook publishers. This sense is conveyed, most notably, by the strong and significant results of concerns about "diminished creativity" in the classroom and "unused professional skills and experience" in the explanation of teachers' overall assessment of NCLB. Said one teacher, "I have said many times that you can take the janitor and he could follow the script and teach. There is no creativity. If you can follow a script, you can teach" (8th grade teacher). Another said, "(NCLB) mandates how you have to teach. You would never tell a doctor or a lawyer how to do their job" (high-school art teacher).

No other issue revealed as much anger among teachers: "I want to put my hands on my hips and stomp my foot and say, 'How dare you? It's a real slap in the face (coming from people)…who really don't know how to do it or haven't had any experience or (enough) education to say, 'We know how to make it happen; here's your recipe…;" (kindergarten teacher). Another suggested that schools were being held hostage to the vanity projects of politicians: "If the program continues to be played out by politicians' ideas about…why California should have higher standards than other states…teachers who have the passion to teach are going to be driven away by…what NCLB is starting to become — more and more driven by numbers rather than by people" (7th grade teacher).

These comments convey, not only the frustrations many teachers feel in the face of external control, but the centrality of workplace autonomy for teaching professionals. Professions are distinguished from other occupations by the level of autonomy practitioners enjoy at work. This autonomy is based on the complexity of professionals' workplace responsibilities, and the specialized training, occupational skills, and experiences that allow professionals to exercise effective judgment in discharging these responsibilities (Freidson 1986).[8]

The sharply critical response of teachers to NCLB can be interpreted as a reaction to the erosion of professional autonomy in three areas over which teachers have traditionally exercised considerable control: materials, pacing, and techniques. As standards and test performance have become dominant features of schooling, textbook publishers have exercised increasing control over both the content and pace of instruction. Even where teaching is not scripted, many schools require teachers to follow scope and sequence plans designed by publishers. Teachers resent that they are discouraged from breaking scope and sequence guidelines, and many continue to bring in their own materials, even in the face of skepticism from colleagues.

The introduction of a large number of tested standards at each grade level has also limited teachers' control over pace. Many feel that they are being asked to cover more material than their students can master. "I can see that my students are struggling…or these particular students are struggling…and I feel like this is a good way to handle it. Okay, but I can't do that because I need to cover what the state and federal government are telling me I need to cover" (8th grade teacher). Similarly, the centrality of high-stakes testing—with its very public penalties for failure to meet performance expectations—has led teachers to deemphasize instructional techniques they consider to be effective in order to concentrate on tested subjects in ways that prepare students for the testing experience. "Teachers do not have the option to do what experience has taught them is best for the 'whole child'" (kindergarten teacher).

Sociologists have sometimes categorized teaching as a "semiprofession," because it is set within a highly regulated bureaucratic context (e.g., Etzioni 1969). However, when the focus shifts to the classroom, it is clear that high-level teaching requires high-level professional skills and judgments. We can see this by looking at the range of skills and judgments teachers mentioned as part of professional practice in the pre-NCLB classroom. Teachers chose materials that they considered developmentally appropriate. They organized the pace of instruction so that materials could be not just understood and memorized, but mastered. They exercised judgment about when understanding was complete, rather than partial. They searched for supplementary instructional materials that enhanced interest and learning. They implemented projects that allowed for depth as well as breadth of coverage. They recognized that education aimed to develop capacities for sustained, complex thinking and vivid expression, not only an increase in short-term retention of textbook materials. They consequently balanced the learning of factual content with the development of higher-order thinking skills. They remained attentive to differences among children in the ways they acquired knowledge and therefore used multiple modes of instruction. Finally, they maintained awareness that schooling has social and emotional as well as cognitive objectives. In each of these areas, the narrow objectives and restricted performance evaluations of NCLB confront the broader objectives and larger repertoire of techniques used by competent teaching professionals.

Social scientists have recognized tendencies both in bureaucratic organization and corporate profit-seeking to rationalize production in efficient, quantifiable ways. These rationalizing projects have led to the "deskilling" of many occupations. In the process of deskilling, capacities once held by workers are transferred to machines, divided among narrower groups of specialists, organized for maximum efficiency, and focused on quantifiable contributions to production (Braverman 1974; Edwards 1979). Professionals have often successfully resisted deskilling by monopolizing access to occupations through rigorous educational programs and by convincing publics that the variation in the tasks they perform and the judgment required to perform these tasks require workplace autonomy. Our data reveal the strong emotions that have been aroused in the contemporary struggle of teaching professionals to resist what they perceive to be the deskilling of their occupation represented by the requirements and incentives of high-stakes testing.

The Reindustrialization of Schooling

In the 19th century, American public schools could properly be described as highly industrialized settings. Classrooms were organized not so much to stimulate the intellect as to create well-disciplined workers. Children were relentlessly taught to be obedient, regular, and precise in their habits. The phrase "toeing the line" still had a literal meaning. The journalist Joseph Rice (1893) visited hundreds of urban classrooms in the eastern United States to collect data for a book. During recitation periods, children were expected to stand on the line, perfectly motionless, their bodies erect, their knees and feet together, the tips of their shoes touching the edge of a board in the floor. The teachers, according to Rice, paid as much attention to the state of their students' toes and knees as to the words coming out of their mouths. "How can you learn anything?" one teacher asked, "with your knees and toes out of order?" The child study and progressive education movements of the late 19th and early 20th centuries were responses to the weaknesses of this form of education. They were intended to break the grip of drilling for industrial work discipline by making the classroom a more inviting space for children and one richer in educationally stimulating opportunities (Cremin 1961).

From a historical perspective, NCLB can be interpreted as part of a process of "reindustrializing" schooling. According to the teachers in our study, it frequently leads to outcomes similar to those found by Joseph Rice more than 100 years ago: classrooms organized around drilling for tests, great concern for memorizing "bite-sized" pieces of knowledge, and perhaps also high levels of alienation among students who are at once fearful and bored.

Teachers are aware that students pass through distinct epistemic levels (King and Kitchener 1994; Mines et al. 1990). While basic skills must be mastered before higher order thinking skills become a predominant focus, cultivation of higher order skills can accompany and enrich work on basic skills, even (and perhaps especially) among younger children. By cutting out "creative detours" and exercises stimulating critical thinking, NCLB addresses basic skills acquisition in a form that can be deadening rather than enlivening for children.

Teachers' concerns about the consequences of NCLB are closely tied to their concerns about the ultimate objectives of public schools. "There are way too many assessments. We don't have time to develop social skills or a love of learning" (kindergarten teacher) "The intent of NCLB is admirable. The result, though, is a huge emphasis on test scores. Now…my incoming class has a much weaker understanding of material, though (some) can score well on standardized tests. I fear for their futures" (5th grade teacher). One teacher predicted that NCLB would have long-term effects on universities because of the style of learning it encouraged: "(Our) students are not able to look at things from multiple perspectives, where students…in my class just five years ago were still in the mindset of (the) creative thinker (who could do this). This generation has been tested, tested, tested, and (some) are going to really struggle when they have to think outside of the test format" (middle school teacher). Another added, "They have lost critical thinking skills, because those skills are not validated at school… Critical thinking could be the rallying cry, because that's what's left out of NCLB" (1st grade teacher).

High-stakes tests were first introduced in the 1980s because educators and business leaders feared that American students were underperforming in relation to their peers in other countries. This system led to improved achievement, particularly in math, for younger students (Loveless 2006). However, we are now reaching a point of diminishing returns, and of heightened student and teacher resistance. If we want our schools to employ teachers who have a passion for teaching, and if we want them to produce students who have an appetite for learning, the strategies developed over the last 20 years to address concerns about American competitiveness will need to be reconsidered. Already schools in some affluent communities are beginning to prioritize standards and to focus attention on a smaller number of "essential" standards, while reintroducing support for higher order thinking skills (see, e.g., CUSD 2006).[9] No one should wish to jettison the gains attributable to the accountability movement, but we may be reaching a point of imbalance in our vision of schooling, one that can be corrected only by a broader and better balanced vision.

Notes

1. We would like to thank Daniel Amador, Chioma Chukwu, Shannon Fay, Ashley N. Koda, Monica Marquez, Linda McAnnally, Kelly R. Miller, Danielle Morad, Natasha Passerello, Richard Rangel, Erin Schultz, Noel Valencia, Eric Vega, Annette Webb, Sheritta Wells, and Scott Wilson for research assistance. We would like to thank Robert A. Hanneman for statistical advice and Patrick Guggino for helpful references on teacher professionalism.

2. In addition, a number of studies of teachers' views of accountability exist from the pre-NCLB era. See Woody et al. (2003). Like ours, these studies suggest that nontested subjects are crowded out by tested subjects, and that teachers believe an overemphasis on standards-based testing has decreased their autonomy and effectiveness in the classroom.

3. AYP is not publicized as much as API. For this reason, many teachers and principals worry, as one teacher told us, "more about API than AYP." Testing related to the construction of the Academic Performance Index is only one feature of California's testing regime. High-school students are required to pass an exit examination, the California High-School Exit Examination (CHSEE) in language arts, writing, and mathematics. Many school districts also administer "benchmark" tests, and some administer the National Assessment of Educational Progress (NAEP).

4. A few teachers (depending on the question, between 1 and 6% of respondents) circled more than five responses on the multiple response questions. The majority of respondents choosing more than five responses chose either six or seven, but a few circled 10 or more responses. We were reluctant to eliminate these respondents from the data analysis because of our relatively small sample. In lieu of introducing a complex (and debatable) weighting system to adjust for the answers of this small number of respondents who chose more than five responses, we made a simplifying assumption: that had these teachers limited their choices to only five, they would have disproportionately chosen the items most frequently chosen by other teachers. Analysis of the choices of these teachers confirms that they were very likely to choose items frequently chosen by other teachers, and added items less often mentioned by other teachers. Infrequently chosen responses do not figure prominently in our analysis, and we therefore feel justified in including the responses of the few teachers who failed to follow our directions. However, we recognize that this procedure inevitably introduces a small amount of measurement error into our data analysis.

5. Nearly half of teachers said state-mandated tutoring programs helped students (43%). These teachers said the tutoring programs helped primarily because they provided extra attention (96%). Among those who said after-school tutoring did not help, the majority thought students were uninterested in tutoring and did not want it (64%). A few also said that group settings were not conducive to effectiveness, tutors were inexperienced, and tutoring methods were not effective.

6. Not all teachers accurately identified their schools as program improvement schools. Two-thirds of the teachers in the sample accurately identified their schools as making adequate yearly progress or as failing in at least some years to make adequately yearly progress. When we grouped teachers according to state designations of their schools' program status, the teachers in program improvement schools continued to be more favorable to NCLB than teachers in schools making adequate yearly progress. However, the differences were not statistically significant.

7. Data were too sparse at a few schools to use hierarchical linear modeling. Using schools in fixed effects models provides an appropriate alternative approach to separating contextual and individual teacher effects.

8. No salaried professional has unlimited autonomy, and it is therefore useful to consider professional autonomy as multidimensional and variable across occupations. The four major dimensions of professional autonomy are control over: (1) the choice of clients, (2) resources, (3) work pace, and (4) techniques. Some professionals, such as university researchers, exercise control over the problems they address. Some professionals, such as self-employed physicians, exercise control over the resources they use to do their work. These forms of control are, however, far from universal among professionals. The great majority of professionals do control the techniques and methods they use to address problems related to their work responsibilities (Derber, Schwartz, and Magrass 1990). For teachers, see also Ingersoll (2003).

9. For an influential discussion of standards "overload," see Marzano and Kendall (1998).

References

Associated Press. 2006. A false picture of academic progress. http://www.msnbc.msn.com/id/12357165.

Bracey, Gerald W. 2003. *On the death of childhood and the destruction of public schools: The folly of today's educational policies and practices.* Portsmouth, NH: Heinemann.

Braverman, Harry. 1974. *Labor and monopoly capitalism: The degradation of work in the 20th century.* New York: Monthly Review Press.

Brint, Steven. 2006. *Schools and societies,* 2nd ed. Stanford, CA: Stanford University Press.

Center for Education Policy (CEP). 2006. *From the capital to the classroom: Year four of the No Child Left Behind Act.* Washington, D.C.: CEP. (March)

Claremont Unified School District (CUSD) Advisory Committee on Quality Education. 2006. *Recommendations* (May). Claremont, CA: CUSD

Cremin, Lawrence. 1961. *The transformation of the school.* New York: Vintage.

Cronin, John, G. Gage Kingsbury, Martha S. McCall, and Branin Bowe. 2005. *The Impact of No Child Left Behind on student achievement and growth.* Lake Oswego, OR: Northwest Evaluation Association.

Derber, Charles, William A. Schwartz, and Yale Magrass. 1990. *Power in the highest degree.* New York: Oxford University Press.

Edwards, Richard. 1979. *Contested terrain: The transformation of the workplace in the twentieth century.* New York: Basic Books.

Etzioni, Amitai. 1969. *The semi-professions and their organization.* New York: The Free Press.

Freidson, Eliot. 1986. *Professional powers.* Chicago: University of Chicago Press.

Fuller, Bruce. 2004. Are test scores really rising? *Education Week* (October 13).

Ingersoll, Richard M. 2003. *Who controls teachers' work? Power and accountability in America's schools.* Cambridge, MA: Harvard University Press.

Kaufmann, David, Susan M. Kardos, Edward Liu, and Heather G. Peske. 2002. Lost at sea: New teachers' experiences with curriculum and assessment. *Teachers College Record* 104: 273–300.

King, Patricia M., and Karen S. Kitchener. 1994. *Developing reflective judgment:Understanding and promoting intellectual growth and critical thinking in adolescents and adults.* San Francisco: Jossey-Bass.

Loveless, Tom. 2006. *How well are American students learning?* Washington, D.C.: The Brookings Institution.

Marzano, Robert J. and John S. Kendall. 1998. *Awash in a sea of standards.* Aurora, CO: Mid-Continent Research for Education and Learning.

McDonnell, Lorraine M. 2005. No child left behind and the federal role in education: Evolution or revolution? *Peabody Journal of Education* 80:19–38.

Mines, Robert A., Patricia M. King, Albert B. Hood, and Phillip K. Wood. 1990. Stages of intellectual development and associated critical thinking skills in college students. *Journal of College Student Development* 31:538–47.

National Commission on Excellence in Education. 1983. *A nation at risk.* Washington, D.C.: Government Printing Office.

Rice, Joseph M. 1893. *The public school system of the United States.* New York: Century.

Sunderman, Gail L., Christopher A. Tracey, Jimmy Kim, and Gary Orfield. 2004. *Listening to teachers: Classroom realities and No Child Left Behind.* Cambridge, MA: The Civil Rights Project at Harvard University.

U.S. Department of Education. 2006. New "Nation's Report Card" shows NCLB is working for all students. Washington, D.C.: USDOE. http://www.ed.gov.

Valencia, Noel, Amy Runion, Kelly R. Miller, and Natasha Passarello. 2005. Teachers' view of the No Child Left Behind Act: A pilot study. Unpublished paper. Department of Sociology, University of California Riverside. (June)

Woody, Elizabeth, Melissa Buttles, Judith Kafka, Sandra Park, and Jennifer Russell. 2003. *Voices from the field: Educators respond to accountability.* Berkeley: PACE Center.

8

Teacher Quality, Educational Inequality, and the Organization of Schools[1]

Richard M. Ingersoll

Few educational problems have received more attention in recent times than the failure to ensure that elementary and secondary classrooms are all staffed with qualified teachers. Since the mid-1980s, dozens of studies, commissions, and national reports have drawn attention to the importance of the qualifications and quality of the teaching force. This concern is understandable. Teachers are a particularly important educational resource, the largest single component of the cost of education in any country is teacher compensation and student educational outcomes ultimately depend on the work of teachers.

Not surprisingly, the issue of teacher quality has also been at the heart of the ongoing national debate over equity in education. Among those concerned with issues of educational inequity, it is widely believed that students from disadvantaged backgrounds do not have equal access to qualified teachers. At least since James Coleman's seminal study, commentators, researchers, and policymakers have long held that the most needy students in the United States—especially those in schools serving poor, minority, and urban communities—are taught by the least qualified teachers (e.g., Coleman 1966; Darling-Hammond 1987; Dreeben and Gamoran 1986; Haycock 1998, 2000; National Commission on Excellence in Education 1983; Oakes 1990; Rosenbaum 1976). Disadvantaged school districts, these critics hold, are unable to match the salaries, benefits, and resources offered by more affluent schools and, hence, have difficulty competing for the more qualified teaching candidates. In turn, unequal access to qualified teachers and, hence, to quality teaching is considered a primary factor in the stratification of educational resources and opportunities to learn, and ultimately, unequal educational and occupational outcomes.

One of the most significant reform efforts designed to address these problems has been the federal No Child Left Behind Act (NCLB), the Elementary and Secondary Education Act revised and reauthorized in January 2002. This legislation set a new and unprecedented goal; namely, to ensure that the nation's public elementary and secondary students are all taught their core academic subjects by highly qualified teachers.

In general, NCLB defines a "highly qualified" teacher as someone who has a bachelor's degree, who holds a regular or full state-approved teaching certificate or license, and who is competent in each of the core academic subjects they teach. There are several means by which teachers can establish "competency" in a subject. They can hold an undergraduate or graduate major or its equivalent in the subject, pass a test on the subject, hold an advanced teaching certificate in the subject, or meet some other state-approved method of evaluation for the subject. In order to assess how well schools are doing in regard to the new requirements and to hold them accountable if they do not meet them, NCLB requires three things of states and school districts: annual report cards; plans for improvement; and disclosure to parents of students taught by underqualified teachers.

This chapter adopts a sociological perspective, one that focuses upon the social organization of teachers' work, to examine the sources of, and responses to, these inadequacies and inequities in teacher qualifications. The thesis of this chapter is that, although ensuring that the nation's classrooms are all staffed with qualified teachers is a perennially important issue in our schools, it is also among the least understood. As a result, most recent reform efforts, such as NCLB, will have difficulty solving the problem of underqualified teachers, especially in disadvantaged schools, because they do not address some of their key causes.

TEACHER QUALITY AND THE ORGANIZATION OF SCHOOLS

The dominant approach, hereafter referred to as the teacher deficit perspective, is that the source of the problem of underqualified teachers primarily lies in deficits in either the quality or the quantity of teachers.

In the first case, underqualified teaching is assumed to be a problem of poor teacher preparation. In this view, the preemployment education and training of teachers in college or university training programs lacks adequate rigor, breadth, and depth. To address this issue many states have pushed for more rigorous teacher education, training, and certification standards to remedy this problem.

In the second case, the problem is assumed to be a result of teacher shortages, due to increasing student enrollments and a "graying" teaching workforce. These problems are deemed most acute in disadvantaged school districts, which have difficulty competing with more affluent schools for the more qualified teaching candidates. In response to this issue, states and school districts have implemented a host of initiatives and programs that attempt to increase the supply of available teachers by recruiting new candidates into teaching. These include a wide range of alternative licensing programs designed to ease entry into teaching and midcareer switch programs such as Troops-to-Teachers designed to entice professionals from other occupations into teaching. Many states have used financial incentives such as signing bonuses, student loan forgiveness, housing assistance, and tuition reimbursement, to aid teacher recruitment (Hirsch, Koppich, and Knapp 2001).

In contrast, the central argument of this study is that fully understanding the problem of unqualified teachers requires not only examining the quantity and quality of the teaching force, but also examining the organizational and occupational characteristics of the social settings within which teachers are employed and work. This perspective, drawn from the sociology of organizations, occupations, and work, is that these kinds of inadequacies and inequities in schools, like many other issues of social stratification, cannot be fully understood without "putting the organization back" into the analysis (cf. Stolzenberg 1978; Hirsch and Lounsbury 1997). From this perspective, the social organization of teachers' work, that is, the manner in which teachers are managed, employed, and utilized, can account for as much of the problem of underqualified teaching as do inadequacies in the supply or training of teachers (see Figure 8.1).

One of the least recognized causes behind inadequacies and inequities in access to qualified teachers is the phenomenon known as out-of-field teaching—teachers assigned to teach subjects for which they have little education or training. This is a crucial factor because highly qualified and well-trained teachers may actually become highly unqualified if, once on the job, they are assigned to teach subjects for which they have little background. This practice has been largely unknown to the public, to policymakers, and many educational commentators and researchers. An absence of accurate data on out-of-field teaching contributed to this lack of recognition, a situation remedied with the release, beginning in the early 1990s, of the Schools and Staffing Survey (SASS) conducted by the National Center for Education Statistics (NCES) of the U.S. Department of Education.

In previous research I have presented SASS data showing that out-of-field teaching is an ongoing and serious problem across the nation, especially in secondary schools (for summaries, see, Ingersoll 1999, 2001, 2003b). NCES analysts have also calculated levels of out-of-field teaching using the same, or similar, data sources and, although different analysts have focused an a wide range of different measures of out-of-field teaching, all have reached the same conclusion: that there are high levels of out-of-field teaching in American schools (e.g., McMillen et al. 2002). Over the past several years the problem of out-of-field teaching has become a major concern in the realm of educational policy and it was specifically targeted by NCLB.

Teacher Deficit Perspective:

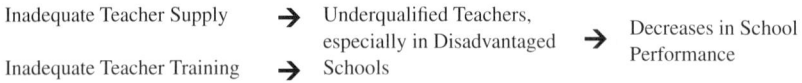

Inadequate Teacher Supply → Underqualified Teachers, especially in Disadvantaged Schools → Decreases in School Performance

Inadequate Teacher Training →

An Organizational Perspective:

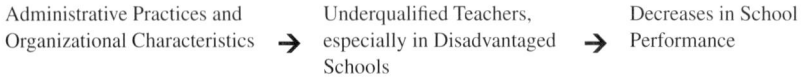

Administrative Practices and Organizational Characteristics → Underqualified Teachers, especially in Disadvantaged Schools → Decreases in School Performance

Figure 8.1 Two perspectives on the causes and consequences of underqualified teaching

Nonetheless, many unanswered questions remain. This analysis will address two sets of these questions:

1. Do some kinds of schools, especially those serving disadvantaged students, have more out-of-field teaching than do others? What is the role of out-of-field teaching in the problem of unequal access to qualified teachers in disadvantaged schools?
2. What are the sources of school-to-school differences in out-of-field teaching? Why are particular schools more likely to have out-of-field teachers?

From the organizational perspective of this study, it is necessary to develop an adequate understanding of which aspects of schools and districts—their policies, administration, or conditions—affect the extent to which schools succeed in providing qualified teachers in their classrooms. Understanding if and how school decision makers can either undermine or foster quality teaching is of vital importance because of the obvious implications for devising reforms, policies, and interventions that address all the key factors at the root of the problem of underqualified teaching.

AN ORGANIZATIONAL PERSPECTIVE

Unlike those employed in the traditional professions, teachers have only limited authority over many key workplace decisions. One key set of decisions in schools concerns the distribution of courses and workloads across faculty. National data have long documented that teachers have little influence or input into which courses they are assigned to teach. The data tell us that decisions that concern the selection and the allocation of teachers to course and program assignments are primarily the responsibility and prerogative of principals and other building-level school administrators (Ingersoll 2003a). These administrators are charged with the often difficult task of providing a broad array of programs and courses with limited resources, limited time, a limited budget, and a limited teaching staff. In this context, principals may find that assigning teachers to teach out of their fields is more efficient and less expensive than the alternatives. Simply put, out-of-field teaching is used by administrators because it is a cheap and convenient way of closing the gap between demands and resources; that is, of making ends meet.

Rather than trying to find and hire a new science teacher to teach a newly state-mandated, but underfunded science curriculum, a principal may find it more convenient to assign a couple of English and social studies teachers to cover a section or two in science. If a teacher suddenly leaves in the middle of a semester, a principal may opt to hire a readily available, but not fully qualified, substitute teacher rather than instigate a formal search for a new fully qualified teacher. When faced with the choice between hiring a fully qualified candidate for an English position and hiring a less qualified candidate who is also willing to coach a major varsity sport, a principal may find it more expedient to do the latter.

Faced with a myriad of such trade-offs and judgments, some degree of teacher misassignment by principals is probably unavoidable. However, while the SASS data have shown that out-of-field teaching is widespread, these data also show there are large school-to-school differences in this practice (Ingersoll 1999). This raises an important question that is at the center of this study: What accounts for school differences in levels of out-of-field teaching?

ADMINISTRATIVE PRACTICES, ORGANIZATIONAL CHARACTERISTICS, AND OUT-OF-FIELD TEACHING

This analysis seeks to build on earlier work by empirically exploring the reasons *why* particular kinds of schools have more or less out-of-field teaching. It investigates the relationships between the degree of out-of-field teaching in schools and a number of possible factors suggested by the above discussion. These include factors suggested by the teacher deficit perspective, such as the extent to which schools experience difficulties in recruiting qualified teaching staff for their teaching job openings, and also factors suggested by an organizational perspective, including a number of administrative practices and organizational characteristics. Below, I describe these latter practices and characteristics.

Hiring Policies

While data from SASS show that school principals have a great deal of control over teacher hiring decisions, the data also show that the central administrations of public school districts often impose standards on these school-level decisions in the form of regulations concerning minimal training requirements for new hires. For example, the data show that about two-thirds of all school districts formally require new teacher hires to hold a college major or minor in the main field to be taught. We would expect such regulations to constrain the capacity of school principals to hire out-of-field candidates for openings. This analysis will examine whether the existence of these kinds of regulations is related to decreases in the amount of out-of-field teaching in schools.

Principal Leadership

The degree to which a school is faced with teacher recruitment and hiring difficulties and the kinds of regulations imposed by district-level administrators may shape a principal's teacher hiring and staffing decisions. An organizational perspective, however, suggests there is also an overlooked role for the leadership skills of principals in the employment, assignment, and utilization of teachers. This analysis will explore this factor by examining whether there is a positive association between the general leadership skill of principals and the degree of out-of-field teaching in schools.

Staffing Practices

Depending upon the constraints within which principals work, the degree of discretion allowed to them, and their leadership skills, there could be numerous options, choices, and strategies available to principals in regard to teacher hiring and assignment. As discussed previously, when faced with difficulty in finding qualified candidates to fill teaching openings, school principals might opt to hire an available but underqualified teacher at the cost of a regular teacher salary, might choose to reassign an existing teacher to cover part or all of the hard-to-staff classes at no additional salary, or might opt to employ a long-term substitute teacher at a relatively low salary. We would expect each of these choices to result in significantly more out-of-field teaching.

Alternatively, rather than resort to the above choices, principals might opt to leave some hard-to-staff teaching openings unfilled and shift student enrollment to existing classes. This would create larger classes, save salary costs, and, presumably, result in less out-of-field teaching. This analysis will examine the relationships between these contrasting managerial choices and the degree of out-of-field teaching that exists in schools.

Teacher Unions

Teacher unions and their work rules are another source of constraint on the staffing decisions of school principals. It is unclear, however, what effect such constraints have on the degree of out-of-field teaching. On the one hand, some opponents of teacher unions have blamed teacher unions for the prevalence of out-of-field teaching. In this view, self-serving work rules promulgated by teacher unions, especially seniority rules, are the main reason that classrooms are staffed with underqualified teachers (Toch 1996).

On the other hand, members and leaders of teacher unions have often opposed the practice of out-of-field teaching and the presence of a teacher union in a school district could have an attenuating effect on the practice of out-of-field teaching. This analysis will test these competing predictions by examining under what conditions the presence of teacher unions is related to the degree of out-of-field teaching in schools.

School Size

School size has been the subject of much attention in recent years and a "small is beautiful" notion is currently popular among many education researchers and policymakers (e.g., Bryk, Lee, and Smith 1990). In earlier analyses of the data (Ingersoll 1999) I found a strong inverse correlation between the size of schools and the amount of out-of-field teaching in schools; smaller schools have more out-of-field teaching than do larger schools. This finding suggests that one possible disadvantage of smaller schools often overlooked in the debates over the relative merits of small and large schools is a greater degree of underqualified teaching. Small schools may find it more difficult to allow staff specialization, and, as a result, teachers in these schools may often be required to be generalists. This study will test whether the association between size and out-of-field teaching holds up across a range of schools and after controlling for other factors.

In sum, the objective of this study is to investigate the sources of underqualified teaching in schools and why particular schools, especially those in disadvantaged communities, are more likely to have out-of-field teaching. The analysis first focuses on establishing the role of out-of-field teaching as a major source of underqualified teachers, especially in disadvantaged schools. I present data showing the distribution of teachers' qualifications and the distribution of out-of-field teaching across different types of schools (e.g., according to student race/ethnicity, poverty and urbanicity). The study then explores the sources of school-to-school variations in out-of-field teaching by investigating which of the above contextual, organizational, and administrative aspects of schools are associated with underqualified teachers in schools.

DATA AND METHODS

As mentioned, the data for this study come from the NCES Schools and Staffing Survey (SASS) (NCES 2005). This is the largest and most comprehensive data set available on the staffing, occupational, and organizational characteristics of elementary and secondary schools. The survey was specifically designed to remedy the lack of nationally representative and comprehensive data on these issues.

Data

The U.S. Census Bureau collected the SASS data for NCES from random samples stratified by state, sector, and school level. To date, five independent cycles of SASS have been completed: 1987–88, 1990–91, 1993–94, 1999–2000 and 2003-2004. Each cycle of SASS includes several sets of separate, but linked, questionnaires for school administrators and for a random sample of teachers within each school. The response rates have been relatively high: 86 percent for schoolteachers and 94 percent for school administrators. The data used in this study are primarily from the 1993–94 SASS. The sample contains about 46,700 teachers employed in about 9,000 public elementary, secondary, and combined (K–12) schools. Throughout, this analysis uses data weighted to compensate for the over- and undersampling of the complex stratified survey design. Each observation is weighted by the inverse of its probability of selection in order to obtain unbiased estimates of population parameters.

SASS is particularly useful for addressing research questions on access to qualified teachers. It has gathered a wide range of information on the characteristics of teachers and the characteristics of schools and school districts across the country. Data were collected, for example, on the subject taught, grade level, and number of students enrolled for each class period in the school day for each teacher sampled. In addition, teachers reported their certification status and the major and minor fields of study for each of their degrees earned at both the undergraduate and graduate levels. From administrators, SASS has obtained a wide range of information on the school demographic characteristics, staffing procedures and difficulties, and administrative practices and organizational characteristics.

Methods

There are two stages to the data analysis and data presentation: the first is concerned with documenting levels of both teacher qualifications and out-of-field teaching across different types of schools, while the second is concerned with examining the sources of school-to-school variations in out-of-field teaching.

One of the difficulties encountered in researching the problem of underqualified teachers has been a lack of consensus on the best standard by which to define a qualified teacher (Ingersoll 2001). Few would argue that teachers ought not to be qualified. Moreover, unlike many other occupations, teaching has a body of empirical research investigating the effects of teachers' qualifications on performance and a number of studies have shown positive effects (e.g., Greenwald et al. 1996). For instance, recent analyses of NAEP data found that 8th grade students whose math teachers had a regular teaching certificate in math, or had a major or minor in math or in math education, scored significantly higher on the 8th grade math test (e.g., Greenberg et al. 2004).

Nevertheless, there remains a great deal of controversy concerning how much education, what types of training, and which kinds of preparation teachers ought to have to be considered qualified in any given field. Underlying this analysis is the premise that adequately qualified teachers ought to have, as a minimal prerequisite, a credential (such as a degree or certificate) in the fields they are assigned to teach. Having a credential and signifying some degree of training or education in a field does not guarantee one is a quality teacher, nor even that one is a qualified teacher, but the assumption underlying this research is that some degree of training is a necessary, if not sufficient, requirement of both.

The first stage of the analysis presents descriptive statistics on levels of teacher education, teacher certification, and teaching experience, and the extent to which these levels vary according to school poverty enrollment level, school minority enrollment level, and school urbanicity. This stage of the analysis also presents data on the extent to which teachers are assigned to teach in fields that do not match their fields of training. For measures of out-of-field teaching, the first stage of the analysis focuses on those teachers without an undergraduate or graduate major or minor in the field taught, for five specific fields (general elementary education, and secondary level mathematics, English, social studies, and science).

The second stage of the analysis is concerned with explaining why particular schools are more or less likely to have different levels of out-of-field teaching. It begins by summarizing descriptive statistics on recent trends in overall levels of teacher supply, demand, and shortages. This stage of the analysis then turns to a multiple regression analysis of the relative impact of various factors on out-of-field teaching, focusing on the secondary level. The subsample includes 23,867 teachers in grades 7–12. It includes all those teaching in any of eight fields, parallel to conventional departmental divisions at the secondary level: English, mathematics, social studies, science, art/music, physical education, foreign language, and vocational education. It excludes those employed in middle schools.

The outcome or dependent variable in this analysis is a second measure of out-of-field teaching—for each secondary-level teacher, the percentage of their daily classes in which they do not have an undergraduate or graduate major or a minor in the field taught. The objective of this portion of the analysis is to examine whether the proportion of secondary-level classes in schools that are taught by out-of-field teachers is related to four groups of independent variables: teacher qualifications, school demographic characteristics, school recruiting and hiring difficulties, and school administrative practices and organization

Table 8.1 Definitions of measures used in the multiple regression analysis of out-of-field teaching at the secondary level

Out-of-field teaching

Percent secondary classes out-of-field: for each 7–12th grade teacher, percentage classes in which teacher does not have an undergraduate or graduate major or minor in field taught. Both academic and education majors/minors are counted (e.g., math and math education) . Measure includes all those teaching in any of eight fields, parallel to conventional departmental divisions at the secondary level: English, mathematics, social studies, science, art/music, physical education, foreign language, vocational education. It excludes those employed in middle schools.

Teacher qualifications

Highest degree: a 4 category variable, where 0 = less than Bachelor's degree, 1 = Bachelor's degree, 2 = master's degree, 3 = above master's degree.

Teaching experience: total years of teaching experience

School demographic characteristics

Poverty enrollment: percentage of students receiving the federal free or reduced-price lunch program for students from families below poverty level.

Minority enrollment: percentage of students that were black, Hispanic, American Indian, Asian and Pacific Islander

Rural: a dichotomous variable where 0=central city or urban fringe/large town and 1=rural/small town

Suburban: a dichotomous variable where 0 = rural/small town or central city and 1 = urban fringe/large town

School recruiting and hiring difficulties

Teaching job openings: a dichotomous variable where 0=school had no teaching job opening(s) that year and 1 = school had teaching job opening(s) that year

Hiring difficulties: On a scale of 0 to 13, sum of 13 teaching fields for which school administrator reported either "somewhat difficult," "very difficult," or "could not fill" in response to item which asked: "how difficult or easy was it to fill the vacancies for this school year in each of the following fields?" The latter include: special education, ESL/ESOL/bilingual education, English, mathematics, social studies, physical science, life science, music, foreign languages, business or marketing, industrial arts, home economics, trade and industry, agriculture.

Administrative practices/organizational characteristics

Major/minor required of hires: on a scale of 1 = not used, 2 = used, 3 = required, school district requirement for new hires having college major or minor in field to be taught, as reported by school administrators.

Principal leadership: on a scale of 1 = strongly disagree to 4 = strongly agree the school mean of 6 items asked of teachers about: whether their principal recognizes staff members for good work; communicates his/her expectations; is supportive and encouraging; backs up teachers; and communicates with teachers about instructional practices. Factor analysis (with varimax rotation method) was used to develop this measure. Item loadings of .4 were considered necessary for inclusion. Items in the factor had high internal consistency (a > .7).

Hiring or assigning underqualified: on a scale of 0 to 4, sum used of 4 possible methods to cover vacancies, as reported by school administrators: hire a less than fully qualified teacher; assign teacher of another subject or grade level to teach the class; assign administrator or counselor to teach the class; use short-term or long-term substitutes. To avoid missing observations, this variable is calculated for all schools, even those without vacancies or without hiring difficulties that, by definition, would not have indicated use of these strategies.

Average class size: school's mean student enrollment per classroom.

Starting teacher salary: normal yearly base salary for teacher with a bachelor's degree and no experience, as reported by school administrators. Divided by 1000, to make units refer to increments of $1000.

Presence of teacher union: a dichotomous variable where 0 = school district has no teacher union and 1 = school district does have one

School size: student enrollment of school. Divided by 100, to make units refer to increments of 100 students.

Table 8.2 Means and standard deviations for variables used in multiple regression analysis of out-of-field teaching at the secondary level

	Mean	Standard deviation
Percent 7–12 grade classes taught by out-of-field teachers	16	35
Teacher qualifications		
Highest degree (scale of 0–3)	1.6	.62
Teaching experience (yrs)	16	9.4
School demographic characteristics		
Percent students in school receiving free-reduced lunch	23	22.8
Percent minority students in school	28	28.5
Percent rural schools	43	
Percent suburban schools	32	
School recruiting and hiring difficulties		
Percent schools with teaching job openings	87	
Hiring difficulties (scale of 0–13)	1.5	1.9
Administrative practices/organizational characteristics		
Major/minor required of hires (scale of 1–3)	2.6	.60
Principal leadership (scale of 1–4)	2.1	.68
Hiring/assigning underqualified (scale of 0–4)	.31	.61
Class size	23	8
Starting teacher salary ($)	23,177	3,358
Percent schools with teacher union	73	
School size	1084	640

characteristics. Table 8.1 provides definitions and Table 8.2 provides summary statistics for these variables.

For measures of teacher qualifications, the regression analysis includes controls for each teacher's highest degree earned and total years of teaching experience. For school demographic characteristics, the analysis includes measures of school poverty enrollment, school minority enrollment, and school urbanicity. For school recruiting and hiring difficulties, the analysis includes a measure to control for whether schools had teaching job openings in the year of the survey and a measure of the extent of difficulty these schools experienced with recruiting qualified faculty to fill their openings for 13 teaching fields. Finally, after controlling for the above teacher and school factors, the analysis includes a number of independent variables reflecting school administrative practices and organizational characteristics. These latter measures include a variable assessing whether the school district has informal or formal rules stipulating that new teacher hires have a major or minor in the main field to be taught. There is a variable representing teachers' ratings of the leadership skills of their principals. This measure is based on teachers' subjective perceptions and, hence, is vulnerable to bias. There is also a variable on the extent to which a school covers hard-to-fill teaching openings by hiring underqualified teachers, reassigning teachers of another subject or grade level, or using short-term or long-term substitutes. Finally, there are variables for both school size and the school's average class size; the normal yearly starting salary provided by the school for new, inexperienced teachers; and whether there is a teacher union in the school district.

Because the data in the analysis are couched at two levels—teacher level and school level—this analysis uses a regression program, SAS' PROC MIXED, that adjusts for the clustering of teachers within schools resulting from the complex multilevel design of the SASS sample. PROC MIXED has the additional advantage of allowing for the inclusion of the survey's design weights.

LEVELS OF TEACHER QUALIFICATIONS AND
OUT-OF-FIELD TEACHING

The data show that most public elementary and secondary teachers have basic education and training (see Table 8.3). Almost all public school teachers have completed a four-year college education. Ninety-nine percent of public school teachers hold a bachelor's degree, and almost half have obtained graduate degrees. Moreover, 94 percent of teachers have regular or full state-approved teaching certificates. The data also reveal some distinct cross-school differences in the qualifications of teachers. Students in schools with a high poverty enrollment, in schools with a high minority enrollment, and in urban schools sometimes have less access to qualified teachers. For example, teachers in high-poverty schools are less likely to have graduate degrees than teachers in low-poverty schools. On the other hand, there is little difference between suburban and urban schools and between high-minority and low-minority schools in the percentage of teachers with graduate degrees.

Disparities in teachers' qualifications are more clear and distinct when these demographic characteristics are combined. For example, teachers in nonpoor/white/suburban schools (hereafter referred to as advantaged schools) are more likely to have graduate degrees and more likely to have full certificates than those in poor/minority/urban schools (hereafter referred to as disadvantaged schools). It is important to note that these data tell us little of the quality of these credentials; there may be inequities in teacher qualifications not revealed here.

However, the most glaring and prominent source of inadequate access to qualified teachers is not a lack of basic education or training of teachers, but rather a lack of fit between teachers' preparation and teachers' class assignments: the phenomenon of out-of-field teaching. Whereas most teachers, even in disadvantaged schools, have a bachelor's degree and a regular teaching certificate,

Table 8.3 Percentage of elementary and secondary public school teachers, by highest degree earned and by highest type of certification, by type of school

	Less than bachelor's degree	Bachelor's degree	Master's degree or more	No certification	Less-than-regular certification	Regular certification
Total	.7	52	47	2	4	94
Poverty enrollment						
Low	.9	45	54	1.5	3	96
High	.6	56	43	4	6	90
Minority enrollment						
Low	.6	51	48	1	3	96
High	.9	52	47	4	7	89
Community						
Rural	.8	58	41	2	3	95
Suburban	.7	46	53	2	3	96
Urban	.7	49	50	3	5	92
Not-poor/white/suburban	.3	41	58	2	2	96
Poor/minority/urban	.2	51	49	7	9	85

Notes:
Less-than-regular certification—includes all those with emergency, temporary, alternative, or provisional certification.
Regular certification—includes all those with probationary, regular, standard, full or advanced certification. (Probationary refers to initial license issued after satisfying all requirements except completion of probationary period)
Low poverty—refers to schools where 15 percent or less of the students receive publicly funded free or reduced price lunches.
High poverty refers to schools where over 80 percent do so.
Low minority—refers to schools where 15 percent or less of the students are minority.
High minority—refers to schools where over 80 percent are. Middle categories of poverty and minority enrollment are not shown.
Not-poor/white/suburban—refers to schools that are low poverty and low minority and suburban
Poor/minority/urban—refers to schools that are high poverty and high minority and urban.

many teachers at both the elementary and the secondary levels are assigned to teach classes in fields that do not match their educational background.

At the elementary school level, the data show that 12 percent of those whose assignment is preelementary or general elementary do not have an undergraduate or graduate major or minor in the fields of preelementary education, early childhood education, or elementary education (see column 1 of Table 8.4). Interestingly, the data also show that beginning elementary teachers are more prone than experienced teachers to be teaching out of their fields (see bottom row of Table 8.4). There are also cross-school disparities: elementary teachers in poor schools and schools serving predominantly minority student populations are more likely not to have a major or minor in the field.

Levels of out-of-field teaching among elementary school teachers vary, however, according to how one defines a qualified elementary teacher. These levels drop significantly when looking at those without certificates; in background analyses (not shown here), 95 percent of regular elementary teachers had regular certificates in the fields of preelementary education or elementary education.

The data also show that levels of out-of-field teaching are higher at the secondary level than at the elementary level. For example, about a third of all public secondary school math teachers have neither a major nor a minor in math, math education, or related disciplines like engineering or physics. About one-quarter of all secondary school English teachers have neither a major nor a minor in English or related subjects such as literature, communications, speech, journalism, English education, or reading education. In science, slightly lower levels—about one-fifth of all public secondary school teachers—do not have at least a minor in one of the sciences or in science education. Finally, about a fifth of social studies teachers are without at least a minor in any of the social sciences, in public affairs, in social studies education, or in history (see columns 2–8 of Table 8.4).

As in elementary schools, there are large cross-school differences in out-of-field teaching in secondary schools. In most fields, teachers in high-poverty schools are more likely to be out-of-field than are teachers in more affluent schools. For example, almost a third of social studies teachers in high-poverty schools, as opposed to 16 percent in low-poverty schools, do not have at least a minor in social studies or a related discipline. Levels of out-of-field teaching are lower in low-poverty and low-minority schools, although these schools are not free of out-of-field teaching. Many teachers in suburban and advantaged schools also teach out of their fields. But misassignment is clearly a major factor behind lack of access to qualified teachers in disadvantaged schools. The poverty and race gaps for out-of-field teaching (in Table 8.4) are distinctly wider than the poverty and race gaps for teacher qualifications (in Table 8.3). In other words, *although teachers in disadvantaged schools are slightly more likely to have fewer qualifications, they are far more likely to be misassigned.*

Table 8.4 Percentage of public school teachers in each field without a major or a minor in that field, by school type and teacher experience.

	Elementary	Secondary						
		English	Math	Science	Life science	Physical science	Social studies	History
Total	12.2	24.1	31.4	19.9	32.9	56.9	19.3	53.1
Poverty enrollment								
Low	11.6	21.8	27.5	17.2	28.9	50.6	16.2	47.1
High	20.8	20.1	37.6	28.0	39.4	68.4	29.6	63.6
Minority enrollment								
Low	8.1	21.7	27.3	17.0	32.1	55.3	18.8	55.4
High	19.5	28.5	37.8	24.6	33.6	54.2	25.5	56.8
Community								
Rural	8.3	23.1	30.2	19.5	34.1	60.2	19.5	56.8
Suburban	14.5	21.8	29.6	21.5	32.1	55.1	16.9	50.6
Urban	14.7	25.3	33.1	16.7	31.8	50.5	21.1	48.0
Not-poor/white/suburb	13.8	.	.	.	.	.	.	.
Poor/minority/urban	21.3	.	.	.	.	.	.	.
Teacher's experience								
Less than 5 yrs	15.2	26.1	31.7	19.7	36.1	56.8	21.3	54.8
More than 25 yrs	11.5	17.8	25.6	13.3	24.5	52.7	14.8	48.7

Notes:

Column 1 —Elementary includes all those teaching in the fields of prekindergarten, kindergarten, or general elementary in grades K–8. It includes those teaching in self-contained classes, where the teacher teaches multiple subjects to the same class of students all of most of the day. It includes K–8 teachers employed in middle schools. It excludes departmentalized teachers who teach subject-matter courses to several classes of different students all of most of the day. Elementary teachers with a major or minor in the fields of preelementary, early childhood education or elementary education are defined as in-field.

Columns 2–7—The teaching fields of English, math, science, and social studies only include departmentalized teachers in grades 7–12. It excludes those employed in middle schools. For details on definitions of these assignment fields and the major/minors defined as in-field in each, see Ingersoll 1999.

Columns 5, 6, and 8 —The estimates for life science, physical science, and history represent the percentage of teachers without at least a minor in *those particular subfields*. For example, in science, teachers (column 4) who hold a minor in any one of the sciences are defined as in-field. On the other hand, in physical science, teachers (column 6)—which includes physics, chemistry, space science, and geology—must hold a minor in one of those physical sciences to be defined as in-field, rather than simply a minor in any science.

High poverty refers to schools where 15 percent or less of the students receive publicly funded free or reduced price lunches. *High poverty* refers to schools where over 80 percent do so.

Low minority refers to schools where 15 percent or less of the students are minority. *High minority* refers to schools where over 80 percent are. Middle categories of poverty and minority enrollment are not shown.

Not-poor/white/suburb refers to schools that are low poverty and low minority and suburban

Poor/minority/urban refers to schools that are high poverty and high minority and urban.

. —too few cases for reliable estimate.

At the secondary level, levels of out-of-field teaching are similar for teachers without a major or minor or teachers without certification in their assigned fields. For example, in background analyses (not shown here), about a third of public secondary math teachers do not have teaching certificates in math—a figure similar to those lacking a major or minor in math (Ingersoll 1999). But focusing on those without certificates can lead one to underestimate the amount of underqualified teaching within broad multidisciplinary fields, such as science and social studies. Teachers in these fields are routinely required to teach any of a wide array of disciplines and subfields within the department. However, simply having a certificate in the larger field may not mean that teachers are qualified to teach all of the subjects within the field. For example, a teacher with a degree in biology and a certificate in science may not be qualified to teach physics. Indeed, as shown in columns 5, 6, and 8 in Table 8.4, within science and social studies there are high levels of within-department, but out-of-subfield, teaching. Over half of those teaching physical science classes (chemistry, physics, earth, or space science) are without a major or minor in any of the physical sciences. Likewise, over half of all those teaching history are without a major or minor in history.

Several points must be stressed concerning these data on out-of-field teaching. First, there is no doubt that some of these out-of-field teachers may actually be qualified even though they do not have a minor or major in the field. Some may be qualified by virtue of knowledge gained through previous jobs, through life experiences, or through informal training. Others may have completed substantial college coursework in a field and even have a certificate but lack a major or minor in that field.

On the other hand, these measures represent a relatively low standard by which to define a qualified teacher. To many observers, even a moderate number of teachers lacking the minimal prerequisite of a college minor signals the existence of serious problems in schools. Indeed, if the definition of a qualified teacher is upgraded to include only those who hold *both* a college major and a teaching certificate in the field the amount of out-of-field teaching substantially increases.

Moreover, these findings are consistent across all five cycles of the SASS data. Despite all the reform efforts reviewed earlier, out-of-field teaching does not appear to be decreasing. Overall for the nation, levels of out-of-field teaching changed little from 1987 to 2004. Moreover, the data reveal that the actual numbers of students affected are not trivial: every year in each of the fields of English, math, and history well over 4 million secondary-level students are taught by teachers with neither a major nor a minor in the field.

It is also important to recognize the implications of these data for explaining the sources of out-of-field teaching. Contrary to the teacher deficit perspective held by many researchers, policymakers, and media commentators, out-of-field teaching is not due to a lack of education or training on the part of teachers. The data show that, while beginning teachers are more prone than experienced teachers to be misassigned, those teaching out of field at either the elementary or secondary level are typically veterans with an average of 14 years of teaching experience, and about 45 percent of out-of-field teachers hold graduate degrees.

THE SOURCES OF OUT-OF-FIELD TEACHING

If not due to inadequacies in the training of teachers, what is the reason for out-of-field teaching? The latter is a widespread phenomenon; the data show that each year some out-of-field teaching takes place in well over half of all secondary schools in the United States and each year over one-fifth of the public secondary teaching force does some out-of-field teaching. But the data also show that there are large school-to-school differences in the extent to which teachers are assigned to teach in or out of their fields of training. This raises a key research question: What accounts for the degree to which school administrators misassign teachers? The standard answer is teacher shortages. Shortfalls in the numbers of available teachers primarily due to increasing student enrollments and a "graying" teaching workforce, this argument holds, have forced many school systems to resort to lowering standards to fill teaching openings, the net effect of which is high levels of out-of-field teaching.

Teacher Shortages

Data from SASS and other NCES data sources show that, consistent with the shortage predictions, demand for teachers has increased since the mid-1980s. Since 1984, student enrollments have increased, most schools have had job openings for teachers, and the size of the teacher workforce (K–12) has increased. Most important, substantial numbers of schools with teaching openings have experienced difficulties with recruitment. However, the data also show there are several problems with the shortage explanation for out-of-field teaching. First, shortages cannot explain the high levels of out-of-field teaching that the data indicate exist in fields such as English and social studies, which have long been known to have surpluses. Second, even when the rates of student enrollment increases were at their peak, in any given field only a minority of the total population of schools actually experienced recruitment problems. Additional analysis I have done indicates that levels of out-of-field teaching were higher in schools reporting more difficulties in finding qualified candidates for their job openings. But the data also indicate that about half of all misassigned teachers in any given year were employed in schools that reported no difficulties whatsoever finding qualified candidates for their job openings that year. These data suggest that shortages and their attendant hiring difficulties are not the sole, nor even the primary, factor behind out-of-field teaching. Rather than simply focusing on macro, demographic sources of this problem, this analysis hypothesizes that the source of out-of-field teaching also lies in the way schools are organized and teachers are managed.

Predictors of Out-of-Field Teaching

This section presents the results of multiple regression analyses estimating the relationship between the dependent variable—the percentage of out-of-field classes—and four groups of independent variables: teacher qualifications, school demographic characteristics, school recruiting and hiring difficulties, and school administrative practices/organizational characteristics.

Table 8.5 displays the results of these analyses. Because school poverty enrollment and school minority enrollment are highly intercorrelated, I tested their effects separately: Model 1 includes a variable for school poverty enrollment, and Model 2 includes a variable for school minority enrollment. Moreover, this part of the analysis focuses solely on the secondary level: Grades 7–12. The data in the previous stage of the analysis (Table 8.4) indicated that levels of out-of-field teaching are more pronounced in secondary schools than in elementary schools. Moreover, to many observers the problem in secondary schools is a more compelling case because classes at the secondary levels usually require a greater level of subject-matter mastery and training on the part of teachers than do those at the elementary-school level and, hence, being taught by an out-of-field teacher could be more consequential for students at that level.

The two control measures of teacher qualifications are both related to the degree to which teachers are assigned out of their fields. Teachers without at least a bachelor's degree are, by definition, out-of-field. Teachers' experience is strongly related; beginning teachers are more likely to be misassigned than are more senior teachers. The data also show that teachers in both high-poverty and high-minority schools are more often out-of-field. However, while teachers in urban schools are more often out-of-field than teachers in rural schools, the difference between out-of-field teaching in urban and suburban schools is not statistically significant (at a 95% level of confidence).

Surprisingly, school hiring and hiring difficulties do not appear to be a major factor related to the amount of out-of-field teaching in the school. In background analyses, I found a significant positive correlation between the degree to which a school has difficulty finding qualified candidates to fill their openings and the degree of out-of-field teaching in the school. But after controlling for other factors in Table 8.5, this relationship becomes weak and statistically insignificant. This finding raises a particularly interesting question: After controlling for these characteristics of teachers and schools, what administrative practices and orga-

TABLE 8.5 Multilevel multiple regression analysis of percent secondary level classes out of field

	Model 1		Model 2	
	(b)	(se)	(b)	(se)
Intercept	41.4*	3.3	44.9*	3.06
Teacher qualifications				
Highest degree	−2.9*	.427	−3.2*	.41
Teaching experience	−.16*	.028	−.15*	.027
School demographic characteristics				
Poverty enrollment	.09*	.015		
Minority enrollment	.	.	.11*	.01
Rural	−3.8*	.919	−2.0*	.93
Suburban	−1.2	.925	−.45	.902
School recruiting and hiring difficulties				
Teaching job openings	−1.7	1.01	−1.53	.956
Hiring difficulties	.03	.183	−.04	.176
Administrative practices/ organizational characteristics				
Major/minor required of hires	−1.9*	.53	−1.7*	.517
Principal leadership	−1.3*	.38	−1.5*	.363
Hiring/assigning underqualified	1.1*	.53	.65	.520
Average class size	−.67*	.033	−.66*	.031
Starting teacher salary (by 1000)	.23*	.107	.04	.104
Presence of teacher union	.84	.77	1.34	.754
School size (by 100)	−.02	.06	−.13*	.058
Proportion of school-level variance explained (Rsq)	.16		.19	
Sample size (N)	18,770		19,921	

*p < .05, (Unstandardized coefficients displayed)

nization characteristics of schools do have an independent association with the average amount of out-of-field teaching in schools?

The analysis shows that several aspects of schools are related to misassignment. For example, school districts vary in the extent to which they impose standards on the teacher hiring process, and these hiring regulations are related to the average degree of out-of-field teaching in schools. The SASS data show that about two-thirds of school districts have formal requirements that new teacher hires must hold a college major or minor in the field to be taught and, as shown in Table 8.5, teachers in schools governed by these district-level policies do less out-of-field teaching.

The data also show that an additional factor associated with the degree of out of-field teaching in a school is the perceived leadership effectiveness of the principal. Schools vary in how well their teachers rate the performance of their principals on attributes of "good" leadership (e.g., principals that recognize good teaching, communicate well, are supportive, and back teachers up). The data in Table 8.5 show significantly less out-of-field teaching occurs in schools in which the teachers highly rate the leadership performance of their principals. It is unclear from this finding which aspects of principals' behavior may be related to their staffing assignment practices and whether the attitudes of teachers toward principals are a cause or effect of such practices.

While the fact of experiencing difficulty in finding candidates to fill teaching vacancies does not have an independent effect on the degree of out-of-field teaching, how school administrators chose to cope with their hiring difficulties does have an effect. The analysis in Model 1 shows more out-of-field teaching in schools that covered their vacancies by hiring less than fully qualified teachers, by reassigning teachers trained in another field to teach the unstaffed classes, or by using substitute teachers. In Model 2 this factor is, however, not quite statistically significant (at a 95 percent level of confidence).

In contrast, other schools administrators might opt to expand class sizes, add additional class sections, or cancel classes rather then use misassignment to cope with staffing difficulties. The analysis shows that average class sizes are strongly related to the degree of out-of-field teaching in schools. Schools with larger classes tend to have less out-of-field teaching.

Finally, the models tested the association of several other characteristics of schools with misassignment. Smaller schools have more out-of-field teaching in Model 2, although this predictor fails to achieve statistical significance in Model 1. Starting teacher salaries are weakly associated with higher levels of out-of-field teaching in Model 1 and fail to achieve statistical significance in Model 2. The presence of a teacher union is not related to the extent of out-of-field teaching in the school in either model.

Notably, these analyses failed to find any factors that accounted for the effects of poverty and minority enrollment. In other words, none of the variables when introduced to the models reduced the estimates for poverty and minority enrollment to a statistically significant extent.

Several cautions and limitations need to be stressed. First, it must be remembered the multivariate findings do not show causality, but represent associations between particular school measures and the degree of out-of-field teaching in schools. Second, the regression models account for only a portion of school-to-school differences in out-of-field teaching. Further research is needed to refine and verify these. If borne out by further analysis, these preliminary findings do, however, suggest important implications for both theory and policy concerning the problem of underqualified teachers.

IMPLICATIONS

The source of the problem of underqualified teachers, according to most researchers and commentators, lies primarily in inadequacies in the quantity of teachers produced (i.e., shortages) and in the quality of the preparation these teaching candidates receive (i.e., low standards for teacher training). Following this teacher deficit perspective, the dominant policy responses have been attempts to upgrade the quality of teachers through more rigorous training and testing and licensing requirements or to increase the quantity of teachers supplied through various recruitment strategies.

In contrast, the central thesis of this study is that fully understanding the problem of unqualified teachers requires not only examining the quantity and quality of the teaching force, but also examining the social organization of teachers' work—that is, the manner in which teachers are managed, employed, and used. Specifically, this analysis shifts attention to the managerial practice of out-of-field teaching and shows that it is widespread, especially in those schools serving disadvantaged communities. Furthermore, the analysis shows that the frequency of out-of-field teaching is not due to a deficit in either the quality or the quantity of teachers. Rather, out-of-field teaching is a common administrative practice whereby otherwise qualified teachers are assigned by school principals to teach classes in subjects which do not match their fields of training or certification. This practice takes place as often as not in schools that do not suffer from teacher recruitment problems due to shortages.

Hence, this analysis suggests that the above kinds of teacher reforms, while perhaps at times highly worthwhile, will not eliminate the problem of underqualified teaching unless they also address the problem of misassignment. In short, recruiting new candidates into teaching and mandating more rigorous training requirements for them will not solve the problem of underqualified teaching if large numbers of such teachers, especially in disadvantaged schools, continue to be assigned to teach subjects other than those for which they were trained. Hence, this analysis suggests that schools are not simply victims. Focusing blame on teachers, teacher training institutions, or inexorable, macro, demographic trends diverts attention from the roots of this problem in the way schools are organized and teachers are managed.

An objective of this analysis was to investigate which aspects of the organization of schools are linked to the degree of misassignment in schools. The results suggest that the extent to which schools face teacher shortages and their attendant hiring difficulties are less crucial factors than how school administrators—especially school principals—respond to and cope with staffing decisions and challenges. In the face of difficulty finding qualified candidates to fill their teaching job openings, some school principals resort to hiring less than fully qualified teachers, assigning teachers of one subject or grade level to teach classes in others, or employing substitute teachers to cover hard-to-staff classes. These decisions, of course, result in more out-of-field teaching. Sometimes these choices and some degree of out-of-field teaching may be unavoidable. But the results also show that school principals vary in their staffing strategies. Sometimes, top-down regulations shape the choices available. For example, school districts that have formal regulations concerning minimal training requirements for new hires have less out-of-field teaching. But interestingly, one of the stronger predictors of the amount of out-of-field teaching in schools is the leadership performance of principals. The measure used for the latter was a composite indicator based on the evaluations of teachers and, hence, is highly subjective. Like the other factors, however, it is highly suggestive. The results also contradict the view that teacher unions are a major source of out-of-field teaching. Schools with unions do not have more out-of-field teaching. Union work rules certainly have an impact on the management and administration of schools, but eliminating teacher unions will not eliminate out-of-field teaching.

What all of these findings collectively suggest is a role for managerial choice, agency, and responsibility—elements that are often overlooked in the educational literature on the sources of underqualified teachers. Improving the assignment of teachers already in schools as a strategy for raising teaching quality is an alternative to trying to modify the quality or quantity of teacher training graduates. It also offers an intervention that can be undertaken immediately, as opposed to the lag time it takes for modifications in the output of teacher training institutions to actually lead to changes in classroom practice in schools. This, of course, has immediate implications for the success of the NCLB mandate to staff all core academic classrooms with highly qualified teachers.

While the data suggest some alternative staffing strategies for school leadership, they do not suggest any of these options will be easy or cost free. Staffing decisions involve some difficult trade-offs and tough choices for school administrators. For example, lowering class sizes, a currently popular reform idea, appears to come at the expense of increasing out-of-field teaching (Stecher et al. 2001, for insightful discussions of the unanticipated outcomes of class-size reduction reforms). Likewise, the data suggest reducing the size of schools, another currently popular reform idea, may also result in more out-of-field teaching.

Note

1. This paper draws from an earlier research report (Ingersoll 2002). This research was supported through a grant from the Field Initiated Studies Program, administered by the former Office and Educational Research and Improvement, U.S. Department of Education. Opinions reflect those of the author and do not necessarily reflect those of the granting agencies.

References

Bryk, A., V. Lee, and J. Smith.1990. High school organization and its effects on teachers and students: An interpretive summary of the research. In *Choice and control in American education.* Vol. 1, *The theory of choice and control in education,* ed. W. H. Clune and J. F. Witte, 135–226. New York: Falmer Press.

Coleman, J. 1966. *Equality of educational opportunity.*

Darling-Hammond, L. (1987). Teacher quality and equality. In *Access to knowledge,* ed. P. Keating and J. I. Goodlad. New York: College Entrance Examination Board.

Dreeben, R and A. Gamoran.1986. Race, instruction and learning. *American Sociological Review* 51:660–69.

Greenberg, E., Rhodes, Xioalan,Ye, and F. Stancavage. 2004. Prepared to teach: Teacher preparation and student achievement in 8th grade mathematics. Paper presented at the American Educational Research Association Annual Meeting, San Diego.

Greenwald, R., L. Hedges, and R. Laine. 1996. The effect of school resources on student achievement. *Review of Educational Research* 66:361–96.

Haycock, K. 1998. Good teaching matters...a lot. *Thinking K-16: A Publication of the Education Trust* 3 (2):3–14.

———. 2000. No more settling for less. *Thinking K-16: A Publication of the Education Trust,* 4 (1):3–12.

Hirsch, E., J. Koppich, and M. Knapp.2001. *Revisiting what states are doing to improve the quality of teaching: An update on patterns and trends.* Center for the Study of Teaching and Policy, University of Washington.

Hirsch, P. and M. Lounsbury. 1997. Putting the organization back into organization theory. *Journal of Management Inquiry* 6:79–88.

Ingersoll, R. (1999).The problem of underqualified teachers in American secondary schools. *Educational Researcher* 28(2):26–37.

———. 2001. Misunderstanding the problem of out-of-field teaching. *Educational Researcher* 30(1):21–22.

———. 2002. *Out-of-field teaching, educational inequality and the organization of schools: An Exploratory analysis.* Seattle, WA: Center for the Study of Teaching and Policy, University of Washington.

———. 2003a. *Who controls teachers' work? Power and accountability in America's schools.* Cambridge, MA: Harvard University Press.

———. 2003b. *Out-of-field teaching and the limits of teacher policy.* Consortium for Policy Research in Education, University of Pennsylvania and the Center for the Study of Teaching and Policy, University of Washington.

McMillen, M., K. Gruber, Henke and McGrath. 2002. *Qualifications of the public school teacher workforce: 1987–88 to 1999–2000.* Washington, D.C.: National Center for Education Statistics.

National Commission on Excellence in Education. 1983. *A Nation at risk: The imperative for educational reform.* Washington, D.C.: Government Printing Office.

NCES (National Center for Education Statistics). 2005. Schools and Staffing Survey (SASS) and Teacher Followup Survey (TFS) Data File. Washington, DC: U.S. Department of Education. Available from http://nces.ed.gov/surveys/SASS/

Oakes, J. 1990. *Multiplying inequalities: The effects of race, social class, and tracking on opportunities to learn mathematics and science.* Santa Monica, CA: RAND.

Rosenbaum, J. (1976). *Making inequality.* New York: John Wiley.

Stecher, B., G. Bohrnstedt, M. Kirst, J. McRobbie, and T. Williams. 2001. Class-size reduction in California: A story of hope, promise and unintended consequences. *Phi Delta Kappan* 82(9):670–74.

Stolzenberg, R. (1978). "Bringing the firm back in: Employer size, employee schooling and socioeconomic achievement." *American Sociological Review, 43,* 813-28.

Toch, T. (1996, February 26). Why teachers don't teach: How teacher unions are wrecking our schools, *U.S. News and World Report.* 62–71.

9

Teaching Quality as a Problem of School Change[1]

Joan E. Talbert and Milbrey W. McLaughlin

INTRODUCTION

No Child Left Behind (NCLB) mandates that all schools have "highly qualified" teachers for the core academic subjects—including English, reading or language arts, math, science, foreign languages, civics and government, arts, history, and geography—by 2005–6.[2] Further it makes available special funds for teacher professional development in schools that fail to meet their improvement goals for two years in a row. Yet, a strategy of staffing all schools with fully credentialed teachers, even when coupled with extra professional development funds, will not be sufficient to turn the tide of poor student performance in our nation's poorest schools and districts. Research on teaching points to the need for social nor mative change in schools serving poor students of color, in particular creating collaborative teacher teams focused on improving student learning—what we call "teacher learning communities."

Drawing on research regarding teachers' work and educational reform in U.S. schools since the mid-1980s, we argue that building school-based teacher learning communities is key to improving education quality and equity. We point to the promise, challenges, and strategies entailed in this approach to improving teaching quality and consider how the federal NCLB legislation enables or constrains local systems' capacity to develop school learning communities. Separate sections focus on:

- How and why teacher learning community is significant in student outcomes;
- The problem of school culture change;
- Strategies for developing teacher learning communities; and
- Challenges for local systems in the context of NCLB.

Evidence for our analysis of teacher communities and challenges for school change comes from several research projects: an OERI-funded study of 16 California and Michigan high schools (1987–92), an NSF-funded study on reform of math and science departments (1993–96), and evaluation research on the Bay Area School Reform Collaborative (BASRC) supported by the Hewlett Foundation (1996–2005). Evidence for our analysis of community-building practices comes primarily from five years of research on a professional development initiative called Students at the Center (SATC) carried out in Chicago, New York, and Philadelphia with funding from the Dewitt Wallace-Reader's Digest Funds (1996–2001). Together these research efforts inform our analysis of productive strategies for improving teaching in schools serving poor students of color and our critique of NCLB legislation.

WHY INVEST IN TEACHER LEARNING COMMUNITIES?

School-based teacher learning communities are essential to the significant improvements in teaching quality and student achievement envisioned by NCLB legislation. The kinds of professional learning and change in practice that are required to improve teaching and close student achievement gaps cannot be achieved solely through a teacher credentialing program, nor through typical teacher training venues. Available evidence suggests, however, that teacher learning communities are able to significantly improve teaching and learning for the students. Findings from research using national educational data and field-based studies indicate that when teachers collaborate to improve instruction, they can achieve a range of desirable student outcomes, including engagement in class and performance on standardized tests, and a narrowing of inequality in student achievement. Case studies of teacher communities in both high-school departments and in elementary schools reveal the professional practices and norms that distinguish these communities and that account for their success in improving student outcomes.

Limits of "Training" for Quality Teaching

The typical teacher credentialing program provides necessary but insufficient grounding for high-quality, equitable teaching in schools. For one, effective professional practice in teaching and in all fields entails sustained learning both through following the development of "best practices" in the profession and through ongoing use of data and evidence from one's own practice. These kinds of learning for quality teaching can be encouraged and modeled in credentialing programs, but they are inherently part of professional practice rather than of preparation for practice. Further, teaching is situated in particular schools and classrooms with particular students, and effective practice depends upon teachers' successful adaptation of instruction to student academic needs, capacities, and learning resources. This kind of professional learning is inherently site-situated and not highly amenable to preservice education. Moreover, teachers' capacity to utilize their knowledge of effective teaching depends upon conditions of teaching in a particular school and district. Effective teaching practices can be inhibited or supported by the curriculum and assessments, by the organization of classes and teachers' work, and by professional norms and leadership. In short, quality teaching depends not just upon the employment of well-prepared teachers but also upon their continued and situated learning and conditions of their work in particular schools (Ingersoll 2005, for further discussion).

District in-service workshops typically are inadequate to address teachers' ongoing learning needs. Staff development sessions usually are tied to special projects or "training" on new curricula. These sessions seldom reflect teachers' particular learning needs but rather the ideas of curriculum developers, state policymakers, or various education experts about what and how teachers should learn. Externally developed professional development opportunities almost never build on teachers' knowledge of day-to-day classroom challenges, such as adapting to particular students and to local parent communities.

Research shows that externally driven professional development efforts are likely to be episodic in their consequences for practice or education reform. They tend to be pasted onto existing instructional and institutional arrangements with little attention to issues of sustaining improvement or deepening practice (Tyack and Cuban 1996). Further, education reform initiatives and the teacher development resources that accompany them can promote incoherence in both school and district instructional offerings when they derive from different in-structional philosophies, use diverse and not always compatible instructional materials, or in other ways represent different approaches to teachers' classroom work (Newmann et al. 1996). Observers of school reform note that schools and districts often adopt many unconnected special projects or fashionable reforms in response to attractive funding opportunities, resulting in a succession of su-perficial and short-lived initiatives that do little to support and sustain teacher learning and improvement.

A more fundamental issue concerns the limited effectiveness of such profes-sional development efforts. Although they can provide resources for teacher learning, they are unlikely to result in improved teaching quality without op-portunities for teachers to situate new knowledge and practices in their own classrooms or school contexts. Moreover, the external resources are not enough to develop professionalism in teaching and accountability for all students' learning. As elaborated later, these goals require change in the professional culture of school-based teacher communities (Louis and Marks 1998; McLaughlin and Talbert 2006). Improved student learning depends upon the kinds of professional learning and changed practice that come from teachers working together to improve instruction for the students in their school.

Teacher Community Effects on Student Outcomes

Statistical support for the claim that school-based professional learning communities improve teaching and learning includes: (1) positive effects of teacher learning community measures on student achievement for both regional and national school samples; (2) strong correlations of teacher learning community indicators with teaching practices that predict student learning gains; and (3) strong correlations of teacher learning community and students' experiences of their school and class.

Using data from the National Longitudinal Study of 1988 (NELS: 88),[3] Valerie Lee and colleagues conducted three studies that consistently showed positive teacher community effects on student achievement gains (Lee and Smith 1995, 1996; Lee, Smith, and Croninger 1997). Each study used multilevel modeling techniques designed to estimate professional community and other school effects on student outcomes. All three studies support the hypothesis that students do better academically in a school where their teachers take collective responsibility for the success of all students. Further, these analyses showed that students' socioeconomic status had less effect on their achievement gains in schools with collaborative teacher communities; in other words, academic performance was less strongly related to social class origins than is typically the case in American schools.

Another study using the NELS: 88 database, conducted by Brian Rowan and colleagues (Rowan, Chiang, and Miller 1997), analyzed effects of teachers' ability, motivation, and work situation on students' achievement. This research found that each factor had an independent effect, with teacher control over instructional decisions and common planning time standing out as school predictors. Further, these school conditions correlate significantly with teacher expectations and other classroom instructional variables that predict student achievement.

Research on high-school professional communities finds significant variation in the strength and character of teacher community across subject departments, and these differences are associated with differential student performance in subjects. For example, our analysis of teacher survey data on professional relations and norms for 16 California and Michigan high-schools showed more variation within high-schools than between them (Talbert and McLaughlin 1994). In a study of students in four case study schools in this sample, we found that student survey ratings of their effort in class and efficacy in the subject were predicted by their teachers' survey ratings of teacher community in the subject department. Using the Longitudinal Study of Youth (LSAY) national database, a national research program that started with 7th graders in 1987, other researchers studied effects of teacher professional community on a range of student academic outcomes in math and science departments. (Yasumoto, Uekawa, and Bidwell 2001). They found that several conditions describing teachers' "professional discussion networks"—communication density, intensity of instructional practice norms, and consistency of practice—intensified the positive statistical effects of good teaching practices on student outcomes. The study provides statistical evidence that teacher learning communities develop knowledge of practice that is beyond the sum of competent and innovative teachers.

Convincing evidence for the claim that teacher learning communities boost student learning also comes from the research of Fred Newmann et al. (1996). In a study from the early 1990s using a national sample of restructured high-schools, they developed elaborate survey and field measures of "authentic instruction," grounded in learning theory, in order to assess effects of instruction on student learning. They also captured teaching norms and teacher interaction through teacher survey measures of "professional community" (shared purpose, collaborative activity in teaching, collective focus on student learning, deprivatized practice, and reflective dialogue). Data for the 24 high-schools in their sample show strong correlations between measures of authentic instruction and student achievement and between professional community and authentic instruction. These relationships show clear connections between how teachers work together and the learning opportunities they provide for their students (see also Louis and Marks 1998).

Our local analysis of teacher community effects on student achievement gains for a sample of schools participating in the Bay Area School Reform Collaborative (BASRC) showed statistically significant effects of a measure of school inquiry practices (Center for Research on the Context of Teaching 2002). Students did better in schools where teachers examined student achievement data together and collaborated to develop and assess interventions.[4] Survey data for a small case study sample of nine schools showed strong correlations between: (1) teacher ratings of collegial inquiry in the school; and (2) student ratings of teacher–student respect, their active role in class, and their academic self-efficacy. Although this sample was small, these data capture the meaning for students of teachers' professionalism and their collaboration to improve teaching.

Available evidence supports the claim that school-based teacher learning communities—school faculties or groups of teachers at a grade level or in a subject department that collaborate to improve instruction for their students—achieve higher quality teaching and learning than is typical in U.S. schools.

How Teacher Learning Communities Improve Teaching Quality

Teacher learning communities enhance students' outcomes because they provide effective learning environments for teachers, organize instruction to provide equitable student learning opportunities, and nurture and sustain a professional service ethic and mutual accountability for all students' success. These characteristics were identified through comparative analysis of different kinds of professional communities that we found in schools; learning communities were distinguished from typical weak communities and strong traditional communities (for discussion of contrasting community types see McLaughlin and Talbert 2001).

In professional learning communities colleagues support each other's learning and together create new knowledge of instructional practices that are effective with their students. Their daily practice embodies standards for effective professional development: (1) focus on instruction and student learning, specific to the settings in which they teach; (2) sustained and continuous, rather than episodic; (3) opportunities for teachers to collaborate with colleagues inside and outside the school; and (4) opportunities for teachers to influence what and how they learn (Hawley and Valli 1999).

Where these conditions for collaborative teachers' work in schools are established, teacher communities develop practices and norms that depart radically from traditional school cultures (McLaughlin and Talbert 2001, 2006, chapter 2). They share evidence from their classroom instruction and improvement efforts to guide changes in instruction to fit the learning needs of particular students in their school. This kind of knowledge development is inherently a school-based learning agenda, since student mix in terms of social class, race, language, immigration status, and academic skills is highly variable across schools in the nation. At the secondary level, these teacher communities also reorganize the curriculum and instruction to increase student access to advanced courses in a subject area (see Guitierrez 1996, for discussion of how a math department "organizes for advancement").

Beyond developing and using knowledge to improve instruction, teacher learning communities stand out for the organizational conditions they establish to support and sustain their collaboration and equitable student learning opportunities. In the school-based learning communities we studied, new teacher induction is an important focus for ensuring quality instruction and for sustaining the professional culture of improvement. For example, a math department we studied organizes teaching assignments so that each new teacher is paired with an experienced teacher so that they can coplan course lessons and form a mentoring relationship. Such teacher communities challenge the common practice of assigning new teachers to lowest-achieving students; by rotating course assignments among the faculty they ensure that students have equitable learning opportunities and teachers learn to teach across the curriculum.

Finally, teacher learning communities establish collegial relationships and norms that engender trust, collaboration, and shared accountability for all students' learning. Teachers in these site-based communities support one another in challenging education conventions that undermine the learning opportunities of some students. For example, math teacher communities that detrack their curriculum are often under attack from parents who perceive this as illegitimate and costly to students' college access; teachers' shared commitments and the moral support provided by the professional community are important in their ability to withstand pressures toward the educational status quo. Collegial support and ongoing learning opportunities for teachers in these communities develop and sustain their commitment to the teaching profession.

Although cumulative evidence from field studies and national survey research points to the educational benefits for students of teacher collaboration on instructional improvement, this mode of professional practice is far from the reality in most American schools. And school-based learning communities usually are not the focus of teacher professional development or of various efforts undertaken to reform the nation's schools. Sociological research on teachers' work and education reform initiatives reveals the kinds of radical change in school culture and teachers' professional practice that are entailed in developing teacher learning communities.

THE PROBLEM OF SCHOOL CULTURE CHANGE

In order to develop teacher learning communities it is necessary to reculture schools—change their technical culture, organizational practices, professional relations, and norms. Teachers' instructional routines, the work organization, and collegial relations in typical U.S. schools contrast significantly with those found in teacher learning communities (McLaughlin and Talbert 2001, 2006). Developing learning communities in schools involves confronting prevalent beliefs that teaching is a matter of transmitting knowledge and that some students will not succeed; reorganizing teachers' work so as not to reward experienced teachers with preferred teaching assignments and to create time for collaboration; and challenging the privacy norm that inhibits teacher knowledge sharing and collaboration to improve instruction for all students. Schools with vibrant teacher learning communities replace the constraints of convention with norms and practices that establish teachers' shared commitment and collaboration to continually improve all students' success.

Technical Challenges for Change

Instruction in most schools follows conventions of teaching—text-focused and teacher-directed, with students working alone on routine assignments and graded "on the curve." Absent conversations about instruction and leadership for improvement, teachers in such professional communities come to understand little about the principles and evidence that ground national and state standards for teaching and learning. They persist with practices that current research evidence deems ineffective. Many teachers water down the curriculum for students with weak academic skills in a well-intentioned attempt to make their class fun or comfortable. In weak professional communities, teachers who work to engage all their students in challenging subject content are the exception.

When well-prepared teachers try alone to change instruction to better serve their students, they often become discouraged and feel constrained by school or department culture and policies. In one of the schools we studied, an innovative social studies teacher who was regarded by administrators to be one of the school's most effective teachers became bored with his teaching career in a weak department and bitter over the fact that he alone was working to improve the quality of student learning. After eight years of teaching, he was planning to change careers rather than to lower his expectations for his students' learning outcomes.. The tendency for teachers to leave teaching when they work in a weak school community is captured by survey data showing a strong (r = .47) relationship between the strength of teachers' professional community and their commitments to the profession (Talbert and McLaughlin 1994).

NCLB's emphasis on the adoption of research-based curricula and use of standardized tests to measure of student learning may enforce instructional traditions rather than encourage innovation. Teachers pressed to implement a curriculum with fidelity and to coach students for tests may see little room or need to work with colleagues to improve instruction.

Organizational Challenges for Change

One challenge for community building in high schools is the common practice in subject departments of tracking teachers according to their subject mastery (Finley 1984; Page 1991; Talbert and Ennis 1990). In typical professional communities, teachers see their own learning in sequential terms, as a series of university courses and advanced degrees. Similarly, they have a hierarchical view of teacher knowledge and expertise for subject instruction that justifies tracking teachers on the basis of their credentials. This practice exacerbates inequalities in student performance, since low-performing students are matched with teachers least prepared to accelerate their content learning. Further, the specialization and stratification of teachers' assignments undermines teacher collaboration on instruction and mutual accountability for student learning and thus the development of teacher learning community.

Lowest-performing schools face a special challenge in building teacher learning communities that come from district patterns of teacher assignment. Typically new and least-prepared teachers are concentrated in a district's least desirable schools because collective bargaining agreements usually allow teachers access to job openings on the basis of their seniority. There is no solid evidence that a "critical mass" of well-prepared and experienced teachers is essential to learning communities, yet studies of these communities document the key role that highly skilled teachers play in the induction of new teachers. Conversely, schools where all or most teachers are weak in subject preparation and experience show least progress on change (CRC 2002). How many or what proportion of expert teachers are needed in a school, department, or grade-level teacher community is not clear, but it is likely that some threshold presence of skilled teachers is needed to support the community's learning and instructional improvement. Although NCLB legislation presses local systems to establish equity of teacher credentials across schools, it only begins to address the patterns of inequality associated with teacher recruitment and placement.

A related problem of high teacher turnover in the hard-to-staff schools presents a different kind of problem for teacher community development, namely that instability undermines social cohesion and sustained teacher collaboration. Statistical analysis of teacher survey data in a 100-school district shows a strong positive effect of mean teacher experience on teacher community strength (.40), with student poverty level controlled; in this district student poverty was correlated –.66 with teacher experience (CRC 2004).

Other organizational challenges for change concern limited opportunity for teacher collaboration in normal school schedules. The importance of organization resources of time and place for teacher collaboration on instruction has been documented repeatedly in research on school communities, yet school and district schedules generally allocate very limited time for teachers to work together on instruction; what time is made available is usually very early in the day or once a week after school. The considerable pressure that NCLB places on lowest-performing schools to raise test scores is likely to shift their use of time further away from teacher collaboration, as after-school tutoring and test preparation take more time. In effect, the federal legislation may have the unanticipated consequence of further undermining these schools' capacity to improve educational outcomes for their students.

Social-Normative Challenges for Change

A tradition of autonomy in teaching works against the formation of teacher learning community in schools. When instruction is considered private practice, teachers resist the idea of collaborating with colleagues on instruction. In general, teachers avoid even discussing teaching and student learning, let alone working together on instructional problems or opening their classrooms to colleague observation and feedback (Little 1982; Lortie 1975; Smylie 1994). The vision of teacher learning communities as sites for improving instruction and student outcomes goes against norms of collegial relations in U.S. schools. School change efforts thus must include strategies to reverse privacy norms in teaching.

Further, school communities sometimes lack a strong service ethic or commitment to serving all of their students, which is a core organizing principle of teacher learning communities. Even when accountability systems press schools to close achievement gaps, teachers sometimes believe that their lowest-achieving students are not able to meet educational standards. School change thus entails changing teachers' beliefs about students' abilities to learn and about the capacity for high-quality instruction to make a difference in the performance of all students.

Public beliefs about effective education often work to enforce traditions and thus to discourage teachers from joining with colleagues to adapt instruction to students and to design curriculum to achieve greater equity in student learning opportunities. Among the social-normative challenges for changing school professional culture then is addressing parent conceptions of teaching quality and equity.

In emphasizing teacher credentials as the standard for judging teaching quality, NCLB may enforce autonomy norms within the teaching profession and discourage the development of a faculty's collective responsibility for student achievement. It signals to the profession and to the public that quality teaching is a matter of individual preparation and expertise, rather than an organizational outcome rooted in collaboration and mutual accountability.

***

Research on the challenges and contexts of educational improvement points to conditions that enable or constrain the development of teacher learning communities in schools, but evidence on *how* they develop is scant. Context resources for teacher learning communities such as grade-level standards for subject instruction, on-site professional development time, and external professional networks—are insufficient for their *development* because they do not bring about change in the culture of teaching. Nor does changing the structure of schools or mandating teacher collaboration create learning communities. In a national study of restructured schools, Fred Newmann et al. (1996) concluded that a school's culture determined effects of structural change on instructional practices, rather than the reverse. In other words, while existing teacher learning communities made good use of structural changes that supported their collaborative work, restructuring of schools did not change the culture of teaching.

DEVELOPING TEACHER LEARNING COMMUNITIES

Changing the culture of American schools toward learning communities requires skilled support of teacher collaboration and learning and strategic administrative leadership. Our research on reform initiatives to create school learning communities and literature on community building in business organizations suggest two broad propositions about the processes of changing school culture:

- A teacher community of practice develops through joint work that is guided by a facilitator who creates an *effective learning environment* for teachers; and
- Teacher learning communities develop, spread, and survive where school administrators and leaders support the culture change process.

The first proposition concerns technical facets of developing a teacher learning community—the "curriculum" and practices for high-quality learning in teacher groups; the second pertains to organizational and normative facets of teacher community building.

Engaging Teachers in Joint Work and Supporting Their Learning

In all instances of significant school culture change that we found, a facilitator from within or outside the school was involved in developing teacher learning community.. This finding is consistent with evidence from research in business organizations that a skilled "community coordinator" is key to developing a community of practice (Wenger, McDermott, and Snyder 2003, p. 80). This individual's role centers on *organizing the group's work* (that is, determining the focus and boundaries for joint work) and *establishing an effective learning environment* for the group.

Getting teachers started on a course of collaborating to improve student learning takes a skilled leader or facilitator to create the impetus and focus of joint work. Because traditions and conditions of teaching push toward autonomy, teachers need a compelling reason to begin collaborating to improve instruction. They also need to learn how to work with colleagues on a problem of instruction and how this work helps them be successful with their students. A skilled facilitator—from inside the school, from the district office, or from an outside teacher educator or reform organization—catalyzes and guides these change and learning processes.

Entry for Joint Work Community-building facilitators that we studied used several different entry points and curricula for developing teacher communities of practice. Each focused teachers' joint work on a particular facet of instruction—assessment data, individual students, and subject discipline. Each entry point offers particular opportunities and challenge for changing a school's professional culture, each requires particular kinds of facilitator knowledge and skills, and each is more or less compatible with NCLB legislation.

Using *student assessment data* as a vehicle for community building is a promising start toward teacher conversations about, and collaboration on, improving teaching and learning. With skilled facilitation, teachers work together at the grade level, subject department, or school levels to assess student performance in various content areas and analyze data to identify areas that need enhanced instruction. Typically they examine patterns associated with student groups that differ in race and language status and those that are associated with strands of the curriculum or outcome standards. Through this process teachers identify students and content areas for interventions designed to improve learning outcomes and close achievement gaps. As the community matures, teachers learn to improve their instruction through cycles of inquiry and collaboration on interventions.

Building a teacher learning community around the use of student assessment data entails developing valid measures of student learning and providing technical training in data analysis and interpretation. A facilitator capable of leading teachers' joint work with student assessment data therefore is one who is knowledgeable about assessing subject-specific learning outcomes and is skilled in data analysis. Our research on BASRC's efforts to promote evidence-based practice across many schools and districts suggests further that a successful facilitator would have authority in the district and be a reputable educator in the region, because he or she must play a liaison role with the district assessment office and broker teacher groups' access to professional knowledge and networks outside the school.

This entry focus is encouraged by NCLB legislation and state accountability systems that press school administrators and teachers to use data on student learning to evaluate and improve instruction. Yet, teachers generally have little preparation or experience in analyzing student assessment data for the purposes of making instructional decisions, and many oppose the use of standardized test data for accountability (Ingram, Seashore Louis, and Schroeder 2004). Thus, although context conditions are ripe for this community building tack, teachers' readiness for this work is generally quite weak.

Using *individual students as entry* focuses teacher's joint work on intense study of individual children and their academic and personal development. Looking at an individual student's work in a teacher group can be a particularly powerful vehicle for developing shared understandings and trust for collaboration. Because the focus is on a particular student's learning, rather than directly on teaching, it offers teachers a safe entry to discourse on instruction. Also, it builds upon their shared professional commitments to serving their students and connects with their interest in particular students in their classroom. By analyzing student work with colleagues, teachers deepen their understanding of individual learners in their classroom and how to better support their growth. Conversations around student learners may open the door to new collegial discussions about norms and ethics of teaching. In particular, they bring into focus the whole child and the learning needs of students who struggle most in traditional school settings. This work thus can leverage a stronger service ethic in the school community and strengthen teachers' commitments to serving all students.

In order to effectively build teacher learning community around this kind of joint work, a facilitator must have considerable experience using one or more protocols for the study of a child in order to guide the conversation in fruitful directions and anticipate habits of mind or dynamics that can undermine the group's learning and progress. Our research on this entry strategy suggests that facilitators specialize in using one or another protocol according to preferences based on the power of their prior learning experiences in teacher groups.

NCLB's emphasis on standardized tests and student achievement in the core academic subjects—over the holistic assessment and broad view of individual development featured in this kind of teacher community work—discourages this approach to community building. Nevertheless, looking at individual students' work is a popular strategy for developing a teacher learning community and over recent decades educators have developed a wide variety of protocols to support the work (MacDonald et al. 2003). Protocols focus teachers' inquiry and discourse on individual students and thus develop their clinical diagnostic skills, much as physicians' joint consultation around a patient case helps them to make professional judgments about care and develop shared standards of practice.

Using a *subject discipline as entry* to community building engages teachers in learning content more deeply, and promotes understanding of how to better support student learning in the subject. Typically teacher groups are formed at grade levels in elementary schools or in subject departments in secondary schools; a facilitator guides the group's learning around particular content areas or curriculum topics. The joint work includes such practices as developing and teaching a lesson and sharing observations, using a standards-based rubric to assess student work and discuss ratings, analyzing student misconceptions in a curricular topic. Through participation in a teacher community focused on subject instruction, teachers learn content more deeply and learn how to better see and guide students' understanding in the discipline. They also experience how knowledge develops in work with colleagues on content instruction and come to see themselves as members of subject professional communities within and beyond their school (see Stein, Silver, and Smith 1998, on identity forming processes in mathematics teaching).

Facilitators effective in developing teacher communities of practice around subject disciplines thus need both deep content knowledge and pedagogical content knowledge and skills for working with both students and teachers. Typically they have extensive experience as learners and leaders in teacher groups; for example, as participants and leaders in the summer institutes of the National Writing Project or other organizations with a strong track record of developing teachers' leadership for educational improvement in a discipline.

Since facilitation around subject instruction moves between the classroom and teacher group sessions, these facilitators also need to develop skills in guiding teachers' learning in the classroom.

Although NCLB's focus on subject matter knowledge as the crux of teacher quality supports a subject focus for community building, investment in school-based learning is discouraged by the legislation's emphasis on credentials as the criteria of teachers' content knowledge and the university as locus for learning. At the same time, however, national networks of subject-rooted professional development organizations, such as the National Writing Project, university-based math projects, and subject professional associations that focus on the development of programs and teacher leadership for school-based professional development, comprise resources that support this strategy.

Regardless of which facet of instruction is used to begin teacher collaboration in a school, the quality of leadership for learning and change is critical to the success of this strategy. In all cases we studied where teacher learning communities developed through joint work, the facilitator created and sustained an effective learning environment for teachers.

Quality of Teacher Learning Environments Skilled teacher community facilitators guide the group's learning and improvement practices in ways that reflect research-based principles of effective learning environments (Bransford, Brown, and Cockings 1999). Like an effective classroom teacher, they establish a learning environment for the teacher group that is:

- *Knowledge-centered*, focusing learners on problems and practices designed to deepen their conceptual knowledge and skills in a content domain;
- *Learner-centered,* attending to individual learners' interests, cultural backgrounds, prior knowledge and skills;
- *Assessment-centered,* creating opportunities for learners to get ongoing feedback on their performance to guide their learning; and
- *Community-centered,* involving peers in joint work that draws upon each person's knowledge and skills to build new understandings and practices.

Regardless of the facet of classroom instruction they use to focus teachers' joint work—subject discipline, students, or assessments—skilled facilitators nurture these conditions for learning. Those we observed brought to their work with school communities not only protocols and other tools to scaffold teachers' joint work, but also a deep understanding of, and experience in guiding learning in groups.

Case studies of facilitators' work with teacher groups inside and outside the school setting and with individual teachers in their classrooms revealed ways in which these principles work to guide teacher learning and improved instructional quality. For example, a math facilitator's work with teachers was learner-centered, in that her knowledge of each teacher as learner guided her decisions about how to facilitate change in math instruction. She established an assessment-centered learning environment for teachers by providing feedback on individual and team work and prompting teachers' reflection on instruction with tools that scaffolded ongoing self-assessment in math instruction (McLaughlin and Talbert 2006, for further evidence).

NCLB legislation, on the surface, appears out of sync with quality standards for teacher learning environments. It implies a view of teaching as curriculum implementation—transmitting a research-based program and testing students for prescribed content knowledge—and learning as mastering curriculum content. Thus, teacher preparation and professional development (earmarked by NCLB for teachers in low-performing schools) would presumably focus on teacher mastery of curricula to be taught and tests to be administered. This view of what teachers need to learn for quality instruction does not warrant the kind of in-depth, ongoing learning in teacher communities that high-quality facilitators support. District and school administrators thus need to promote high standards for professional development and invest resources in those who can provide it for their teachers and schools.

Although well-designed group activities and protocol are necessary to spur change in teaching culture toward community practice, they are not sufficient. In our research we found teacher communities where practice was procedural and learning was shallow—what Chris Argyris (1982) termed "single loop learning," even when the group had skilled guidance in using a particular protocol. Absent strong leadership for school culture change, it appears that conventional norms of teaching prevail and joint work remains on the margins of professional practice.

Leading School Culture Change

Community building is not just about creating or defining new work for teachers to do collaboratively and establishing principles for learning in the community, that is, technical conditions and processes of change. It is also about addressing the organizational and normative challenges for change highlighted earlier.

Because of their positional authority, school administrators set the stage for starting and sustaining the community development process. They can use organizational resources and persuasion to leverage teachers' initial involvement in facilitated work to build communities of practice. And they can broker resources from within and outside the system. School administrators who made a difference for teacher learning community development in schools we followed, for example: created collaboration time and defined how it would be used; assigned teachers to courses and classes to achieve students' equitable access to high-quality instruction; used base budget slack and categorical funds to support teacher community work and innovation; identified and hired skilled teacher educators and facilitators outside the system; invested in developing a wide range of student assessment data and supported its use by teachers and teacher teams to improve their instruction; and supported teachers' participation in local, state, and national professional networks and high-quality off-site professional development.

In leading school culture change, administrators and other school leaders address norms of professional practice in the school—and in subcommunities of the school defined by subject departments or interdisciplinary learning communities (SLCs) in high schools. They create focus, vehicles, and legitimacy for teachers to depart from private classroom practice and support them to engage conflicts between conventional routines and innovations to improve educational quality and equity. Research and reflection on effective school-change practice has identified several stages of administrative leadership entailed in moving from typical schools to school learning communities (CRC 2002: McLaughlin and Talbert 2006; Mohr and Dichter 2001). School leaders play particular roles in supporting faculty transitions from what we call "novice" to "intermediate" to "advanced" stages of learning community. During the "novice stage" of community development, change focuses on building social trust and norms for group decision making. At the "intermediate stage," change centers on sustaining collaborative work when the pay-offs are uncertain and the faculty fears that its work is unproductive. Once an advanced or mature school learning community has developed, the principal's role shifts to sustaining the community and its work. Effective leadership practices address the challenges for change at each stage (for further analysis see).

Many schools involved in initiatives that aim to develop a teacher learning community do not move from the novice to the intermediate stage, and most do not transition to an advanced stage after several years (McLaughlin and Mitra 2003). They become stuck at a stage of collaborative work that falls short of teacher learning community practice. This reality highlights the need for clearer understanding of the problem of change. The stagnated development of a teacher community reflects in part the weak leadership for change among school administrators and their limited opportunities to learn how to be effective in these roles. It also testifies to the complex challenges entailed in developing teacher learning communities widely in U.S. schools.

School leadership for change also involves managing disappointing outcomes, regardless of the stage of professional community development. A community learns through examining the mismatch between goals and performance—that is, they confront the "brutal facts" about student learning in their school (Shon 1983). However, candid description and discussion of shortfalls in student learning can trigger angry responses from parents and community. This anger erodes teachers' willingness to highlight disappointments as well as celebrate successes. Making failure public has presented an ongoing challenge for schools working to develop teacher learning communities.

NCLB legislation that labels some schools as failing generally pulls schools away from long-term investment in building professional capacity. Many BASRC schools that worked to move their schools out of "underperforming" status, for example, were distracted from an agenda to develop collective responsibility for improving student achievement and instead focused on implementing subject curricula with "fidelity" and adding test-prep routines. Schools' efforts to boost scores quickly worked against community development and innovation when they turned the spotlight on individual teachers' classroom outcomes and curriculum implementation as the primary reform strategy.

***

Developing teacher learning communities entails reculturing schools. And the knowledge and skills of teacher community facilitators and administrators are essential to schools' capacity to change teachers' deep-seated beliefs and practices that inhibit instructional innovation and to engender organizational learning. These capacities for school change depend, in turn, on conditions and investments of local and state policy systems in developing a focused and coherent strategy to develop professional communities in schools that are capable of continually improving their students' learning environments (Gamoran et al. 2003; McLaughlin and Talbert 2006). In this view, all local education stakeholders are implicated in a learning agenda to improve teaching quality and equity in the nation's schools, since system leadership for change depends upon the support of their community partners. Necessary investments to improve teaching quality—by federal, state, and local education authorities—go well beyond the scope and level defined by No Child Left Behind legislation.

CHALLENGES FOR LOCAL SYSTEMS IN THE CONTEXT OF NCLB LEGISLATION

NCLB legislation has brought teaching quality to the fore of our nation's education reform agenda. However, the federal legislation misses the mark in its emphasis on preservice training and credentials as criteria of high-quality teachers and the best vehicle for improving educational quality and closing achievement gaps among students. Although responsive to research-based evidence that well-prepared teachers are unequally distributed across U.S. schools and districts, the federal legislation fails to address both the significant ongoing learning demands of teaching and the ways in which schools typically undermine teaching quality and equity.

Some school and district leaders feel pressed to respond quickly to state and federal accountability systems and perceive a trade-off between pursuing the goal of building teacher learning communities and responding to these external accountability demands. Norms of collective responsibility and collaborative teaching practice develop slowly, yet high-stakes accountability systems demand fast, significant improvement in student achievement. The press for immediate gains in test scores pushes a pace of change that can undermine the development of school learning community. A community of practice preoccupied with test scores may chose to stick with known practices and make the most of them, rather than adopting or creating new modes of instruction. Leaders are challenged to find a balance that protects the community from the consequences of failure, but also furthers experimentation and the use of data to evaluate change. Organizational theorist James March (1991) terms this tension the "exploration/exploitation tradeoff" and sees the proper balance between them as a primary element in system survival and success.

The development and vigor of teacher learning communities across a school system depend upon a local learning agenda to support this vision of school change. Districts need to develop strategies to promote and sustain school-based learning communities and responses to NCLB that use opportunities and minimize the potentially negative consequences of the legislation. The national agenda to improve teaching quality and equity requires the mobilization of resources for change and professional learning at all levels of the system. Table 9.1 indicates the general nature of system resources for changing technical, organizational, and social-normative conditions of school culture toward professional learning communities.

Technical Resources

Technical resources include coherent instructional policies, professional development, and a robust assessment system.

Coherent Instructional Policies Teacher communities of practice are more likely to develop and to learn ways of improving instruction when the local system has instructional policies that are aligned to standards for student performance and when administrators convey coherent, consistent messages to schools about, for example, high-quality learning outcomes in mathematics at the 4th grade level. Yet, public school teachers practice in a complex policy environment of regulations, rules, resources, expectations, past investments, and community expectations whose incoherence can undermine effective instruction and collaboration (Berends, Bodilly, and Kirby 2003). District leadership plays a key role in managing the policy environment to create coherent messages and supports for instruction (McLaughlin and Talbert 2002).

Table 9.1 Developing a school-based teacher learning community: Functions, challenges, and resources for change

| Facet of teacher's work and context | Developing teacher learning community in schools | | |
	Functions	Challenges for change	Resources for change
Technical	Knowledge development and use Instructional design for equity	Instructional routines and policies that constrain innovation	Skilled facilitator; coach Coherent instructional policies and professional development Robust assessment system Professional networks and knowledge resources
Organizational	New teacher induction; mentoring Equitable teacher assignment	Teacher "tracking" practices Need for critical mass of highly skilled teachers High teacher turnover in least desirable schools Schedule/time constraints on collaboration	Resource alignment with teacher and student learning goals Administrator brokering of resources (experts, time, external networks, etc.) District policy and supports for teacher learning and school change (e.g., knowledge capture)
Social-normative	Cohesion and mutual accountability Support for breaking institutional norms Professional commitment sustained	Norm of teacher autonomy Teacher competition for desirable assignments Public enforcement of education traditions	Administrator/school leadership for professional change Political leadership for community support of change and teacher collaboration

Source: From Talbert, Joan E. and Milbrey W. McLaughlin. 2005. Teaching quality as a problem of school change: A local agenda to develop teacher learning communities. Prepared for the Sociology of Education Section's conference, No Child Left Behind, American Sociology Association annual meeting, Philadelphia, August 12.

Professional Development The development of teacher learning communities depends upon the system's vision for high-quality and equitable teaching and upon its knowledge of how professionals learn. An effective local learning system to support school communities of practice includes a cadre of facilitators skilled in guiding school change and employed to provide on-site technical support of teachers' collaboration and learning to improve instruction.

The development of skilled practitioners to nurture school change and teacher learning requires change in the typical district's professional development system and partnering with local professional development organizations, higher education, or intermediary reform organizations. As we noted earlier, it is likely that NCLB inhibits change by directing resources toward traditional training focused on curriculum implementation.

Robust Assessment System An assessment system that supports analysis of a range of student outcome data aligned with grade-level standards is a key technical resource for a learning system. This is the basis for learning at all levels of the district system and for communication and accountability between levels. A data system that provides a comprehensive account of students' progress toward academic outcomes and guidance for instruction includes both formative and summative data generated on a regular basis. Formative assessments provide teacher communities with information on student performance and outcomes of their instructional innovations. They also point to needed changes and guide student-focused instruction by identifying areas of need for individual students in a class. Summative measures and data document patterns of achievement within and across schools by such student demographics as ethnicity, economic status, and English language proficiency are data that provide teacher communities, school administrators, and district staff and administrators with evidence of their progress on both quality and equity goals. A learning system has the technology to deliver information in a timely, user-friendly manner so that everyone from the area manager to the classroom teacher can access to up-to-date information.

NCLB demands the use of assessments data for local accountability and thus is a potential catalyst for system change. However, it is up to each local agency to develop the kind of assessment system that can track all children's performance on standardized tests and all students' learning needs within a discipline and grade level.

Organizational Resources

The allocation of district resources of all kinds—base budgets, titled funds, personnel, equipment, and space—determines the system's capacity to develop teacher learning communities in schools. District administrators think about and allocate resources differently when these decisions are made with an eye to supporting vital teacher learning communities as opposed to ensuring compliance with bureaucratic regulations or accommodating political pressures.

Resource Alignment A learning system stance directs administrators to map the totality of district resources from public and private sources for professional development and to assess both their coherence and equitable distribution. Key to building teacher learning communities is the integration of resources to provide support for school change and high-quality learning opportunities across the system

Equitable Teacher Assignment In addition to recruiting and developing highly qualified professionals, the equitable placement of the most skilled teachers and administrators in district schools is of central importance to the system's capacity to improve teaching quality and equity. Creating incentives for these teachers and principals to take on assignments in the most difficult schools and providing intensive supports for their success are among the organizational strategies that districts can use to develop strong learning communities in schools serving the lowest-performing students.

Capturing Clinical Knowledge Organizational designs for capturing local knowledge of effective professional practice also support the development and learning of school-based teacher communities. Strong learning communities in district schools are resources for system learning when they are charged and authorized to develop and share knowledge of their improvement practices and effective instructional designs. The use of teachers' clinical knowledge for school and district system improvement is powerful because it provides concrete, situated illustrations of principles for professional practice. A local learning system brokers both clinical and research-based knowledge of effective practice and provides teachers and school leaders with access to skilled professionals within and outside the system.

Social-Normative Resources

District leadership for developing school-based teacher learning communities—and more broadly a local learning system—provides essential normative and political support for change. Managing organizational change to support professional learning includes modeling an inquiry stance and creating a data culture. It also takes political leadership to protect the investments required by a learning system. As one district's technology director put it: "The technical part—that's fairly standard. The toughest piece is changing the culture of the way people do things…" (quoted in Mieles and Foley 2005, 28).

Leadership for Professional Change Moving to a local learning system that uses data to inform decisions requires profound changes in teachers' and principals' professional culture, as highlighted in this chapter. Changes involve not only expectations that educators will use a variety of evidence to make decisions about practice but more significantly that practice will be deprivatized, that is, moved into the public view of colleagues and the community (e.g., Petrides and Nodine 2005). Leadership to motivate and support this kind of cultural shift has been rare in American school districts because a learning posture and uncertainty associated with it can be perceived as out of line with the popular image of a confident, competent leader. NCLB's accountability pressures and threats

198 • Joan E. Talbert and Milbrey W. McLaughlin

may have increased administrators' tendency to avoid taking an inquiry stance. Yet, without this leadership, the candid, evidence-based reflection on practice essential to instructional change carries risks for both teachers and principals. The relative scarcity of this kind of district leadership, more than inadequate technology or knowledge resources, impedes the development of comprehensive and fully functioning district learning systems.

Political Leadership System leaders face the challenge of building stakeholders' support for radical change in school culture and in approaches to teacher learning and educational improvement. These stakeholders include everyone from parents to members of the school board, the business community, and the civic elite. An engaged public plays an indispensable role in school reform and support for public education (Hill, Campbell, and Harvey 2000), and the agenda to build teacher learning communities in schools presents particular challenges for public engagement (McLaughlin and Talbert 2006). These challenges include involving the public in learning and debate around the equity agenda for instructional change and shifting views of professional learning to include teacher collaboration in school communities. Parents and community members need opportunities to move beyond old notions of education and teachers' work to understand basic tenets and challenges of new professional practice in schools.

Stakeholder support for teacher learning and change is ultimately critical to the success and survival of teacher learning community. Civic support of specific reform efforts and of the public schools plays a crucial part in teachers' sense of being valued for their efforts. Conversely, community ignorance about local needs, teachers' professional goals, and plans for more effective classroom practices is a barrier to getting parents and the community behind teachers' efforts. In many instances, stakeholders simply have no information about what teachers are up to. But beyond that, prevalent ideas about "the way things used to be," outmoded mental models of school, often thwart teachers' initiatives and learning goals.

Engaging public support for teacher learning communities hinges on the development of political consensus for the equity goals that motivate such communities and new understandings about how teachers learn together to improve student achievement. Although NCLB puts forth a competing conception of teacher quality, it has framed the challenge of improving teaching quality in schools where students perform poorly. System leaders thus might use the federal legislation as an opportunity to leverage school culture change and a local learning system to improve teaching quality and equity.

Notes

1. This chapter is a revised version of a paper presented at the No Child Left Behind Conference of the American Sociological Association's Section on Sociology of Education, Philadelphia,

August 12, 2005. Research summarized here was funded by the U.S. Department of Education, the National Science Foundation, the Dewitt Wallace-Readers Digest Funds, the William and Flora Hewlett Foundation, the Annenberg Foundation, the Johnson Foundation, and the Stuart Foundation during the period 1987–2005. Opinions expressed do not necessarily reflect those of the granting agencies. We are grateful to the many organizations, educators, administrators, and research colleagues who contributed to the body of research that grounds our analysis and to two anonymous reviewers of an earlier draft of the chapter.

2. NCLB legislation defines a highly qualified teacher as one who has a college degree, a teaching certificate, and competence in each of the subjects being taught (demonstrated by having a major or an advanced certificate in the subject or by passing a test in the subject). See Ingersoll (2005, this volume) for further discussion.

3. NELS: 88 is a federal research program that follows a national sample of students who were 8th graders in 1988 through their education and into the workforce. During 1988–92, the program surveyed students and teachers and tested students every two years, yielding data for students and their teachers at 8th, 10th, and 12th grades.

4. This analysis used a school survey measure of "inquiry practices" and estimated its effect on 2001 SAT-9 scores after 1998 SAT-9 scores were controlled. Results were consistent for two samples of BASRC schools: 18 schools for which mean teacher survey ratings were analyzed and 52 schools for which a reform coordinator's ratings were used. For details, see Center for Research on the Context of Teaching (2002), *Bay Area School Reform Collaborative: Phase One (1996–2001) Evaluation*. Stanford, CA: Stanford University. These evaluations and the instruments they employed are available at: http://www:stanford.edu/group/CRC/.

REFERENCES

Argyris, C. 1982. *Reasoning, learning, and action*. San Francisco: Jossey-Bass.

Bransford, J. D., A. L. Brown, and R. R. Cocking, eds. 1999. *How people learn: Brain, mind, experience, and school*. Washington, D.C.: National Academy Press.

Center for Research on the Context of Teaching. 2002. *Bay AreaSschool Reform Collaborative: Phase one (1996–2001) Evaluation*. Stanford University. Stanford, CA:Author.

Finley, M. K. 1984. Teachers and tracking in a comprehensive high-school. *Sociology of Education* 57:233–43.

Fullan, M. 2001. *The new meaning of education change*, 3rd ed. New York: Teachers College Press.

Gamoran, A., C. W. Anderson, P. A. Quiroz, W. G. Secada, T. Williams, and S. Ashmann. 2003. *Transforming teaching in math and science. How schools and districts can support change*. New York: Teachers College Press.

Guitierrez, R. 1996. Practices, beliefs and cultures of high-school math departments: Understanding their influence on student learning. *Journal of Curriculum Studies* 28:495–529.

Hawley, W. D.,and L.Valli. 1999. The essentials of effective professional development: A new consensus. In *Teaching as a learning profession: Handbook of policy and practice*, ed. L. Darling-Hammond and G. Sykes, 127–50. San Francisco: Jossey-Bass.

Hill, P. T., C. Campbell, and J. Harvey. 2000. *It takes a city. Getting serious about urban school reform*. Washington, D.C.: Brookings Institution.

Ingersoll, R. M. 2005. The problem of underqualified teachers: A sociological perspective. *Sociology of Education* 78 (2):175–78.

Ingram, D., K. Seashore Louis, and R. Schroeder. 2004. Accountability policies and teacher decision making: Barriers to the use of data to improve practice. *Teachers College Record* 106 (6):1258–87.

Lee, V. E. and J. B. Smith. 1995. Effects of high-school restructuring and size on gains in achievement and engagement for early secondary school students. *Sociology of Education* 68:241–70.

———.1996. Collective responsibility for learning and its effects on gains in achievement for early secondary school students. *American Journal of Education* 104:103–47.

———. R. G. Croninger.1997. How high-school organization influences the equitable distribution of learning in mathematics and science. *Sociology of Education* 70:128–50.

Levitt, B., and J. G. March. 1988. Organizational learning. *Annual Review of Sociology* 114:319–40.

Lieberman, A. and D. R. Wood. 2003. *Inside the National Writing Project: Connecting network learning and classroom teaching*. New York: Teachers College Press.

Little, J. W. 1982. Norms of collegiality and experimentation: Workplace conditions of school success. *American Educational Research Journal* 19:325–40.

Lortie, D. C. 1975. *Schoolteacher: A sociological study.* Chicago: University of Chicago Press.

Louis, K. S. and H. M. Marks. 1998. Does professional community affect the classroom? Teachers' work and student experiences in restructuring schools. *American Journal of Education* 106:532–75.

McDonald, J. P., N. Mohr, A. Dichter, and E. C. McDonald. 2003. *The power of protocols: An educator's guide to better practice.* New York: Teachers College Press.

March, J. G. 1991. Exploration and exploitation in organizational learning. *Organizational Science* 2 (1):71–87.

McLaughlin, M. W. and D. Mitra.2003. *The cycle of inquiry as engine of school reform: Lessons from the Bay Area School Reform Collaborative.* Stanford, CA: Stanford University, Center for Research on the Context of Teaching.

McLaughlin, M. W. and J. E. Talbert. 2001. *Professional communities and the work of high-school teaching.* Chicago: University of Chicago Press.

———.2003. *Reforming districts: How districts support school reform.* Seattle, WA: University of Washington, Center for the Study of Teaching and Policy.

———.2006. *Building school-based teacher learning communities: Professional strategies to improve student achievement.* New York: Teachers College Press.

Mieles, T. and E. Foley. 2005. *From data to decisions: Lessons from school districts using data warehousing.* Providence, RI: Annenberg Instutute for School Reform.

Mohr, N. and A. Dichter. 2001. *Stages of team development: Lessons from the struggles of site-based management.* Providence, RI: Brown University, Annenberg Institute for School Reform.

Newmann, F. et al. 1996. *Authentic achievement: Restructuring schools for intellectual quality,* San Francisco: Jossey-Bass.

Petrides, L. and E. Nodine (with L. Nguyen, A. Karaglani, and R. Gluck). 2005. *Anatomy of school system improvement: Performance-driven practices in urban school districts.* San Francisco: NewSchools Venture Fund.

Rowan, B., F-S. Chiang, and R. J. Miller. 1997. Using research on employees' performance to study the effects of teachers on students' achievement. *Sociology of Education* 70:256–84

Shon, D. 1983. *The reflective practitioner.* New York: Basic Books.

Smylie, M. 1994. Redesigning teachers' work: Connections to the classroom. In *Review of Research in Education,* ed. L. Darling-Hammond, 20. Washington, D.C.: American Education Research Association.

Stein, M. K., E. A. Silver, and M. S. Smith. 1998. Mathematics reform and teacher development: A community of practice perspective. In *Thinking practices in mathematics and science learning,* ed. J. G. Greeno and S. V. Goldman, 17–52. Mahwah, NJ: Lawrence Erlbaum.

Stone, C., J. Henig, B. D. Jones, and C. Pierannunzi.2001. *Building civic capacity: The politics of reforming urban schools.* Lawrence, KS: University Press of Kansas.

Talbert, J. E. and M. Ennis. 1990. Teacher tracking: Exacerbating inequalities in the high-school. Stanford, CA: Stanford University, Center for Research on the Context of Teaching.

——— and M. W. McLaughlin. 1994. Teacher professionalism in local school context. *American Journal of Education* 102:123–53.

Togneri, W. and S. E. Anderson. 2003. *Beyond islands of excellence: What districts can do to improve instruction and achievement in all schools.* Washington, D.C.: Learning First Alliance.

Tyack, D. B. and L. Cuban. 1996. *Tinkering toward utopia.* Cambridge, MA: Harvard University Press.

Wenger, E. 1998. *Communities of practice: Learning, meaning, and identity.* Cambridge, UK: Cambridge University Press.

———, R. McDermott, and W. M. Snyder. 2003. *Cultivating communities of practice.* Cambridge, MA: Harvard Business School Press.

Yasumoto, J. Y., K. Uekawa, and C. E. Bidwell. 2001. The collegial focus and high-school students' achievement. *Sociology of Education* 74:181–209.

Part IV
School Choice and Parental Involvement

10

False Promises

The School Choice Provisions in NCLB[1]

Douglas Lee Lauen

STRATIFICATION AND EQUALITY OF EDUCATIONAL OPPORTUNITY

Scholars have long debated the extent to which education enhances mobility chances or simply maintains existing patterns of inequality. On the one hand, social scientists have argued that mobility based on achievement, rather status maintenance, is a hallmark of the U.S. social system (Blau and Duncan 1967). The U.S. educational system has been characterized as one with "contest," rather than "sponsored" mobility. Unlike the British system, in which elites induct a select group of youth at an early age to groom them for high-status positions, youth in the United States compete in multiple contests, with every effort taken to keep students in the game (Turner 1960). Alternative views argue that through hidden curriculum and tracking, the U.S. system "cools out" the mobility aspirations of disadvantaged students, thereby reinforcing, rather than overturning, existing patterns of stratification (MacLeod 1995; Oakes 1985; Rosenbaum 1976).

If the United States is indeed characterized by mobility through achievement, one must consider the rules of the game. To establish the legitimacy of contest mobility regimes and maintain social control, participants must believe that differential outcomes, and the rewards that flow from these outcomes, are due not to differential access to the resources necessary to compete in the contest, but rather to effort and merit. In order for success in school to be viewed as an effective mechanism to attain the rights and privileges of high status, all students must have access to high-quality teachers, curricula, and schools.

Promoting equality of educational opportunity was a persistent goal of U.S. education policy throughout the 19th and 20th century. Expanding access has taken various forms over time: it has extended schooling in rural areas; ensured that immigrants attended common schools in urban areas; addressed school desegregation; and, as some have argued, expanded school choice. Though expansion of educational opportunity has been a hallmark of the U.S. system, structural inequality and entrenched power dynamics have made providing students with the same starting point a highly contentious area of public policy. Due to the relatively high level of inequality in American society and the de-centralized nature of the educational system, efforts to use education policy to reduce inequality have faced political opposition and myriad difficulties in policy implementation. While there is often widespread agreement among the public and policymakers that students *should* receive equal access to education, implementing reform has often foundered on entrenched interests seeking to maintain their advantages (Hochschild and Scovronick 2003).

The expansion of school choice through vouchers, charter schools, and NCLB has been framed by advocates as a way to enhance equality of educational op-portunity; critics claim that school choice would reduce, rather than increase, educational opportunities for disadvantaged students. The stakes of this debate have been raised now that school choice is being funded and encouraged through federal policy. The D.C. Opportunity Scholarship program, begun in the 2004–5 school year, currently serves about 1,700 students who each receive up to $7,500 in federal funds to enable them to attend one of 68 private schools (about two-thirds of which are religiously affiliated) (Wolf et al. 2006). A policy that affects many more students and schools is the school choice provision in NCLB, which requires that students in schools that have failed to make adequate yearly progress (AYP) in consecutive years be given the option of transferring to a school that has done so. The implication of this provision is that because states and local school districts have failed to provide adequate access to educational resources to low-income children, the federal government must use its authority to regulate student enrollment policy.

In order to justify what has become a significant incursion of federal gov-ernment power into educational policy since the original ESEA law was passed in 1965, the president and Congressional leaders sought to instill in the public and other members of Congress a sense that urgent reform was required to fix a dysfunctional educational system. The image of "freeing" students from "failing" schools was central in this effort. For example, upon introducing his educational agenda on January 23, 2001, President George W. Bush said: "American children must not be left in persistently dangerous or failing schools. When schools do not teach and will not change, parents and students must have other meaning-ful options."[2]

Not surprisingly, the exertion of federal authority over student enrollment policy has proved controversial and implementation of these provisions has been uneven across local school districts. In fact, one could argue that the school choice provisions have been remarkably ineffective. Despite the fact that 3.3 million students were eligible for NCLB transfers in the 2003–4 school year, only 31,500, or 1 percent of eligible students actually transferred to a school that was making AYP (U.S. Government Accountability Office 2004).

The purpose of this chapter is to assess the extent to which public school choice either through local or federal policy is likely to expand equality of educational opportunity. I begin by outlining some important design principles for school choice programs. I discuss the challenges local districts have faced when attempting to comply with the NCLB transfer mandates. I conclude by drawing implications for NCLB's 2007 reauthorization and for future research on NCLB choice.

THE PROMISES AND PERILS OF SCHOOL CHOICE

The most common and least controversial policy of assigning students to schools is by geographic catchment area, with all students in a given set of neighborhoods going to the same neighborhood school. This policy is the norm in American education, in which local school district officials determine which students attend which schools through drawing attendance area boundaries. Neither parents nor school principals have much choice over enrollment decisions.[3] School choice advocates criticize this type of school enrollment policy for creating monopolistic conditions in which students are essentially a captive clientele. This view holds that these monopolistic conditions stifle both diversity of educational approach and educational excellence. In 2003, about 74 percent of students in grades 1–12 attend an assigned public school (Wirt et al. 2004). Ten years previously, in 1993, about 80 percent of students attended an assigned neighborhood school, one indication of the erosion of support for assigned public schools through the 1990s and early 2000s.

School choice advocates seek to replace the neighborhood-based school with a wide variety of schools tailored to fit the needs and interests of various student groups. Advocates argue that school choice can help parents both find a school that better fits their child's educational needs and potentially leverage school reform by promoting competition among schools for students. For example, a cultural divide between teachers and poor parents has been identified as a barrier to school improvement (Comer 1988; Lareau 1989;). A goal of school choice policy, therefore, is to bridge this divide by allowing schools to recruit parents aligned with their educational approaches. This should promote parent satisfaction and trust if teachers and administrators adhere to these approaches and serve the needs of the students (Bryk and Schneider 2002). Moreover, some have argued that schools in which educational values are aligned among staff, parents, and students may produce more functional learning communities (Bryk et al. 1993; Coleman and Hoffer 1987;). Therefore, choice has the potential to raise parent satisfaction, student engagement, and improve the incentives that influence school leaders.

Choice, if paired with deregulation of curricular foci, could promote a better match between family values and school mission. Promoting innovation of educational approach increases the likelihood of a match between student and family interests and a school's educational approach. If one assumes that the needs of students and families vary too much to be served by one type of school, a goal of school choice policy is to subvert the common school ideal, which promotes a unitary conception of educational values. In its place, choice policy promotes a wide variety of schools, each tailored to a particular conception of educational values, with the ability to attract students and families based on shared values: the "interests of children are best served in a decentralized polity giving maximum scope to free, chosen, communal relationships that are generally organized on a small scale" (Coons and Sugarman 1978, 2). School choice advocates have argued that it is not the state's place to enforce conformity to one set of values: "Our problem today is not to enforce conformity; it is rather that we are threatened with an excess of conformity. Our problem is to foster diversity, and the alternative [vouchers] would do this far more effectively than a nationalized system" (Friedman 1962, 97).

Education organized around a plurality of value commitments raises the possibility that school choice might harm social cohesion. While some voucher proponents have advocated reforms to create a system of pluralistic value competition—education as a "marketplace of ideas" (Coons and Sugarman 1978, 102)—the fact that education is a public good paid for by tax dollars makes political contestation over curricular content inevitable. As controversies over the teaching of evolution suggest, matters of curriculum involve deeply held value commitments. Because schools are one of society's most important institutions of socialization and national identity, school curricula are fiercely contested.

From an egalitarian standpoint, therefore, school choice is problematic because it threatens the common school ideal of educating children of many different social, racial, and achievement backgrounds in the same institution. It has been argued that the common school has benefits for social cohesion and perhaps even peer effects on test scores if low ability and high-ability students share classrooms. Therefore, allowing students to exercise school choice to attend schools that better suit their values, racial/ethnic preferences, or abilities, would harm social cohesion and may have negative spill-over effects on the students who remain in neighborhood schools. Expanding school choice could promote "creaming" (i.e., more advantaged students would be more likely to take advantage of school choice and leave less advantaged students in failing schools). Given that the social isolation of disadvantaged groups has been shown to harm student outcomes, one could predict that school choice could increase inequality in test scores, college enrollment rates, and incomes over time.

From a meritocratic standpoint, on the other hand, school choice could promote equity. The fact that highly motivated parents and children are able to gain access to alternatives to their neighborhood schools can be viewed as unproblematic assuming the admission rules are fair. In other words, in its ideal form school choice replaces the current system of school stratification based on race and class with one governed by merit, measured by test scores, effort, grades, or some other criteria. This could improve the incentives for families to seek out schools that serve their interests and for schools to attract and hold students who place a high-value on learning (Coleman 1992). Therefore, access to high-ability peers becomes a result of a fair process rather than some combination of ascriptive characteristics.

While my characterizations of these two divergent viewpoints may be roughly hewn, these perspectives are critical to understanding whether expanding school choice will increase or decrease social inequality through changes in access to educational opportunities.

As we might expect from the decentralized educational system in the United States, choice policy varies somewhat across the country. Most areas of the country allow some degree of choice within school districts, most states allow charter schools, and vouchers are quite rare. NCLB choice, which has largely been implemented within (rather than across) school districts, can be viewed as a form of intradistrict choice that has been mandated by the federal government onto local school districts.

NCLB CHOICE IMPLEMENTATION

I begin my discussion of NCLB choice implementation by first discussing the legal and regulatory framework of NCLB and providing a nationwide overview of the difficulties school districts have had with implementing the transfer provisions of the Act. Following this, I describe in some detail what is known about Chicago's implementation of the transfer provisions. To place Chicago's compliance with federal mandates into perspective, I draw on research I conducted on the history and current operation of school choice programs in Chicago (Lauen 2006).

The Legal and Regulatory Framework of NCLB Choice

NCLB choice is a form of intradistrict choice mandated by federal law and implemented by local school districts. The NCLB school transfer provisions, which only apply to schools receiving Title I funds, are designed as a negative incentive for underperforming schools. They are triggered when a high-poverty school fails to make "adequate yearly progress" (AYP) for two years in a row.

AYP applies to standards set by states (and subject to the approval of the U.S. Department of Education) in reading and math. AYP describes an improvement trajectory leading to 100 percent proficiency in both subjects for all students by the 2013–14 school year, measured by testing results from students in grades 3–8. A school can be judged as not making adequate yearly progress for failing to meet performance targets or for failing to test 95 percent of their students. In addition, schools can miss AYP for not testing at least 95 percent of students in a number of subgroups—major ethnic/racial groups, the economically disadvantaged, limited English proficient students, and students with disabilities—or if the average subgroup score fails meet a certain threshold.[4] If a school fails to make AYP in two consecutive years, it must offer students the opportunity to attend another public school in the same district or one nearby that is making AYP.[5] A school forced to provide NCLB transfers must do so until it succeeds in meeting AYP in two consecutive years. Students who transfer to a receiving school must be allowed to stay through the highest grade offered in the school. In implementing school transfer policies, the Act requires that local school districts (LEAs) give low-income and low-achieving students priority in school transfers in the event that not enough spaces in eligible schools are available.

Based in part on comments regarding regulation and additional questions to the U.S. Department of Education, in February of 2004 the department provided additional guidance to states attempting to implement the laws requirements (U.S. Department of Education, 2004). While additional funding would provide a positive incentive for schools receiving NCLB transfer students, the law does not require Title I funds to "follow the child."[6] LEAs must spend an amount equal to 20 percent of its Title I allocation on choice-related transportation or tutoring, with no less than 5 percent of this allocation going to either transportation or tutoring. LEAs may delimit student transfer options to designated transportation zones to reduce costs. However, LEAs are not required to provide transportation to students whose original school is no longer in improvement status.

LEAs are not required to change admission requirements in schools with specialized missions (like arts magnets, science and math academies, and selective enrollment schools) even if these schools are the only ones identified by the district as eligible to receive transfers. They may, however, give NCLB transfer students priority in charter school lotteries. LEAs must not use lack of capacity to deny students the transfer option, but may take capacity under consideration in deciding which choices to make available. LEAs with a lack of capacity must create new capacity for NCLB transfers by building new classroom space, erecting portables, building new schools, starting charter schools, developing distance learning programs, sending students to another school district, or contracting with private schools. Finally, LEAs subject to desegregation orders are not exempt from the NCLB transfer provisions. They must attempt to comply with both the dictates of the order and the transfer provisions.

Nationwide Overview

The NCLB transfer provisions have been called among the hardest provisions in the Act for local school districts to implement (Casserly 2004). They require districts to identify schools that have failed to make AYP for two consecutive years; identify schools that are both eligible to accept transfers under the Act and have the space available for student transfers; notify parents of their eligibility for a school choice transfer; set up a selection process to assign students to schools in the event that more students apply for transfers than can be accommodated; and provide transportation for transferring students. In some districts, this process is relatively straightforward and involves very few students. Three cities in Texas, for example, Houston, Dallas, and Austin, had no schools that were in "school improvement" status in 2003–4,[7] so these districts did not have to create a transfer process. Philadelphia, on the other hand, had 74 percent of the schools in improvement status, and was forced by NCLB to set up elaborate transfer program (Casserly 2004).

Nationwide, about 1 percent of eligible students in both the 2003–4 and 2004–5 school years actually switched schools through NCLB choice (Center for Education Policy 2005; U.S. Government Accountability Office 2004). About 15 percent of school districts had schools designated to offer NCLB transfers in 2004–5, and large urban districts tended to have more schools facing this sanction (Center for Education Policy 2005). In large urban districts, NCLB transfers have been a small but rising percentage of the overall student population. These figures are based on a survey of the 50 largest urban districts in 2003–4, 44,373, or 3.8 percent of eligible students who requested a NCLB transfer (Casserly 2004). Of these requests, 17,879, or 40.3 percent, were granted. For comparison purposes, the number of NCLB transfer requests granted by these large urban districts in 2002–3 was 5,661 (Casserly 2004).

According to a survey of state and school district officials, finding enough space in schools meeting AYP to satisfy requests, identifying eligible families in a timely manner, and communicating with parents were the most challenging barriers to implementing the choice provisions (Center for Education Policy 2005). Capacity constraints were particularly severe in some rural districts with only one school and in overcrowded urban districts where large proportions of schools were in improvement status. Interdistrict choice is a potential solution to this problem, but virtually no districts have been willing or able to create cross-district agreements to allow interdistrict NCLB transfers (Brown 2004).

Notifying families of their options in a timely manner has been a particular challenge due to testing, data cleaning, and reporting schedules. Given the high stakes attached to testing results, the complex NCLB achievement and testing participation criteria for each subgroup, and recent scandals involving mistakes in test scoring (e.g., Duchesne 2000), states must carefully scrutinize student, subgroup, and school test scores to ensure accuracy. While NCLB has increased the demand for accuracy, there has been a concurrent demand for results to be processed more rapidly. To ensure that testing results reflect what students have learned in a school year, students are typically tested as late in the spring as possible. Providing adequate notification to families eligible for NCLB transfers, however, requires results to be processed in a matter of months, before the next school year. This presents problems for most school districts. According to a survey of large urban districts, no district had testing results processed by the end of the 2002–3 school year, and more than half did not have results by the beginning of the next school year (Casserly 2004).

Lack of adequate notification is one barrier that contributes to the broader challenge of parent participation in the NCLB transfer program. While NCLB is designed to serve disadvantaged families, it is precisely these families that are the least likely to know whether they are eligible for a transfer. A survey in Massachusetts found that most parents whose children qualify for an NCLB transfer do not know whether their child's school is in improvement status and is thus required to offer their child a transfer. Specifically, only one in four parents of eligible children correctly identified the improvement status of their school (Howell 2004).

Evidence suggests that uptake for NCLB transfers has been low because parents have strong commitments to local schools and may be getting conflicting signals from the overlapping federal, state, and district accountability regimes. Opinion surveys consistently indicate that public school parents think highly of the schools their children attend, but not highly of schools in general. For example, in 2004 more than two-thirds of public school parents gave the school their oldest child attends a grade of "A" or a "B." Less than one-quarter of public school parents, however, gave public schools in the nation as a whole a grade of "A" or "B" (Rose and Gallup 2004). This suggests that parents might be willing to support efforts like those called for in NCLB to reform schools in general, but may resist efforts to punish or reform their own child's school. Despite high levels of parent satisfaction among those whose children attend schools of choice (Gill 2001, 128–37), most parents prefer reforming the existing school system to creating expanding school choice. Poll figures suggest that even if their child's school was in NCLB improvement status, only a small minority of parents would opt to exercise school choice. The vast majority (85%) of parents preferred that instead of choice, additional efforts should be made to improve their neighborhood school (Gill 2001).[8]

Some evidence also suggests that parents do not believe that the alternatives to their home school are markedly better. In some cases, this is understandable because state and federal quality designations sometimes vary. In some cases, states may recognize a school as being a school of excellence, but because of the underperformance of one subgroup, or because of the test participation rate of a particular subgroup, the school may miss AYP standards. In other cases, it may be that districts identify schools as NCLB transfer options that are only marginally better than the sending schools themselves.

Scholars have questioned the effectiveness of relying on an accountability program that can lead to an overly broad definition of school failure. In other words, if large majorities of schools are deemed to be "failures" by NCLB rules, then the stigmatizing effect of the label may be limited. If, however, only a small proportion of schools are deemed as failing to meet a more relaxed set of standards, then arguably the stigmatizing effect would be more likely to lead to productivity improvements. For example, in 2003 75 percent of Florida's elementary schools were deemed as failing to meet AYP, whereas only 10 percent of schools in 2002 received failing marks under the state's A++ accountability plan (which, as noted above, offered vouchers to students in failing schools) (West and Peterson 2006). A study of Florida's A++ program found that schools facing, or at risk of facing, the voucher threat produced positive impacts on school performance; schools at risk of facing sanctions through NCLB, however, did not produce similar effects (West and Peterson 2006). This provides some evidence in support of the hypothesis that targeted sanctions work better than overly broad ones. Further study is needed to determine the extent to which (1) the proportion of schools facing a sanction; (2) the type of choice offered (public versus private); or (3) the extent of state and local commitment to providing teeth to negative sanctions through policy implementation are the most effective at bringing about school improvement through stigmatization and negative sanctions.

In summary, the low NCLB transfer rates stem from several sources: (1) capacity constraints; (2) the logistical hurdles inherent in meeting both annual testing and notification requirements; (3) strong commitment to local schools; (4) race and class disparities in access to information about school quality; and (5) the fact that federal and state accountability regimes send conflicting signals about the quality of local schools.

In summary, the NCLB choice provision is explicitly linked to school accountability, it requires LEAs to use Title I funds for transportation, and forbids overcrowding from preventing student transfers. To provide more institutional detail and a sense of how policy implementation can evolve over time, I now turn to a more in-depth examination of one case.

CHICAGO CASE STUDY

Chicago is a highly segregated city with a predominantly low income and minority student population. Its schools were once decried by William Bennett (former Secretary of Education under President Reagan) as the "worst in the nation" (Johnson 1987). While some strides have been made to reform schools and improve student achievement, large numbers of the city's schools remain on

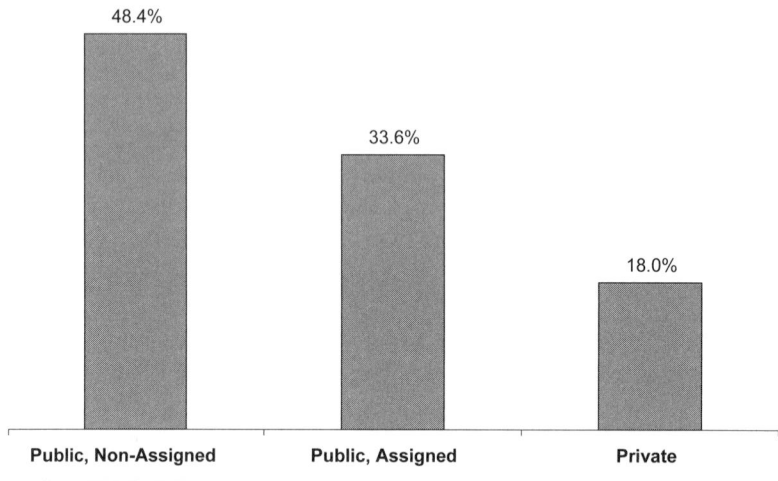

Figure 10.1 Chicago secondary school enrollment, by school type, 2000. *Note:* Data on private school enrollment is from author calculations of 2000 IPUMS data. Data on nonneighborhood public school enrollment is from author calculations of CPS administrative data.

academic probation and are deemed to be underperforming by local and federal standards. The District is currently identified by NCLB as being in "improvement" status for failing to meet goals in math.

Chicago has a large intradistrict high-school choice program in which public or private school choice is the norm. About half of secondary students exercise public school choice and almost one-fifth attend a private high school (see Figure 10.1). Public alternatives include career academies, selective enrollment college preparatory high schools, magnet schools and programs, charter schools, and military academies; private alternatives are predominantly Catholic schools. Only about one-third of secondary students in Chicago attend an assigned public school. The district also runs a liberal open enrollment transfer program which allows high-school students to attend any high school in the district on a space-available basis.

The Emergence of School Choice from Desegregation

Chicago's history with school choice began as a response to the problem of school segregation. Though Chicago formally desegregated its school system in 1874, due to real estate practices, public housing policy that situated projects in black neighborhoods, and a neighborhood schools policy, Chicago's schools were segregated de facto (Hess 1984). Despite calls for action from community groups, policy recommendations in reports by academic experts, student boycotts, and the constant threats of federal civil rights enforcement, the Chicago school board refused to implement any substantial school desegregation policy between 1960 and 1980 (Peterson 1976). Unlike in the South, where National Guard troops escorted black students through the hallways of Little Rock High School, the federal role in enforcing civil rights in Chicago was minimal. After passage of the Civil Rights Act in 1964, Chicago became an early test case in enforcement of the Act's provisions. When the Office of Education withheld federal education funds from Chicago due to the board's inaction on school integration, Mayor Daley complained to President Johnson, who quickly intervened on Chicago's behalf. The funds were quickly released (Hess 1984; Peterson 1976). Johnson's intervention set a precedent. At least in key Democratic strongholds like Chicago and other northern cities, the federal role in enforcement would be an empty threat until 1980, the turning point for both the history of desegregation and school choice in Chicago.

To avoid a federal lawsuit, in 1980 the District negotiated a consent decree with the U.S. Department of Justice to create a voluntary transfer program called "Options for Knowledge" to entice students away from segregated schools. Creating and maintaining integrated schools was a central goal of this program, so transfer requests were evaluated to determine the impact of a student transfer on the racial composition of the sending and receiving schools. Applications to schools under this program were sorted by grade, race, and gender. Students were chosen by lottery if schools or programs were oversubscribed. The plan established a standard to guide student reassignment and transfers: if a school was more than 70 percent of one race or ethnicity, then it was considered segregated and was subject to student reassignment policies including boundary changes and racial/ethnic quotas on incoming student transfers. Therefore, what emerged in Chicago was a program that sought to expand school choice, while also regulating schools' racial mix.

Mayoral Takeover and a Turn Towards Selectivity

During the mid- to late 1990s, Mayor Richard M. Daley, Jr. used authority granted to him by a school reform law in 1995 to close chronically underperforming schools and open new schools.[9] In Chicago and other cities during the 1990s, professional discretion and union control gave way to a business-led movement to give authority to big city mayors who then hired technocrats, businessmen, and military leaders to run schools. The reform act was passed by a Republican legislature and informed by extensive input from Chicago United and the Civic Committee of the Commercial Club, both influential Chicago-based business organizations (Klonsky 1995). The mayor, and Paul Vallas, the mayor's former budget director (who was himself not a professional educator) tightened accountability for both students and schools. They put an end to social promotion, the practice of promoting students from one grade to the next whether or not students performed at grade level on standardized tests. In 1997, for example, 11,000 students were retained in the 3rd, 6th, and 8th grades due to poor performance on standardized tests in reading and math (Roderick et al. 1999). Vallas also used his expanded authority to use standardized test scores as a basis for evaluating schools and closing them for chronic underperformance.

Neighborhood schools, which had not fared well under the "Options for Knowledge" program, were further stigmatized by rising academic standards. One study found that schools on probation for low test score performance lost the highest proportion of their attendance area student enrollment to schools of choice (Duffrin 2001). As neighborhood high schools gained poor reputations, families with the information and ability to negotiate the school choice process (or pay for private schooling) sent their children elsewhere. Those students who had fewer options or special needs became disproportionately represented in neighborhood high schools. In South Shore High School, once a school with a good reputation in an integrated middle-class neighborhood, for example, a reporter found that a typical classroom of 28 students had 10 to 12 students with learning disabilities or behavior disorders (Duffrin 2001).

Given the poor reputation of many neighborhood schools in Chicago, the Daley regime sought to close dysfunctional schools, open new schools in their place, and build new school buildings. Between 1995 and 2004, 22 schools were closed and 53 schools opened. Of those that opened, only 16 had attendance areas, and 37 were schools of choice such as charters, magnets, and selective enrollment high schools. One objective in creating these new schools was to change the image of the Chicago public schools from one of fraud, mismanagement, and failure to one of performance and innovation. Daley and Vallas sought to keep more middle-class families in the city and attract students from the private sector to the district's selective enrollment schools and programs. The administration built eight new selective enrollment high schools, expanded International Baccalaureate programs (a selective high-school program leading to a high-school diploma set to a worldwide standard), and created math/science/technology academies in schools with large outflows of attendance area students. In addition, the school district created fee-based preschool programs and neighborhood set-asides in gentrifying neighborhoods in an effort to entice young professionals to consider sending their children to the public schools.[10]

Features of the Existing System

Several features of Chicago's existing school choice regime are worth noting before exploring the District's implementation of the NCLB transfer provisions. At least in part because most high schools have an application process to admit some or all of their students, students with social and academic advantages are more likely to participate in public school choice programs in Chicago.

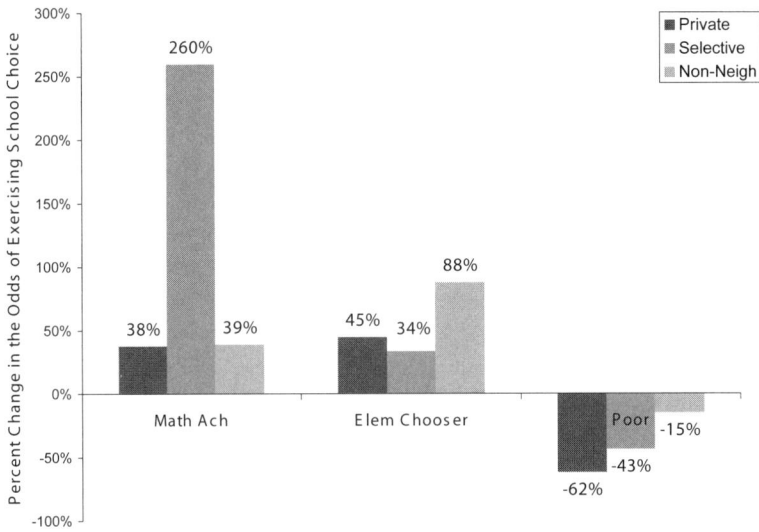

Figure 10.2 Effect of measures of student social and academic status on high-school choice, 2000. *Source:* Lauen (2006). 2000–2001 Chicago public schools administrative data. 9th grade destinations of 8th grade public school students only. Effects shown control for gender, race-ethnicity, special education status, age, number of previous school moves, and measures of elementary school context.

Students with higher prior achievement, and students with parents who had successfully negotiated the elementary school choice process, are more likely to attend a private or public alternative to their assigned public high school (Figure 10.2). Poor students (measured by whether the student was eligible for a free or reduced priced lunch), on the other hand, are less likely to exercise private or public high-school choice.[11]

There is also evidence that, consistent with prior research (Glazerman 1998; Saporito and Lareau 1999; Schneider and Buckley 2002), parents in Chicago choose schools based on race. Net of assigned high-school average achievement, nonblack families tend to avoid neighborhood high schools with high percentages of black students (Figure 10.3). This suggests that high-minority schools, no matter how productive, may be at a disadvantage in Chicago's system of school choice.

Ideally, we would like to be able to separate parent racial and class preferences from their preferences for high-performing schools. It could be that parents assume that schools serving disadvantaged student populations are of low quality. The evidence from Chicago is that parents prefer high schools with high-compositional quality, defined as a composite of aggregate achievement, safety, mobility, poverty, motivation, and attainment measures. (These school-level measures are all highly correlated.) The evidence also suggests, however, that parents are also likely to avoid enrolling their children in highly productive

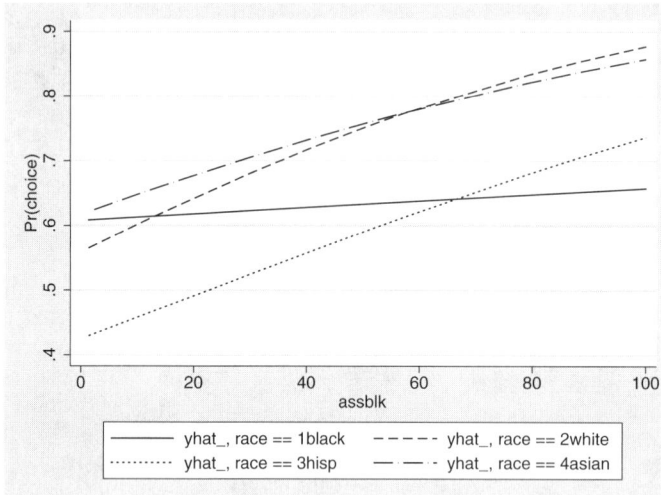

Figure 10.3 Effect of percentage black students on propensity to exercise school choice, by race-ethnicity, 2000. *Source:* Lauen (2006). 2000–2001 Chicago public schools administrative data. 8th grade public school students only. Effects shown control for student-level covariates such as prior achievement, poverty, and race-ethnicity, and neighborhood high-school average achievement.

assigned high schools. This could be because parents are unaware that, controlling for student background, prior educational experiences, and elementary school quality, disadvantaged high schools in Chicago tend to produce higher 8th to 9th grade test score gains.[12] Figure 10.4 displays the opposite effects of compositional quality and productivity.

In summary, Chicago's existing system of school choice emerged from school desegregation. At first, policymakers focused on expanding educational opportunities for black students in segregated schools. After a mayoral takeover of the school system in the mid-1990s, however, the focus of school choice policy shifted somewhat to expand educational opportunities for high-achieving students. By the year 2000, choice of high school in Chicago was designed as a "winner-take-all" system, with high-achieving students receiving a disproportionate share of the benefits of school choice (Lauen 2006). There is evidence to support the hypothesis that parents are sensitive to school quality differences; unfortunately, whether due to lack of access to school quality information or due to assumptions that schools serving disadvantaged students are of low quality, families seem to be avoiding schools with relatively high-productivity levels.

Chicago and NCLB Choice

Elected and appointed officials have been openly critical of NCLB and the transfer provisions. Mayor Daley has been quoted as arguing that NCLB should have given

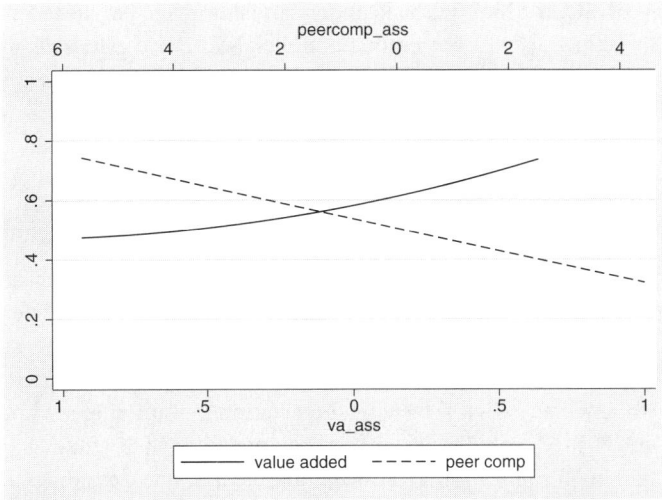

Figure 10.4 Effect of assigned school peer composition and productivity on propensity to exercise school choice, by poverty level, 2000. *Source:* Lauen .2006. 2000–2001 Chicago public schools administrative data. 8th grade public school students only. Effects shown control for student-level covariates such as prior achievement, poverty, and race-ethnicity. Peer composition is a principal components measure of assigned high-school characteristics such as percent poor, mobility rate, and average achievement. Productivity is defined as the average residual 8th to 9th grade test score gain, controlling for student background and elementary school quality.

schools more time to improve before they were subject to the transfer threat: "it's 'ridiculous' to think schools can improve 'overnight....Many of the schools are not performing. Everybody knows that,' Daley said. 'We know it. Where are you going to go? To another non-performing school? You can't.'" (Rossi and Spielman 2002). Arne Duncan, the CEO of the Chicago Public School system (CPS), has expressed doubt that NCLB would improve student learning and was "burdensome...complex and impractical" (Rossi 2003b).

The U.S. Department of Education official responsible for overseeing the transfer provisions of NCLB, Nina Reece, said, "Based on every single news report and discussion we've had with the city of Chicago, we feel, when it comes to choice, they are not looking at creative ways to extend capacity and meet the needs of students in low-performing schools" (Rossi 2003a). Two options for complying with federal mandates include providing trailers for students on the grounds of schools making AYP and creating interdistrict agreements for transfers across district lines. Duncan has been quoted as saying that CPS has no funds to purchase trailers and that he hasn't asked neighboring districts to accept CPS transfers because, "I don't think yellow school buses from Chicago would be well-received" (Rossi 2003a).

From these exchanges in the newspapers, it seems fair to characterize the attitude of important elected and appointed officials as being hostile to the transfer provisions of NCLB. This is perhaps understandable given that the federal share of funding is low, federal requirements under NCLB are extensive, and that NCLB labels large portions of Chicago's schools as in need of improvement, a problem that policymakers had been attempting to address in various ways for at least the past 10 to 15 years.

According to data provided by the Illinois State School Board, in the 2003–4 school year, three-quarters of elementary schools and 90 percent of high-schools failed to make AYP. In subsequent years, the proportion of elementary schools failing to make AYP fell to two-thirds; the high-school proportion fell and then increased to 94 percent (Table 10.1). By the 2005–6 school year, 64 percent of elementary school students and 94 percent of high-school students attended schools that failed to make AYP according to federal guidelines. Approximately 256,000 students were eligible by federal regulation to transfer to a school making AYP in 2005–6.[13] In a district with approximately 436,000 students enrolled in the fall of 2005 eligible for a transfer under NCLB, it is clear that CPS faces implementation problems; short of shutting down all schools that missed AYP, it is impossible for the district to find spaces for all students eligible for an NCLB transfer under federal guidelines.

For 2003–4, the first year of NCLB choice implementation, CPS determined that 1,100 spaces would be made available by lottery to eligible students, which for this year was determined to be 270,000 students. Approximately 19,000 students entered the lottery. Lottery winners were given one day to decide whether

TABLE 10.1 Selected NCLB statistics, Chicago, 2003–6

	School Year		
	03-04	**04-05**	**05-06**
Panel A, Federal definitions			
Elementary			
% of schools that failed AYP	75%	65%	64%
% of students in schools that failed AYP	80%	70%	64%
High School			
% of schools that failed AYP	90%	84%	92%
% of students in schools that failed AYP	90%	84%	94%
Panel B, Chicago implementation of NCLB transfers			
Eligible students (as defined by CPS)	270,757	2,500	1,100
Applications	19,246	5,933	267
Spaces made available	1,100	440	550

Source: Percent of schools failing AYP from author calculations of data provided by the Illinois State Board of Education. Chicago implementation of choice transfer policy from newspaper reports, e-mail communication with CPS officials, and Center on Education policy reports (Center for Education Policy, 2005, 2006).

to accept a choice seat (Rossi 2003b). For the 2004–5 school year, CPS changed eligibility rules and determined that about 2,500 students were eligible for 440 slots. About 5,933 students applied for these slots (Center for Education Policy 2006). It is clear that the decline in the number of students eligible for a choice transfer was due not to a large decline in the number of schools subject to the choice sanction, but to a redefinition of eligibility by local officials. In 2005–6, the definition of eligibility was further restricted to students in three schools that both missed AYP and had been identified for closure under the CPS account-ability regime; 550 slots were made available to students in these three schools, but only 267 students applied for an NCLB transfer to one of 20 schools that were making AYP.[14] This left more than 800 students who chose to attend schools in neighborhoods adjacent to their old schools, none of which were making AYP (Grossman 2005). The number of students applying for NCLB transfers has been falling (Table 10.1). No high-school students were given the opportunity to exercise NCLB choice during the 2004–5 and 2005–6 school years.

In addition to capacity constraints, CPS has had difficulty identifying schools that were significantly better than those subject to the choice sanction. Students in Chicago could only choose from schools that had, on average, very high poverty levels. The average proficiency level of the receiving schools in Chicago, while generally higher than the sending schools, was significantly below the average proficiency level of the pool of potential receiving schools (Kim and Sunderman 2004). Of the 11 schools slated to be receiving schools of students affected by school closures in the spring of 2002, however, six were identified as needing improvement and eligible for choice in the fall of 2002 (Rossi and Spielman 2002). In some cases, receiving schools had worse test scores than some of the sending schools (Rossi 2003b). In at least one case, this was the case because the receiving school had not been in existence long enough to be subject to the choice sanction.

Illinois state law prevents local school districts from complying with some federal mandates. Though federal regulations state that local school districts must allow NCLB transfers even to overcrowded schools, Illinois state law forbids such an action. State law also prevents NCLB transfer students from taking precedence in admissions to academically selective schools (Center for Education Policy 2006).

In summary, Chicago is a large and diverse urban school system that has been struggling for many years to improve student learning. NCLB choice is but a small portion of the choice transfers that exist in a district in which 30 percent of elementary school students and 60 percent of public school students attend a public school of choice. Despite the fact that NCLB was perhaps designed with school districts like Chicago in mind, the ability of federal officials to force compliance with the law's dictates has been limited. For four years local officials have been largely free to craft policies that severely constrain the number of

NCLB transfer slots and limit the pool of eligible students that has little, if any, resemblance to federal regulations.

IMPLICATIONS FOR REAUTHORIZATION

Rather than encouraging the rise of new school forms that could expand educational opportunity, the NCLB transfer provisions are a blunt system of negative sanctions. Without careful attention to mid-course modifications informed by additional research in exactly how school choice leads to benefits to students, NCLB choice is likely to hold an empty promise to American school children.

To be most effective, school choice policy must encourage innovation, reform, and productivity while also promoting (or at least not harming) social cohesion, accountability, and equity (Levin 2004; National Working Commission on Choice in K–12 Education 2003). Policy aimed at promoting a diverse array of educational options must, therefore, regulate enough to maintain social cohesion and ensure that public dollars are being put to productive use, but not so much that schools cannot innovate, take risks, and reach populations aligned with their mission. If enough new (or reconstituted) schools enter the market, policy must also create a level playing field to foster competition between new entrants and existing schools (National Working Commission on Choice in K–12 Education 2003). This involves providing both new and old schools with adequate and equitable funding, budgetary control, and the flexibility to hire and fire teachers aligned with reform objectives. The goal of policy would be to allow teachers and families to focus on a shared mission and the technical core of education—teaching and learning—while also fostering competition among educational providers and ensuring quality standards.

In short, the state must use its powers at the federal, state, and local levels to ensure innovation and competition in education while also holding schools accountable, promoting social cohesion, and protecting the rights of students to gain equal access to educational opportunity. Some of these powers include: maintaining an adequate and equitable flow of funding to schools; providing or paying for transportation to schools that are outside a student's neighborhood; providing extra funds to schools with harder to serve student populations; funding parent information centers and social marketing campaigns to facilitate an efficient and equitable school-to-parent matching process; promoting a mix of schools with a variety of selectivity criteria and lotteries for student admission; holding schools accountable for their "value added" (the achievement gain for the students who remain in the school long enough to produce a treatment effect); widely disseminating the performance measurement results; and closing schools with persistent failure records or records of financial malfeasance.

It would be hard to conclude from the early phase of NCLB choice that the policy as currently implemented is living up to the rhetoric of "liberation" used by the framers of the Act. The choice provisions are difficult for many, if not most, districts to implement, give struggling schools only one year to improve before facing sanctions, and penalize too many schools for the sanction to be effective. The vast majority of students who desire a school transfer are not being allowed one. Testing schedules, capacity constraints, the large variation in state standards, and the high-between-district variation in access to high-quality alternatives represent substantial barriers to the prospect of NCLB transfers actually improving the plight of students in low performing, high poverty schools.

Absent significant changes in the implementation of the transfer provisions, and perhaps regulatory and legislative action, NCLB choice will probably have very little effect on educational reform. Because local school districts have a great deal of latitude in designing transfer programs, those districts that want to use the negative sanction will have legislative cover to do so and those that do not will be able to design programs that render the negative sanction impotent. Until state and local officials see evidence that negative sanctions work and that school choice is directly related to educational achievement, state and local resistance is also likely to remain strong.

The implementation difficulties of the NCLB school choice provisions likely stem from several sources. First, school choice is a flash-point issue in American educational policy. It threatens the interests of powerful actors in the educational system, such as teacher unions and school boards. There is ample evidence that the NCLB transfer provisions have been resisted by powerful local actors. Second, school choice threatens the cherished notion of the common school ideal. NCLB school choice may have had such a limited impact because of strong parental loyalty to neighborhood schools. Third, the potential costs and benefits of school choice are poorly understood. As a consequence, it is not clear what system of regulation and incentives should be employed to achieve the appropriate balance of educational equity and efficiency. This suggests that the NCLB transfer policy has been ineffective simply because it was poorly conceived and implemented. Finally, it could be that the federal role in education policy is too limited to present a credible threat to local entities that ignore legal mandates. Further research is needed to test the tenability of these propositions.

NCLB dramatically alters the balance of governmental authority in education, away from local control and toward state and federal control. While it fails to set national standards and test these standards with a national test, it provides a common set of negative sanctions. Based on local and state resistance to NCLB, the limits of this expanded federal role are being severely tested. The fact that the federal share of education spending was 8 percent in 2003 indicates that the federal role is limited. Furthermore, because this federal share varies across states (from 4% to 18%), the leverage federal power can exert over education at the local level may also vary.[15]

A good indication of the limits of federal power in education, and a substantial limitation of the NCLB Act, is the inability of the federal government to set national standards and hold states accountable to these standards with a national test. The wide fluctuation of standards across the states results in the problem that cities with high proportions of schools in need of improvement are not necessarily those cities with the lowest NAEP scores (Casserly 2004).[16] Therefore, while NCLB is informed by the "liberation" hypothesis, in which students are to be freed from failed schools, the federal government cannot ensure the quality of standards across states, much less the quality of particular schools slated by local districts to accept NCLB transfers. To ensure comparability of educational opportunity across states, federal policymakers should carefully scrutinize state standards. As it stands now, the easiest way to ensure that maximum number of schools in a state meets AYP is to water down state academic standards and tests.

This suggests that the ability of federal authority to enforce compliance is sharply limited. Compliance with NCLB offers a good case study of the difficulty of enforcing federal accountability provisions in a loosely coupled educational system (Meyer and Rowan 1977). It is clear in Chicago at least that local officials are seeking to maintain the charade of minimal compliance with federal mandates in order to continue receiving federal funds.

There is some evidence that the Bush administration is using low transfer rates under NCLB as justification for a nationwide voucher program. Margaret Spellings, Secretary of the U.S. Department of Education, recently touted the Bush administration's $100 million "Opportunity Scholarship" program at a Christian school in New York. She said,[17]

> In some districts, public school choice is non-existent because no public schools are meeting state standards and waiting lists for charter schools are out the door. I've heard stories about parents cramming into rooms like this one to draw numbers to see which students will make it off the waiting list. You shouldn't need to win the lottery to send your child to a high-performing school…. More than 1,700 schools around the country have failed to meet state standards for five or six years in a row. And many of these schools are in districts where public school choice isn't a real option. We're proposing a new $100 million Opportunity Scholarship Fund to help thousands of low-income students in these schools attend the private school of their choice or receive intensive one-on-one tutoring after school or during the summer.

If passed by the Congress, the scholarship program would be offered to students in the restructuring phase of NCLB. The fact that private schools would become options could increase participation rates (Howell 2004), but given the mixed results from voucher experiments and studies of private schools (Neal 1997; Lubienski and Lubienski 2006), substantially improved student outcomes are not likely. In addition, providing vouchers to private schools would raise the question of whether private schools funded in part by public funds should be subject to the same accountability framework as public schools. This is not likely to be something private schools would accept; without this, however, public and private schools would not be on an even playing field, and vouchers could lose support if funds were spent without appropriate evaluation and accountability.

CONCLUSION

NCLB represents a dramatic shift in federal education policy aimed at expanding equal access to educational opportunity for poor students. While the initial ESEA legislation focused on infusing federal funds into poor schools to address resource inequalities, NCLB focuses on the issue of school quality and whether poor children and those from traditionally underserved populations are learning what they need to know to succeed. The Act assumes that schools can spur complete proficiency in all students, including the disadvantaged and those with special educational needs. This, while it may be impossible without dramatic improvements in the early childhood education system, parent participation, and antipoverty programs, is a laudable goal.

Unfortunately, NCLB relies on blunt negative sanctions on low performing schools and must rely on local school districts to implement what is in many districts across the country an unworkable set of transfer policies. Schools are given only one year after being labeled as at-risk of facing the choice sanction to make changes in practice and improve student achievement in all the necessary subgroups. The elaborate formula used to define whether or not a school is meeting AYP labels so many schools as "in need of improvement" that the sanction becomes meaningless.

With the 2007 reauthorization of NCLB fast approaching, more research is urgently needed to test the tenability of these hypotheses with particular attention to whether and how NCLB choice promotes educational opportunity for those who transfer and encourages competition among schools. Research is also needed to determine the extent to which families offered a transfer receive the information and time to make an informed choice, receive opportunities to transfer to qualitatively better schools, and become integrated into the academic and social life of their receiving schools.

Notes

1. A paper prepared for the Sociology of Education Section No Child Left Behind Conference, August 14, 2005. The author gratefully acknowledges support from the Alfred P. Sloan Center on Parents, Children, and Work and the contributions of Jeffrey Henig, Barbara Schneider, and two anonymous reviewers for their comments on a previous draft. The views expressed in this chapter are solely the responsibility of the author. Working paper. Please do not cite without permission. ©Douglas Lee Lauen.

2. Quote is from a White House press conference transcript: http://www.whitehouse.gov/news/releases/2001/01/20010123-2.html (accessed May 26, 2006).

3. Many parents do, however, take school quality into consideration when determining where to live. National estimates suggest that about one-quarter of parents report moving to their current neighborhood for the schools (Wirt et al. 2004).

4. Exceptions to this rule are made if there are too few students in a subgroup to provide statistically reliable results. The minimum subgroup size is determined by each state.

5. Schools that fail to meet AYP for three years in a row must allow students free after-school tutoring. Schools failing to make AYP for five years face school restructuring. School restructuring may include conversion to a charter school or contracting out to a private management organization.

6. Of course, if enough poor students enter a new school, it is possible that the receiving school could become eligible for Title I funds. This would then make the school subject to school choice transfer provisions, however.

7. "School improvement" status is the designation for schools that fail to make AYP in two consecutive years.

8. This 2004 Phi Delta Kappan poll found that 54 percent of parents oppose vouchers to choose private schools at public expense, while 42 percent favor them. There is some evidence, however, that those who favor vouchers care more about this issue than those who oppose them. When asked whether knowing that a candidate for a national office supports vouchers, 43 percent said that this position would make supporting that candidate more likely, while only 37 percent said it would make supporting that candidate less likely (Rose and Gallup 2004).

9. The mayoral takeover occurred just seven years after a radical decentralization reform plan passed the legislature in 1988.

10. Some analysis indicates that this policy has yet to bear fruit. In neighborhoods with the highest levels of gentrification, white enrollment in the school system has decreased rather than increased. As one observer noted, "Yuppies don't have kids, they have dogs" (Weissman 2002).

11. Figures are from multilevel models that control for a number of student- and school-level models. See Lauen (2006, chapter 5) for tables and more details.

12. School productivity is defined as the average student-level residual from the following OLS test score gain model: $ij01ij2ijjjij$, where ij is the 9th grade reading test score (in grade-equivalent units) for student i who attended elementary school j in 8th grade; ij is the ith student's 8th grade reading test score (in grade-equivalent units); ij is a vector of student background characteristics such as poverty, gender, and race/ethnicity; jj is a vector of elementary school fixed effects to control for prior school quality differences; and ij is the student-specific error component of test score gain. High-school k's value added measure, k, is defined as the within-high-school average of the student-level residual: $kikk$. This specification of the value added model was proposed by Cullen et al. (2005). Defining and measuring school productivity is a contentious area of educational policy; further research is needed to determine the validity of this particular specification of the productivity of Chicago's neighborhood high-schools.

13. This figure is the result of author calculations based on data provided by the state. It is not shown in the table because comparable figures are not available for previous years.

14. CPS later offered the unaccounted for slots to students in 15 other of the lowest performing schools. Data on the number of students who applied for transfers from this group are unavailable.

15. Figures are from author calculations of state-level federal funding shares and are based on 2003 Census Bureau statistics. (U.S. Census Bureau 2005)

16. NAEP, or the National Assessment of Educational Progress, is a national test that is "low stakes." In other words, states are not currently held accountable for subpar performance on NAEP.

17. Remarks published online at http://www.ed.gov/news/pressreleases/2006/04/04052006.html (accessed on May 26, 2006)

References

Blau, Peter M. and O. D. Duncan. 1967. *The American occupational structure.* New York: John Wiley.

Brown, Cynthia G. 2004. *Choosing better schools: A report on student transfers under the No Child Left Behind Act*. Technical report. Washington, D.C.: Citizen's Commission on Civil Rights.

Bryk, Anthony, Valerie E. Lee, and Peter B. Holland. 1993. *Catholic schools and the common good*. Cambridge, MA: Harvard University Press.

Bryk, Anthony S., and Barbara L. Schneider, 2002. *Trust in schools: A core resource for improvement*. New York: Russell Sage Foundation.

Casserly, Michael. 2004. Choice and supplemental services in America's great city schools. In *Leaving no child behind? Options for kids in failing schools*, ed. Frederick M. Hess and Chester E. Finn, 191–211. New York: Palgrave Macmillan.

Center for Education Policy. 2005. *From the capital to the classroom: Year 3 of the No Child Left Behind Act*. Technical report. Washington, D.C.: Center for Education Policy.

———. 2006. *From the Capital to the Classroom: Year 4 of the No Child Left Behind Act*. Technical report. Washington, D.C.: Center for Education Policy.

Coleman, J. S. 1992. Some points on choice in education. *Sociology of Education* 65 (4):260–62.

Coleman, James Samuel, and Thomas Hoffer. 1987. *Public and private high schools: the impact of communities*. New York: Basic Books.

Comer, J. P. 1988. Educating poor minority children. *Scientific American* 259 (5):42–48.

Coons, John E., and Stephen D. Sugarman. 1978. *Education by choice: The case for family control*. Berkeley: University of California Press.

Cullen, Julie B, Brian A. Jacob, and Steven Levitt. 2006. *The effect of school choice on participants: Evidence from randomized lotteries*. Econometrica. 74 (5): 1191-1230.

Duchesne, Paul D. 2000. 8,000 passed test after all: Scoring firm blamed for basic-skills test error that kept hundreds from graduating. *Star Tribune (Minneapolis MN)*, July 29, 1A.

Duffrin, Elizabeth. 2001. Why kids flee. *Catalyst Chicago*, December.

Epstein, Noel (ed), *Who's in charge here? The tangled web of school governance and policy.* Denver and Washington, D.C.: Education Commission of the States; Brookings Institution Press.

Friedman, Milton. 1962. *Capitalism and freedom*. Chicago: University of Chicago Press.

Gill, Brian P. 2001. *Rhetoric versus reality: what we know and what we need to know about vouchers and charter schools*. Santa Monica, CA: Rand Education.

Glazerman, Steven. 1998. Determinants and Consequences of Parental School Choice. Doctoral dissertation, University of Chicago.

Grossman, Kate. 2005. Parents declining to send children to top schools: Only a quarter of kids from closing schools apply for open schools. *Chicago Sun-Times*, April 27, News, 34.

Hess, G. Alfred. 1984. Renegotiating a multicultural society—Participation in desegregation planning in Chicago. *Journal of Negro Education* 53 (2):132–46.

Hochschild, Jennifer L., and Nathan B. Scovronick. 2003. *The American dream and the public schools*. New York: Oxford University Press.

Howell, William. 2004. Fumbling for an exit key: Parents, choice, and the future of NCLB. In *Leaving no child behind? Options for kids in failing schools*, ed. Frederick M.Hess and Chester E. Finn, 161–90. New York: Palgrave Macmillan.

Johnson, Dirk. 1987. Chicago leads way in city school woe. The *New York Times*, December 9, 7.

Kim, Jimmy and Gail Sunderman. 2004. *Does NCLB provide good choices for students in low-performing schools*. Technical report. Cambridge, MA: The Civil Rights Project at Harvard University.

Klonsky, Michael. 1995. GOP clears field, Daley runs with the ball. *Catalyst Chicago*, September.

Lareau, Annette. 2000. *Home advantage: Social class and parental intervention in elementary education*. 2nd edition. Lanham, Md: Rowman and Littlefield Publishers.

Lauen, Douglas L. 2006. Opportunity for all? The hidden causes and consequences of school choice in Chicago. PhD diss. Univ. of Chicago.

Levin, Henry. 2004. *Multiple choice questions: The road ahead*.

National Working Commission on choice in K-12 education. 2003. School choice doing it the right way makes a difference (228–255). Tech. rept. Washington, D.C.: Brookings Institution.

Lubienski, Christopher, and Sarah Theule Lubienski. 2006. *Charter, private, public schools and academic achievement: New evidence from NAEP mathematics data*. Technical report. National Center for the Study of Privatization in Education, New York, NY.

MacLeod, Jay. 1995. *Ain't no makin' it: Aspirations and attainment in a low-income neighborhood*. Boulder, CO: Westview Press.

Meyer, J. W. and B. Rowan. 1977. Institutionalized organizations: Formal structure as myth and ceremony. *American Journal of Sociology* 83 (2):340–63.

National Working Commission on Choice in K-12 Education. 2003. *School choice: Doing it the right way makes a difference*. Technical report. Washington, D.C.: Brookings Institution.

Neal, Derek. 1997. The effects of Catholic schooling on educational achievement. *Journal of Labor Economics* 15:98–123.

Oakes, Jeannie. 1985. *Keeping track: How schools structure inequality*. New Haven, CT: Yale University Press.

Peterson, Paul E. 1976. *School politics, Chicago style*. Chicago: University of Chicago Press.

Roderick, Melissa, Anthony S. Bryk, Brian A. Jacob, John Q. Easton, and Elaine Allensworth. 1999. *Ending social promotion*. Technical report. Chicago: Consortium on Chicago Schools Research.

Rose, Lowell C., and Alec M. Gallup. 2004. The 36th annual phi delta kappa/Gallup poll of the public's attitudes toward the public schools. *Phi Delta Kappa* 86 (1): 41–52.

Rosenbaum, James E. 1976. *Making inequality:The hidden curriculum of high-school tracking*. New York: Wiley.

Rossi, Rosalind. 2003a. Feds: City falling short of school transfer goals. *Chicago Sun-Times*, October 27, News Special Edition, 10.

———. 2003b. To Duncan, no child left behind law is "burdensome" and "impractical." *Chicago Sun-Times*, August 29, News Special Edition, 12.

———. Fran Spielman, 2002. Daley protests student transfers. *Chicago Sun-Times*, July 17, News Special Edition, 5.

Saporito, Salvatore, and Lareau, Annette. 1999. School selection as a process: The multiple dimensions of race in framing educational choice. *Social Problems*, 46(3), 418–439.

Schneider, Mark, and Buckley, Jack. 2002. What Do Parents Want From Schools? Evidence From the Internet. *Educational Evaluation and Policy Analysis*, 24(2), 133–44.

Turner, R. H. 1960. Sponsored and contest mobility and the school-system. *American Sociological Review* 25 (6):855–67.

U.S. Census Bureau. 2005. *Public education finances, 2003*. Technical report. Washington, D.C.: U.S. Census Bureau.

U.S. Department of Education. 2004. *Public school choice: Non-regulatory guidance*. Washington, D.C.: U.S. Department of Education.

U.S. Government Accountability Office. 2004. *No Child Left Behind Act: Education needs to provide additional technical assistance and conduct implementation studies for school choice provision: Report to Secretary of Education*. Washington, D.C.: U.S. Government Accountability Office.

Weissman, Dan. 2002. Gentrifiers slow to buy CPS. *Catalyst Chicago*, February.

West, Martin R., and Paul E. Peterson. 2006. The efficacy of choice threats within school accountability systems: Results from legislatively induced experiments. *The Economic Journal*, 116(March): C46–C62.

Wirt, J., Choy, S, Rooney, P, Provasnik, S., Sen, A., and R. Tobin, R. 2004. *The condition of education 2004*. Washington, D.C: U.S. Department of Education.

Wolf, Patrick, Babette Butmann, Michael Puma, and Marsha Silverberg. 2006. *Evaluation of the DC opportunity scholarship program: Second year report on participation*. Washington, D.C.: U.S. Government Printing Office. U.S. Department of Education, Institute of Education Sciences.

11

When School Choice Leaves Many Children Behind

Implications for NCLB from the Charlotte–Mecklenburg Schools

Roslyn Arlin Mickelson and Stephanie Southworth

The No Child Left Behind (NCLB) Act seeks to enhance equality of educational opportunity, close achievement gaps, and improve academic achievement through market inspired reforms. Among its many provisions, NCLB gives families the opportunity to transfer their children from low-performing to high-performing schools by giving them an opt-out choice.[1] Advocates of school choice consider a student's opportunity to transfer to be a central component of equality of educational opportunity. Furthermore, the choice to transfer from a low-performing school will ultimately improve the quality of instruction and student outcomes for those remaining in the underperforming schools through the discipline of market forces (Chubb and Moe 1991; Godwin and Kamerer 2002; Peterson and Hassel 1998).[2] Market mechanisms will stimulate schools to improve and attract the "clientele" they need to survive.

NCLB is emblematic of the key principles found in the contemporary market-inspired school reform agenda. These principles include standards, accountability, and choice. Under NCLB, for the first time the federal government has established specific national standards for schools and their students, and sanctions for not meeting these standards. Sanctions range from labeling a school as low performing to withholding federal aid to states where schools fail to meet the law's goals. One key provision holds that after two consecutive years in a low-performing school, students are eligible to transfer to a public school of their choice in either their own district or a neighboring district (if that district agrees to take them). The opt-out provision is the focus of this chapter.

This chapter explores whether NCLB's choice option facilitates or hinders the realization of the law's equity and excellence goals.Drawing from a case study of school reform in Charlotte, North Carolina, this chapter examines early experiences with transfer options in the Charlotte-Mecklenburg School (CMS) district. The experiences of CMS illustrate how larger social, economic, and political contexts shape and constrain the implementation of standards-based reforms like NCLB in general and, in particular, the transfer option's capacity to improve academic achievement and enhance educational equity.

NCLB AND THE CHOICE THEORY OF SCHOOL IMPROVEMENT

The formal goals of NCLB are to improve the overall quality of education, to provide equality of educational opportunity to all students, and to eliminate group differences in educational outcomes. Advocates of NCLB believe its requirements for rigorous curricula, teaching, and learning standards and accountability strike the right balance of incentives and sanctions (Ali 2004; Taylor 2003). Some educators and civil rights advocates support NCLB because they view it as a federal policy that expresses the moral and legal imperative to provide equality of educational opportunity to all youth.

A general critique of NCLB notes that the legislation fails to take into account how the social, political, and economic sources of unequal educational achievement that lie beyond the school's walls affect what goes on within them. Acknowledging that contextual factors contribute to unequal educational achievement is not equivalent to excusing unequal school-related opportunities to learn. This critique is especially relevant to schools in rural areas and central urban communities where the material realities of daily life make teaching and learning extremely difficult.

NCLB's opt-out provision is also a source of concern to many observers. Districts reluctant to fully implement transfer policies could limit transfers to certain schools in the district, limit the number of spaces available, delay notification to parents, or provide tepid announcements without affirmative outreach to parents of eligible students. In addition, a number of factors could prevent parents from transferring their children from low-performing to high-performing schools and thus limit NCLB's expected utility as a vehicle for enhancing equality of educational opportunity or school improvement.

STANDARDS AND ACCOUNTABILITY IN NORTH CAROLINA

Several state governments instituted standards and accountability reforms for K–12 and higher education years before NCLB required all states receiving federal aid to do so. Under the leadership of Governor Jim Hunt, North Carolina became one of the first of these early states. The centerpiece of North Carolina's own public education restructuring efforts was its 1996 school-based management and accountability program known as the New ABCs of Public Education framework (North Carolina 2004b). In fact, much of NCLB's standards-based reforms are foreshadowed in North Carolina's reforms.

The ABC framework established growth and performance standards for grades K–8 beginning in 1996. Students in grades 3 through 8 are assessed by annual end-of-grade (EOG) tests in reading, mathematics, and writing. High-school students are tested in five mandated subjects. Their assessments are called end-of-course (EOC) tests. EOG and EOC tests are aligned with the state's curricular standards in the tested subjects. Students' scores on EOG and EOC tests are rated as 4 if they exceed proficiency, 3 if they are proficient, 2 if their test performance is below proficiency, and 1 for nonproficient performance (North Carolina 2004b).

Schools with students who meet growth standards are rewarded with accolades from the state and monetary bonuses for their staff. Schools failing to meet growth and performance standards receive help from assistance teams sent by the North Carolina Department of Public Instruction (NCDPI). Ultimately, schools that do not improve will be taken over by the state. School results are sent home for parents, and school by school ABC results are reported to the public in *A Report Card for the ABCs of Public Education* made available on the NCDPI's website. After two consecutive years of low performances, the ABC Framework permits parents to transfer their children to a high-performing school from a low-performing one.

After the passage of NCLB in 2002, several components of the ABC Plan were modified or added to conform to the federal law. These two assessments and standards programs remain complementary but not identical. For instance, the ABC rating can conflict with NCLB labels. Elementary and middle school EOG tests in reading and mathematics are used for both NCLB and ABCs rating, but results are calculated differently. NCLB looks at performance at the school level disaggregated by group; the ABC Plan assesses schoolwide performance averages in addition to growth scores. Therefore, it is possible for a school to meet its ABC goals but fail to make AYP according to NCLB's standards (Helms 2004b).[3]

DESEGREGATION, RESEGREGATION, AND CHOICE IN CMS

Any assessment of Charlotte-Mecklenburg's experiences with standards-based reforms, testing, accountability, school choice, and opting out of low-performing schools must consider the district's past and present struggles to provide equality of educational opportunity in the shadows of its Jim Crow educational legacy. In 1971 the U.S. Supreme Court upheld Judge James McMillan's orders to desegregate CMS using mandatory intradistrict busing along with other remedies (*Swann v. Charlotte-Mecklenburg Schools*, 1971). From roughly 1974 to 1992, CMS used mandatory busing to achieve racial balance in almost every school (S. S. Smith 2004). As a result of the mandatory busing, almost all students in CMS attended a racially desegregated school during some portion of their academic careers, and a majority of both whites and blacks spent most of their education in desegregated schools (Mickelson 2001).

Pressure to End Desegregation

The broad social and political coalition supporting desegregation began to weaken by the late 1980s (Mickelson and Ray 1994). Most of the mandatory busing plan was dismantled in 1992. It was replaced with voluntary desegregation strategies, the most prominent of which was a controlled-choice system of magnet schools (Charlotte-Mecklenburg Schools 1992). For its first five years, the magnet program experienced mixed success in voluntarily desegregating the district. The magnet plan's race-sensitive guidelines for admissions became the basis of a lawsuit filed by white suburban parents who challenged the constitutionality of the entire desegregation plan (*Capacchione et al. v. Charlotte-Mecklenburg School* 1999). In 1999 a judge declared CMS unitary, and after several years of appeals, the U.S. Supreme Court refused to review the lower court's unitary rulings (*Capacchione et al. v. Charlotte-Mecklenburg Board of Education* 2002).

The 2001 Family Choice Plan

In April 2001, a year before the U.S. Supreme Court's final disposition of the Charlotte desegregation case, CMS adopted a race-neutral pupil assignment plan built around neighborhood schools, beginning in the 2002–3 school year (CMS 2001a). Named the Family Choice Plan, this policy essentially was a neighborhood schools assignment plan with a race-neutral choice option among nearby magnet schools. Provisions offered in the Family Choice Plan included: (1) the choice between a guaranteed seat in a neighborhood school or enrollment in a magnet school with an open seat; (2) granted options to transfer to high-performing schools to students attending schools with concentrations of poor-performing or low-income students; and (3) maximum utilization of all school seat capacities (Helms 2003a, 2003b).

Critics of the Family Choice Plan saw a number of potential problems with it. First, due to neighborhood racial and social class homogeneity, the Plan would likely result in resegregation of many more CMS schools.[4] Second, poor, low-performing students would likely be concentrated in schools segregated by race and social class, making it even more difficult to educate them (Natriello 1999). Third, because sites for the existing schools were chosen to meet the needs of the

30-year-old desegregation plan, the guarantee of a seat in a neighborhood school would almost certainly lead to overcapacity in the suburbs and undercapacity in the central city. Fourth, the unbalanced distribution of highly qualified teachers in the schools and other key resources would privilege middle-class white suburban students and disadvantage poor and minority students who lived in the center city. Fifth, together such conditions would militate against providing equitable, high-quality opportunities to learn for all children in CMS and thus violate the school board's promise to ensure equity after the Family Choice Plan was implemented.

In response to the serious likelihood that the Family Choice Plan could undermine the district's ability to provide a quality education to all students, the school board adopted an Equity Plan (CMS 2001b). The Equity Plan's core provisions included identification of high-poverty, low-performing schools as "Equity Plus II" schools (EPII). EPII schools were guaranteed smaller teacher–student ratios, teachers in them were to be paid a premium of several thousand dollars per year above their base salary, and teachers were to receive tuition for advanced degrees. EPII schools were promised bond funds for renovations and funds for additional learning equipment and supplies. The final piece of the Equity Plan was the opportunity for parents to opt-out of EPII schools and enroll their children in a higher performing school if they so chose.

In fall 2002 a newly unitary CMS populated its schools based on its neighborhood school-based Family Choice assignment plan. The same year, the President signed NCLB into law. By 2004 CMS students enrolled in low-performing schools were guaranteed the choice to transfer to high-performing schools by CMS's Equity Plan, by North Carolina's ABCs of Public Education Policy, and by the federal government's No Child Left Behind law.

RESEARCH QUESTIONS

The implementation of the transfer option in CMS provides an opportunity to examine initial equity and quality effects of the opt-out provisions found in CMS's Equity Plan, the state of North Carolina ABC's, and the federal No Child Left Behind Act. Specifically, this chapter seeks to answer the following questions:

1. Are there historical legacies or material constraints that affect the implementation of transfer provisions?
2. Do eligible CMS families choose to opt-out of low-performing schools?
3. Is there evidence from CMS that opting-out of a low-performing school improves educational equity (measured by less school poverty, more resources, less segregation, and higher school performance)?
4. What does the early CMS experience with opting-out suggest about

NCLB's transfer provisions potential for enhancing educational equity and improving opportunities to learn for all children?

DATA AND METHODS

This chapter's data come from a multimethod, longitudinal case study of school reform in the Charlotte-Mecklenburg Schools conducted since 1987 by Mickelson and her colleagues. This phase of the case study examines CMS's record of equity and excellence in the post-*Swann* era. The authors collected and analyzed official documents and public use electronic data provided by CMS and the North Carolina Department of Public Instruction (NCDPI).

FINDINGS

Unitary Status, Choice, and Resegregation

CMS became noticeably more resegregated during the first year of the Family Choice Plan's operation, 2002–3. To be sure, CMS had drifted toward resegregation during the 1990s; however, unitary status and the Family Choice Plan rapidly accelerated that process. Table 11.1 presents the changing demographics and racial balance of CMS schools during the first and second years of postunitary status. An examination of the demographic shifts between 2001 and 2002 (the last year CMS operated under court-mandated desegregation) and 2003 and 2004 (the second year as a unitary district) suggests the rapid pace of resegregation. Between the 2001–2 and the 2003–4 school years, 22.6 percent fewer elementary schools, 7.4 percent fewer middle schools, and 20.6 percent fewer high schools were racially balanced; 9 percent more elementary schools, 3 percent more middle schools, and 16.6 percent more high schools were racially identifiable as black; 11.6 percent more elementary schools, 4.5 percent more middle schools, and 4 percent more high schools were racially identifiable as white.[5]

Table 11.1 Changes in CMS racial demographics by school level, 2001–2 (prior to unitary status) through 2003–4 (Two years postunitary status)*

% Change from 2001–2 ... through 2003–4	Elementary	Middle	High
Racially balanced	−22.6	−7.4	−20.6
Racially identifiable black	+9.0	+3.0	+16.6
Racially identifiable white	+11.6	+4.5	+4.0

* Based on ± 15 percent CMS black population for each year.
Source:. Charlotte-Mecklenburg Schools, Class Counts, May 2002; Charlotte-Mecklenburg Schools, Monthly Membership at End of Month One, September 17, 2002; September 18, 2003.

Achievement and Concentrated Poverty

Improved school achievement is, of course, a critical measure of school success according to NCLB. The resegregation of CMS is relevant because of the correlations among high concentrations of poverty in schools with large numbers of ethnic minority youth and low achievement on standardized tests. The race-neutral pupil assignment plan created scores of schools where it was more difficult to achieve AYP due to the high concentrations of poor students in the schools. And as predicted by CMS's own consultant (Natriello 1999), the achievement levels of all CMS students were affected by the mean socioeconomic status of the schools they attended. In the case of students who attended schools with concentrated poverty, achievement was adversely affected even after controlling for students' race and their social class backgrounds. The opposite relationship was true as well; attending a low-poverty school positively affected achievement irrespective of students' race and their own social class background.[6]

Table 11.2 shows the percentage of CMS elementary and middle school students who passed their North Carolina EOG (reading and math composite scores for grades 3 through 8), and high-school students who passed their EOC tests (composites of history, algebra, and English) with either a ranking of 3 (proficient) or 4 (highly proficient) for 2002–3 and 2003–4. Table 11.2 presents disaggregated scores by the poverty level of the school, the students' own SES, and their race. The results illustrate the well-known association between school SES, student characteristics such as race and SES, and academic outcomes. Table 11.2 shows that low-income students and black students are less likely than more prosperous and white students to receive a proficient score on their standardized tests. In both years, the scores also reflect the effects of school socioeconomic status on achievement: irrespective of an individual student's racial background and family income, on average, students attending high-poverty schools perform worse than otherwise similar students attending low-poverty schools.

Sociologists have long known that both the student's own socioeconomic status and the mean SES of the school affect school processes and outcomes. Rumberger and Palardy (2005) used NAEP data to demonstrate that in southern schools, the mean SES of the school is far more powerful than family SES in predicting achievement. The relationship between schools with concentrated poverty and low performance is a central rationale for CMS's Equity Plan's opt-out provisions. Yet what if students who wish to opt out of their low-performing school cannot do so because there are no seats available to them in more successful schools? The chapter now turns to this dilemma.

Over- and Underutilization of School Facilities

When CMS began operating its Family Choice Plan in 2002–3, the school system's extant schools—built over 30 years in certain locations consistent with

Table 11.2 Percent passing North Carolina statewide tests by school poverty level, student poverty, and student race, 2002–3 (Year 1 unitary status) and 2003–4 (Year 2 unitary status)†

| Student group | % Passing by school poverty level | | | | | |
| | High | | Moderate | | Low | |
	2003	2004	2003	2004	2003	2004
Elementary schools						
All students	62	66	77	84	91	93
Low income	60	63	65	71	69	72
Not low Income	77	82	89	90	94	95
Black	60	64	70	74	74	77
White	76	79	90	92	94	94
Hispanic	59	69	69	78	75	82
Middle schools						
All students	54	55	70	73	88	91
Low income	50	51	55	59	64	74
Not low Income	69	72	84	86	93	94
Black	60	52	70	63	74	74
White	74	77	88	88	93	94
Hispanic	55	56	60	67	82	84
High schools						
All students	23	28	46	48	71	72
Low income	21	24	27	33	34	35
Not low Income	27	34	56	56	76	78
Black	22	25	36	37	39	42
White	62	51	70	69	82	83
Hispanic	25	26	48	48	61	60

Elementary and Middle School Poverty Formula: ≥ 75% High-; 74–26% Moderate; ≤ 25% Low
High-school formula: ≥ 55% High; 54–26% Moderate; ≤ 25% Low
† Elementary and Middle School Scores are math and language composites; High school scores are Algebra, English, and History composites
Source: NC DPI End-of-Grade Test Results 2002–3, 2003–4

the demands of the ongoing desegregation plan—became the building blocks for the new neighborhood school-based Family Choice Plan. In other words, the school system's physical capacity was already cast in concrete! Nevertheless, the extant seating capacities, library, cafeteria, and gymnasium spaces were called upon to accommodate the students guaranteed the option of attending their neighborhood schools. Certainly, new schools would be built once bonds were passed by voters, land was purchased, and contractors hired. Meanwhile, explosive growth in suburban neighborhoods meant that because the Family

Choice Plan guaranteed seats to families who chose their neighborhood schools, suburban schools became filled well over capacity, leaving no seats for transfer students. At the same time, many inner city neighborhood schools became underutilized.

Despite overcapacity problems, during the Family Choice Plan's first year of operation (2002–3), the majority of families (85%) received their first or second choice of schools. Among families who did not, however, blacks were the most likely not to receive any of their three choices, resulting in these children attending their unselected neighborhood school. Black families were also the least likely ethnic group to name their neighborhood school as one of their choices (Helms 2002). In the second year of the choice plan's operation, the overutilization in some suburban schools was so extreme that the school district capped their enrollment. This action further blocked access to the high-performing suburban schools for those families wishing to opt out of their own low-performing/high-poverty schools. In the third year of the plan's operation, almost 60 percent of white students indicated their neighborhood school was their top choice, while about one in four black students made the same decision (Smolowitz 2005).

Under- and overutilization patterns are related to a given school's racial and socioeconomic composition. As Table 11.3 indicates, in the 2002–3 academic year, all but one of the 39 underutilized schools were racially imbalanced in terms of minority students. (Here we calculated imbalance summing black, Asian, Hispanic, and other ethnic minority students into one "minority" category.) Of the 33 overutilized schools, 6 were racially identifiable minority, 13 were racially balanced, and 14 were racially identifiable white.

In the second year of the choice plan (2003–4) underutilization was less of a problem, but overutilization remained a critical one even though several new elementary schools were opened in the suburbs. Ironically, as new schools opened in suburban areas, the problem of elementary school overutilization became relatively more pressing in high—poverty areas: two-thirds of the overutilized elementary schools are EPII schools. Table 11.3 indicates that in the second year of the choice plan all six of the underutilized elementary schools, one of the two middle schools, and all six of the underutilized high schools were racially identifiable minority. With one exception, all of the underutilized schools have EPII status. Overutilized schools rarely have EPII status. The bottom line is clear—opting-out provisions failed to provide either the promised equity or the excellence safety valves to CMS students in low-performing schools because no seats were available to them in high-performing schools.

Do Parents Utilize Their Choice-Out Option?

The theoretical rationale for offering transfer options to parents whose children attend low- performing schools is twofold: an option to transfer to a better school

Table 11.3 Utilization of seat capacity by school level, racial composition of student population, and equity plus status, CMS 2002–3 to 2003–4

2002–2003	RIM	RB	RIW	RIM	RB	RIW	RIM	RB	RIW
Underutilization of capacity									
Level	Elementary			Middle school			High school		
Range	(52% –79%)			(57% –79%)			(76% –89%)		
N	25	1	0	8	0	0	5	0	0
N Equity Plus	24	0	0	8	0	0	5	0	0
Overutilization of capacity									
Level	Elementary			Middle school			High school		
Range	(102% –139%)			(102%–111%)			(116%–131%)		
N	3	7	3	0	3	5	3	3	6
N Equity Plus	0	0	0	0	0	0	0	0	0
2003–2004	RIM	RB	RIW	RIM	RB	RIW	RIM	RB	RIW
Underutilization of capacity									
Level	Elementary			Middle school			High school		
Range	(62%–79%)			(61% –80%)			(72%–88%)		
N	6	0	0	1	1	0	6	0	0
N Equity Plus	2	0	0	1	0	0	6	0	0
Overutilization of capacity									
Level	Elementary			Middle school			High school		
Range	(102%–139%)			(102%–111 %)			(116%–131%)		
N	33	14	16	6	4	4	3	5	2
N Equity Plus	22	0	0	0	0	0	0	0	0

RIM = racially isolated minority
RB = racially balanced
RIW = racially isolated white
Source: CMS (2002a)

fosters greater educational equity and excellence; and low-performing schools will be galvanized to improve in order to keep their student clientele. In the second year of the CMS Equity Plan's operation (2003–4), the opt-out option was available to students attending low-performing schools. Yet, very few parents of the 9,600 eligible students even inquired about the program as of January 2003, the end of the application period for the 2003–4 school year (Educate! 2003). Eighteen months later in 2004, fully 92 percent of the eligible families did not exercise their choice to exit from the low-performing schools: only 658 (8%) of the 8,200 eligible students accepted last minute transfers to new schools (Helms 2004c; Smolowitz 2004).

What kinds of schools were chosen by families who transferred their children out of low-performing schools? Only a handful of the transferring students gained seats in the top-performing schools, many of whose seat capacities were capped due to their extreme enrollment. Of the 658 students who opted-out of their low-performing schools, a majority transferred to schools with modestly better records of test performance. A number of the schools they chose were magnet programs. But a substantial minority of students transferred to other low-performing schools (Smolowitz 2004).

It is not clear why only 8 percent of eligible families availed themselves of their choice to opt-out of a low-performing school. Several potential explanations include the well-publicized overcapacity problems at the high-performing schools. Another possible reason is that the parents of students attending high-poverty schools tend to be undereducated or non-English speaking adults who are the least likely to become involved in their children's education without outreach efforts (Ream 2005). Lack of timely information was also a problem. In January 2003, CMS did not provide sufficient targeted information about transfer options to parents of students who were qualified under North Carolina's ABC plan (Helms 2003b). The following year, students who were eligible to transfer under NCLB received the necessary information about their options in August just days prior to the opening of the 2004–5 school year (Smolowitz 2004).

The End of School Choice in CMS

By the fall of 2005, CMS's school board recognized that, in fact, there was very little choice for anyone in Charlotte. CMS's Family Choice Assignment Plan was renamed the Student Assignment Plan before its second anniversary of operation (Helms 2004a) and by the fall of 2005 the board formally dropped choice as an alternative. Parents who wanted their children to go to a school other than their home school had to request an application and hope that their child was high on the list. The vast majority of students attend their neighborhood school. There was some choice for those who competed for the limited number of seats in magnet schools, but for most students, there was no real choice. The extensive overcrowding in high-performing suburban schools led to so few seats being available for transferring students, the Family Choice Plan was eliminated to conform with reality.

DISCUSSION

The reality with which CMS had to conform was the fact that school choice never was an equity option for CMS students—not in 1992 when the magnet school plan replaced mandatory busing and not in 2002 when the Family Choice Plan replaced the *Swann* court order as the basis for school assignments. This chapter has examined the implementation of the option to transfer from low- to high-performing schools in CMS. This choice option was instituted in a school system undergoing massive restructuring in the wake of 30 years of court mandated desegregation. The consequences of ending desegregation and switching to a neighborhood school-based assignment plan generated the contentious context in which the transfer option was implemented.

In this discussion, we return to the questions that shaped this chapter. We first asked what, if anything, the case study of CMS suggests about the role of contextual factors in the successful implementation of school reform policy. The historic legacy of CMS's struggle for school desegregation, the desegregation plan's domination of the community's politics for three decades—especially how the plan influenced where schools were built—the political and legal struggles that culminated in the 2002 unitary decision, all left many people emotionally bruised, embittered, and distrustful of people from different racial and social class backgrounds and highly skeptical of school reforms. At the same time, the changing nature of the county's economy, the growth of, and demographic shifts in its population, and the suburbanization that followed these changes meant that CMS's return to neighborhood schools led to resegregation and over- and underutilization of school capacity. These factors became part of a volatile and complicated social and political context that made the implementation of the transfer policy an impractical and untenable strategy to generate educational equity and improved achievement.

While in theory, students in high-poverty, low-performing schools could transfer to better ones, in reality, the CMS's extant infrastructure could not sustain the numbers of transferring students required to make the opt-out provisions a genuine tool of educational equity or school improvement. Students in low-performing schools were compelled to stay there. Ironically, at the same time that transferring out became essentially an empty promise in CMS, the other elements of the Equity Plan—additional resources for high-poverty schools—disappeared when a fiscally conservative Republican majority replaced the Democratic majority on the County Commission. With the ascension of the Republican majority, cuts in CMS's budget precluded funding for the Equity Plan (C. Smith 2002; White 2003).

Our second and third questions concern whether eligible families opted-out of low performing schools and transferred their children to higher performing ones. Very little information is available about the results of the transfer option. The low transfer rates in both the first and second years the option was available suggest that the vast majority of eligible students remained in their low-performing schools. Available evidence from CMS indicates that parents do not always transfer their children to better performing schools. We do not know the reasons for this fact. But at a minimum, parents' choices appear to undercut the rationale for utilizing the transfer option as an equity safety value or as a tool for overall school improvement. Future research will shed light on this question as well.

Finally, we asked what the CMS experience suggests about the transfer option as a tool for fostering greater educational equity and excellence. Our findings suggest it has not had a positive effect on either educational excellence or equity for students in low performing schools. From a policy perspective, the CMS experience suggests that NCLB's transfer provision is unlikely to operate as its designers envisioned. Even if all parents of eligible students exercised their rights to transfer their children, there are simply not enough seats in higher-performing schools to accommodate the eligible students. Without a seat in better school, neither the hypothesized school improvement nor educational equity dynamic of NCLB will operate as planned. The implications of CMS's experiences point to the importance of considering local conditions, contexts, and histories for likely consequences—intended and unintended—of federal education policies. From a substantive perspective, given what we know about the restricted opportunities to learn in high-poverty schools, and the importance of school SES for achievement it is unlikely that the mere existence of NCLB's transfer option will do anything to improve the opportunities to learn for students who remain in their underperforming schools.

CMS's political and legal struggles that culminated in the 2002 unitary decision, ending 31 years of court ordered desegregation, left many citizens distrustful of people from different racial and social class backgrounds and highly skeptical of school reforms. At the same time, suburban population growth and demographic shifts meant that CMS's return to neighborhood schools hastened resegregation and triggered the school capacity over- and underutilization crises.

In local school districts across the United States, political, social, and demographic factors like those that complicated CMS's transfer policy will make the NCLB transfer option an untenable strategy to enhance educational equity and improve achievement. The case study of CMS's experiences with the transfer option suggests how race, socioeconomic status, school quality, and choice intersect in ways that disadvantage poor children and students of color. NCLB's transfer provision has not facilitated greater educational excellence or equity in CMS. The vast majority of the CMS students in low-performing schools will be there next year. NCLB's opt-out provision has left them behind.

Notes

1. This chapter is a revised and updated version of the authors' article, "When opting-out is not a choice: Implications for NCLB from Charlotte, North Carolina." *Equity and Excellence in Education* 38:1–15, 2005. The research reported in this article was supported by grants to the first author from the Ford Foundation (985-1336 and 1000-1430) and from the National Science Foundation (RED-9550763 and REC-0208290).
2. We interchangeably use the concepts of choosing to opt-out and transfer out of low-performing schools.

3. Discrepancies between state and NCLB proficiency results occur elsewhere, for example Florida (Pinzur 2003).
4. As of 2001 when the school board made this decision, CMS was still operating under the *Swann* court order to desegregate and the majority of CMS schools were still desegregated, although each year since 1992 more schools were becoming racially isolated. Critics saw the school board's decision to craft the 2001 Family Choice Plan based on neighborhood schools as an abdication of its responsibility to desegregate the schools while still under a court mandate to do so. Proponents of the Family Choice Plan viewed the school board's decision as appropriate for the political climate.
5. Table 11.1 shows the effects of the return to neighborhood schools on racial balance soon after CMS became unitary in 2002. We do not show the racial composition of schools and levels of resegregation for the most recent years because: (a). the demographics of the district have changed rapidly as the Hispanic and Asian populations have grown and the white population has decreased, thereby making a calculation of racial balance and imbalance complicated, and (b) several new schools have opened as racially imbalanced white because they were built in disproportionately white areas where there has been tremendous overcapacity problems.Both reasons make a comparison of school segregation levels in 2002 with levels in 2007 difficult to interpret.
6. Using 1997 CMS survey data, Mickelson (2001) demonstrated that even after controlling for school effects and students' family background, prior achievement, peer academic orientation, effort, race, and gender, attending segregated minority elementary schools negatively affected. grades and test scores and secondary school track placements.

References

Ali, R. 2004. Keynote remarks to sociology of education section No Child Left Behind Conference. Meetings of the American Sociological Association. San Francisco, CA, August.
Capacchione et al. v. Charlotte-Mecklenburg Schools. 1999. 57 F. Supp.2d 228 (W.D.N.C.).
———. 2002. U.S. 122 S. Ct. 1537, 152 L.Ed.2d 465.
Charlotte-Mecklenburg Schools. 1970–99. Monthly reports. Author.
———. 1992. Minutes of the school board meeting, March 31. Charlotte-Mecklenburg, NC: Author.
———. 1996–2002b. *Class counts.* Charlotte-Mecklenburg, NC: Author.
———. 2001a. *Board Resolution 2001,* April 3. http://www.cms.k12.nc.us/studentassignment/board-resolution2001.asp (accessed May 31, 2002).
———. 2001b. *Board resolution 2002–2003*, July 31. http://www.cms.k12.nc.us/studentassignment/boardresolution02-03.asp (accessed May 31, 2002).
———. 2001c. *2002–2003 student assignment plan*, July 30. Charlotte-Mecklenburg, NC: Author.
———. 2002a. *Monthly membership reports.* 2001–2004. Charlotte-Mecklenburg, NC: Author.
———. 2002b. *Teacher statistics as of May 22, 2002.* Charlotte-Mecklenburg, NC: Author.
———. 2006. *CMS fast facts.* Charlotte-Mecklenburg, NC: Author.
Chubb, J. E., and T. M. Moe. 1990. *Politics, markets, and American schools.* Washington, D.C.: Brookings Institution.
Educate! 2003. CMS elementary schools by race and SES concentration, 2003–2004. *Choices* March 6:1.
Godwin, R. K., and F. Kemerer. 2002. *School choice tradeoffs. Liberty, equity, and diversity.* Austin: University of Texas Press.
Helms, A. D. 2002. Blacks less likely to get choice of schools. *Charlotte Observer*, March 20, 1A.
———. 2003a. Parents' choice may clinch schools' fate. *Charlotte Observer*, January 5, 4A.
———. 2003b. Parents in dark on "out" choice. *Charlotte Observer*, January 28, 1B.
———. 2003c. In-demand schools shut choice door. *Charlotte Observer*, March 24, 1A.
———. 2004a. Becoats resigns from CMS. *Charlotte Observer*, January 29, 1B.
———. 2004b. What's working and what's not. *Charlotte Observer*, July 21, 4M–7M.
———. 2004c. Only 658 of 8,200 take CMS transfer. *Charlotte Observer*, August 24, 3B.
Mickelson, R. A. 2001. Subverting *Swann*: First- and second-generation segregation in the Charlotte-Mecklenburg Schools. *American Educational Research Journal* 38 (2):215–52.

———. C. A. Ray. 1994. Fear of falling from grace: The middle class, downward mobility, and school desegregation. *Research in Sociology of Education and Socialization* 10: 207–38.

Natriello, G. 1999. Consultant remarks to the Charlotte-Mecklenburg school board. September 28.

No Child Left Behind Act of 2001. (2002). Pub. L. No.107-110, 115 Stat.1425, 20 U.S.C. §§6301 et seq.

North Carolina Department of Public Instruction (NCDPI). 2004a. *Results of the 2002–2003 and 2003-2004 EOG and EOC tests*. http://disag.ncpublicschols.org/ (accessed January. 25, 2005).

North Carolina Department of Public Instruction (NCDPI). 2004. *Evolution of the ABCs.* Raleigh, NC: Division of Accountability Services.

Peterson, P. E., and B. C. Hassel. 1998. *Learning from school choice.* Washington, D.C.: Brookings Institution.

Pinzur, M. 2003. State schools fail to meet new federal test standards: Federal, state results differ. *Miami Herald,* August 8.

Ream, Robert. 2005. *Uprooting children. Mobility, social capital, and Mexican American underachievement.* New York:. LFB.

Rumberger, R., and J. Palardy. 2005. Does resegregation matter? The impact of social composition on academic achievement in southern high schools. In *School resegregation: Must the South turn back?* ed. J. C. Boger and G. Orfield, Chapel Hill: University of North Carolina Press.

Smith, C. 2002. With less state money on way, CMS looks for cuts. *Charlotte Observer,* October 3, 4B.

Smith, S. S. 2004. *Boom for whom? Education, desegregation, and development in Charlotte.* Albany: State University of New York Press.

Smolowitz, P. 2004. Last minute transfers leave schools in limbo *Charlotte Observer,* September 10, 7B.

———. 2005. 71% of students in assignment lottery get 1st choice. *Charlotte Observer,* March 11, 8A.

Swann v. Charlotte-Mecklenburg. 1971. *402 U.S. 1*

Taylor, W. 2003. Title I as an instrument for achieving desegregation and equal educational opportunity. *North Carolina Law Review* 81:1751.

White, H. L. 2003. CMS's uphill funding battle. *The Charlotte Post,* March 20, 1A.

12

Nonpromotional School Change and the Achievement of Texas Students

Possible Public School Choice Outcomes under NCLB

A. Gary Dworkin and Jon Lorence

Under the No Child Left Behind Act of 2001, schools that repeatedly fail to meet AYP goals are subject to severe consequences, including redirection of some of their Title I funds for the hiring of outside consultants, the removal of staff, and reorganization as a charter school. After two years of failure to meet adequate yearly progress (AYP) schools are required to offer public school choice to the parents of their students. The student would be able to take the tax dollars and apply them to enrollment in any school that was meeting its AYP goals. The intended consequence of the school choice component of the law is to provide students in low-performing schools, those identified under NCLB as "in need of improvement" (INOI), with an improved opportunity to learn and consequently perform better on the state-mandated, standardized tests. Using longitudinal, statewide, student-level data from Texas, we ask whether students who transfer from failing schools to higher-performing schools subsequently improve their test scores. We also investigate whether schools that exceed their AYP goals affect the performance of the transferring students.

There are several underlying assumptions of the school choice policy of NCLB. First, it is assumed that students will perform significantly better if they transfer from an INOI school to one that meets its AYP goals. Second, the policy rests on the assumption that higher-performing schools meet their AYP goals because they have teachers who are both more competent and more motivated to work diligently to help their students meet high academic standards. Furthermore, there is an assumption that, despite its voluntary nature, higher-performing schools will welcome students from INOI schools without reservations about how such children's performances might affect the AYP of the receiving school.

However, there are plausible rival explanations for the difference in the achievement of INOI schools and the schools that meet their AYP goals. There could be a selection bias among the students who transfer out of low-performing schools such that only those whose parents have more social and economic capital or educational resources will initiate transfer requests. Perhaps students who are the highest test scorers among their classmates, or who are the most motivated to do well academically will be the ones whose parents initiate transfer requests. If these conditions hold, then the school choice option cannot be a universal solution for children in low-performing schools.

There could also be home advantages among the students who attend higher-performing schools such that even with comparable teaching staffs the schools that are not identified as INOI produce higher test scores because of such factors as parental social capital, economic advantage, stable neighborhoods, or lower crime rates. If this is the case then the assumption of differentials in teacher ability and commitment can be questioned. Some schools meeting AYP goals may have difficulty bringing lower-performing students up to the level of their core student body.

NCLB assumes that administrators in higher-performing schools are rational actors in selecting the brightest and most committed teaching staff who rely upon those educational practices that work to raise achievement. Nevertheless, the school choice option assumes that such school administrators will show altruism in accepting students coming from low-performing schools when such students could adversely affect AYP objectives of the receiving campus for the coming year. As rational actors, the school administrators may be selective in considering transfer applicants from INOI schools, thereby limiting the choice options of parents. This is especially likely because NCLB makes acceptance of transfer applications voluntary and affords higher-performing schools the option of accepting applicants only if there is space available.

Other assumptions underlying NCLB's school choice option are that parents will be notified about their options; that they will make rational choices based principally on what is best for their children's test scores; and that they are free from significant economic and geographical constraints not to do otherwise. It is plausible, however, that many of the most at-risk children come from homes where the parents do not have the time or resources to investigate school options; to determine whether the receiving school is appropriate for their children; and may have more priorities that are essential to their survival and that of their children than to explore school choices. Any of these plausible alternatives militate against the effectiveness of NCLB not to leave children behind.

DISINCENTIVES FOR SCHOOLS MEETING AYP

Under NCLB, schools meeting their AYP goals are under no obligation to accept students leaving a low-performing school, especially if it is necessary for them to cross school district lines to do so. Further, accepting students from INOI schools could result in a reduced probability of meeting one's own school's AYP goals for the next year. Schools with high accountability ratings receive numerous benefits that contribute to the acquisition of intangible organizational capital (Black and Lynch 2005; Von Pischke 1996) that is characterized by high faculty morale, considerable collegiality, lower turnover and burnout rates, and smooth, efficient, and effective organizational operation. Greater organizational capital also results in financial capital that schools receive under accountability systems providing cash rewards to schools (and sometimes principals and teachers) that exceed accountability standards. Furthermore, under the Texas Accountability System, schools that achieve the highest rating of "Exemplary" (schools that meet or exceed a 90 percent passage rate) are exempted from some accountability standards and are subject to the completion of less paperwork (see page 5 in each *Accountability Manual* for the years 1994 through 2006).

High-performing schools are showcased by districts, the state, and even the U.S. Department of Education, receiving praise, visits from other school district personnel, and given commendations by the state and the district. The status honor bestowed upon such schools also accrues to the teachers, raising their morale. However, schools that accept children from failing campuses risk the loss of those benefits as they face the potential of lowered test scores. In addition, having to work with new, low-performing children may exacerbate staff stress levels and teacher burnout rates (Dworkin 2001). These changes increase the social cost of school operation and diminish the level of organizational capital in the school. These costs may make schools meeting their AYP goals more reluctant to accept children from low-performing campuses. To illustrate, Wells (2002) reported that low-income students in urban public schools have been denied enrollment in nearby suburban schools.

DISINCENTIVES FOR INOI SCHOOLS

Schools that fail to meet their AYP goals have rational-choice reasons not to notify the parents of their students of the school choice option. Failing schools often have wide standard deviations in test scores among their students, with many students having scores that meet passing thresholds. Schools that fail to meet their AYP goals by relatively small percentages will have a nontrivial number of students who had scores that contributed to the school's attempt to meet its AYP goals. It is most likely that the students whose parents opt for school choice may be disproportionately drawn from those higher test scorers. Their loss is likely to diminish even further the school's chances of meeting future AYP goals (Dworkin 2005). The loss of their higher-scoring students and most involved parents is likely to diminish further those factors that contribute to teacher morale, collegiality, and retard turnover. It is thus in the school's best interest to attempt to keep parents uninformed about school choice options.

DISINCENTIVES FOR PARENTS

Parents most likely to take advantage of the public school choice option would have to weigh several factors. The parents must be informed of the available school choice options, which Stullich et al. (2006) note may be problematic.[1]

A family may undergo economic hardship if school choice involves a residential transfer or the students may encounter a social cost if friends are to be left behind because of the change of school. The process of transfer also involves parental efforts and potentially time away from work to investigate the receiving school. We would not expect many parents of children who are doing well academically in their present school to opt to transfer their children. It is likely, however, that the children who would change schools under the NCLB choice option have parents who are more actively involved in their children's education than are those who elect to keep their children in failing schools.

We have portrayed some of the assumptions underlying the school choice option in NCLB and have suggested plausible rival conditions that challenge the likelihood that the intended outcomes of school choice under NCLB will be achieved. Using statewide, longitudinal, student-level achievement data, this paper offers a partial test of plausible outcomes of school choice on student achievement. The paper contrasts the hypotheses based on NCLB's school choice assumptions with those of rival assumptions that are based on resource allocation and rational choice models. These models suggest that schools, in the presence of scarce resources, will attempt to maximize the achievement gains of students who will have a greater impact on a school's accountability rating rather than provide extra resources to students in need who will have less of an impact on school accountability. We ask:

1. Will students transferring from an INOI school to one meeting AYP improve their test performances compared with students who remain in INOI schools?
2. Does the extent to which a receiving school exceeds its AYP standard affect the performance of incoming transfer students?

The Cost of Mobility

Underlying NCLB recommendations is the assumption that moving from a lower-performing school to a school with a higher academic rating will improve student learning outcomes. However, this assumption contradicts previous research that indicates an adverse effect on students' educational performance as a result of changing schools. Most studies indicate that student mobility has potentially negative effects on student learning outcomes, as well as the likelihood of high school completion. Work by Alexander, Entwisle, and Dauber (1996); Roderick and Camburn (1996); Rumberger (2003); Rumberger and Larson (1998); and Rumberger, Larson, Ream, and Palardy (1999) has examined the interplay between mobility, especially "nonpromotional school changes" (school changes that are not associated with grade level changes) and academic risk. Such nonpromotional mobility can occur when families change residences, either because of the demands of employment or because of housing needs and financial pressures. Some nonpromotional mobility occurs when students or their parents initiate a change of schools because of academic difficulties or social and behavioral problems. Finally, school systems initiate some nonpromotional changes when they transfer disruptive, dangerous, or otherwise problem youth from a regular campus to an alternative school designed to address the needs of such youth. Using the National Longitudinal Educational Study of 1988–94, Swanson and Schneider (1999) considered the timing and three different forms of mobility of high-school students: "changers" (who change residence, but do not change schools); "movers" (who change schools, but do not change residence); and "leavers" (who change both residence and school). Students who moved late (after 10th grade) were likely to experience the most negative effects of mobility on their achievement and the likelihood of dropping out of school. Researchers have reported that school mobility can have negative effects on academic achievement, although it may be academic failure that leads to the nonpromotional move rather than the move leading to academic failure. Rumberger et al. (1999) have noted that dropouts are more likely than nondropouts to have made one or more nonpromotional school changes.

Regardless of the reason for switching schools, any school mobility may be disruptive. School change in itself results in weakened attachments to schools, a factor implicated in greater dropout behavior. Additionally, school change can result in the loss of social capital that could be converted into influence in schools and access to information about school organization as it impacts opportunities to learn (Coleman 1988). Further, mobility, especially within the school year, means that students fail to experience the continuities in instruction, often missing key lessons upon which they will be tested. Even intragrade mobility results in the loss of teacher knowledge about the strengths and weaknesses of individual children that can help tailor instruction and academic enrichment. However, Alexander et al. (1996) reported that while the academic achievement of mobile students is lower than that of students who do not make nonpromotional school changes, prior home disadvantages and low achievement are seen as being the cause of mobility, rather than the mobility being a cause of current low achievement.

Alternatively, it is often assumed that at-risk students will do better after transferring to higher-performing schools. For example, minority and low-income students enrolled in significantly higher-performing schools made up of mostly white, middle-class students perform better on standardized tests than do students in schools overwhelmingly populated by children from low-income families, especially if the school is low performing. Much of the research is based on comparisons between students enrolled in low-performing schools and those in higher-performing schools, without regard to migration from one type of school to the other. Coleman (1988) has suggested that higher-SES students possess greater amounts of social capital that facilitates higher academic aspirations and achievement. It is possible that peer and school effects might also accrue to their more economically disadvantaged classmates. However, Dreeben and Barr (1988) have held that peer-group attitudes toward achievement are likely more salient in adolescence than in the elementary grades.

There can be structural and curricular differences in higher-performing and more middle-class schools, too (Dreeban and Barr 1988; Hallinan 1988; Pallas, Entwisle, Alexander, and Stulka 1994). Teachers in higher-performing, middle-class schools may expect more from their students, teach more broadly and cover more difficult topics. All students in the class, including those transferring from low-performing schools, could benefit from this level of instruction. Thus, the effect of transferring could result in an ultimate improvement in academic achievement, once the effects of mobility per se are removed. However, if the transferring student belongs to a group whose numbers on campus are such that AYP is not disaggregated to them, teachers may be reluctant to allocate school resources and time to their academic needs (Dworkin et al. 2000).

RESEARCH DESIGN

The data we have available to simulate the longitudinal effects of the choice option under NCLB predates the current law, although the current law is fashioned on the basis of the Texas Accountability System. Our data consist of the test records and student information on every child in the State of Texas between 1994 and 2002, the period when the Texas Assessment of Academic Skills test (TAAS) was the standard by which schools and children were assessed. The TAAS was a criterion-referenced test tied to state-specified curricular standards. Students were tested in grades 3 through 8, and again in grade 10. The TAAS test in grade 10 was an exit test that determined whether a high-school student would graduate with a diploma or only receive a certificate of course completion. Each year well over 2 million Texas students took the TAAS test. The state also maintained additional data on about 4 million students each year (including students in grades that were not tested). The data for the present paper was drawn from selected grades within all of the state data sets.

Accountability systems under NCLB have been in place for only a few years. Most were approved by the U.S. Department of Education during 2004 and have subsequently undergone revisions. Many states that previously did not have high-stakes testing or that did not rely on standardized tests are in an early stage in the implementation of their accountability systems. Although some low-performing schools have been required to offer public school choice to their students, there is currently little data available on the extent to which student transfers under the school choice plan will have long-term benefits. Especially lacking is longitudinal, statewide data on the achievement of students who move from INOI schools to those meeting AYP. However, Texas has extensive, student level, statewide data on the effects of its accountability system, which served as the basis for NCLB. Using Texas data it is possible to simulate the effect of transfers on student achievement using the individual test results from the 1994 to 2002 Texas Assessment of Academic Skills tests, the state mandated standardized tests required of all eligible public school students.

The following are reasons to rely upon the Texas accountability system and the longitudinal TAAS data: (1) In the absence of sufficient data to examine the academic effects of public school choice on student achievement, it is necessary to explore data that represent a reasonable surrogate to test the two research questions. The Texas Accountability System served as the basis for the creation of No Child Left Behind. (2) Like NCLB, the Texas system relies on standardized tests that assess learning based on an array of state-specified curricular goals. While Maine uses a portfolio of indicators, most states rely on a single criterion-referenced test, or on a norm-referenced test that has been supplemented with additional, criterion-referenced like items. The same test is to be administered annually, beginning in grade 3 through high school. (3) Results of the test must be disaggregated to student subgroups, including those identified in terms of race-ethnicity, subsidized lunch, special education, and limited English proficiency statuses. (4) The results of the test should be high-stakes, at least for schools, school personnel, and school districts, although many of the states have made the test high-stakes for students, too, affecting promotion to the next grade and graduation. (5) Additionally, schools that fail to meet state-specified passage rates must face consequences, including the potential of school choice for parents, removal of staff, and ultimate reorganization or closure. (6) The threshold for acceptable passing rates must rise over time, thereby making it increasingly more difficult for schools to meet the passing standard. However, rewards, including financial ones, are offered to schools that exceed passing thresholds. (7) Finally, it should be mandated that all or most all students are to be tested, with sanctions against schools that hold back from testing their students whose likelihood of test passage is problematic. These are the characteristics present in both the Texas Accountability System and NCLB.

During the years that the TAAS was used, the Texas Education Agency rated schools on the TAAS passing rate for all students tested and for subgroups, including African American, Hispanic, non-Hispanic white, low-income, and students with limited English proficiency. Graduation rates and student attendance also were incorporated in the campus and district accountability ratings. Schools that had passing rates below the minimum standard for that year were deemed "Low Performing," and could face staff removal, reorganization, and closing if they continued to fail to meet the standard. Schools and districts performing above the standard were given monetary rewards, sometimes including bonuses to teachers, principals, and school superintendents

The passing standard for the exit-level TAAS was maintained at a level equivalent to correctly answering 70 percent of the items that appeared on the October 1990 exit-level test. Raw scores were adjusted so that this level of proficiency corresponded to a Texas Learning Index (TLI) score of 70. Beginning in 1994, test results in reading and math in grades 3 through 8 were also scaled in a manner that aligned the passing standard in these grades with achieving a TLI of 70 on the exit level test. The percentage of correct responses needed to pass the TAAS varied yearly and by grade level because of variations in test item difficulty. For example, on the year 2000 reading test in grade 8, a passing TLI score of 70 corresponded to a percent correct score of 64.6, whereas in mathematics only 60 percent correct was required to obtain a TLI of 70. While the test that Texas is using under NCLB is not the TAAS, but the Texas Assessment of Knowledge and Skills (TAKS), there are only three years of data on that test, with the first year (2003) being one in which the test was benchmarked and was not used for accountability. Consequently, many schools and students probably did not take that year's test seriously. We elected to address our questions using the longitudinal database consisting of TAAS scores.

The Texas Education Agency supplied us with student-level TAAS test score data for the years 1994 through 2002. Each year approximately 280,000 third grade students took the TAAS test. The present study examines three cohorts of students who were in Texas schools each of the years between grades 1 and 5. The different cohorts are needed because passing rate standards for schools changed over the years that the TAAS was administered. Table 12.1 displays the passing standards for the Texas Accountability System during the years that the TAAS test was the measure of student achievement. During 1994, the first year that the TAAS-based accountability system was in place, and 1995, schools were deemed "Low Performing" if their TAAS passage rate was below 25 percent of the students tested. The Texas Education Agency put greater pressure on districts in 1995 to increase testing rates, with the result that the number of low-performing schools increased three-fold that year. Standards for an "Academically Acceptable" and "Recognized" status were lower in 1994 than in 1995, too. Between 1996 and 2000 the threshold for "Academically Acceptable" rose by five points per year, from 30 percent to 50 percent. Between 1998 and 2002,

Table 12.1 TAAS passage standards for campus and district accountability ratings: 1994–2002*

Test Year	Exemplary passing standard	Recognized passing standard	Academically acceptable passing standard	Low performing passing standard	Number of low performing elementary schools
	%	%	%	%	
1994	At least 90	65–89.9	25–64.9	Below 25	54
1995	At least 90	70–89.9	25–69.9	Below 25	150
1996	At least 90	70–89.9	30–69.9	Below 30	109
1997	At least 90	75–89.9	35–74.9	Below 35	67
1998	At least 90	80–89.9	40–79.9	Below 40	59
1999	At least 90	80–89.9	45–79.9	Below 45	96
2000	At least 90	80–89.9	50–79.9	Below 50	134
2001	At least 90	80–89.9	50–79.9	Below 50	100
2002	At least 90	80–89.9	55–79.9	Below 55	166

* Passage rates are based on performances by each subgroup of students and the entire student body on the reading, math, and in the grades offered, the writing test. Actual accountability is also affected by attendance and dropout rates, particularly in higher grades.
Source: The Texas Education Agency (Department of Accountability, Reporting, and Research) , 1994 through 2002, Accountability Manuals.

when the TAAS was last administered, the threshold for a "Recognized" school remained at 80 percent passage. During each year that the TAAS was used the threshold for an "Exemplary" school had been 90 percent passage. Increases in the threshold levels for "Academically Acceptable" often resulted in more schools being deemed "Low Performing."

Besides demarcating changes in the passing thresholds for state accountability ratings, the three cohorts represent changes in teaching practices that became more aligned to the state test. The early cohort took their first TAAS exam as 3rd graders in 1994 and their 5th grade exam in 1996. During that time low-performing schools were those with passing rates below 25 percent in 1994 and 1995 and 30 percent in 1996. The early years of implementation of the accountability system and the use of the TAAS was marked by a large test score gap between minorities and majority group students and a comparative absence of alignment of curricula and testing. The second cohort took their first TAAS test as 3rd graders in 1998 and their 5th grade test in 2000. Between those years low-performing schools had passage rates below 40 percent in 1998 and 50 percent in 2000. Substantial curricular alignment had occurred and the gap between groups had narrowed significantly. The third cohort took their first TAAS test as 3rd graders in 2000 and their 5th grade test in 2002, the last year that the TAAS was administered. During this time period the test score gap continued to narrow and debates about the validity of TAAS results intensified (Haney 2000;

Toenjes et al. 2002; Toenjes and Dworkin 2002). It was also during this last time period that (1) the state adopted legislation intended to end social promotion of students who failed the reading section of the TAAS as 3rd graders and (2) the federal legislation, No Child Left Behind, was passed. Analyses in this study will compare and contrast findings for these three cohorts.

Given the negative association between mobility and student achievement reported in the literature, we imposed best-case conditions on the data to be used. Students who change schools frequently miss out on significant amounts of instruction and much continuity of curricula; they tend to perform less well than students who are not mobile or make fewer moves. On the Texas Assessment of Academic Skills the effect of one move within a school year is associated with a decrease of about 2.0 TLI points, or an effect size decline of .13 of a standard deviation (Dworkin et al. 1998). The effect of movement in middle and high school is more profound. More frequent movements are associated with even greater negative effects. Thus, in the present study we have restricted our analysis to students who make no moves between grades 1 and 5 and those who make only one move, that being between grades 3 and 4. By requiring the movers to take their 3rd grade TAAS test in the sending school and subsequent TAAS tests in the receiving school, we have a baseline (premove) measure of student achievement that can be compared with postmove test scores. Because the move itself is associated with a decline in TAAS scores, we rely upon the 5th grade test as the postmove measure, giving students two years to adjust to their new school.

During the 1990s, many school districts in Texas began to experiment with strategies to reduce school size and to ease the transitions from elementary to middle to high school. Some districts separated 4th and 5th graders in intermediate schools; other districts created early education centers for student in pre-K, kindergarten, and grades 1 or 2. Some districts also segregated 9th graders, putting them into academies of their own, while some administrators sought to ease the transition from elementary to middle school by placing 6th graders in their own school. The result of these practices has been that many students changed schools during the elementary years because the grade levels taught at their own schools changed. When students change schools without separating from their classmates and even their teachers, we have elected to redefine such changes as distinct from the school changes that would be associated with public school choice. Thus, students who remained in the same school throughout their elementary years and students who moved with their classmates to a new campus as a result of a redesignation of the grade level of their previous school have been coded as nonmovers.

While we can determine whether a student changed schools, it is not possible from the data to ascertain their motivation for such changes. However, we can decipher whether the change constituted a movement from a low-performing school to some other school, or from a school that had met accountability standards for that year to a similar school or one where the students were performing better or worse on the Texas required standardized test. Therefore it is possible to select students who might likely resemble those whose parents will make use of the public school choice option under NCLB. In order to estimate the exercise of NCLB's parental choice option on achievement it is clear that some selectivity must be considered. Not all parents choose to transfer their children from a failing school and not all failing schools will provide parents with the choice option. We therefore decided to exclude children whose parents frequently transfer them from school to school, as the impact of an NCLB public school choice option cannot be distinguished from the instabilities of frequent mobility behavior. The optimal cases for the simulation of the school choice option under NCLB in the data set we have are students who remained in the same elementary school from 1st to 3rd grade, made a single school change in grade 4, and remained in the new school for the rest of their elementary careers—that is through grade 5. Additionally, we specify that the student must have taken the standardized test each year (grades 3 through 5). These students will be compared with similar children who made no school transfers during the five years of their elementary school experiences.

Patterns of Student Mobility

The full data set from which our analysis data were drawn consists of 234,290 students in the early cohort (1994–96), 226,427 students in the middle cohort (1998–2000), and 224,410 in the late cohort (2000–2002). However, the data include students who could not satisfy our selection criteria. The data include Asian-American and Native-American students, groups upon which AYP would not be disaggregated in Texas, students who did not remain in the public schools beyond the 3rd grade, and students who were not tested each year. Our attempt to reproduce a sample that resembles students whose parents might take advantage of the choice option requires us to include only students who were enrolled in Texas schools from grades 1 to 5 and who took the TAAS test each time it was offered to their grade level. In light of the evidence against nonpromotional mobility, we deleted students who made more than one move during their elementary school careers. In fact, we selected only students who remained in the same elementary school from grades 1 to 3, either moved in grade four or continued in the same school, and made no moves after fourth grade.

Table 12.2 displays the patterns among students who attended Texas public schools between grades 1 and 5 and who took a TAAS test in grades 3 through 5. The table is based on African-American, Hispanic, and non-Hispanic white students, both participating and not participating in the federal subsidized lunch program. The sample size for the early cohort was 76,971 students, while the sample for the middle cohort was 71,581 students, and the sample for the late cohort was 78,331 students. As would be expected, fewer students were mobile in the three cohorts, compared with the population statistics for all cohort members. A total of 21.5 percent of the African-American students, 15.7 percent of the Hispanic students, 18.3 percent of the non-Hispanic white students, and 19.0 percent of the low income students were mobile. The mobility rates in the middle and late cohorts resembled those of the early cohort. In the middle cohort, 22.3 percent of the African Americans, 16.0 percent of the Hispanics, 17.8 percent of the non-Hispanic whites, and 18.3 percent of the low income students were mobile. Finally, in the late cohort, 20.4 percent of the African Americans, 15.7 percent of the Hispanics, 18.5 percent of the non-Hispanic whites, and 17.5 percent of the low income students were mobile.

The table presents six types of mobility patterns, reflecting student movement among schools that are categorized by their ratings under the Texas Accountability System. The system incorporates passage rates on the TAAS test for all students and cognizable subgroups. The ratings are "Low Performing," "Academically Acceptable," "Recognized," and "Exemplary." The movement patterns include (1) "Level Moves" in which students transfer to and from schools with the same accountability rating; (2) "Downward Moves," where the rating of the sending school is higher than that of the receiving school; and a series of upward moves, including (3) "Movement from Low Performing to Acceptable"; (4) "Movement from Low Performing to Recognized or Exemplary"; (5) "Movement Acceptable to Recognized or Exemplary"; and (6) "Movement from Recognized to

Table 12.2 Ethnic and poverty status in elementary school campus mobility patterns: 1994–2002 (Students with scored TAAS tests in grades 3 through 5)

	Early Cohort (1994–96)			
	African American (n = 8,068) %	Hispanic (n = 22,401) %	Non-Hispanic white (n = 46,502) %	Low income (n = 27,806) %
Campus movers	24.3	17.6	20.8	21.6
Level move: No rating improvement	14.6	9.0	11.2	11.6
Move: Down in campus accountability	2.2	1.0	1.2	1.5
Move: Low-performing to acceptable (meets AYP)	0.6	0.2	0.0	0.3
Move: Low performing to recognized or exemplary	0.2	0.1	0.0	0.1
Move: Acceptable to recognized or exemplary	6.1	6.7	6.3	7.4
Move: Recognized to exemplary	0.6	0.6	2.1	0.7

(*continued*)

Middle Cohort (1998–2000)				
	African American (n = 7,747) %	Hispanic (n = 24,449) %	Non-Hispanic white (n = 39,385) %	Low income (n = 29,865) %
Campus movers	22.3	16.0	17.9	19.1
Level move: No rating improvement	9.3	6.2	7.2	7.6
Move: Down in campus accountability	3.5	2.1	1.2	2.5
Move: Low performing to acceptable (meets AYP)	0.0	0.1	0.0	0.0
Move: Low performing to recognized or exemplary	0.0	0.0	0.0	0.0
Move: acceptable to recognized or exemplary	7.4	5.5	4.5	6.4
Move: Recognized to exemplary	2.1	2.1	5.0	2.6
Late Cohort (2000–2002)				
	African American (n = 7,832) %	Hispanic (n = 31,167) %	Non-Hispanic white (n = 39,332) %	Low income (n = 3 4,399) %
Campus movers	20.5	15.7	18.4	17.6
Level move: No rating improvement	7.3	5.2	9.5	6.1
Move: Down in campus accountability	1.8	1.6	0.7	1.7
Move: Low performing to acceptable (meets AYP)	0.3	0.4	0.0	0.4
Move: Low performing to recognized or exemplary	0.2	0.1	0.0	0.1
Move: Acceptable to recognized or exemplary	7.1	4.1	2.5	4.9
Move: Recognized to exemplary	3.8	4.3	5.7	4.4

Exemplary." While "Level Moves" is the modal form for all groups in each of the three cohorts, downward movements and movements from "Acceptable" to "Recognized" or "Exemplary" are the second most common move.

FINDINGS

The analyses presented in this chapter represent an estimation of possible outcomes for students who attempt nonpromotional transfers out of low-performing elementary schools. The findings reflect the historical effects on reading and mathematics performances in Texas in the years prior to and during the initial implementation of NCLB.

The Effects of Mobility Patterns on Student Achievement

Both school level variables and the characteristics of individual students are used to predict the academic performance of Texas elementary school children. The means and standard deviations of the variables used in the analyses for the three cohorts are presented in Table 12.3. Note that, with the exception of the test scores, all student-level traits are binary variables. Only students with complete data on all variables are analyzed. Also deleted from the analyses were schools (and their students) with fewer than five tested children. Even with these data restrictions, over 70,000 students from approximately 2,500 schools were studied in the three time periods examined. The average number of children with complete data per school was about 29 in each of the three years with outcome measures. The hierarchical linear regression modeling (HLM) framework popularized by Raudenbush and Bryk (2002) was used to analyze the data because individual students were nested within schools, thus violating the assumption of independent observations underlying traditional ordinary least squares methods. Analyses are separated for each of the three cohorts because schools were subject to different levels of rigor in accountability standards during the three time periods. The rising accountability standards based on passing rates simulates the changes in AYP standards that are specified under NCLB. Schools also utilized different strategies to address the achievement gaps between minority and majority students and between students in poverty and noneconomically disadvantaged children. Pooling the cohorts would therefore mask changes in standards, incentives to raise academic performance, and pedagogical approaches.

   Although the specific effects of student movement across schools of various academic ratings are of primary concern, we first discuss the effects of other predictors of test performance. Table 12.4 gives the unstandardized coefficients and their levels of statistical significance for the determinants of TAAS reading scores. As was evident in Table 12.1, the cutoff for schools to receive an "Academically Acceptable" rating was lower during the years that the early cohort was in grades 3 through 5 than when the middle cohort was in those grades; likewise the cutoff for the middle cohort was lower than for the late cohort. Further, the gaps among groups of students were wider for the early cohort than for subsequent cohorts (Toenjes et al. 2002). Lower TAAS passage rates necessary for a school to avoid being labeled Low Performing could mean that schools were able to ignore the needs of some failing students, especially if such students did not belong to a group upon which test data were disaggregated. Consequently, Table 12.4 examines the factors that affect reading achievement separately for

Table 12.3 Means and standard deviations of variables in three cohorts used for hierarchical linear analyses

	Cohort 1 Early accountability		Cohort 2 Middle accountability		Cohort 3 Late accountability	
	Mean	*SD*	*Mean*	*SD*	*Mean*	*SD*
School-level variables						
Low-performing rating	.01	.07	.01	.11	.01	.10
Acceptable rating	.49	.50	.43	.49	.27	.44
Recognized rating	.29	.46	.34	.47	.39	.49
Exemplary rating	.21	.41	.22	.42	.33	.47
Ln number of students	6.24	.45	6.23	.44	6.23	.45
Ln mobility rate	2.96	.41	2.95	.42	2.93	.42
Ln expenditures/pupil	8.23	.18	8.36	.19	8.44	.19
% Students African American	14.81	21.96	14.62	21.51	13.97	20.48
% Students Hispanic	40.42	33.30	42.35	33.47	45.26	33.47
% Free/ reduced price lunch	57.11	29.31	57.32	29.34	58.53	29.55
Mean years teacher experience	11.86	2.67	11.96	2.83	11.78	2.98
N	2,463		2,485		2,641	
Student-level variables						
5th Grade reading score	86.12	12.43	88.98	11.35	91.09	9.51
5th Grade math score	82.71	10.05	86.01	7.61	87.22	5.77
3rd Grade reading score	79.75	13.99	84.20	10.48	85.33	10.29
3rd Grade math score	77.77	13.27	80.06	10.45	81.07	10.53
African American student	.12	.32	.11	.31	.10	.30
Hispanic student	.32	.47	.34	.47	.40	.50
White student	.56	.50	.55	.50	.50	.50
Female student	.51	.50	.51	.50	.51	.50
Free/reduced price lunch	.40	.49	.40	.49	.44	.50
Limited English proficiency	.03	.17	.03	.16	.03	.18
Special education	.07	.25	.04	.21	.03	.18
At-risk student	.31	.46	.25	.43	.19	.40
Gifted/talented student	.17	.38	.18	.38	.18	.38
Move down	.03	.18	.05	.21	.04	.19
Move same level	.10	.31	.08	.28	.08	.27
Move: Low perform to acceptable	.00	.03	.00	.03	.00	.06
Move: Low perform to rec/exemplary	.00	.01	.01	.10	.00	.02
Move: Accept to rec/exemplary	.03	.17	.03	.17	.04	.19
Move: Recognized to exemplary	.01	.09	.01	.10	.01	.12
N	72,017		70,900		77,584	

Table 12.4 The effects of school characteristics, student characteristics, and student mobility patterns on Texas reading achievement scores among three cohorts

	Cohort 1 Early accountability		Cohort 2 Middle accountability		Cohort 3 Late accountability	
	Coef.	Sig.	Coef.	Sig.	Coef.	Sig.
School-level effects						
Acceptable rating	2.99	.012	4.46	.000	.96	.107
Recognized rating	4.95	.000	6.05	.000	2.12	.000
Exemplary rating	5.54	.000	7.00	.000	3.18	.000
Ln number of students	.97	.000	.38	.040	.77	.000
Ln mobility rate	.15	.481	.19	.288	.21	.114
Ln expenditures/pupil	.66	.125	.23	.530	.90	.001
% Students African American	.00	.642	−.02	.000	−.00	.259
% Students Hispanic	.01	.123	.01	.227	−.00	.799
% Free/reduced price lunch	−.04	.000	−.04	.000	−.03	.000
Mean years teacher experience	−.07	.009	−.05	.042	.04	.043
Student-level effects						
3rd Grade reading score	.43	.000	.51	.000	.46	.000
African American student	−1.54	.000	−2.45	.000	−1.98	.000
Hispanic student	−.84	.000	−.91	.000	−.56	.000
Female student	.85	.000	.78	.000	−.05	.363
Free/reduced price lunch	−.86	.000	−.98	.000	−1.01	.000
Limited English proficiency	.31	.347	.26	.444	−1.13	.000
Special education	−4.69	.000	−1.61	.000	−1.00	.000
At-risk student	−5.12	.000	−5.20	.000	−3.87	.000
Gifted/talented student	2.83	.000	3.33	.000	2.75	.000
Move down	−.32	.334	−.90	.000	−.55	.015
Move: Same level	−.31	.114	−.53	.009	−.58	.001
Move: Low perform to acceptable	2.77	.148	−.76	.623	1.05	.269
Move: Low perform to rec/exempl.	1.57	.320	4.59	.178	2.96	.002
Move: Accept to rec/exempl.	−.43	.073	−.03	.902	−.14	.459
Move: Recognized to exemplary	.37	.335	−.25	.475	−.24	.355
Intercept	81.70		83.12		88.73	
Initial variation due to interschool differences	14.53		15.40		14.01	
% School variation explained	68.55		70.82		73.45	
% Student variation explained	46.24		43.77		41.06	
Number of students	72,017		70,900		77,584	
Number of schools	2,463		2,485		2,641	

each cohort. Fifth graders attending schools with Acceptable, Recognized, and Exemplary ratings usually obtained significantly higher scores than children enrolled in Low-Performing schools (the reference group not included in the equation). However, mean reading scores of children enrolled in Low-Performing schools in the Late Accountability cohort did not differ significantly from students attending schools with an Acceptable rating. Moreover, the average difference in test scores between students in Low-Performing schools and children attending Recognized and Exemplary schools was about half the size observed in the two earlier cohorts. The fact that the achievement gap between the Low-Performing schools and the three higher-rated campuses decreased by the spring 2002 TAAS reading test (the time students in the third cohort were tested) suggests that teachers in Low-Performing schools may be devoting more effort to help ensure that their students do well on the mandatory state test.

Only a few of the school-level variables exerted a statistically significant effect on individual student test scores. Schools with greater numbers of students evidenced higher reading scores in each of the three cohorts. Insofar as the natural logarithm of the number of students in a school is the independent variable, the positive impact of school size on reading scores tends to diminish in magnitude as the number of students increases. Schools with greater percentages of economically disadvantaged students (as measured by enrollment in the free/reduced price federal lunch program) obtain fewer correctly answered reading questions. Average years of experience among teachers working at the school also affected individual reading performance, but inconsistently. Schools with more experienced teachers reduced the reading scores of students in the first two cohorts; however, in the third cohort, students attending schools with more experienced teachers obtained higher reading scores. Only in the second cohort did the racial composition of the student body exert a statistically significant impact on reading scores. Children in schools with greater percentages of African-American students obtained lower reading scores. An increase in the logarithm of the total amount of expenditures per pupil resulted in significantly higher reading scores only among students in the third cohort.

The effects of individual student characteristics on individual reading scores were more consistent than those of the campus level variables. Students with higher 3rd grade reading scores obtained higher scores on their 5th grade reading test. Students classified as being in a gifted/talented program also evidenced relatively more correctly answered reading items in 5th grade. Females in the first two cohorts obtained slightly higher reading scores than boys, but by the third cohort test, boys' scores were not appreciably different from those of the girls. Several student characteristics were observed to negatively affect performance on the reading tests. Both African-American and Hispanic students obtained lower reading scores than non-Hispanic white students (the omitted group). Likewise, economically disadvantaged students reported lower scores than children not participating in the federal school lunch program. Children classified as being in special education and at-risk (i.e., students with a high probability of dropping out of school according to state-defined criteria) also did not fare as well on the reading test. Students with limited English did as well on the 5th grade reading test as children with no language deficiency, at least in the first two cohorts. But in the third cohort students with limited English obtained somewhat lower reading scores. We suspect that schools may have excluded students with severe English problems from testing in the first two cohorts; however, as the state began to tighten the exemption requirements by the third cohort, more children whose initial language was not English were tested.

Table 12.4 also examines the effects of student mobility patterns on reading achievement. While it is expected that some mobility will have an effect on achievement during the year of school change and even the next year, the data suggest that the effect of mobility persists two years after the school change. However, the effect of changing schools depends on the performance level of the school to which a student transfers, as well as that of the school from which a student exited. To illustrate, students who moved to a lower-performing school or to a school with a similar performance rating evidenced somewhat lower reading scores. Similarly, moving from a Low-Performing to an Acceptable school had no significant impact on TAAS reading scores. Only among students in the third cohort, did transferring from a Low-Performing school to a Recognized or Exemplary school result in greater reading achievement. Movement from an Academically Acceptable or Recognized school to schools with higher ratings was not associated with improved reading performance.

The net effects of school-level and student predictors on the mathematics performance of Texas 5th graders are presented in Table 12.5. The impacts of many of the variables are similar to those observed on reading scores, although a few differences occurred. For example, the percentage of economically disadvantaged students attending a school was associated with lower mathematics scores only among children in the second cohort. Moreover, years of teacher work experience had no significant effect on the number of correctly answered mathematics questions. Whereas Hispanic children obtained significantly lower reading scores than non-Hispanic white students, Hispanic children in the second cohort slightly outperformed white students on the TAAS math exam. Fifth graders with limited English proficiency also obtained higher math scores in the first and second cohorts.

The effect on mathematics performance of moving to different schools was also similar to the effect of school transfers on reading scores. Attending a school with a lower academic rating was associated with lower performance on the state's mathematics test. Transferring from an Acceptable or Recognized school to a campus with a higher academic rating had little effect on math performance, as was the case with reading. Moving to a school with an academic rating comparable to the originating school led to a reduction in the number of correctly answered mathematics questions. Enrolling in a school with an Acceptable rating

TABLE 12.5 The effects of school characteristics, student characteristics, and student mobility patterns on Texas mathematics achievement scores among three cohorts

	Cohort 1 Early accountability		Cohort 2 Middle accountability		Cohort 3 Late accountability	
	Coef.	Sig.	Coef.	Sig.	Coef.	Sig.
School-level effects						
Acceptable rating	3.09	.003	2.57	.002	1.49	.011
Recognized rating	4.64	.000	4.02	.000	2.28	.000
Exemplary rating	5.21	.000	4.54	.000	2.91	.000
Ln number of students	.31	.080	−.21	.159	.29	.006
Ln mobility rate	−.01	.962	.19	.204	.09	.370
Ln expenditures/pupil	.39	.397	−.49	.099	.60	.002
% Students African American	−.03	.000	−.01	.001	−.00	.160
% Students Hispanic	−.00	.422	.01	.000	−.00	.711
% Free/reduced price lunch	−.01	.131	−.01	.001	−.00	.369
Mean years teacher experience	−.04	.069	−.01	.540	.01	.264
Student-level effects						
3rd Grade mathematics score	.40	.000	.35	.000	.29	.000
African American student	−1.39	.000	−1.08	.000	−.71	.000
Hispanic student	−.13	.185	.27	.001	.10	.063
Female student	.17	.001	.36	.000	.15	.000
Free/reduced price lunch	−.57	.000	−.41	.000	−.32	.000
Limited English proficiency	.87	.002	.75	.003	−.95	.000
Special education	−3.96	.000	−1.15	.000	−.68	.000
At-risk student	−3.84	.000	−3.23	.000	−1.89	.000
Gifted/talented student	1.47	.000	1.17	.000	1.21	.000
Move down	−.94	.001	−.76	.000	−.63	.000
Move: Same level	−.57	.004	−.70	.000	−.29	.008
Move: Low perform to acceptable	.06	.959	3.76	.000	.41	.673
Move: Low perform to rec/exemplary	2.06	.404	4.05	.050	2.44	.000
Move: Accept to rec/exemplary	.05	.821	.23	.137	−.01	.930
Move: Recognized to exemplary	.48	.118	−.27	.325	−.22	.105
Intercept	78.56		82.41		84.93	
Initial variation due to interschool differences	14.54		15.39		14.15	
% School variation explained	69.25		55.86		56.50	
% Student variation explained	66.96		38.43		41.40	
Number of students	72,017		70,900		77,584	
Number of schools	2,463		2,485		2,641	

after attending a Low-Performing school was associated with an increase of about 4 TLI points, but only among students in the second cohort.

These findings reveal that school-level variables account from between 56 percent to over 70 percent of the variation in both mean reading and mathematics scores across campuses. The fact that the models account from between 40 percent to 67 percent of the variability in the test scores of individual students indicates that other predictors have been omitted. An important feature of Tables 12.4 and 12.5 is that they reveal that most of the variation in student reading and mathematics scores occurs within schools. Only about 14 percent to 15 percent of the total variability in student test scores can be attributed to differences among schools. Most of the variation in test scores results from students who attend the same schools. These data indicate that, were it possible to equalize the average performance of all Texas schools, but allow differences to remain in test performance among students in the same schools, overall inequality of state test scores would decrease by only 14 percent to 15 percent. Even if all schools had the same mean TAAS scores in reading or mathematics, major differences in all test outcomes would continue to exist. Alternately, if the differences in test scores among individual students could be equalized such that every student in a school had the identical test result, but average test scores were allowed to vary across schools, the overall variation in Texas test scores would decrease by approximately 85 percent. We view this as an important finding because it contradicts an implicit assumption underlying NCLB; that is, many schools do not meet accountability standards because most of the students attending low-performing schools are failing. Although there are certainly some schools with a large number of students who do poorly on required examinations, a much larger percentage of failing students are dispersed throughout all schools. Simply shutting down a small number of low-performing schools would likely have little impact on raising the overall academic achievement for the overwhelming number of Texas students.

DISCUSSION AND CONCLUSIONS

Until enough data are gathered on the long-term effects of school choice options in NCLB, it will be necessary to use surrogate measures to assess the effect of changing accountability standards on the performance of students in different school settings. The data we used from the Texas Education Agency included samples of all 3rd-grade students who took the state mandated, criterion-referenced test, the Texas Assessment of Academic Skills (TAAS) between 1994 and 2002. We tracked student performances throughout their elementary school years. The present study examined the effects of mobility on student achievement, with special attention to students who changed from schools that were low-performing to others that were meeting accountability criteria.

This study investigated two research questions: (1) whether children transferring from INOI schools to ones that meet AYP goals will improve their test results, and (2) the minimum performance level difference between the sending and receiving school required for the transferring students to improve their test performances. Because NCLB mandates progressively higher passing rates for all subgroups of students that eventuate in 100 percent of the students passing the standardized test by the 2013–14 academic year, this study addressed the questions by relying on three cohorts of students, drawn from time periods that had different test passing standards for school accountability.

One problem we faced in the current study is that the TAAS data contained no information on the motivation of students to make nonpromotional transfers. However, examining some of the known characteristics of students whose parents might take advantage of the public school choice option in NCLB, we restricted our sample to students who might transfer for academic reasons, rather than because their parents made frequent moves. Because mobility is associated with decreases in achievement, consequently we included students who either made no school transfers throughout elementary school or made only one transfer. Those making transfers were to have taken an initial TAAS test as 3rd graders in the sending school and TAAS tests in grades 4 and 5 in the receiving school. Comparisons were then made on test score changes from 3rd to 5th grade, disregarding test scores in grade 4 because they would be distorted by the transition from one school to another. The three cohorts, student in grades 3 through 5 in 1994–96, 1998–2000, and 2000–2002, consisted of approximately 75,000 students each.

One-fifth of all students in the cohorts made nonpromotional school changes during the time periods, rates that are lower than those reported nationally by Rumberger and Larson (1998). However, their data were based on many students changing schools for reasons other than to attend better-performing schools. We found variations in transfer rates differ by ethnic groups and students in poverty, with African Americans and students on subsidized lunch status having higher mobility rates.

School transfers have variable impacts on reading and mathematics achievement two years after the move. Moving from a school that was INOI to one that was Academically Acceptable or just meeting its AYP goals tended to produce lower achievement than staying in the low-performing school, and the total effect was additive to the negative consequences of making any move. This pattern persisted even as passing standards rose across the cohorts. Likewise, moving downward in accountability and moving to a school performing at a similar level to the sending school were both associated with diminished achievement relative to being immobile. Transferring to a Recognized or Exemplary school, or a campus that substantially exceeds its AYP goal, was the only school change that was associated with significantly improved achievement that offset the negative consequences of any mobility. Enrolling in schools with higher academic ratings after attending a Low-Performing school, however, did not consistently result in higher test scores. This kind of school transfer was associated with a positive effect only in the third cohort, once the accountability system's passing standards had risen significantly. Thus, as accountability standards rise, only then are parental choice options likely to result in substantially improved student achievement, and only for students transferring to schools that are among the better performers. However, as passing rates needed for a school to meet or surpass AYP levels continue to rise under NCLB, it is likely that the demand for transfers to the better-performing schools will outstrip the supply of such schools, resulting in many students being left behind in the lower-performing campuses. This is most likely to occur by 2013–14 when AYP standards mandate test passage of 100 percent of the students. By then, assuming that there has been no retrenchment in the resolve to "leave no child behind," there may be many schools left behind.

Observations by Coleman (1988), Dreeben and Barr (1988), Hallinan (1988), and Pallas et al. (1994) suggest all students in higher-performing schools will do better than in lower-performing schools because of a broad and rich content of instruction and higher teacher and peer expectations. All students in the class, including those transferring from lower-performing schools, may benefit from the higher-performing school. Thus, transfers to better schools may offset any negative effects of mobility. The fact that we selected students who took the test each year might have mitigated any negative effects of tokenism, especially among students moving to higher-performing schools. To be included in the data set precluded the kind of gaming most common among Texas schools—exclusion of the student from testing. Since the tokens were tested, they were most likely provided with the same assistance that other students were given. NCLB mandates that no more than 5 percent of the students can be excluded from testing. In the future, when NCLB standards for AYP also mandate that all tested students must pass the examination, and that relatively few will be exempted from the test, it is likely that tokens will receive the enrichment and resources that nontokens obtain. What may continue to be a strategy for higher-performing schools is to deny enrollment requests from students seeking to leave INOI schools. While school districts are not permitted under NCLB to deny school choice, individual campuses within districts can still cap their enrollments (Stullich et al. 2006). It is in the interest of higher-performing schools to teach well even those students who come from INOI schools; but it is also in their best interest to refuse to enroll them or to exempt them from testing (unless the state negatively sanctions low testing rates). All such practices permit high-achieving schools to protect the organizational capital they have amassed and thereby maintain morale, efficiency, and effectiveness (Black and Lynch 2005).

The present research, although only a surrogate for the yet-to-be collected data on the longitudinal effects of NCLB, leads us to conclude that parents of students who take advantage of public school choice to leave a school that is in need of improvement should consider how much higher is the academic rating of the school to which they will transfer their children. One lesson from these data is that, if public school choice is offered, the move should be to a much better performing school and not to one that merely makes AYP. Simply transferring from a low-performing school to one that is merely adequate may result in diminished academic achievement relative to not making a transfer. The cost to achievement of the nonpromotional transfer offsets the small differences between schools that are meeting minimal AYP goals and those that are INOI.

Note

1. In a recent assessment of Title I prepared for the Institute of Education Sciences, Stullich et al. (2006, 66) noted that of the approximately 3.9 million students attending schools that had failed to meet their AYP goals for two consecutive years, only about 38,000 changed schools under the school choice option of NCLB. Many reasons account for the underuse of the choice option, including (1) the distance children might have to travel to leave a failing neighborhood school; (2) the apparent lack of openings at schools meeting AYP; and (3) the reticence of low-performing schools to notify parents that they had a school choice option (in 2004–5 some 39 percent of the districts failed to inform their parents about choice options). Further, the authors observed from the unpublished *National Longitudinal Study of NCLB, District Survey* that "Fifty-eight percent of districts with high schools identified for improvement reported that they were not offering the school choice option at the high school level, as did 46 percent at the middle school level and 30 percent at the elementary level" (Stullich et al., 65). Finally, in 2004–5, some 71 percent of the districts that did notify parents of the choice option for their children waited until it was either so close to the opening of school that moving to another campus would have been very difficult, or waited until after the school year had begun, making a move all but impossible (Stullich et al. 67).

References

Alexander, K. L., D. R. Entwisle, and S. L. Dauber. 1996. Children in motion: School transfers and elementary school performance. *Journal of Education Research* 90 (1): 3–12.

Black, S. E. and L. M. Lynch. 2005. Measuring organizational capital in the new economy. In *Measuring capital in the new economy*, ed. Carol Corrado, John Holtiwanger, and Daniel Sichel, 205-234. Chicago: University of Chicago Press.

Coleman, J. S. 1988. Social capital in the creation of human capital. *American Journal of Sociology* 94:S95–S120.

Dreeben, R. and R. Barr. 1988. Classroom composition and the design of instruction. *Sociology of Education* 61 (3):129–42.

Dworkin, A. G. 2001. Perspectives on teacher burnout and school reform. *International Journal of Education* 2 (July):69–78.

———. 2005. The No Child Left Behind Act: Accountability, high-stakes testing, and roles for sociologists. *Sociology of Education* 78 (2):170–74.

Dworkin, A. G., J. Lorence, L. A.Toenjes, and A. N. Hill. 1998. Evaluation of academic performance in the Houston Independent School District. Unpublished research report to the Center for Houston's Future.

———, P. Purser, and A. Sheikh-Hussin. 2000. Modeling the effects of changing demography on student learning: Applications designed to change school district practices. In *Challenges of urban education: Sociological perspectives for the next century*, ed. K. A. McClafferty, C. A.Torres, and T. R. Mitchell, 195–226. Albany, NY: State University of New York Press.

Hallinan, M. T. 1988. School composition and learning: A critique of the Dreeben-Barr model. *Sociology of Education* 61 (3):143–46.

Haney, W. 2000. The myth of the Texas miracle in education. *Education PolicyAnalysis Archives* 8 (41). http://epaa.asu.edu/epaa/v8n41.

Pallas, A. M., D. R. Entwisle, K. L. Alexander, and M. Francis Stulka.1998. Ability-group effects: Instructional, social, or institutional? *Sociology of Education* 67 (1):27–46.

Raudenbush, S.W. and A. S. Bryk. 2002. *Hierarchical linear modeling: Applications and data analysis methods*, 2nd ed. Thousand Oaks, CA: Sage.

Roderick, M. and E. Camburn. 1996. Academic difficulties during the high school transition. In *Charting reform in Chicago: The students speak*, . 47–65. Chicago: The Consortium on Chicago School Research.

Rumberger, R. W. 2003. The causes and consequences of student mobility. *Journal of Negro Education* 72:6–21.

––––– and K. W. Larson.1998. Student mobility and the increased risk of high school dropout. *American Journal of Education* 107 (1):1–35.

–––––, R. K. Ream, and G. J. Palardy. 1999. *The educational consequences of mobility for California students and schools*. Berkeley, CA: Policy Analysis for California Education ED 441 040.

Stullich, S., E. Eisner, J. McCrary, and C. Roney. 2006. *Implementation of Title I*. Vol. 1 of *National assessment of Title I interim report*. Washington, D.C.: U.S. Department of Education, Institute of Education Sciences.

Swanson, C. B. and B. Schneider.1999. Students on the move: Residential and educational mobility in America's schools. *Sociology of Education* 72 (1): 54–67.

Texas Education Agency (Department of Accountability Reporting and Research). *Texas accountability manual: The accountability rating system for Texas public schools and school districts*. Austin, TX : Author. (individual manuals for 1994 through 2002)

Toenjes, L. A. and A. G. Dworkin. 2002. Are increasing test scores in Texas really a myth, or is Haney's myth a myth? *Education Policy Analysis Archives* 10 (17): http://epaa.asu.edu/epaa/v10n17

–––––, J. P. Lorence, and A. N. Hill. 2002. High-stakes testing, accountability, and student achievement in Texas and Houston. In *Bridging the Achievement Gap*, ed. J. E. Chubb and T. Loveless, 109–30. Washington, D.C.: The Brookings Institution Press.

Wells, A. S. 2002. Reactions to the Supreme Court ruling on vouchers: Introduction toan online special issue. *Teachers College Record*, http://www.tcrecord.org (ID Number: 10949).

13

Research Meets Policy and Practice

How Are School Districts Addressing NCLB
Requirements for Parental Involvement?

Joyce L. Epstein

The No Child Left Behind Act provides federal funds to improve schools serving children from economically disadvantaged families and communities. In addition to well-publicized requirements for high-quality teachers, achievement tests, and accountability for the progress of major subgroups of students, NCLB includes important requirements for district leaders to develop district-level and school-based policies and programs for more effective parental involvement. The regulations in NCLB's Section 1118 on parental involvement reflect advances in sociological and educational theories about district leadership for school improvement.

Historically, there have been notable pendulum swings in assessments of the contributions of district leaders to school improvement. Some have labeled district leaders irrelevant and inadequate managers of school reform; others have called them essential guides for improving schools (Coburn 2003; Datnow, Hubbard, and Mehan 2002; Fullan 2001; Learning First Alliance 2003; Mac Iver and Farley 2003) and for strengthening programs of school, family, and community partnerships (Chrispeels 1996; Epstein 2001, Sanders 2005). The consensus across studies is that district leaders are responsible for creating a culture of reform with all schools and that they must not allow one school to improve while others decline (Burch and Spillane 2004).

The new understanding of effective district leadership emphasizes shared, distributed, or democratic leadership and teamwork for school reform (Fullan 2001; Pounder, Reitzug, and Young 2002). In practice, shared leadership typically refers to collaborative work conducted by administrators and teachers. Although educators know that family and community involvement is important, educators often are reluctant to share leadership with parents and community members. Most teachers and administrators have not been prepared in college courses to conduct collaborative work (Darling-Hammond and Bransford 2005; Epstein and Sanders 2006; Leithwood and Prestine 2002). Most districts do not offer effective inservice education on new strategies for organizing school, family, and community partnerships (Epstein et al. 2002).

Despite these gaps in the education of educators, NCLB requires district leaders to organize effective partnership programs and to share leadership for children's education with parents. Specifically, Section 1118 specifies that districts *must* provide professional development and ongoing technical assistance to help schools implement programs that inform families about state standards and tests, guide parents to support student achievement at home, communicate messages in languages parents can understand, resolve other "barriers" or challenges that limit the involvement of economically disadvantaged and linguistically diverse parents, and build the capacity of both schools and parents to conduct and improve programs.

The law also outlines several optional activities that districts *may* conduct, including establishing district-level advisory councils; providing parents with literacy classes, leadership training, and transportation and child care to attend school meetings and workshops; scheduling meetings at varied times to increase parental participation, working with businesses and community partners; and adopting model approaches to help organize partnership programs.

The specifications in NCLB redirect district leaders from simply monitoring schools' compliance with the law to actively guiding schools to improve the quality and results of their partnership programs (Cowan 2003; U.S. Department of Education 2004).

FRAMEWORK OF POLICY INSTRUMENTS

The required and optional actions in NCLB for district leadership on partnerships can be understood with a theoretical framework that outlines a range of policy instruments for school reform. McDonnell and Elmore (1991) identified important differences of mandates that require and regulate actions; inducements that reward or sanction actions; capacity building that increases knowledge and skills for action; and system changing that reassigns decision making activities to new groups or individuals. NCLB includes all four policy instruments to guide district leaders on varied ways to improve programs of family and community involvement.

NCLB's Section 1118 includes the mandates for actions districts must take, outlined above. Title I, Part A includes inducements for action through funding that districts must allocate to schools to implement effective school-based parental involvement programs. The funding is tied to sanctions, which federal monitors may impose if districts fail to meet the requirements. Overall, the law states its goal to build capacities of district leaders, school leaders, and parents to plan, implement, and evaluate productive family involvement through the required professional development activities. District leaders who implement the required actions could help all schools develop more equitable programs of involvement by involving families who are typically labeled "hard to reach." Such actions would produce system-changing behaviors at the district level and in all schools (Epstein 2005; Epstein and Sheldon 2006).

Additional system-changing requirements are legislated in other sections of NCLB that require district leaders to offer parents of eligible students options to change schools and select supplemental services if their child's school fails to meet state standards for achievement or for safety for two years or more (see chapter 10 by Lauen and chapter 11 by Mickelson and Southworth in this volume). These options change the way decisions about student placements are made in school districts.

NATIONAL NETWORK OF PARTNERSHIP SCHOOLS

Although NCLB specifies that research-based programs should be implemented, the law does not indicate how the actions can be accomplished. Most district leaders need help in enacting NCLB Section 1118 and other requirements for family and community involvement. Studies and field tests are required in order to understand the structures and processes that enable districts and schools to develop and sustain effective partnership programs. In this study, we draw from data collected by the National Network of Partnership Schools (NNPS) at Johns Hopkins University, which includes a large number of school districts that share an interest in improving school, family, and community partnerships.[1]

NNPS guides districts to use research based approaches to understand family and community involvement and to help schools develop goal-linked programs that will help more students succeed in school (Epstein et al. 2002). Of course, not all leaders apply new knowledge or use handbooks, tools, or professional development training with the same speed or effectiveness. The variations in district leadership permit NNPS to study whether and how particular practices contribute to the quality of district partnership programs over time. We asked two main research questions:

- How are school districts addressing NCLB's requirements for family involvement? Are the requirements in Section 1118 for districts reasonable and attainable?
- How do district leaders' efforts on partnerships affect their reports of

the quality of their schools' programs of family and community involvement?

DATA

Data were collected in 2004 on end-of-year *UPDATE* surveys from 69 U.S. school districts in NNPS. Of these, 51 districts also provided data in 2003, permitting longitudinal analyses of progress in districts' partnership program development. The districts, ranging in size from one school to over 200 schools, were located in urban, suburban, and rural communities in 24 states.[2] They had been members of NNPS for from one year (20.8%) to eight years (11.1%). *UPDATE* surveys are required by NNPS to renew membership and services for the next school year. Therefore, all districts that returned the surveys were, in effect, restating their interest in improving their partnership programs.

Measures

In NNPS, district leaders for partnerships are guided to assume two major responsibilities, which also are required by NCLB. They are expected to establish district-level leadership and directly assist individual schools with their partnership programs, as measured by the following scales.

Dependent Variables

Leadership This measure of 13 items (α = .79) assessed the extent to which district leaders organized their work by setting up an office, identifying a budget, writing a leadership plan, writing or reviewing policy on parent involvement, and conducting other district-level activities.

Facilitation This scale of 16 items (α = .92) gauged the extent to which district leaders directly assisted individual schools to form an Action Team for Partnerships, write annual plans, evaluate progress, share ideas, and conduct other school-based activities.

Solve challenges to increase involvement Six items (α = .71) identified whether district leaders actively helped schools address basic challenges to reach more diverse families or left the schools on their own to solve problems. Challenges included involving parents who do not speak or read English; getting information to families who cannot attend school meetings; providing opportunities to volunteer at school and other locations; preparing teachers to guide families on helping children with homework; ensuring that diverse families are represented on school committees; and identifying community resources for school improvement.

Report of schools' progress A single item asked district leaders for the number of schools making "good progress" on partnerships. This number was transformed into the percentage of all schools that were assisted with work on partnerships.

Independent Variables

The explanatory variables in this study included measures that were of interest in prior studies of district leadership on partnerships.

Demographic characteristics The size of the district (number of schools) and poverty level (the percentage of students receiving free- or reduced-price meals in the district) were statistically controlled.

Collegial support for partnerships This 13-item scale (α = .93) reported the average level of cooperation (from none = 1 to a lot = 4) that district leaders for partnerships reported receiving from colleagues at the district level, in schools, from parent organizations, and from others in the community.

Program development tools and guidelines This 7-item scale (α = .87) reported district leaders' average ratings of helpfulness (from not helpful = 1 to very helpful=4) of major tools and materials for program development, including a comprehensive handbook, newsletters, books on best practices, website information, monthly communications, and other connections with NNPS.

Evaluation tools A 6-item scale (α = .53) identified whether district leaders used tools designed to help them evaluate district and school partnership programs, including reflective documentations, on-site inventories, and survey instruments.

Other NCLB requirements A 10-item scale (α = .79) assessed leaders' reports of whether the district, as a whole, was addressing specific NCLB requirements. One item in this scale—*communicate in languages that parents can understand*—had the greatest variation across districts. It is used as an explanatory variable in selected analyses of district leaders' work on partnerships.

RESULTS

Districts varied on the nature and extent of their leadership and facilitation activities for developing district-level and school-based programs of family and community involvement. They implemented an average of 7.37 activities to organize their offices and their work on partnerships. Some (16.9%) conducted 11 to 13 district-level leadership activities, whereas others (19.7%) conducted only 1 to 4 of the actions listed. District leaders also reported conducting an average of 7.25 facilitation activities to directly assist schools in developing their partnership programs. About 24 percent conducted 13 to 16 activities, whereas

14.1 percent reported that, as yet, they conducted *no* (0) actions to assist individual schools.

A few NCLB requirements were almost universally addressed, such as having a policy on parental involvement (85%) and providing information to parents about their child's achievement test scores (98.4%). By contrast, only 51 percent of the district leaders said their districts were working well to communicate with families in the languages parents speak at home..

District Leaders' Work

OLS regression analyses were conducted to test whether districts in NNPS improved their leadership and facilitation of schools from 2003 to 2004, as shown in Table 13.1. Districts' demographic characteristics of size and poverty level did not significantly affect the number of leadership or facilitation actions conducted by district leaders for partnerships. Some leaders in large and small, affluent and poor districts successfully set up their offices and worked with schools on partnerships, whereas other leaders lagged on these actions.

Table 13.1 also shows the importance of sustaining work on program development. District leaders who conducted more leadership actions in 2003 also did so in 2004 ($\beta = 539$, p < .001), and those who previously assisted their schools continued to do so in 2004 ($\beta = 629$, p < .001).

After accounting for their prior work in 2003, district leaders who reported strong collegial support for partnerships ($\beta = 208$, p < .10) and who used and found helpful more NNPS tools for program development ($\beta = 347$, p < .001)

Table 13.1 Variables affecting district-level leadership and facilitation from 2003 to 2004

	NCLB requirements for districts			
	Leadership structure		Facilitation of schools	
	β	(t)	β	(t)
District characteristics				
Size of district (# schools)	– .085	NS	–.050	NS
Percent free or reduced-price lunch	.156	NS	– .025	NS
Program components				
Prior year's leadership structure .539	.532	(4.24)***	—	
Prior year's facilitation of schools	—		.629	(5.78)***
Collegial support (district, school, family)	.176	NS	.208	(1.89)+
NNPS program tools and guidelines	.325	(2.66)**	.347	(3.17)***
Adjusted R²		.501		.597

Standardized regression coefficients are shown.
+p<.10, *p<.05, **p<.01, ***p<.001
Source: 2003 and 2004 UPDATE surveys, N=51 districts in NNPS for at least 2 years

significantly increased the number of facilitative activities they conducted to assist schools. Useful tools and guidelines also helped leaders organize their own work on partnerships (β = 325, p < .01). About 50 percent of the variance in leadership and nearly 60 percent of the variance in facilitation were explained by prior work on partnerships, collegial support, and the use of helpful tools and materials. These basic factors helped explain district leaders' attention to the requirements listed in NCLB Section 1118 to improve programs of parental involvement.

Solving Challenges To Involve All Families

Table 13.2 explores the influences on district leaders' efforts to help schools address challenges to reach more diverse families, as required by NCLB. The results indicate that district leaders who worked with schools to address challenges in 2003 continued to provide schools with ideas to involve all families in the next school year (β = .379, p < .01).

Over and above the work of the prior year, district leaders were more likely to give schools ideas for addressing key challenges to involve parents from all racial, educational, and socioeconomic groups if the district, as a whole, was addressing the NCLB requirement to communicate in understandable languages with all families (β = .264, p < .10) and if the leaders for partnerships used more NNPS evaluation tools (β = .296, p < .05).

The size of the district and poverty level of students did not influence whether leaders for partnerships worked with schools on solving challenges to reach all families or left it up to the schools alone. The district's history of attention to challenges, priority for communicating in languages families understand, and the use of evaluation tools explained 40 percent of the variance in whether district leaders directly assisted schools to work on challenges to reach all families.

Table 13. 2 Influence on district leaders to help schools meet challenges to involve all families

	β	(t)
District characteristics		
Size of district (# schools)	.278	(1.98)[+]
Percent free or reduced-price lunch	−.151	NS
District program components		
Prior year's attention to meet challenges	.379	(2.56)**
District's emphasis on communicating with all parents	.264	(1.82)[+]
NNPS evaluation tools	.296	(2.05)*
Adjusted R^2		.407

N=51 districts in NNPS for at least two years. Standardized regression coefficients are shown. +p<.10, *p<.05, **p<.01
Source: 2003 and 2004 UPDATE surveys

Schools' Progress on Partnerships

District leaders reported whether their schools were making *little, some,* or *good progress* on partnerships. Table 13.3 shows that neither the size nor poverty level of the district significantly affected leaders' reports of their schools' progress. By contrast, leaders' actions of *leadership* and *facilitation* had strong, but varying effects on their reports of schools' progress on partnership program development.

Column 1 of Table 13.3 shows that the extent of district leadership to organize an office, budget, and plans for partnerships was important for how leaders reported schools' progress (β = .343, p < .01). Those who conducted more leadership actions reported that more of their schools were making good progress on partnerships. Column 2 shows even more dramatic effects of leaders' direct assistance to schools on reports of schools' progress (β = .575, p < .001) and of the level of collegial support on schools' progress (β = .283, p < .05). District facilitation and collegial support—two measures that indicate whether district leaders made contact with schools and witnessed the work on school-based partnership programs—explained more than twice the variance as the more distal measure of leadership structure (43% compared to 20%) in reports of schools' progress on partnerships.

Contrasting Correlates of District :eadership

Not every leadership action is equally important for the quality of district-level partnership programs. Analyses were conducted to "unpack" the above results. NCLB requires districts to have a parental involvement policy. In addition, NNPS asks district leaders to write a leadership plan each year that schedules their actions at the district level and in assisting schools on partnerships.

Table 13.3 Influence of district leadership and facilitation on reports of schools' progress in family and community involvement

	β	(t)	β	(t)
District characteristics				
Size of district (# schools)	.052	NS	.060	NS
Percent free or reduced-price lunch	−.098	NS	−.048	NS
Program Components				
District leadership structure	.343	(2.31)*	—	
Facilitation of schools' action teams	—		.575	(4.88)***
Collegial support (district, school, family)	.278	(1.87)	.283	(2.23)*
Adjusted R₂		**.203**		**.433**

Standardized regression coefficients are shown.
+p<.10, *p<.05, ***p<.001
Source: 2004 *UPDATE* surveys; N=69 districts

TABLE 13.4 Contrasting correlates of district policies and written plans with NCLB requirements

Leadership actions on partnerships linked to NCLB requirements (Sec. 1118)	Have a district policy Mean .85 (s.d. .36)		Have a written plan Mean .58 (s.d. .50)	
	r	sig.	r	sig.
Have a district budget	.222	ns	.543	***
Conduct professional development for schools	.042	ns	.317	**
Disseminate best practices	.088	ns	.440	***
Make connections with colleagues to coordinate family involvement	.084	ns	.472	***
Facilitate schools' Action Teams for Partnerships (scale)	.176	ns	.552	***
Use NNPS evaluation tools (scale)	.101	ns	.378	**

N = 69 districts
+ < .10; *< .05; **< .01; ***<.001
Source: UPDATE 2004

Table 13.4 shows that leaders with written plans were significantly more likely to fulfill other requirements in NCLB's Section 1118 for district leadership on parental involvement. Those with detailed schedules were more likely to identify a budget for partnerships ($r = .543$, $p < .001$), conduct professional development ($r = .317$, $p < .01$), actively facilitate their schools ($r = .552$, $p < .001$), disseminate best practices ($r = .440$, $p < .001$), and conduct other activities to increase district-level and school-level capacities for productive parental involvement. Having a policy was not significantly correlated with any of the other actions by district leaders.

These patterns are due, in part, to the greater variation among districts in writing detailed plans than in having a policy. Although most districts (85%) had a policy, just over half (58%) of the district leaders fulfilled NNPS's requirement to write a detailed work plan in 2004. The results reinforce the importance for district leaders to go beyond the minimum of having a policy to increase the quality of their leadership and facilitation of programs of partnership.

DISCUSSION

This study presents the first quantitative analyses of whether and how well districts are addressing NCLB requirements for improving programs of family involvement. The data collected in 2004, as NCLB completed its 2nd full school year, showed that most districts in NNPS had started to address NCLB's requirements for district leadership on parental involvement. The results point to four policy-related conclusions that could help other districts organize more effective leadership for partnerships.

1. *Writing a policy is important but not sufficient for districts to conduct viable partnership programs.* Most districts in NNPS had formal policies on parental involvement and were trying to disseminate information to parents on their children's achievement and on schools' status in making adequate yearly progress (AYP), as required by NCLB. Fewer were addressing more difficult challenges of helping schools communicate with families who did not speak English and helping families become involved in ways that could increase students' achievement in school subjects. Some others (14%) had taken no steps to directly assist schools in developing educators' and parents' capacities to create comprehensive school-based partnership programs.

The results suggested that having a district policy on parental involvement was just one step on a much longer path to partnerships. Another document—a detailed plan for leadership and facilitation—was associated with the enactment of more NCLB requirements for district leadership on partnerships.

2. *A district leader for partnerships must be assigned to enact a district-wide partnership program.* Each district in this study had a leader for partnerships who served as a "key contact" to researchers at Johns Hopkins University for guidance on their work on partnerships. By contrast, other districts may have policies for parental involvement, but have *no one* assigned to lead this component of school organization and school improvement. This kind of "unstaffed mandate" would not be tolerated in schools working to improve their reading or math curricula, where curriculum coaches or consultants are expected. By contrast, many districts have lagged in assigning leaders for partnerships to guide schools in this work.

Assigning a leader for partnerships still was not enough to ensure high-quality partnership programs. District leaders must take action to improve their partnership programs. In this study, leaders varied widely in the number and quality of activities they conducted. Leaders did more to organize work and facilitate schools if they had strong collegial support, used research-based program development and evaluation tools and materials, and sustained their efforts over time. Further, leaders who directly assisted their schools were more likely to report that the schools were making good progress in their programs of family and community involvement.

3. *District leaders for partnerships need support from others to conduct districtwide partnership programs.* Neither a district policy on partnerships nor an assigned leader was enough to ensure a high-quality partnership program. This study showed that collegial support from other district leaders, school principals, educators, families, and from tools and guidelines offered by NNPS helped some district leaders for partnerships do more to assist schools and to report progress on partnerships. The results suggest that collegial contacts and using research-based tools for program development and evaluation may increase the seriousness of purpose of leaders' work on partnerships.

4. *The four policy instruments embedded in NCLB Section 1118 are influencing leadership for parental involvement.* This study suggests that NCLB's mandates for partnerships are beginning to affect district leaders' awareness and actions. The scales and measures showed that leaders were able to distinguish between mandates that they were and were not addressing. In written comments, respondents recognized the legitimacy of NCLB's mandates by noting that they wanted to improve their programs in the next school year by providing more staff development on partnerships, getting more principals on board, and helping all schools fully implement their action plans for partnerships.

NCLB inducements in the form of Title I targeted funds are beginning to influence district leaders' actions on family and community involvement. District leaders rated whether there were not enough funds for partnerships or whether their programs were adequately or well funded. More adequate funding was correlated with more district-level leadership activities (r = .433, p < .001) and with more actions to facilitate schools on partnerships (r = .363, p < .01).

NCLB requirements for capacity building were enacted by district leaders who conducted professional development on partnerships for school teams, including teachers, administrators, parents, and community partners and other workshops and presentations on family involvement for district colleagues. District leaders who provided team training for schools' Action Teams for Partnerships reported higher quality partnership programs overall (r = .365, p < .004).

Finally, system-changing actions were emerging. Many district leaders were using tools and materials to improve their work on partnerships and to help schools organize their programs and practices. Some were addressing challenges to help schools involve families who would otherwise be excluded from exchanges and decisions about their children's education. Many were guiding schools to write annual goal-oriented action plans with activities that involved families with their children to improve achievement in reading, math, attendance, and other indicators of success in school, as directed by NCLB (see Brownstein et al. 2006 for award winning programs that apply research in practice at http://www.partnershipschools.org in the section "Success Stories").

Limitations and Future Studies

Although this study provides new knowledge about district leaders' work on partnerships in response to NCLB, it is limited by the lack of comparable data from districts that were not members of NNPS. We cannot say if or how well other districts are addressing NCLB requirements for parental involvement. The data provided some useful clues, however, because districts in this study varied widely in their leadership activities. Those that used fewer program development and evaluation tools, for example, conducted fewer leadership and facilitation activities and had weaker partnership programs. These districts may be more like many other districts that are struggling to enact NCLB requirements. Still, studies are needed of matched samples of NNPS and non-NNPS districts to clearly show whether targeted tools, guidelines, and networking on partnerships increase districts' responses to NCLB requirements.

A second limitation is that this study examined only data from district leaders, not reports from the schools in these districts. Separate studies have shown that schools' Action Teams for Partnerships that reported receiving support from their district leaders conducted more family involvement activities, reached more diverse families, and implemented more NCLB requirements for family involvement (see Sheldon 2005; chapter 14 in this volume; Sheldon and Van Voorhis 2004). New studies are needed that examine the "nested" systems of districts and their schools to learn whether and which district leadership actions contribute significantly to the quality of schools' partnership programs, over and above what schools do on their own. With appropriate samples of schools nested within districts, researchers could use Hierarchical Linear Modeling (HLM) analyses to separate the independent effects of district policies and actions from the effects of leadership and support that occurs at the school level.

CONCLUSION

NLCB Section 1118 appears to be raising district leaders' awareness and encouraging action on partnerships. The regulations for parental involvement require attention to the structure of district leadership and to processes for planning, implementing, and evaluating programs and practices of partnerships at the district level and in all schools. In this study, data from districts showed that with time, collegial support, and helpful guidelines and tools, district leaders addressed more NCLB requirements for family and community involvement. By their actions, these leaders are showing that districts can meet the spirit and the letter of the law.

Notes

1. This work was supported by a grant from the National Institute of Child Health and Human Development (NICHD). The author's opinions do not necessarily reflect the policies or positions of the funding agency. The author thanks Kenyatta J. Williams for data management for this project.
2. The U.S. districts providing 2004 UPDATE data were in AL, AR, CA, FL, GA, KY, LA, MA, MD, MI, MN, MO, NC, NJ, NY, OH, OK, PA, SC, TN, TX, UT, WA, and WI.

References

Brownstein, J. I., M. Maushard, J. Robinson, M. D. Greenfeld, and D. J. Hutchins. 2006. *Promising partnership practices 2006*. Baltimore: Johns Hopkins University Center on School, Family, and

Community Partnerships. (See annual collections of practices in the section Success Stories) http://www.partnershipschools.org.

Burch, P. and J. Spillane. 2004. *Leading from the middle: Midlevel district staff and instructional improvement.* Chicago: Cross City Campaign for Urban School Reform.

Chrispeels, J. H. 1996. Evaluating teachers' relationships with families: A case study of one district. *The Elementary School Journal* 97:179–200.

Coburn, C. 2003. Rethinking scale: Moving beyond numbers to deep and lasting change. *Educational Researcher,* 32:3–12.

Cowan, K. T. 2003. Parental involvement. In *The new Title I: The changing landscape of accountability,* K. T. Cowan and C. J. Edwards (eds.), 139–49. Washington, D.C.: Thompson.

Darling-Hammond, L. and J. Bransford. 2005.. *Preparing teachers for a changing world: What teachers should learn and be able to do.* San Francisco: Jossey-Bass.

Datnow, A., L. Hubbard, and H. Mehan. 2002. *Extending educational reform: From one school to many.* New York: Routledge Falmer.

Epstein, J. L. 2001. *School, family, and community partnerships: Preparing educators and improving schools.* Boulder, CO: Westview Press.

———. 2005. Attainable goals? The spirit and letter of the *No Child Left Behind Act* on parental involvement. *Sociology of Education* 78 (2):179–82.

——— and M. G. Sanders. 2006. Prospects for change: Preparing educators for school, family, and community partnerships. *Peabody Journal of Education* 81(2):81–120.

———, M. G. Sanders, B. S. Simon, K. C. Salinas, N. R. Jansorn, and F. L. Van Voorhis, 2002. *School, family, and community partnerships: Your handbook for action.* 2nd ed. Thousand Oaks, CA: Corwin.

——— and S. B. Sheldon. 2006. Moving forward: Ideas for research on school, family, and community partnerships. In *SAGE Handbook for research in education: Engaging ideas and enriching inquiry,* ed. C. F. Conrad and R. Serlin, 117–37. Thousand Oaks, CA: Sage.

Fullan, M. 2001. *Leading in a culture of change.* San Francisco: Jossey-Bass.

Learning First Alliance. 2003. *Beyond islands of excellence: What districts can do to improve instruction and achievement in all schools.* Baltimore, MD: ASCD. http://www.learnignfirst.org/lfaweb/rp?pa=doc anddocId=62.

Leithwood, K. and N. Prestine. 2002. Unpacking the challenges of leadership at the school and district level. *The educational leadership challenge: Redefining leadership for the 21st century,* ed. J. Murphy, 42–64. Chicago: University of Chicago Press.

Mac Iver, M. and E. Farley. 2003. *Bringing the district back in: The role of the central office in improving instruction and student achievement.* CRESPAR Report #65. Baltimore, MD: Center for Research on the Education of Students Placed at Risk.

McDonnell, L. M. and R. F. Elmore.1991. Getting the job done: Alternative policy instruments. In *Education policy implementation,* ed. A. R. Odden, 157–84. Albany: State University of New York Press.

Pounder, D., U. Reitzug, and M. D. Young. 2002. Preparing school leaders for school improvement, social justice, and community. In *The educational leadership challenge: Redefining leadership for the 21st century,* ed.J.Murphy, 261–88. Chicago: University of Chicago Press.

Sanders, M. G. 2005. *Building school-community partnerships: Collaboration for student success.* Thousand Oaks, CA: Corwin Press.

Sheldon, S. B. 2005. Testing a structural equations model of partnership program implementation and family involvement. *The Elementary School Journal,* 106:171–87.

——— and F. L. Van Voorhis. 2004. Partnership programs in U.S. schools: Their development and relationship to family involvement outcomes. *School Effectiveness and School Improvement,* 15: 125–48.

U.S. Department of Education. 2004. *Parental involvement, Title I, Part A: Non-regulatory guidance.* Washington, D.C.: Author.

14

Getting Families Involved with NCLB

Factors Affecting Schools' Enactment of Federal Policy[1]

Steven B. Sheldon

Current federal education policy, the No Child Left Behind (NCLB) Act, seeks to raise overall student achievement and reduce the disparity in school achievement between white and minority students. To accomplish these goals, NCLB proposes a wide range of mechanisms including regular standardized testing of students, ensuring the presence of high-quality teachers in classrooms, and increasing parental involvement in students' education. The aspect of NCLB that mandates that schools set up processes to include more families in their children's education has remained largely ignored in most discussions about the efficacy of this legislation.

Title I, Sec. 1118 of NCLB requires schools that receive funds for serving students from low-income families to implement activities that help foster greater family and community involvement. Schools are required to create policies stating that family and community involvement are valued goals at the school, include families on school decision- and policy-making committees, provide information to parents to help them understand academic content and achievement standards, train educators in how to reach out to parents and implement programs connecting children's home and school, and communicate in languages and at reading levels accessible to all families. In addition, NCLB encourages schools to develop partnerships with community-based organizations and businesses in order to help all students learn and achieve in school.

Inclusion of family involvement is a valuable component of efforts to improve student achievement. Studies on family involvement have concluded that students' home environments and family involvement are important predictors of a variety of academic and nonacademic outcomes (Henderson and Mapp 2002;

Jordan, Orozco, and Averett 2001). Current explanations for why parents get involved emphasize individual characteristics of parents such as race, income, and personal beliefs (Desimone 1999; Hoover-Dempsey and Sandler 1997; Lareau 1988). These influences on parent involvement, while important, are difficult or impossible to affect. Studies are needed that can help identify the influences on parent involvement that can be affected by the actions of teachers and administrators.

Research shows that educators' efforts to improve school–home relationships can have a positive effect on levels of parent involvement (Epstein and Dauber 1991; Simon 2004; Van Voorhis 2003) and student outcomes (Epstein 2001; Sheldon and Epstein 2004, 2005). Kerbow and Bernhardt (1993) found that teacher contact often leads minority parents to become involved in their children's schooling. Others have shown that having a strong schoolwide approach to school, family, and community partnerships can also facilitate parent involvement (Sheldon and Van Voorhis 2004). Research that can identify school characteristics that help develop high-quality partnership efforts have the potential to impact parental involvement.

LOOKING AT CURRENT PARTNERSHIP EFFORTS

Almost unanimously, educators and school officials recognize the important role of parents in shaping student motivation and achievement in schools. It is also an area many teachers struggle with greatly. According to a recent MetLife survey of teachers (Markow and Martin 2005), teachers reported that interacting with parents is an area where they have the least training and experience the greatest anxiety. In order to help teachers more effectively raise student achievement and improve educational equity, both overarching goals of NCLB, we need research that identifies ways that schools can invest attention and resources to promote a supportive school context for family and community involvement.

To help structure and coordinate their involvement efforts, many schools have joined the National Network of Partnership Schools (NNPS) to develop effective partnership programs using a research-based framework. As members of NNPS, schools are provided tools and guidelines for establishing, maintaining, and improving schoolwide partnership programs that reach out to families of all students. The guidance provided to schools is based on the theory of overlapping spheres of influence and a framework of six types of involvement (Epstein 2001). This theory argues that schools, families, and communities serve as important contexts for children's learning, and that greater coordination among these environments benefits children's education and development. The NNPS framework provides schools with strategies to promote greater communication and collaboration between students' schools, homes, and communities.

As a first step in establishing a partnership program, schools must form an Action Team for Partnerships (ATP). The ATP members include teachers, school administrators, parents, community members, and, at the high-school level, students. This team functions as an "action arm" of the school improvement team, responsible for organizing and implementing each of the school's involvement activities (Epstein et al. 2002).

One of the primary responsibilities of the action team is to create annual action plans for family and community involvement that link these partnership activities to specific goals listed on the school improvement plan. Schools are encouraged to set two academic goals, one nonacademic goal, and a partnership goal as the focus of their partnership activities. For each partnership goal, ATPs are expected to use Epstein's framework of six types of involvement in order to create a comprehensive partnership approach for improving student success. Schools with comprehensive programs of partnership implement activities for all six types of involvement: (1) parenting; (2) communicating; (3) volunteering; (4) learning at home; (5) decision making; and (6) collaborating with the community (Epstein et al. 2002). This typology provides a structure around which a school can organize and evaluate its efforts and activities to involve parents in their children's education.

In addition, NNPS asks schools to confront challenges associated with involving *all* families in their children's education. Because research shows that there is variation in parent involvement according to the education levels of the child, educational attainment of the parents, family structure, and family race or ethnic culture (Astone and McLanahan 1991; Delgato-Gaitan 1992; Lareau 1988), schools in NNPS are encouraged to examine their partnership practices and assess the nature and degree to which they reach out to all of their students' families. In doing so, schools can inform and involve parents across racial, educational, and socioeconomic groups so that all families can actively support their children's education.

In this study, longitudinal data are used to examine the effects of school characteristics and processes on the enactment of NCLB guidelines for family involvement. The study draws upon data from schools in NNPS to understand how principals affect policy enactment over time and whether the schools' reports of district support for partnerships help schools improve the extent to which they enact NCLB regulations for family involvement. In addition, the study investigates attributes of schools' ATPs to see whether this aspect of school organization affects the degree to which schools are involving families in students' education, as written in NCLB.

METHODS

This study relied on the analyses of survey data, collected from a diverse set of schools. In order to test the hypotheses about the effects of school organization, principal leadership, and district support on schools' enactment of federal family involvement policy. Analyses were conducted on a sample of schools working to develop programs of school, family, and community partnerships that can help improve academic and non-academic student outcomes.

Procedure

In the spring of 2004, schools in NNPS received the annual *UPDATE* survey to complete and return to Johns Hopkins University. By completing and returning the *UPDATE* survey, schools renewed their membership in NNPS for the 2004–5 school year and continued to receive NNPS materials and services. The *UPDATE* survey asks schools to report on school characteristics and reflect upon the implementation of their partnership program. Members of the action team report on the quality of their program implementation, the extent to which they are working on challenges to family and community involvement, the extent to which they receive support from the school community and district for partnerships, the extent to which teachers support parent involvement, and the extent to which parents are actively involved in their children's education.

Sample

Six hundred and two schools returned an *UPDATE* survey in 2004 (69.4% return rate). Of these schools, 462 had been in NNPS for more than one year and returned an *UPDATE* survey in 2003. Thirteen schools were removed from the sample because they either served students in kindergarten through 12th grade or because the grade level of the school was not reported. The remaining sample (n = 449) consisted of schools located in large urban (42.0%), small urban (23.9%), suburban (22.5%), and rural (11.6%) areas. Seventy-nine percent of the schools were elementary and PK–8 schools, 13.6 percent were middle schools, 0.9 percent were middle and high schools, and 6.7 percent were high schools. Finally, over three-quarters of the schools reported that they received Title I funds.

Variables

Dependent Variable

NCLB enactment Thirteen items were taken from the 2003 and 2004 *UPDATE* surveys to measure schools' enactment of the NCLB policy requirements for parent involvement. These items were chosen because they correspond to the family involvement requirements found in Section 1118 of Title I in NCLB (see appendix). Because the items did not use a common response scale, each one was converted into standardized scores with a mean of zero and a standard deviation of 1. This measure of enactment is the average of the 13 items in 2003 ($\alpha = .79$) and 2004 ($\alpha = .79$).

Independent Variables
Independent variables include school background, action team organization, principal effects, and district effect.

School background
School level: Schools were categorized as elementary schools and secondary schools. Those serving grades PK–6 and PK–8 were coded "1" to represent elementary schools. Middle schools (grades 4–8), middle/high schools (grades 4–12), and high schools (grades 9–12) were grouped and coded "0" to represent secondary schools.
Large urban: Schools located in large urban, central city areas were coded "1." The remaining schools were coded "0."

Action team organization
Team structure: Schools that organized their Action Team for Partnerships as a single body, without creating committees, focused on either school goals or the six types of involvement, were coded "1." Schools whose action team formed subcommittees were coded "0."
Meeting frequency: A single item measured the frequency of schools' action team meetings. On a scale of 1 to 5, schools reported whether their action team met: "never," "1–2 times," "A few times," "Monthly," or "More than monthly."

Principal effects
Principal turnover: Schools reported the number of principals they have had over the past three years. Higher numbers reflect less stability in the administration of a school.
Principal support for partnerships: Respondents reported the degree to which the principal supported the partnership program at their school. This measure was the sum of eight items ($\alpha =.83$), coded 1 or 0, asking whether or not the principal provided various types of support. The items include: Is an active member of the ATP; provides time for ATP members to meet and work; allocates funds for ATP activities; and brings community partners and resources to the school.

District effect
Reported district support for partnerships: Action teams reported the extent to which their district offices provided six types of support for partnerships ($\alpha=.88$) including: Provided technical assistance on partnerships, provided funds for partnership programs, and evaluated or helped the school evaluate the quality of their partnership program. Each type of support was rated as: 1 "Not Provided," 2 "A Little Helpful," 3 "Helpful," or 4 "Very Helpful." This scale is the mean of the six items.

RESULTS

Data analyses began with descriptive analyses of trends and bivariate relationships of variables. Means and standard deviations of the measures used in this study are presented at the bottom of Table 14.1. In 2004, about half of the schools in this study organized their ATPs by subcommittees, while the others structured the work of the ATP as a single group. On average, schools reported that the ATP met between "a few times" and "monthly." There was no significant relationship between the way a school organized its action team and the frequency of meetings.

Respondents generally viewed principals as supportive of the partnership efforts at their schools. On average, principals provided over six of the eight types of support. On average, schools in this sample reported having relatively stable leadership over the past three years. Three-quarters of the schools (73.6%) had one principal in three years, 23.5 percent had two principals, and 2.9 percent of the schools had three or more principals in three years. As shown in Table 14.1, schools with more stability in school leadership tended to report higher levels of support for the ATP and partnership efforts from the principal in 2004 ($r = -.226$, $p \leq .000$).

Schools in this sample also reported that, overall, their districts were supportive of partnerships. On average, schools reported that their districts provided four of the six types of support. According to the schools in this sample, the support received from their districts on partnerships was somewhat helpful ($M = 2.45$). The correlation coefficient between principal support and district support was statistically significant ($r = .130$, $p \leq .007$), suggesting that principals are more likely to support partnerships at their school when the district conducts more helpful activities related to partnerships.

Table 14.1 also shows other important correlations. Elementary schools tended to be located in large urban areas ($r = .092$, $p \leq .053$) and reported greater principal support for partnerships than did secondary schools ($r = .137$, $p \leq .004$). Compared to schools in other locales, large urban schools reported greater support from their districts for partnerships ($r = .184$ $p \leq .000$). Also, schools with greater principal support for partnerships tended to have action teams that met more frequently ($r = .285$, $p \leq .000$) and reported a greater likelihood that the ATP was organized according to committees ($r = -.115$, $p \leq .019$).

The strongest predictor of the extent to which schools were meeting NCLB requirements for family and community involvement in 2004 was the enactment of these processes in 2003 ($r = .548$, $p \leq .000$). Elementary schools reported greater enactment of NCLB in 2004 ($r = .302$, $p \leq .000$), as did schools with actions teams that met more frequently ($r = .338$, $p \leq .000$). Zero-order correlations suggest that the principal is important to partnership program enactment. Schools with more principal turnover in three years had less NCLB enactment ($r = -.170$, $p \leq .000$), while schools whose principals provided more support for partnerships

TABLE 14.1 Means, standard deviations, and correlations

	School level	Large urban	Meeting frequency	Team structure	Principal turnover	Principal support	Reported district support	NCLB 2003	NCLB 2004
School level	—								
Large urban	.092*	—							
Meeting frequency	-.023	.019	—						
Team structure	.052	-.040	-.023	—					
Principal turnover	-.031	-.013	-.040	.044	—				
Principal support	.137**	.006	.285***	-.115*	-.226***	—			
Reported district support	.075	.184***	.094*	.032	-.026	.130**	—		
NCLB 2003	.199***	-.156**	.156***	-.060	-.103*	.215***	.129**	—	
NCLB 2004	.302***	-.064	.338***	-.060	-.170***	.452***	.253***	.548***	—
Mean	.78	.42	3.33	.50	1.30	6.63	2.45	-.01	-.02
Standard Dev.	.42	.49	.92	.50	.525	1.94	.89	.57	.57

N = 462 Schools
* p ≤ .05, ** p ≤ .01, *** p ≤ .001
School level: Elementary schools=1, Secondary schools =0
Large urban: Yes = 1, No = 0
Team structure: Single team/no committees = 1, committee structure = 0

were more in compliance with the parental involvement requirements of NCLB ($r = .452$, $p \leq .000$). Finally, reported district support was associated with greater NCLB enactment ($r = .253$, $p \leq .000$).

To examine the influences on NCLB enactment, stepwise multiple regression analyses were conducted. Preliminary tests showed that receiving Title I funds did not predict NCLB enactment, and this variable was not included in the models reported here. Removal of Title I status from the regression models did not change estimations of the effect the remaining factors have on schools' NCLB enactment. Model 1 of Table 14.2 shows that elementary schools were in greater compliance with regulations to create partnerships than were secondary schools ($\beta = .290$, $p \leq .000$). Model 2 of Table 14.2 exhibits that ATPs structured as a single team without committees tended to enact NCLB less than those with subcommittees ($\beta = -.084$, $p \leq .057$), and those schools in which the action team met more frequently reported greater NCLB compliance ($\beta = .340$, $p \leq .000$). The action team variables explained 12 percent of the variance in schools' 2004 NCLB enactment, over and above school level.

Model 3 in Table 14.2 demonstrates that the principal and district play an important role in helping schools meet NCLB regulations for parent involvement. Schools with greater principal turnover tended to implement fewer NCLB requirements ($\beta = -.086$, $p \leq .035$). Schools in which the principal supported the work of the action team on partnerships reported greater enactment of parent involvement activities ($\beta = .305$, $p \leq .000$), as did schools that reported greater support for partnerships from their district offices ($\beta = .223$ $p \leq .000$). Having these forms of support explained an additional 15 percent of the variation in schools' implementation of NCLB requirements for family involvement.

Model 4 of Table 14.2 shows that, after accounting for NCLB enactment in 2003, several school factors remained significant predictors of NCLB implementation in 2004. Not surprisingly, schools that were in greater compliance with the NCLB requirement for parent involvement in 2003 tended to be in greater compliance in 2004 ($\beta = .396$, $p \leq .000$). After controlling for prior levels of enactment, elementary schools continued to do more work on partnerships than secondary schools ($\beta = .170$, $p \leq .000$). In addition, schools with ATPs that met more regularly, that received greater principal support for partnerships, and that reported greater support from their district offices tended to report higher levels of compliance from one year to the next ($\beta = .183$, $p \leq .000$, $\beta = .256$, $p \leq .000$, and $\beta = .165$, $p \leq .000$, respectively). This model explained almost half of the variation found in schools' enactment of family involvement practices in 2004.

DISCUSSION

This study adds new information to previous research on factors associated with stronger enactment of the parent involvement requirements in NCLB and is the

Table 14.2 OLS analyses of the effects of partnership program components on NCLB enactment in 2004

	Model 1	**Model 2**	**Model 3**	**Model 4**
Background				
School level	.290***	.301***	.247***	.170***
Large urban	−.076	−.094*	−.140***	−.058
Action team				
Meeting frequency	—	.340***	.225***	.183***
Team structure	—	−.084*	−.048	−.022
Principal effect				
Principal stability	—	—	−.086*	−.061
Principal support	—	—	.305***	.256***
District effect				
Reported district support	—	—	.223***	.165***
Prior enactment				
NCLB 2003	—	—	—	.396***
Adj. R-square	.081	.202	.351	.487

N = 462 schools
* p ≤ .05, ** p ≤ .01, *** p ≤ .001
School level: Elementary schools=1, Secondary schools = 0
Large urban: Yes = 1, No = 0
Team structure: Single team/no committees = 1, committee structure = 0

first to conduct longitudinal analyses on the NCLB family involvement requirements. The study shows the importance of having a school context supportive of school, family, and community partnerships to improve outreach to families and increase levels of family and community involvement at school. Three aspects of the school context were related to NCLB enactment: team functioning, principal support, and district support.

Family and community partnership programs benefit when schools have a coordinated approach to developing strong connections with families. As members of NNPS, schools in this study were encouraged to set up an ATP to plan partnership activities that would help them meet school improvement goals. When these teams met on a regular basis, they were more likely to have implemented NCLB requirements. Having an ATP that meets regularly, at least monthly, may increase the likelihood that schools can organize and implement their partnership efforts. The ways in which schools structured their action teams, whether as a single group or as several goal-oriented committees, was not associated with NCLB enactment once the principal's and district support were taken into consideration.

Principal stability and support are critical for a school to effectively implement family and community involvement activities and programs. Although research has linked principal turnover to schools with greater student mobility, children from families with lower incomes, and greater teacher turnover (Griffith 1999), studies have not connected this measure with schools' ability to implement parental involvement reform programs. This study shows that the more schools changed principals over three years, the less likely they were to enact the family involvement aspects of NCLB. This relationship was not significant once the school's prior level of NCLB enactment was taken into consideration, suggesting that strong partnership programs are less susceptible to the disruptions that accompany frequent change in school leadership.

The measure of the amount of support principals provided their action team was among the strongest predictors of how well schools were implementing the family involvement aspects of NCLB. The finding that principal support is associated with improved program implementation concurs with research on other types of school reform (Berends et al. 2002; Newmann, King, and Youngs 2000) and confirms previous research showing the important role principals have in promoting family and community involvement activities in schools (Van Voorhis and Sheldon 2004).

District support for partnerships may be crucial for meeting the demands for parent involvement in the NCLB law. In this study, schools that reported greater and more effective support for partnerships from district leaders were more likely to implement NCLB requirements. Previous research has shown with cross-sectional data that schools reporting more support for partnerships from their district also tended to report strong partnership programs and greater implementation of NCLB requirements for family involvement (Sheldon 2005). By using longitudinal data, this study lends strong support to the notion that school reforms will be better implemented when these actions are supported systemically.

Limitations

The analyses provide insight into how schools might better implement federal policy regulations to involve families and communities in students' education. The study, however, cannot make claims about the extent to which enactment of NCLB requirements for family involvement affect student learning or success in school. Future studies should test whether the NCLB measure used in this study is connected to student outcomes such as achievement test performance or attendance. Also, despite the fact that the sample includes schools at all grade levels and locales, this study would be strengthened by introducing a matched comparison group of non-NNPS schools to the analyses. Nevertheless, the findings are instructive to any school interested in making family and community involvement an integrated component of the school improvement program.

The results of this study demonstrate that schools' abilities to meet the family involvement requirements of NCLB benefit significantly from an organized, systemic approach to partnerships. Schools are more likely to have well

APPENDIX

APPENDIX Table 14.A NCLB guidelines for parental involvement and corresponding measures of partnership program development

	NCLB guidelines for parental involvement	UPDATE measure
Section 1118, subsection b1	Each school…shall jointly develop with, and distribute to, parents of participating children a written parental involvement policy, agreed on by such parents, that shall describe the means for carrying out the requirements of subsections (c) through (f).	We wrote a One-Year Action Plan for partnerships for the 2002–3 school year. We wrote a One-Year Action Plan for partnerships for the 2003–4 school year.
Section 1118, subsection c3	…involve parents in an organized, ongoing, and timely way, in the planning, review, and improvement of programs under this part,…	How many parents or community liaisons were members of the Action Team for Partnerships?
Section 1118, subsection c4A-C	…provide parents of participating children—timely information about programs a description and explanation of the curriculum in use at the school, the forms of academic assessment used, and the proficiency levels students are expected to meet." opportunities for regular meetings to formulate suggestions and to participate in decisions related to the education of their children	How well did your school's ATP share information about the partnership program with the PTA or PTO and all families?
Section 1118, subsection d	…jointly develop with parents a school-parent compact that outlines how parents, the entire school staff, and students will share the responsibility for improved student academic achievement and the means by which the school and parents will build and develop a partnership to help children achieve state standards	How well did your school's ATP implement partnership activities that support school improvement goals?

(Continued)

APPENDIX Table 14.A Continued

	NCLB guidelines for parental involvement	UPDATE Measure
Section 1118, subsection d2	Address the importance of communication between teachers and parents on an ongoing basis through, at a minimum annual parent-teachers conferences in elementary schools frequent reports to parents on their children's progress reasonable access to staff, opportunities to volunteer and participate in their child's class, and observation of classroom activities.	% of teachers who conducted at least one p-t conference with each students' family % of teachers who utilized parents as volunteers in class, at school, or at home To what extent did the school send positive communications periodically to all parents about their children's work and accomplishments? To what extent did the school recruit and train parent/family volunteers to conduct activities that support school improvement goals?
Section 1118, subsection e3	Shall educate teachers, pupil services personnel, principals, and other staff in the value and utility of contributions of parents and in how to reach out to, communicate with, and work with parents as equally partners	To what extent did the school prepare teachers to guide families on how to talk with, monitor, and interact with their children about homework?
Section 1118, subsection e5	Shall ensure that information related to school and parent programs, meetings, and other activities is sent to parents in a format and, to the extent practical, in a language the parents can understand	To what extent did the school communicate with all families, including those who do not read or speak English well?
Section 1118, subsection e13	…may develop appropriate roles for community-based organizations and businesses in parent involvement activities	To what extent did the school identify and use community resources and services to help meet school improvement goals? Develop ways for student to contribute to the community?

implemented programs and experience greater parent participation when they have a goal-oriented team working on partnership practices that meets regularly, principal leadership that is stable and supportive of the partnership program, and when the school's efforts to connect with students' families are also valued and assisted by the school district. These activities and characteristics are accessible to all schools, making the establishment of strong school, family, and community partnerships, and therefore, compliance with this aspect of NCLB, attainable throughout the nation.

Note

1. This work was supported by a grant from The National Institute of Child Heath and Human Development to the Center on School, Family, and Community Partnerships at Johns Hopkins University. The opinions expressed are the author's and do not necessarily reflect those of the funding agency. Correspondence should be sent to 3003 N. Charles Street, Suite 220, Baltimore, MD, 21218 or e-mail at ssheldon@csos.jhu.edu.

References

Astone, N. and S. McLanahan. 1991. Family structure, parent practices, and high school completion. *American Sociological Review* 56:309–20.

Berends, M., J. Chum, G. Schuyler, S. Stockly, and R. J. Briggs. 2002. *Challenges of conflicting school reforms: Effects of New American Schools in a high-poverty district.* Santa Monica, CA: RAND.

Delgato-Gaitan, C. 1992. School matters in the Mexican-American home: Socializing children to education. *American Educational Research Journal* 29:495–513.

Desimone, L. 1999. Linking parent involvement with student achievement: Do race and income matter? *Journal of Educational Research* 93:11–30.

Epstein, J. L. 2001. *School, family, and community partnerships: Preparing educators and improving schools.* Boulder, CO: Westview.

———. 2005. Attainable goals? The spirit and letter of the no child left behind act on parental involvement. *Sociology of Education* 78:179–82.

——— and S. L. Dauber. 1991. School programs and teacher practices of parent involvement in inner-city elementary and middle schools. *Elementary School Journal,* 91:289–305.

———, M. G. Sanders, B. S. Simon, K. C. Salinas, N. R. Jansorn, and F. L. Van Voorhis. 2002. *School, family, and community partnerships: Your handbook for action.* 2nd ed. Thousand Oaks, CA: Corwin.

Feuerstein, A. 2000. School characteristics and parent involvement: Influences on participation in children's schools. *Journal of Educational Research,* 94:29–40.

Griffith, J. 1999. The school leadership/school climate relation: Identification of school configurations associated with change in principals. *Education Administration Quarterly* 35 (2):267–91.

Henderson, A. T. and K. L. Mapp. 2002. *A new wave of evidence: The impact of school, family, and community connections on student achievement.* Austin, TX: Southwest Educational Development Laboratory.

Hoover-Dempsey, K. V. and H. M. Sandler. 1997. Why do parents become involved in their children's education? *Review of Educational Research* 67:3–42.

Jordon, C., E. Orozco, and A. Averett.2001. *Emerging issues in school, family, and community connections.* Austin, TX: National Center for Family and Community Connections with Schools/Southwest Educational Development Laboratory.

Kerbow, B. and A. Bernhardt. 1993. Parent intervention in the school: The context of minority involvement. In *Parents, their children, and schools,* ed. J. Coleman and B. Schneider, 115–45. Boulder, CO: Westview.

Lareau, A. 1988. Social class differences in family-school relationships: The importance of cultural capital. *Sociology of Education* 60:73–85.

Markow, D. and S. Martin. 2005. *The MetLife survey of the American teacher: Transitions and the role of supportive relationships*. MetLife, Inc.

Newmann, F. M., M. B. King, and P. Youngs. 2000. Professional development that addresses school capacity: Lessons from urban elementary schools. *American Journal of Education* 108:259–99.

Sheldon, S. B. 2005. Testing a structural equation model of partnership program implementation and family involvement. *Elementary School Journal* 106:171–87.

———— and J. L. Epstein. 2004. Getting students to school: Using family and community involvement to reduce chronic absenteeism. *School Community Journal* 14:39–56

————. 2005. Involvement counts: Family and community partnerships and math achievement. *Journal of Educational Research* 98:196–206.

———— and F. L. Van Voorhis. 2004. Partnership programs in U.S. schools: Their development and relationship to family involvement outcomes. *School Effectiveness and School Improvement* 15:125–48.

Simon, B. S. 2004. High-school outreach and parent involvement. *Social Psychology of Education* 7:185–209.

Van Voorhis, F. L. 2003. Interactive homework in middle school: Effects on family involvement and science achievement. *Journal of Educational Research* 96 (6):323–38.

———— and S. B. Sheldon. 2004. Principals' roles in the development of U.S. programs of school, family, and community partnerships. Accepted for publication in the *International Journal of Educational Research*.

Part V

Federal Involvement, NCLB, and the
Reduction of the Achievement Gap

15

Learning from Philadelphia's School Reform

The Impact of NCLB and Related State Legislation[1]

Elizabeth Useem

For researchers seeking to examine the effects of the school and district interventions spelled out in the 2002 federal No Child Left Behind (NCLB) legislation, there is no better place to look than Philadelphia's public school system. The district, the nation's ninth largest with 174,000 pupils, has become a veritable research and development test-bed for judging NCLB's effectiveness in improving urban schools. In Philadelphia's case, NCLB reinforced preexisting state legislation that widened state prerogatives to intervene in distressed districts. Unlike a number of other state and district leaders, Philadelphia's education leaders have embraced both the spirit and substance of the requirements and options laid out in NCLB. At a regional NCLB "summit" held in Philadelphia in April 2006, U.S. Secretary of Education Margaret Spellings applauded the district's "great results" and "long-standing support for No Child Left Behind" (Snyder 2006).

NCLB specifies a range of graduated interventions, ranging from mild to moderate to strong, that can be applied by states to districts and to schools that are chronically in need of improvement. Some of the strongest steps that can be taken include a state takeover of a district, the imposition of a mandatory curriculum on a school, the "reconstitution" or reorganization of a school's staff, the outsourcing of a school's management to nonprofit organizations and for-profit education management organizations (EMOs), or the conversion of a district school to a public charter school (Brady 2003). Policymakers in the district, pushed initially by state leaders, have drawn freely from this broad mix of policy tools to attack the problem of persistently low student achievement.

Beginning with the Commonwealth of Pennsylvania's takeover of the School District of Philadelphia in December 2001, the Philadelphia public schools have experienced, to varying degrees, the strong interventions outlined above. These actions occurred simultaneously with the passage of NCLB, and were based on two pieces of state legislation supported by Governor Tom Ridge: Act 46, passed in 1998, allowed the state to take over districts with serious fiscal or academic problems and to institute a broad range of radical interventions; and Act 16, enacted in 2000, another takeover bill aimed at 11 districts with low levels of student academic performance (Boyd and Christman 2003; Maranto 2005). The options for interventions in these bills were similar to those that were subsequently laid out in NCLB.

No single reform strategy has guided policy in Philadelphia since the state takeover. Instead, state and local education leaders have relied on the three broad classes of policy instruments outlined by Hannaway and Woodroffe (2003): market-based mechanisms, accountability and incentive structures, and school capacity building. In doing so, they (1) adopted a multipronged strategy of creating of a diverse "portfolio" of types of schools; (2) applied top-down pressure to schools by implementing NCLB's accountability system; and (3) implemented a number of initiatives, such as more qualified teachers, a core curriculum, smaller classes in the early grades, to build schools' capacity for self-improvement. The fact that Philadelphia, an underfunded district serving largely poor and minority students, has deployed so many policy tools from the NCLB arsenal makes it a particularly rich case study of the law's impact.

THE BACKGROUND

The state of Pennsylvania took over the Philadelphia school system in December 2001 citing the district's fiscal and academic "distress" as a rationale for the takeover. In taking this step, legislators amended the Pennsylvania School Code to give the district's School Reform Commission (SRC), the new five-member governance unit that replaced the existing school board, sweeping powers to change district policies and procedures.

In the spring of 2002, a majority of SRC members voted to implement a complex "diverse provider model" (Hill, Campbell, and Harvey 2000), one that reflected the faith of former Governor Tom Ridge and Governor Mark Schweiker in the ability of market forces to reinvigorate public education, and one that reflected a philosophical strand underlying NCLB. Despite the angry opposition of community, student, and labor groups, the SRC outsourced the management of 46 of the district's 264 schools to seven different external organizations (Bulkley,

Mundell, and Riffer 2004; Travers 2003). The organizations chosen to manage or partner with the 46 low-performing schools included:

- Three for-profit EMO firms: Edison Schools, Inc.; Victory Schools; and Chancellor Beacon Academies (each allocated approximately $850 extra per pupil);
- Two universities: Temple University and the University of Pennsylvania (each given $450 extra per pupil);[2]
- Two locally based nonprofits: Universal Companies, a community development organization, and Foundations, Inc., a reform support organization (each given approximately $650 extra per pupil).

In addition, in this first stage of the reform, the SRC voted to establish a separate Office of Restructured Schools (ORS), and placed 21 low-performing "Restructured" schools under its jurisdiction. These schools were given an additional $550 per pupil to implement (and pilot) the district's core curriculum and a host of other reforms. Another four schools were designated to convert to independent charter schools, and 16 more ("the Sweet 16") were given additional resources to continue their successful change efforts. In all, 86 of the district's lowest-performing elementary and middle schools were assigned to an intervention treatment of some sort. (High schools were not included in this round of the reform.)

Three months after the SRC had launched the diverse provider model and the restructuring initiative it hired Paul Vallas, the former CEO of the Chicago Public Schools, as the district's new CEO. Vallas accepted and expanded on the market-based tools initiated by the SRC—the privatization of school management, increased outsourcing of central office work, and aggressive growth of charter schools (56 by fall 2007). By the end of the 2005–6 school year about a third of the city's 325 public schools were under some form of private management, either as public charter schools or schools whose management had been contracted out to external groups. Vallas integrated charter school growth with a broad strategy of school development and construction. Vallas and the SRC increased the number of formal partnerships with external companies and nonprofit groups to manage or work with schools and created an extensive set of accelerated options and magnet schools across the district.

Although the market mechanisms are part of the district's options, many of Vallas's centrally directed reforms have been aimed at the heart of teaching and learning: expanded preschool programs; smaller classes in the early grades; a mandatory core curriculum in four major subjects; more plentiful supplies of texts and other curricular materials; longer daily periods of instruction in literacy and math; six-week formative Benchmark tests assessing student mastery of the curriculum (introduced into Philadelphia by the Edison model); and extended learning time for struggling students after school, on Saturdays, and in summer school.[3] His team introduced a sophisticated Instructional Management System (IMS) for teachers, enabling them to use technology to access detailed information on their students, the curriculum, lesson plans, and curriculum resources (Gehring 2005). Further, the administration escalated its programs to train and support current and aspiring principals.

Efforts by the SRC and the Vallas administration to "turn the district around" relied not just on creating market-based choice options and on investing in an array of school supports but relied also on top down-pressures to hold school leaders and staffs accountable for results. Like school personnel across the country, Philadelphia's school-based administrators have been under pressure to meet NCLB's Adequate Yearly Progress (AYP). District leaders have created other measures to assess student and school performance as well: six-week formative Benchmark assessments in literacy, math, and science (monthly for Edison-run schools) broken down by classroom and teacher; a "SchoolStat" system of multiple school indicators of climate and achievement displayed monthly by regional administrators at meetings with their principals; and School Assistance Teams that monitor the performance of low-performing schools and provide support for their improvement efforts.

As education leaders around the country grapple with the prospect of applying strong remedies to the more than 1,000 schools identified as needing "corrective action," they might look to Philadelphia to get a sense of their options and of some short-term lessons learned. This paper synthesizes findings from a broad-based research project about the effectiveness of Philadelphia's reform.

DATA AND METHODS

A collaborating group of scholars from five institutions, led by Research for Action in Philadelphia, has been gathering and analyzing data since the inception of Philadelphia's reform in 2001 through a multipronged research and public awareness project, *Learning from Philadelphia's School Reform.* We have completed papers and reports on governance, teacher quality, and civic engagement, each of which details the data and research methods used for that piece of the work.[4] We have used a mixed-method methodology, including interviews with district administrators, principals and teachers, and case studies in eight schools.

On the quantitative side, we have analyzed an extensive longitudinal district-wide data set of all teachers in the district in our effort to assess the impact of efforts to recruit and retain qualified teachers (Neild, Unseem, Lesnick, and Travers 2003; Neild, Useem, and Farley 2005: Useem, Offenberg, and Farley 2007). For this paper, we worked with researchers at the Consortium for Chicago School Research in an analysis of annual TerraNova student test score data from the spring of 2003 to the spring of 2005. RFA subsequently collaborated with researchers at the RAND Corporation in longitudinal "value-added" analysis of student achievement under the reform, using data from the Pennsylvania System of School Assessment (PSSA) and TerraNova tests from 2002 to 2006 (Gill et al. 2007).

Findings to Date

The School Reform Commission The replacement of Philadelphia's mayoral-appointed school board with a powerful School Reform Commission made up of three appointees of former Republican Governor Mark Schweiker and two appointees of current Democratic Mayor John Street has had several positive effects. The relative absence of a contentious and narrowly focused school board has freed up CEO Vallas to direct his attention to solving district problems without being distracted by board divisions and interventions that so often bedevil urban superintendents. SRC members have for the most part given the appearance of working well together, have voted unanimously on most matters, have set a professional tone at their meetings, and have worked hard at their [unpaid] jobs as commissioners (Useem, Christman, and Boyd 2006). Disagreements among them—reported to be fierce at times—have largely been kept behind closed doors. Chairman James Nevels, founder of an investment firm, has emerged as a key figure in the rollout of the reform.

Further, because the SRC has extraordinary power conferred on it by the state takeover legislation and by NCLB, it has been able to move with alacrity and boldness, thereby accelerating experiments with reform strategies. Although the state takeover took away teachers' right to strike, the SRC and Vallas early on established effective working relationships with the Philadelphia Federation of Teachers (PFT), particularly since the renegotiation of its four-year contract with the district in the fall of 2004. Between the time of the takeover in December 2001 and the early months of 2006, the combination of comparative political tranquility alongside aggressive implementation of sweeping change fulfilled the hopes of the SRC's initial supporters and won over many early opponents.

The actions of the SRC and Vallas have, of course, not been free of controversy. Although the initial turbulence surrounding the wisdom and efficacy of the diverse provider model subsided quickly after Vallas's arrival, for example, it has remained a point of contention both within the SRC and district offices as well as among community and advocacy groups. Moreover, during much of 2006 and to the present, budget cutbacks and school safety issues have chilled the relationship between Vallas and the SRC and the PFT.

The "Hybrid Model" of School Governance

The waning of vocal public dissatisfaction with outsourcing made it easier for the district to expand the diverse provider model in the second and third years of the reform and to outsource other core educational functions (Bulkley and Gold 2006; Gold, Christman, and Herold 2005). By the end of the 2004–5 school year, the SRC had voted to:

- Contract with for-profit national firms to run all of the system's seven disciplinary schools;
- Outsource special small schools for overage adolescent students to one for-profit and two nonprofit entities;
- Contract with a for-profit national company to run an extended day program for up to 1,400 6th grade students in 10 schools;
- Delegate management of one of the district's comprehensive high schools to a local nonprofit, Foundations, Inc.;
- Contract with four for-profit companies to assist with the transition of 12 high schools into small high schools;
- Sign agreements with five different "big name" partners (Microsoft, the Franklin Institute, the University of Pennsylvania, the National Constitution Center, the College Board) to develop and run new or restructured high schools in conjunction with the district and to establish a small high school with peace-oriented studies in partnership with the Philadelphia Citizens for Children and Youth (PCCY);
- Convert a middle school to a charter high school managed by an external nonprofit group;
- Contract with a national company to write a standardized high-school curriculum in core subjects and with a second national firm to write the science curriculum for the primary grades.

These and other decisions by the SRC and Vallas led to a "blurring of the boundaries" between the public and private sectors in the area of school management and other services and made Philadelphia a national leader in creating a "hybrid model" or "joint venture" in such "cross-sectoral" relationships (Christman et al. 2005; Gold, Christman, and Herold 2007; Snyder and Mezzacappa 2005; Whittle 2005).

The introduction of the hybrid public/private approach in Philadelphia can, in part, be attributed to the belief of former Governors Ridge and Schweiker and their appointees on the SRC that competition among private providers would spur educational innovation and improve management while simultaneously giving parents more options. It was also a pragmatic response by district leaders to the performance pressures of NCLB. In the view of Vallas and the SRC, the privatization of educational functions is a way to accelerate reform by bringing in much-needed managerial and technological expertise, new ideas, an entrepreneurial spirit, and material resources. The model rolled out in Philadelphia not only dovetailed with the rationale that market forces could bring change more quickly and efficiently, but also fit the hardnosed assumptions underlying NCLB that low performing schools often need to be "rescued" by external entities who may bring the will and skill that is often missing in those schools (Brady 2003).

Paul Vallas, whose career has been entirely in the public sector, appears to be the ultimate pragmatist. On the day of his appointment as CEO, he declared, "I'm for what works whether it's private or nonprivate." It should be noted that Vallas tried to cut back the outsourcing of school management to external contractors, and, early in his tenure, also tried to have the district be the sole provider of supplemental education services for underperforming students.

Internal District Management of the Diverse Provider Model

Philadelphia's groundbreaking experience with the administration of a diverse provider "hybrid" model already offers some important lessons on implementation for districts that are choosing to outsource low-performing schools to external management groups as a form of corrective action under NCLB. In certain respects, Philadelphia has done a good job in creating conditions where this kind of "joint venture" in public/private management can work reasonably well. In other respects, the district has to contend with the downsides that can accompany the outsourcing of public services. The issues surrounding the "hybrid" model, discussed below, have been described and analyzed in a series of publications from Research for Action (Bulkley and Gold 2006; Bulkley, Mundell and Riffer, 2004; Christman et al. 2005; Gold et al. 2007).

What Works Between 2002 and 2007, the district created an environment of constructive collaboration with the external managers (often referred to in a shorthand way as "partners" or "providers" by district officials and the managers themselves). The partners and other observers we interviewed attributed this to several factors. First, Vallas and the SRC actively supported the work of the external organizations. A central office administrator overseeing the partnerships claimed, "This is not going to fail because we got in your way." Vallas and the SRC constantly articulated the value of the original partnerships and energetically pursued new collaborative opportunities. As one EMO leader put it, "[without this leadership], it could easily have been derailed. Otherwise, it could have failed in the first year."

Second, the district created a single point of contact—initially called the Office of Development—that cleared away bureaucratic obstacles faced by the providers. The Office of Human Resources worked hard as well to facilitate the provider organizations' efforts to staff their schools. This troubleshooting and overall support created the relational glue that made it possible for the providers to work in a large bureaucratic system and to become, in the words of both district and

EMO officials, "part of the fabric of the district." As one high-placed official in the district told us, "It was hard for the EMOs to believe that we weren't out to get them, but eventually they did [believe that] and most come to us for advice."

Third, the agreement among the district and partners to keep discussions about ongoing work behind closed doors meant that partner groups could make mistakes and learn from them without seeing the details played out in public. No obvious wedges were driven among the partners partly because the district avoided making invidious comparisons among the providers in a public way.

Fourth, the Office of Development and other parts of the bureaucracy developed an openness to outside groups. As one insider put it, "[The openness] is a real shift, because the district was always very tight and very closed and very vain about their own stuff…, you know 'nobody can do it better than we can kind of thing.'… It is a huge shift on the district's part to be able to embrace and engage these outside entities as partners." The fact that key staffers in the Office of Development were also very competent was extremely important.

Lastly, the fact that the district formalized the partnerships through contracts that were approved by the SRC helped clarify their relationship. After the first year of the diverse provider model, the district terminated its contract with Chancellor Beacon Academies, a for-profit EMO, for non-performance in the five schools to which it had been assigned.

What's Been Difficult RFA researchers have outlined Philadelphia's experience with the challenges of outsourcing aspects of school management (Bulkley et al. 2006; Bulkley et al. 2004; Christman et al. 2005; Gold et al. 2007). They point to the following issues:

Confusion about roles and responsibilities Uncertainty about roles and responsibilities existed because the outsourced schools still had limited autonomy. When the SRC contracted with the external organizations in 2002, they established a system of "thin management" that left certain administrative responsibilities in the hands of the district but delegated others to the provider groups. The two universities chose to be "partners" rather than school "managers," a role that gave them less authority in school governance than the other groups. They had to rely more on persuasion rather than on the exercise of overt power in implementing their instructional program and professional development with the teachers and principals in their schools.

Under the system of "thin management" that applied to the first set of partnerships, the district retained authority over school budgeting, the management of facilities, school safety, food services, special education regulations, the overall school calendar, the code of conduct for students and teachers, the evaluation processes for employee, and decisions about reconfigurations of grades (e.g., adding or losing grades) or school closings. School staffing followed the regulations established by the district and the Philadelphia Federation of Teachers (PFT). The external providers exercised authority over professional development activities and the curriculum, as long as the latter was aligned with the district's curriculum frameworks, state standards, and state assessments. Providers were free to adopt all or part of the district's core curriculum and materials. Principals were hired by the district but providers played a major role in their selection.

Principals report to and are evaluated by two sets of administrators—the provider and their regional district superintendent. This has proved to be a "gray area" in the division of responsibilities from the start of the reform effort and it still remains a point of confusion.

Accountability While the district has written accountability measures into the contracts with external school managers, one informant for this study who was familiar with contracts in other cities characterized the Philadelphia contracts as somewhat "vague." The Accountability Review Council (ARC) mandated by the state concluded that it had "not been able to identify instructional or other accountability criteria that the EMOs were expected to meet with the additional funds—other than operating the schools" (Accountability Review Council, 2007, p. 22). The district's method of accountability of its contractors appears to rely less on a labor intensive strategy of enforcing strict adherence to performance indicators and more on developing trusting relationships with these partners. According to economist Elliot Sclar (2000), this phenomenon is typical of relationships between public agencies and private service providers. Paradoxically, he argues, the trust that is built up over time can in turn make it more difficult to hold the contractor accountable or even to terminate a contract.

The writing and monitoring of contracts is also challenging for the district because so few of its administrators are experienced and skilled in that area. Goldsmith and Eggers (2004) have argued persuasively that as public agencies outsource more and more of their work they must hire a new cadre of specialists in contract management.

Cost Managers of companies and public administrators often claim that outsourcing makes sense when the work can be done at less expense by outside firms who work in competitive markets. In the case of school management, however, that argument does not apply. The two EMOs and two of the nonprofits now get an additional $750 per pupil annually (university partners get less), far more, say, than is commonly given to federally funded Comprehensive School Reform organizations. Transactional costs—legal and administrative expenses associated with contracting out services—add to the bill.

Further, costs are not held down by a competitive market. Few organizations have a track record in turning around high-poverty urban schools, and they are not, at this point, eager to take on a large number of schools in a district with a history of low performance. In Philadelphia, the providers have developed a collaborative relationship, facilitated by regular meetings run by the Office of Development and the administrative units that succeeded that office. They are not competing with one another for an expanded market share. Instead, competition has taken the form of not wanting to be the laggard among the partner groups in test scores. Still, some district leaders argue that the diverse provider model has introduced a competitive spirit among providers and between the providers and district-run schools.

The district's primary rationale for privatization of school management in Philadelphia has been that it brings in leadership talent, entrepreneurial skills, and innovative ideas—all in short supply in the district—in order to speed up reform. As Vallas put it at a district-sponsored conference on partnerships:

> Partnerships help address leadership gaps.... The issue is not really financial. The key struggle is leadership. Who will manage the process of schools converting to high schools? We need to give management partners the responsibility of managing the creation of new high schools.... We can't wait 5 to 10 years.... We need to institutionalize change now, and that's where private providers and the diversified management model allow us to accelerate the change.

The difficulty for the district of assessing costs versus benefits will come to the fore in 2007 when the SRC decides whether or not to renew the five-year contracts of the EMOs. They will be faced with a number of questions: How much of a gain in student performance will be necessary in order to justify the additional costs of paying for the providers? What decision should be made if the gains among providers' schools are uneven or no higher than gains of district-run schools? Can continuation of contractors with uneven performance be justified in other ways such as acting as a spur to innovation and competition across the district? The SRC's decision will take place within a context of competing political pressures, since the EMOs are expected to draw on political alliances at the state legislative level as they have in the past as they press for renewal of their contracts.

Teacher Quality

The SRC and the Vallas administration have tried to boost schools' capacity to improve instruction by improving the recruitment, the credentials, and retention of teachers. This endeavor has been fueled by the NCLB mandate that all children be taught by a "highly qualified" teacher by June 2006. Prior administrations had not given this issue priority in their own ambitious reform programs. At the time Vallas arrived in Philadelphia in 2002, fewer than half of the new teachers were certified and fewer than half were staying in the district after three years on the job (Neild et al. 2003, 2005). To his credit, Vallas quickly grasped the seriousness of the deteriorating staffing situation and the importance of compliance with the NCLB rules. He chose a capable team that put in place aggressive strategies to recruit and retain able new teachers and worked to change rigid staffing policies. Civic leaders became active in the district-sponsored Campaign for Human Capital, an entity that charted the course of the Human Resource reforms (Thomas and Akinola 2004).

The district revamped its marketing efforts in ways that have attracted more qualified candidates. The percentage of the district's teachers who are certified has risen from 89.9 percent in 2002–3 to 95.3 percent in 2006–7. The proportion of *new* teachers who are certified has risen from 54.8 percent in 2002–3 to 92.4 percent in 2006–7 (Useem, Farley, and Offenberg 2007). Retention of new teachers improved as well due to the use of new teacher coaches, better training and accountability measures for principals in the area of teacher retention, support from the new core curriculum, and a more intensive induction program. New teachers are now much more likely to stay all the way through their first year on the job. Only 73 percent in 2002–3 completed their first year compared to more than 90 percent in subsequent years. Vacancies have plummeted. In the spring of 2006, only 20 to 30 classroom vacancies existed out of a teaching staff of more than 11,000 teachers.

Another key effort was developing multiple alternative certification programs aimed at training new teachers working on emergency permits or Intern certificates. Use of these programs—still a stopgap but superior to the former system of hiring "apprentice teachers" who were not part of any organized alternate route program—helped account for the dramatic decline in the number of classroom vacancies.

Most importantly, the SRC and Vallas negotiated a new four-year contract with the Philadelphia Federation of Teachers in the fall of 2004 that made serious inroads on one of the most cherished perquisites of veteran teachers—the automatic right to transfer among schools based on seniority. The contract established school-based hiring of all new teachers, a practice that had been strenuously opposed by the PFT and long wished for by school reformers (Neild et al. 2003; Useem and Farley 2004). Philadelphia had a cumbersome centralized system of assigning new teachers to schools in which applicants and schools had no chance to review one another in advance. The hiring of new teachers occurred late in the summer and into the fall, in part because transfers had to be processed first when vacancies were filled. These antiquated processes led to attrition in applicant pools over a hiring season, and to dissatisfaction among many new teachers who were placed in schools that were a poor fit for them.

Knowing that it faced a possible teachers' job action on the issue of school-based hiring and transfer rights, the SRC worked hard during 2004 to win civic support for its stance on these questions. In this campaign, its members could point to the pressure from NCLB on teacher quality issues as part of the rationale for its position. In the end, a union that had been weakened by the state takeover—the PFT's right to strike had been taken away in that legislation—made significant concessions. The contract that emerged laid out a complicated set of hiring and transfer rules, but the agreement represented an historic change in the system's policies for hiring and assigning teachers to schools (Neild et al. 2005). At the same time, the district began an expedited and modernized hiring process. While not anticipated, a new spirit of district-PFT collaboration has marked the implementation of this contract.

Major challenges remain. Inequities exist in the distribution of qualified teachers across schools. As in most districts, the neediest schools have the least experienced and the least-credentialed teachers. The incentives to attract teachers to these schools remain anemic. The district faces a serious shortage of certified special education teachers and has a shortage of minority teachers as well. Long-term teacher retention rates remain low (Useem et al. 2007).

Still, the forces set in motion by the state legislation that was a precursor to NCLB and by NCLB itself have clearly made a difference in Philadelphia's effort to stabilize and upgrade its teaching staff.

Student Test Score Results

Student achievement in the elementary and middle grades, as measured by two standardized tests, has improved since the onset of the reform in 2002. District-wide scores on the Pennsylvania System of School Assessment (PSSA) over the first four years of the reform have increased in the tested grades (5th and 8th) at the elementary and middle levels (see Table 15.1). From 2002 to 2006, the percentages of students scoring in the proficient and advanced categories in reading increased by about 11 percentage points for 5th and 20 percentage points for 8th graders. In mathematics, gains have been more impressive: 5th

Table 15.1 School District of Philadelphia: District-wide PSSA results for grades 5, 8, and 11—percentage of students scoring advanced or proficient

		Spring 2002 to Spring 2006					
	Grade	2002	2003	2004	2005	2006	Change in Percentage Points 2002-06
Reading							
	5	20.8%	23.4%	31.6%	35.1%	31.7	10.9
	8	24.1%	30.4%	41.2%	39.6%	44.5	20.4
	11	28.7%	30.1%	27.0%	30.6%	33.2	4.5
Math							
	5	18.7%	23.1%	30.7%	45.8%	41.4	22.7
	8	17.9%	19.7%	30.9%	39.4%	37.0	19.1
	11	23.6%	21.6%	22.9%	23.1%	26.9	3.3

graders' scores increased about 23 percentage points over the four-year period while 8th graders increased about 19 points. Scores for 11th graders, however, whose experience with the reforms began only in 2004–5, rose only slightly over that same period with gains of just over 3 percentage points in math and 4.5 points in reading.

Despite the improvement in PSSA test scores in the 5th and 8th grades, district officials have been quick to note that absolute score levels remain comparatively low, and that much more work would be needed to close achievement gaps with students in suburban districts. The percentage of students scoring in the proficient and advanced categories in the three tested grades in reading in 2006 ranged from a low of about 33 percent of 11th graders to a high of more than 44 percent of the 8th graders. In math, the percentages ranged from about 27 percent of 11th graders scoring at those levels to—the bright spot—about 42 percent of 5th graders doing so (up from about 19 percent in 2002).

The results from another set of standardized tests—the nationally normed TerraNova exams—in grades 3 through 10 in four subjects between fall 2002 and fall 2006 show improvements in district performance as well but indicate a general flattening of scores in fall 2006. Score trends vary among subjects and grades. If the scores from the fall 2002 administration of the test are used as a baseline, gains in the elementary and middle grades are substantial, particularly in mathematics (School District of Philadelphia, 2005a). If the spring 2003 baseline is used—as we do in the sub-group analyses described below—gains are notable but less robust.[5] In the fall of 2006, approximately 39 to 40 percent of the students in grades 3–10 scored at or above national averages in reading, language arts, and math (Snyder, 2007). In a fall 2005 administration of the test, to grades 3 through 8, between 43 and 46 percent of students scored at grade level, depending on the subject area (School District of Philadelphia 2005b).

The number of School District of Philadelphia schools meeting all of their NCLB-mandated Adequate Yearly Progress (AYP) targets, using PSSA test score data and other mandated indicators, rose from 22 in 2002 to 131 in 2006 (49 percent of its schools) despite progressively more stringent standards for meeting that target. The number of schools making AYP that were managed by external providers declined between 2004 and 2006 (Accountability Review Council, 2007). Graduation rates, a component of AYP for high schools, have improved modestly but are still very low (Neild and Balfanz, 2006).

Little progress has been made in closing achievement gaps between student subgroups—those belonging to racial and ethnic minorities, students with disabilities, English language learners, and economically disadvantaged students. —and white students. The Accountability Review Council's report (2007) noted that between 2002 and 2006, all sub-groups registered gains in the percentage of students scoring advanced and proficient on the PSSA tests but the gap between their scores and those of white students remains substantial.

Vallas and his team have attributed improved test scores to the new core curriculum that is aligned to state standards and assessments, teachers' use of six-week Benchmark tests that chart students' progress during the year, and longer instructional blocks of time for language arts and math both during the school day, after school, and during the summer. He also credited the work of district School Assistance Teams that worked with low-performing schools on a Guided Self Study that assisted their school improvement efforts. Researchers at Johns Hopkins University who have analyzed math test score gains between 5th and 8th grades attribute the gains to "increased coherence and coordination of curricula, increased focus on student outcomes, and increased resources for low-performing schools" (M. A. Mac Iver and D. J. Mac Iver 2005, 13; D. J. Mac Iver and M. A. Mac Iver 2006).

Test Score Results by Intervention Type

In order to look at longitudinal trends and subgroup variations in student test-score data, Research for Action contracted with John Easton and Steve Ponisciak at the Consortium on Chicago School Research to analyze student test scores using 5th and 8th grade test-score data from TerraNova examinations between 2003 and 2005.[6] This team examined the patterns of achievement demonstrated by the original 86 low-performing schools that received additional resources or aggressive interventions to see if these schools showed gains in achievement at a higher rate than other district schools.

Using test-score data supplied by the district, Easton and Ponisciak compared scores in the 86 lowest-performing schools with that of other district schools, using TerraNova data from three different time points—spring 2003, spring 2004, and spring 2005. They also compared test scores among the 86 schools, grouping them in one of four categories. These categories included: 19 schools run by the Office of Restructured Schools (ORS); 41 schools run by school management providers, including both for-profit and nonprofit organizations; and 15 of the 16 schools (dubbed the "Sweet 16") that received extra financial resources to continue their school improvement efforts.[7] In assigning schools to these sub-groups, only those schools that had stayed with the same provider or intervention treatment from 2002 to 2005 were classified in one of three groups—ORS, Sweet 16, or in the school management provider group in the analysis. The 11 schools that migrated from one provider or intervention to another during that period were labeled "drifters" in our analysis.[8]

The ORS schools served as a useful natural comparison group to those run by external managers and partners since they were similar to the outsourced schools in demographics and achievement indicators. Like the externally managed schools, they also received additional resources ($550 per pupil), albeit a lower amount than the EMOs, partly because they had no overhead expense and received certain services from the district.

Figures 15.1 to 15.8 (appendix) show the percentage of students in grades 5 and 8 scoring at or above national norms on the TerraNova math and reading tests over time and the percentage of students scoring in the bottom national quartile. These data reveal complex patterns. Students at the 86 schools did not show significantly different trends in scores on the TerraNova exams than other district schools. The data are suggestive that in the case of 8th grade math, students in the low-performing schools showed greater gains than students in the rest of the district's schools, with the schools run by external managers and the Sweet 16 schools showing the most substantial gains over the two-year period studied. Overall, however, using a rigorous standard of statistical significance (.01 level), these analyses found no significant differences in student scores or decreases in the percentage of students in the bottom quartile by intervention strategy. A reading of the figures reveals that no one strategy stands out as being especially effective.

Using different test scores—PSSA, not TerraNova—and methodologies, Mac Iver and Mac Iver (2006) came to conclusions similar to those of Easton and Ponisciak. They conducted a "value added" analysis of student learning gains in math, using 5th and 8th grade PSSA scores, breaking down results by EMO. They looked at test score growth of three cohorts of students who attended high-poverty schools with an 8th grade: Cohort 1 began 5th grade in 1999–2000 and then experienced one year of EMO or district-led reforms in math during 2002–3 as 8th graders; Cohort 2 experienced the reforms during both 7th and 8th grades (2002–3 and 2003–4); and Cohort 3 students were taught under the new reform regime during 6th, 7th, and 8th grades (2002–3 through 2004–5). The researchers found that students in Edison-managed schools did not significantly outperform students in district-managed high-poverty schools. Growth among students in non-Edison EMO schools was significantly lower than the gain in district-run schools, with the exception of Cohort 3 students in new K–8 schools run by Temple University who showed significant growth in math as 8th graders in 2005.

A subsequent study by researchers at the RAND Corporation, in collaboration with RFA, used value-added analyses of individual student gains between 5th and 8th grade in the years between 2001 and 2006, combining scores from both the PSSA and TerraNova tests and comparing outcomes by provider (Gill et al., 2007). Their findings, like those of Easton and Ponisciak and Mac Iver and Mac Iver, showed that student achievement growth in the privately managed schools did not exceed that of other district students. Schools run by the district's Office of Restructured Schools did, however, outpace other schools in raising student achievement levels.

The Accountability Review Council (2007), using school-level data, concluded as well that student achievement gains in privately managed schools did not keep up with growth in district-managed schools in either reading or math, particularly between 2005 and 2006.

These studies showing that external providers, despite having added resources, have not been more effective than the district in raising student achievement pose a challenge to those members of the SRC who have supported the EMO concept and who must calculate the costs and benefits of the diverse provider model as they consider its continuation. The varying perspectives of SRC members on this issue are illustrated by the comments of two of its members as they weighed a decision on whether to award two more schools to Edison in May 2005. These comments foreshadow the debate that is taking place in 2007 as EMO contracts come up for renewal. One of the two SRC members opposing the resolution, Sandra Dungee Glenn, put it this way:

> I am against giving two schools to Edison. I got a report from the Chief Academic Officer and I think there is insufficient data to draw valid conclusions about overall performance on EMOs so far.... I see a very mixed performance, in my view.... Our Restructured schools do better on most of those indicators than the Edison schools. And in some subject areas in some schools, other providers do better. We need a bigger overall review of the EMO experiment. I am not sure they are accelerating school improvement more than other groups. Edison is not so outstanding that they should get two more schools.

James Gallagher, one of the three SRC members voting in support of contracting with Edison for additional schools countered:

> We inherited a district that was failing its students.... We still have a culture of failure. We need to chase [after] additional EMOs and charters and new ideas. We inherited a monopoly that did not work, and in many ways is not working. Edison has done rather well. Keep in mind that we gave Edison the most difficult schools....We must be open to innovation and to every outsider who wants to help us. We have a long way to go.

SUMMING UP

The current wave of reform in Philadelphia bears the imprint of NCLB's press for immediate action aimed at improving low-performing schools and districts. The law, along with Pennsylvania's state takeover legislation that was a precursor to NCLB, increased the arsenal of radical options available to state and city political and educational leaders who oversee public schools in the Commonwealth. They have used these options in Philadelphia. Not only did the state execute the largest takeover to date of any U.S. school district, but its new governance group, the School Reform Commission, has set up the nation's most extensive experiment with the privatization of schools and the outsourcing of educational services to private corporations.

It is important to note here that the reform-oriented administration of Superintendent David W. Hornbeck worked hard from 1994 to 2000 to establish academic standards, a new accountability framework, and the beginnings of a core curriculum. But his efforts, particularly the use of a performance index to measure school progress, met with considerable internal opposition. An arbitration board defeated his attempts to reconstitute two low-performing schools. Hornbeck and his team operated without the benefit of NCLB pressures for academic improvement and the accompanying intervention tools now available to CEO Vallas and the SRC. Moreover, Hornbeck had to answer to a School Board, a more fractious body than the SRC.

The legal running room allowed by NCLB along with the new governance structure has enabled CEO Paul Vallas and the SRC to undertake a host of interventions drawn from three sets of policy tools, all encouraged by NCLB: market-oriented solutions encouraging parent choice such as the expansion of charter schools and magnet programs; top-down pressure and sanctions through an NCLB-mandated accountability regime; and bottom up support in building schools' capacity to deliver sound instruction by, for example, improving the quality and stability of the teacher workforce. The interaction of Vallas's legendary "hyperactive passion," the steady leadership of the SRC, and the immediacy of NCLB pressures for schools to make Adequate Yearly Progress has created a climate favorable to rapid change.

Thus far, a good deal has been accomplished. Test scores through the 8th grade have improved, with gains in math being particularly notable, attributed in part to the new system for managing instruction—a core curriculum and associated Benchmark tests and longer blocks of time for literacy and math along with extended time for learning after school and in the summer for struggling students. The district and teachers' union have established a détente, even as the union's contract has been changed in ways that allow for greater control over staffing decisions at the building level. The recruitment and retention of qualified teachers has improved markedly. Preschool programming has expanded. The conversion of most middle schools to K–8 schools is well underway as is the creation of smaller high schools, new magnet high schools, and an array of enriched or accelerated learning programs in neighborhood schools. Charter schools are now integrated into the district's school development plan. The most ambitious school construction and renovation program in decades has begun.

Civic support for the reforms thus far was reflected in a fall 2005 editorial in the *Philadelphia Inquirer* which talked about "the caffeinated pace of change" and how the district was becoming a "model of success," quite different from "the bad old days of the 1990s." The editorial noted that the original plan of governors Ridge and Schweiker that would have turned management of the district's central office over to for-profit firms had "thankfully, faded from view," and that

Vallas "had put a whole new twist on school choice with his other partnerships" (*Philadelphia Inquirer,* September 7, 2005, 18).

Still, controversies and divisions, never absent from this latest wave of reform, became more pronounced during the fourth and fifth years of the effort, particularly after a budget deficit surfaced in the latter half of the 2005–6 school year. Mayor John Street became highly critical of Paul Vallas for running a deficit, and only three of five SRC members voted for his contract renewal in the summer of 2006. During the 2006–7 school year, civic and parent groups along with other grassroots organizations renewed their objections to the contracting out of school management, citing its cost and lack of evidence of effectiveness. An upsurge of high-profile assaults on teachers during the 2006-07 school year along with widespread concerns about school safety and discipline in general also created a testier political and administrative environment in the district.

By 2008, the year the SRC has designated as a target for meeting important performance goals, researchers will have assembled comprehensive evidence about the effectiveness of the state takeover and the SRC and Vallas-initiated reforms. Several research groups—at the district, RFA, and Johns Hopkins University—will be reporting on how the reforms are playing out at the school level, including how well teachers are using the core curriculum, Benchmark tests, and the longer blocks of time in literacy and math. Information on the degree to which teachers are forming bonds of collaboration and relational trust in their buildings, a key to school improvement, will become available as well. The district has also commissioned an external evaluation of its efforts to improve the quality of school principals' leadership. These and other studies should make it possible for the SRC, state leaders, and public stakeholders to make an informed assessment of the effectiveness of the wave of change in Philadelphia schools that began with the 2001 state takeover.

Although it is always risky to state that improvements in an urban school district will be long-lasting, it does appear at this point that Philadelphia's public school leaders may now be passing "a point of no return" in institutionalizing a set of far-reaching changes. The one major piece of the reform that is likely to be pared back is the contracting out of school management to private providers. But the other bold actions—including the elimination of most middle schools, the deliberate depopulation of large high schools, the growth of greater school choice through charter schools and magnets, the creation of greater curricular coherence, the extended learning time for struggling students, the upgrade in teacher quality, the enhancement of preschool education—hold the prospect of staying in place for a reasonable stretch of time. Without the pressures and options created by NCLB, efforts for change would quite likely have been more anemic, more contentious, and slower paced. Barring a further worsening of its fiscal situation, by 2008 Philadelphia's schools will look very different in some crucial ways than they did in 2001.

APPENDIX

Analysis of Student Achievement Gains in the "Original 86" Low-Performing Schools by Type of Intervention

The "Original 86" lowest-performing schools were identified by the School Reform Commission after the state takeover and targeted for intervention. The graphs that follow show changes in student scores on 5th and 8th grade Terra-Nova standardised math and reading tests in these low-performing schools at three points in time: Spring 2003, Spring 2004, and Spring 2005. The graphs plot changes in (1) the percentage of students scoring at or above national norms; and (2) the percentage of students scoring in the bottom quartile.

The number of schools for each intervention strategy in the graphs represents those schools that have been *consistently managed* under than management structure for the past three years. The "Drifter" category was created to include those schools that have operated under at least two different management structures over the past three years or were closed. The intervention strategies used in the graphs are defined below.

School Management Providers: Forty-one schools operated by Educational Management Organizations: Edison Schools, Inc., Victory Schools, Inc., Universal Companies, Foundations, Inc., and two universities: the University of Pennsylvania and Temple University. School Management Providers received additional per pupil funding between $450 and $881 (origianl number: 46 schools).

Office of Restructured Schools: Nineteen schools managed by the school district's newly created Office of Restructured Schools received an additional $550 per pupil funding (original number: 21 schools).

"Sweet 16": Fifteen schools designated to receive an additional $550 per pupil funding during 2002–2003 (and reduced amounts in later years) but no change in management structure (original number: 16 schools).

"Drifters": Eleven schools which we have designated as "drifters" because they have been operating at least two differnt management structures since the reform began. This includes three schools originally designated as transitional charters. Additional funding was inconsistent if it occurred at all. Two of the "drifter" schools closed in 2003. The initial analysis includes the data for all 11 schools in 2003 and only 9 schools in 2004 and 2005. Future anaylsis will examine testing data for only the 9 schools.

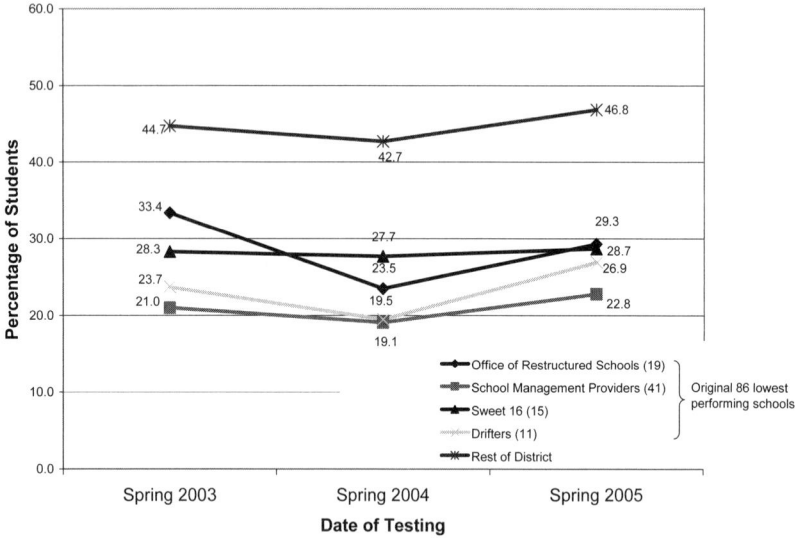

Figure 15.1 School District of Philadelphia, TerraNova 5th grade reading scores. Percentage of students scoring at or above national norms by intervention strategy.

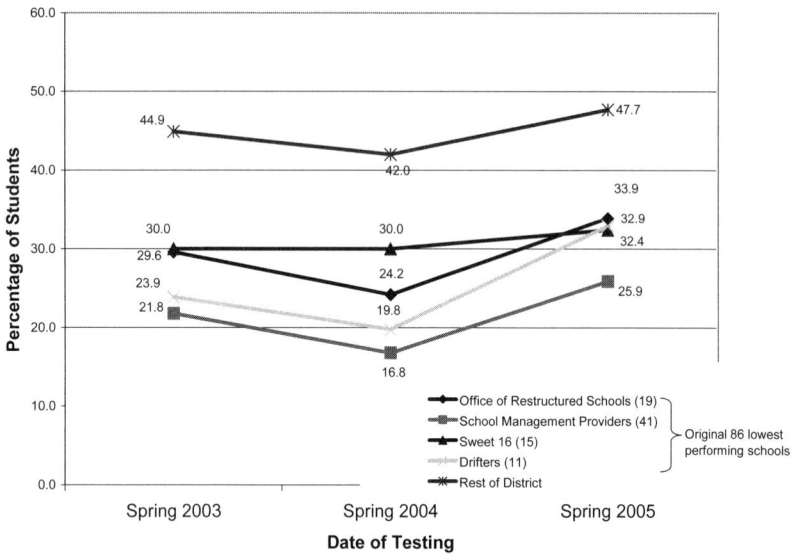

Figure 15.2 School District of Philadelphia, TerraNova 5th grade math scores. Percentage of students scoring at or above national norms by intervention strategy.

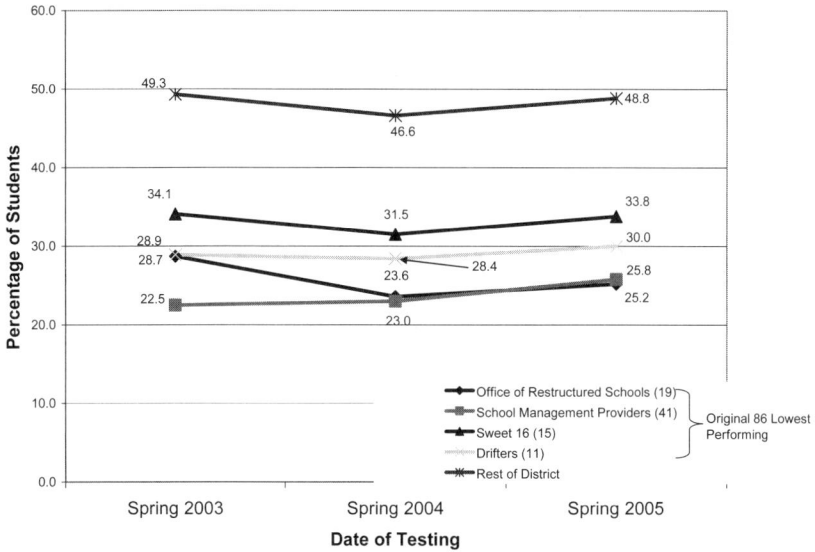

Figure 15.3 School District of Philadelphia, TerraNova 8th grade reading scores. Percentage of students scoring at or above national norms by intervention strategy.

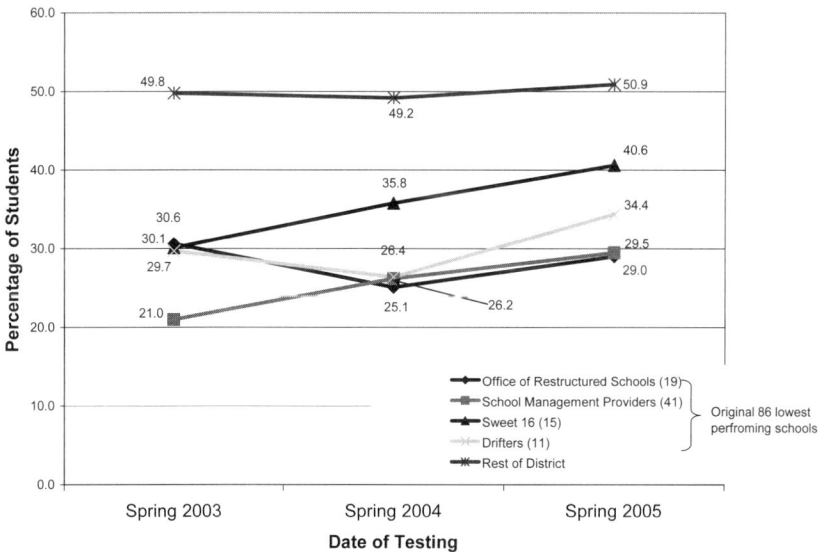

Figure 15.4 School District of Philadelphia, TerraNova 8th grade math scores. Percentage of students scoring at or above national norms by intervention strategy.

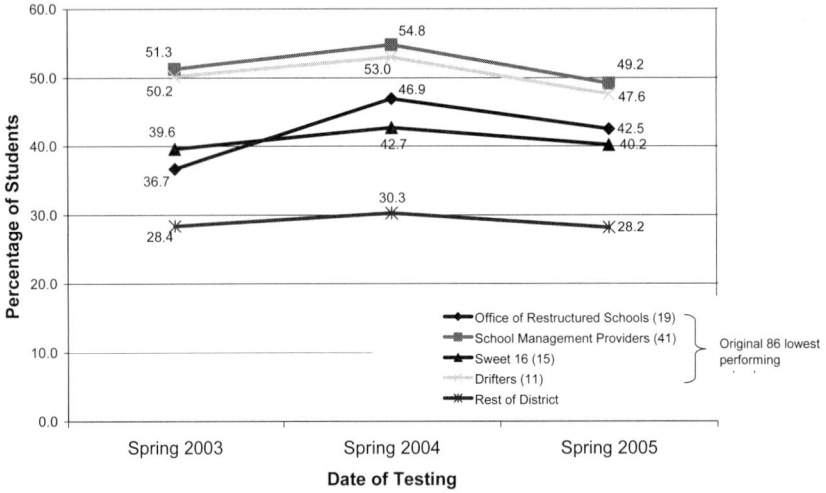

Figure 15.5 School District of Philadelphia, TerraNova 5th grade reading scores. Percentage of students scoring bottom quartile by intervention strategy.

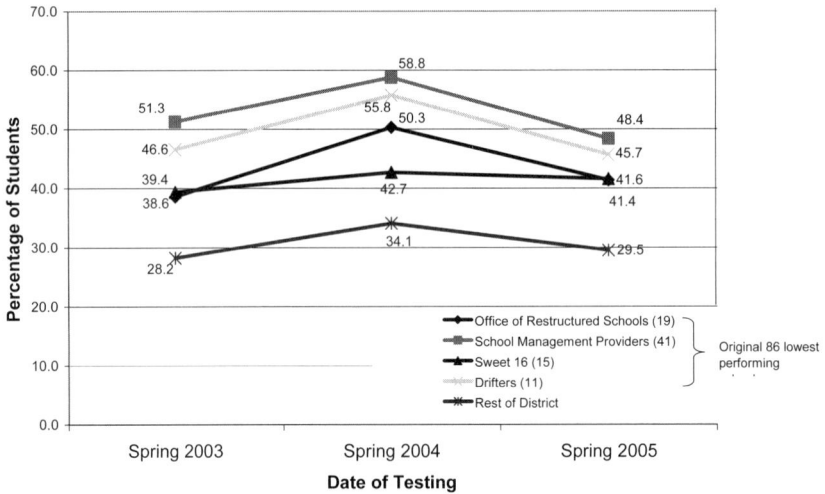

Figure 15.6 School District of Philadelphia, TerraNova 5th grade math scores. Percentage of students scoring bottom quartile by intervention strategy.

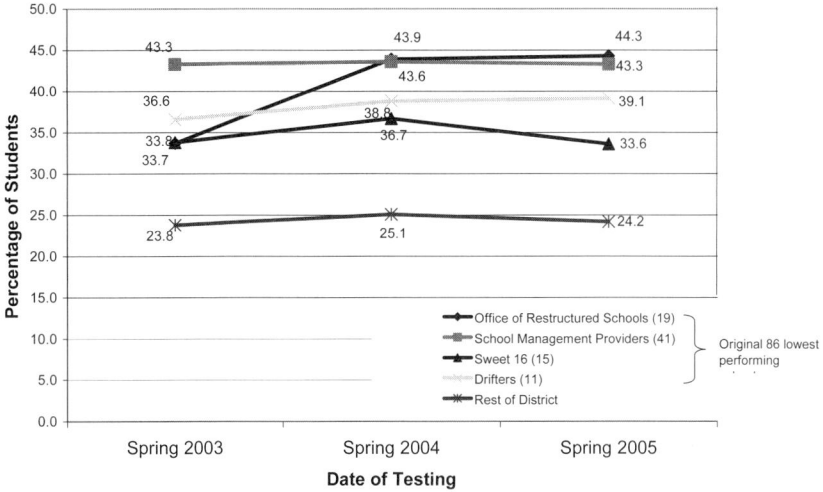

Figure 15.7 School District of Philadelphia, TerraNova 8th grade reading scores. Percentage of students scoring bottom quartile by intervention strategy.

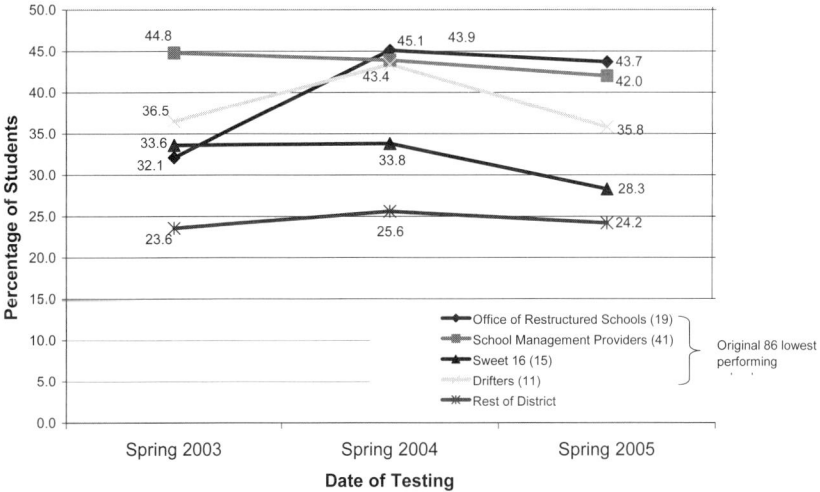

Figure 15.8 School District of Philadelphia, TerraNova 8th grade math scores. Percentage of students scoring bottom quartile by intervention strategy.

Notes

1. This paper was originally presented at the No Child Left Behind Conference sponsored by the Sociology of Education Section of the American Sociological Association, August 12, 2005, in Philadelphia. The paper, initially titled "Learning from Philadelphia's School Reform: What Do the Research Findings Show So Far?" has been revised and updated for this volume.

   This research synthesizes the collaborative work of a group of scholars, led by Research for Action (RFA), conducted from the spring of 2002 to the present. The *Learning from Philadelphia School Reform* project includes seven additional researchers from RFA: Suzanne Blanc, Jolley B. Christman, Eva Gold, Maia Cucchiara, Benjamin Herold, Leah Mundell, Morgan Riffer, and Gretchen Seuss. Six researchers from the University of Pennsylvania have also contributed to the project: Kira Baker, Sarah Costelloe, Elizabeth Farley, Joly Lesnick, Ruth Curran Neild, and Elaine Simon. Other researchers include Katrina Bulkley from Montclair State College, John Easton and Steve Ponisciak from the Consortium for Chicago Research, Eva Travers from Swarthmore College, and Robert Offenberg, an independent consultant.
2. After the first year, the SRC adjusted the amount of additional funding per pupil given to the providers. The two for-profit firms and the two local non-profits were allocated $750 per pupil.
3. Low-performing students are required to attend after-school extended day programs (32,000 students in grades 1-9), Saturday classes, and summer school (50,000 students).
4. These reports are all available on RFA's website:http://www.researchforaction.org.
5. TerraNova tests were first administered in the fall of 2002, just after some of the new wave of reforms had begun. Because the test was meant to be for diagnostic purposes (Accountability Review Council, 2005) and because they differed in format and in time of year from other administrations of the tests, we chose only to use data from the spring administrations for our longitudinal comparisons. Some researchers are wary of fall-administration tests because of the falloff in learning among low-income students during the summer compared to their more advantaged counterparts.
6. We chose the 5th and 8th grades because these are the grades that are also tested by the PSSA and are used by the state to make a determination of whether the schools as made Adequate Yearly Progress (AYP).
7. Comparisons of the TerraNova results were not made among the different management providers because the number of schools assigned to some providers was so small.
8. Two of these schools closed in 2003; the initial analysis includes the data for all 11 schools in 2003 and only 9 schools in 2004 and 2005.

References

Accountability Review Council. 2005. *Report to the School Reform Commission: the status of academic performance in the School District of Philadelphia for the 2003–04 school year.* Philadelphia: School District of Philadelphia
———. 2007. *The status of academic performance in the School District of Philadelphia for the 2005–06 school year. Report to the School Reform Commission.* Philadelphia: School District of Philadelphia.
Boyd, W. L. and J. B. Christman. 2003. A tall order for Philadelphia's new approach to school governance: Heal the political rifts, close the budget gap, and improve the schools. In *Powerful reforms with shallow roots: Improving America's urban schools,* ed. L. Cuban and M. Usdan, New York: Teachers College Press.
Brady, R. C. 2003. *Can failing schools be fixed?* Washington, D.C.: Thomas B. Fordham Foundation.
Bulkley, K. and E. Gold. 2006. Bringing the private into the public: Changing the rules of the game and new regime politics in Philadelphia public education. Paper presented at the annual meeting of the American Educational Research Association, San Francisco.
———. L. Mundell, and M. Riffer. 2004. *Contracting out schools: The first year of the Philadelphia's diverse provider model.* Philadelphia: Research for Action.
Christman, J., E. Gold, and B. Herold. 2005. *Privatization "Philly Style": What can be learned from Philadelphia's Diverse Provider Model of school management?* Philadelphia: Research for Action.

Gehring, J. 2005. Big district priorities. In *Electronic transfer: Moving technology dollars in new directions. Technology Counts 2005*, ed. 38–39.Bethesda, MD: Education Week.

Gill, B., Zimmer, R., Christman, J., and Blanc, S. (2007). *State takeover, school restructuring, private management, and student achievement in Philadelphia.* Washington, D.C.: RAND Corporation and Philadelphia; Research for Action.

Gold, E., J.Christman, and B. Herold. 2007. Blurring the boundaries: A case study of private sector involvement in the Philadelphia public schools. *American Journal of Education* 113(2): 181–212,.

Goldsmith, S. and W. D. Eggers. 2004. *Governing by network: The new shape of the public sector.* Washington, D.C.: Brookings Institution Press.

Hannaway, J. and N. Woodroffe. 2003. Policy instruments in education. In *Review of Research in Education* 27: 1–24, ed. R. E. Floden. Washington, D.C.: The American Educational Research Association .

Hill, P. T., C. Campbell, and J. Harvey. 2000. *It takes a city: Getting serious about urban school reform.* Washington, D.C.: Brookings Institution Press.

Mac Iver, D. J., and M. A. Mac Iver. 2006. Effects on middle grades' mathematics achievement of educational management organizations and new K-8 schools. Paper presented at the annual meeting of the American Educational Research Association, San Francisco.

Mac Iver, M. A., and D. J. Mac Iver. 2005. Which bets paid off? Preliminary findings on the impact of private management and K–8 conversion reforms on the achievement of Philadelphia students. Paper presented at the annual meeting of the American Political Science Association, Washington, DC.

Maranto, R. 2005. A tale of two cities: School privatization in Philadelphia and Chester. *American Journal of Education* 111 (2): 151–90.

Neild, R.C. and Balfanz, R. (2006). *The unfulfilled promise: The dimensions and characteristics of Philadelphia's dropout crisis, 2000–2005.* Philadelphia: Philadelphia Youth Network/Philadelphia Youth Transitions Collaborative/Project U-Turn.

Neild, R. C., E. L.Useem, and E. Farley. 2005. *The quest for quality: Recruiting and retaining teachers in Philadelphia.* Philadelphia: Research for Action.

———, E. Useem, J. Lesnick, and E. Travers. 2003. *Once and for all: Placing a highly qualified teacher in every Philadelphia classroom.* Philadelphia: Research for Action.

School District of Philadelphia. 2005a. Philadelphia public schools see three-year trend in students scoring at or above national averages on TerraNova. News release, June 16. Philadelphia.

———. 2005b. For fourth year in a row, Philadelphia public school students scoring at or above national averages increases. Philadelphia. December 21.

Sclar, E. D. 2000. *You don't always get what you pay for: The economics of privatization.* Ithaca, NY: Cornell University Press.

Snyder, S. 2006. A $100 million incentive to improve teaching. *Philadelphia Inquirer*, April 28,

Snyder, S. (2007, Feb. 22). *Philadelphia Inquirer.* Philadelphia schools' national scores hit plateau.

———. D. Mezzacappa. 2005. Schools' $80 million bet. *Philadelphia Inquirer*, April 24, A1.

Socolar, P. 2005. Edison in line for two more schools. *Philadelphia Public School Notebook* Summer:1.

Thomas, D. and M. Akinola. 2004. *The campaign for human capital at the School District of Philadelphia [Case].* Cambridge, MA: Harvard Business School.

Travers, E. F. 2003. *The state takeover in Philadelphia: Where we are and how we got here.* Philadelphia: Research for Action.

Useem, E.L., J. B. Christman, and W.L. Boyd. 2006. *The role of district-level leadership in making radical reform work: Philadelphia's education reform under the state takeover, 2001–2006.* Philadelphia: Research for Action and Temple University, Mid-Atlantic Educational Laboratory for Student Success, College of Education.

——— and E. Farley. 2004. *Philadelphia's teacher hiring and school assignment practices: Comparisons with other districts.* Philadelphia: Research for Action.

———, R. Offenberg, and E. Farley. (2007). *Closing the Teacher Quality Gap in Philadelphia: New Hope and Old Hurdles.* Philadelphia: Research for Action.

——— and R. C. Neild. 2005. Supporting new teachers in the city. *Educational Leadership* May:44–47.

Whittle, C. 2005. The promise of public/private partnerships. *Education Leadership* February:34–36.

16
Can NCLB Close Achievement Gaps?[1]

David J. Armor

INTRODUCTION

The boldness of the No Child Left Behind (NCLB) Act is epic, and its goals and scope are unprecedented in American education. States must design assessment and accountability systems and set academic standards so that, by 2014, all schools within a state attain 100 percent proficiency for all major racial, income, language, and disability subgroups. Schools must demonstrate annual gains in achievement toward the full proficiency goal, and there must be sanctions for schools that fail to meet annual yearly progress (AYP) requirements. States must develop programs and policies to help students in failing schools, including options to choose nonfailing schools. Needless to say, NCLB has been controversial, and criticism has come from many quarters.

The basic ideas behind NCLB are noble and worthy of support from everyone who cares about racial equity and the quality of American education. Unfortunately, there is a good chance that the act will fail in its current form, although not for the reasons offered by its many critics. The most widespread criticism is lack of funds to accomplish these goals. This paper argues that the problem is not due to a lack of money, but rather to a lack of technical knowledge about how to attain equal proficiency for all groups.

Existing achievement gaps are not caused by schools; they are caused by powerful family risk factors that impact children well before they enter school, and they continue to operate throughout the school years. This does not mean that school programs cannot overcome the disadvantages from family background, but it is fair to say that, at the present time, there is no consensus on explicit education policies and practices that promise to work. A school staff cannot simply go to a shelf and find a set of policies and programs that have been tested and proven.

Most educators are familiar with this problem, although there is understandable reluctance to acknowledge it for fear of being accused of having "the soft bigotry of low expectations." However, expectations are not bigotry if they are based on sound science, and the pervasive influence of family characteristics on cognitive skills and learning—and the difficulty of overcoming deficiencies that children bring to the schoolhouse—is well-grounded in the behavioral sciences.

While I endorse the goal of equal proficiency for all, we should acknowledge that the knowledge and technology for doing so is still being developed, and this will take time—more time than allowed by the law. In the meantime, progress towards this goal should be measured by achievement growth rather than equal proficiency. This approach is now being tested by the U.S. Department of Education in two states, although it is not clear that the type of growth models allowed will solve the problems raised here.

GROWING COMPLAINTS

The controversy over NCLB has been growing as states are finding it increasingly difficult to meet the achievement gains required by the law. In 2004, 30 percent of schools nationwide failed to make AYP, which dropped to 24 percent in 2005 but was back up to 26 percent in 2006 (National Education Association [NEA] 2006). The most common complaints fall into three categories: money, excessive testing, and federalism.

Perhaps the most frequent complaint is lack of federal funds to implement the law, particularly to reduce class sizes and increase teacher quality. In other words, NCLB is an "unfunded mandate."[2] The NEA, joined by school districts in three states, has filed a lawsuit over this issue. It is hard to take the funding complaint seriously, however. While some new funds are necessary for implementing NCLB, the federal government provides less than 10 percent of the total $500 billion K–12 education budget; the rest comes from state and local agencies. If states agree with the goals and assumptions of NCLB, and if their current policies are not doing the job, why would they not want to pay for the necessary improvements? Perhaps that's why so few states have joined the NEA lawsuit.

The complaint about excessive reliance on standardized tests has been made most recently by the State of Connecticut. The argument is that high-stakes testing will cause teachers to "teach to the test," which means narrowing content to focus solely on topics covered by the tests. However, this complaint seems a bit hollow when we consider that virtually every school system in the nation routinely administers standardized tests at most grade levels. The issue is not testing itself, but what I call the three S's: standards, sanctions, and sunshine. States must set standards used by all local districts, school districts must be held accountable for meeting those standards, and test scores for all groups must be published. Assuming that states agree with the fundamental goals of NCLB, how would anyone know if achievement gaps are being closed for a given state unless standard are set, progress is measured, and results are published?

Finally, the issue of federalism raises the question of who is in charge of education policy. The issue was raised forcefully by Utah, which has threatened to withdraw from NCLB at the cost of losing all federal funds. A bipartisan Task Force of state legislatures studied NCLB last year, and in a February report they concluded that the NCLB was an unconstitutional federal intrusion into a policy area delegated to the states. [3] Significantly, the Task Force was in strong agreement with the goals of NCLB but disagreed with many of the NCLB's specific requirements. In effect, it said that achievement gaps should be eliminated, but let the states do it in their own ways and in their own time. Assuming states agree with the goal, who will hold the states accountable for actually doing so if not the federal government?

THE REAL PROBLEM

If we can attain equal proficiencies simply by setting standards and holding schools accountable, why is there so much controversy? The problem is that no one knows how to close these achievement gaps. There are many ideas and theories about how to raise achievement, and some are backed up by hard evidence (reviewed below). When school interventions do raise achievement, however, the gains are usually small and they occur for everyone. At this time there is no proven education intervention that can be implemented on a large scale and that will produce equal proficiency by raising achievement for minority children faster than white children. I say faster because that is precisely what must happen if equal proficiency is to occur by 2014, as I will demonstrate shortly.

The achievement gap has been in existence since the beginning of aptitude and achievement testing, and it is still large despite massive investments in many different educational policies and programs. It was once thought that a combination of segregation and unequal school resources caused the gaps. After the dual school system was dismantled and school resources greatly equalized, achievement gaps remained. School reformers then turned to remediation, with billions of dollars spent on compensatory education, preschool programs like Head Start, and similar interventions. While the achievement gap did diminish somewhat during the 1970s and early 1980s, perhaps due in part to desegregation and remediation programs, the achievement gap stagnated and then widened again during the late 1980s.

Figure 16.1 shows the percentage of 8th graders who scored at or above the "basic" level on the NAEP math achievement test between 1990 and 2005. Over this 15-year period the percentage of black and Hispanic students at or above basic increased significantly, but the rate also increased for white students. Over this extended period the black–white gap did not change at all, the white–Hispanic gap diminished by only 3 points, and the gaps remain very large.

The picture is actually worse for 8th grade reading, where very little change has occurred for any group. Blacks increased by only 8 points compared to 6 points for whites, and the gap remains at 30 percentage points. Likewise, in 4th grade reading the black–white gap has diminished by only 4 points and remains at 34 percentage points. The picture is a bit brighter for 4th grade math scores, where blacks have closed the gap by 11 points but the gap in basic math achievement is still 29 percentage points.

These recent NAEP trends demonstrate the major problem with NCLB. School improvements have raised minority math scores considerably, but they have also raised white scores. If the rates of black and white improvement between 2000 and 2005 are projected to 2014, blacks will still be more than 20 points behind whites in 8th grade math achievement. Assuming that white students continue to gain about 1 point a year, their historical average, then black students will have to gain more than 5 points per year to catch up with whites by 2014, and even then they would only be at 90 percent passing. The situation is similar for reading achievement at both grade levels.

The state accountability systems required by NCLB are not a panacea for the gap problem. Accountability will probably increase achievement levels, and in fact several studies show that NCLB-type accountability has already raised achievement to some extent (Gordon and Armor 2004; Hanushek and Raymond 2004). But the effects are small and so far they have benefited white as much as black students.

How are educators going to raise minority achievement faster than white achievement in order to close the gaps by 2014? Of course, one way to do this is to set standards considerably lower than the basic level defined by the NAEP. There are suggestions that some states have done this. [4] Assuming that a state sets reasonably high standards like those used for the NAEP, current knowledge does not tell us how to attain full proficiency for all students, much less how to raise black and Hispanic achievement faster than white achievement. There are reasons why this knowledge is hard to come by, and it has to do the powerful influence of the family on cognitive skills.

THE READINESS PROBLEM

There is considerable evidence now that the achievement gap is well-established by the time a child starts school. There are several good sources of national data supporting this conclusion. One is the Children of the National Longitudinal Study of Youth (CNLSY) and the other is the Early Childhood Longitudinal

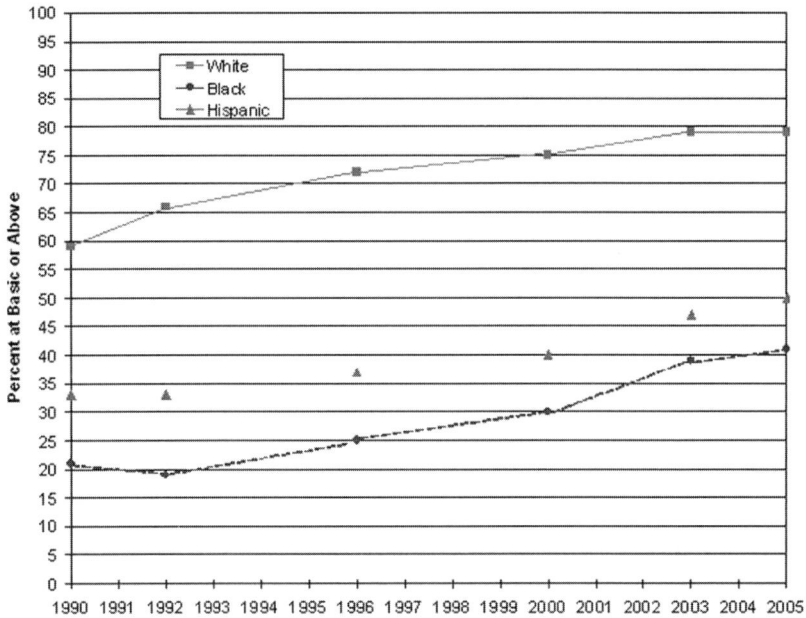

Figure 16.1 Percent basic or above on the NAEP 8th Grade Math Test. *Source:* U.S. Department of Education, Nations Report Card.

Study (ECLS). The CNLSY measures cognitive skills of children starting at age 3 using the Peabody Picture Vocabulary Test (PPVT); the ECLS uses reading and math achievement tests designed specifically for young children and tracks children from Kindergarten to 5th grade and beyond.

Figure 16.2 shows the black–white achievement gaps for kindergarten-age children in standard deviations. The PPVP gap at age 5 is 1.2 standard deviations, while the ECLS kindergarten gap in math achievement rises from .63 to .71 standard deviations from fall to spring.[5] While the ECLS kindergarten gap is somewhat smaller than the 8th grade NAEP gap, it is quite similar to the NAEP 4th grade math gap in 2003. It is likely, therefore, that the math gap does not reach its full magnitude until more complex math topics (e.g., algebra) are introduced in the 7th and 8th grades.[6]

These are important finding for at least two reasons. It tells us that schools do not cause achievement gaps, and it directs us to look to families for the true causes of the gap.

FAMILY RISK FACTORS

Why is the gap so large at the start of schooling, just as large as in higher grades? Clearly, school characteristics cannot explain these preschool gaps. Evidence is accumulating that early achievement gaps can be traced directly to a number

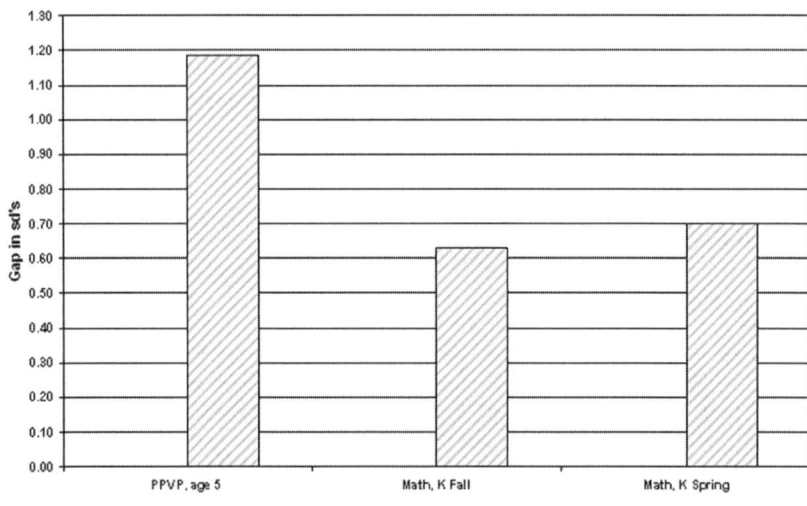

Figure 16.2 Black–white gap at start of schooling. *Source:* NLSY, ECLS.

of family risk factors that operate early in a child's life (Armor 2003). The risk factors are not merely the well-documented socioeconomic status cluster, such as parent education, income, and poverty (SES). Risk factors also include other family characteristics such as parents' IQ, family structure (one or two parents), number of siblings, nutrition factors, and especially parenting behaviors involving instruction (cognitive stimulation) and nurturance (emotional support).

Figure 16.3 shows the simple correlations (light bars) and standardized effects (dark bars) for ten of the most important family risk factors on verbal ability based from the CNLSY. The standardized effects are coefficients from a multiple regression that controls for all family effects simultaneously. They represent the independent effects of each factor controlling for the other nine factors. Breast feeding can be considered a nutrition factor but it may also be an indicator of nurturance.

All risk factors have sizable correlations with verbal scores, but the traditional SES factors—income, parent education, and family structure—have much weaker effects than mother's IQ and the parenting behaviors of cognitive stimulation and emotional support. This is important because most studies of school programs do not measure these non-SES family characteristics. Another point is that all of these family factors influence a child's cognitive development throughout the school years, and they make it all the more difficult for school programs to overcome these family effects.

Regarding independent effects, mother's IQ has the single largest independent effect. But the cumulative independent effects of all the other risk factors combined actually exceed the importance of mother's IQ. Mother's IQ is not

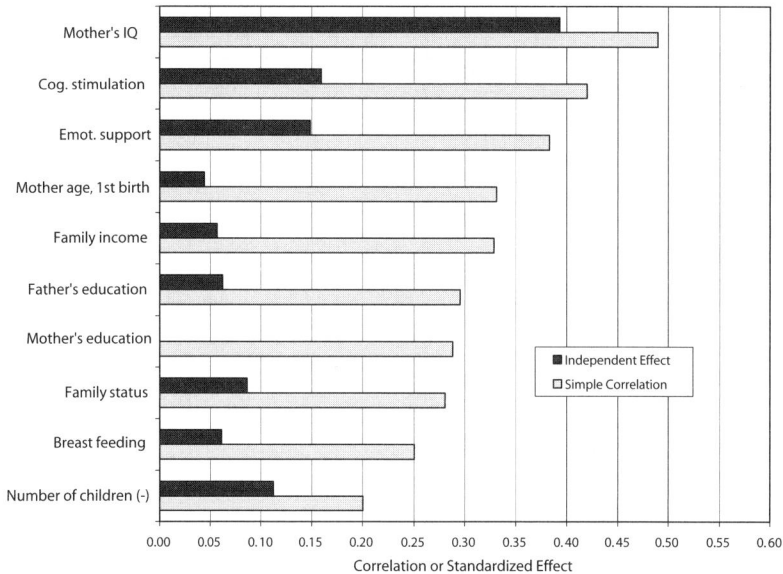

Figure 16.3 Effect of family risk factors on age 5 PPVT. *Source:* 1996 CNLSY.

necessarily a genetic effect; smarter mothers may do many things to create an environment more conducive to learning.

Given the importance of family risk factors in the development of cognitive skills, what can we say about the importance of these family factors in causing racial gaps in achievement? Figure 16.4 reveals very large black–white differences for all 10 of the risk factors. For many of the factors black children have twice the risk of white children: having two parents, family income, mother's education, teen mothers, and breast feeding. While differences in mother's IQ, cognitive stimulation, and emotional support may appear smaller, they are standardized measures with national means of 100 and standard deviations ranging from 12 to 15. Thus all three of these critical factors show race differences exceeding two-thirds of a standard deviation.

Given that family risk factors are highly correlated with achievement and that large black–white differences exist on all of the risk factors, how much of the black–white achievement gap is explained by family risk factors? Figure 16.5 shows what happens to the black–white test score gap at age 11 (6th grade) when various factors are statistically removed. One age 11 test is the PPVT and another is a composite of more conventional reading and math achievement scores.

Family risk factors alone explain about half of the black-white gap on the age 11 PPVT and three-fourths of the age 11 composite achievement gap (darkest bars). Since there are many idiosyncratic factors that influence a child's cognitive

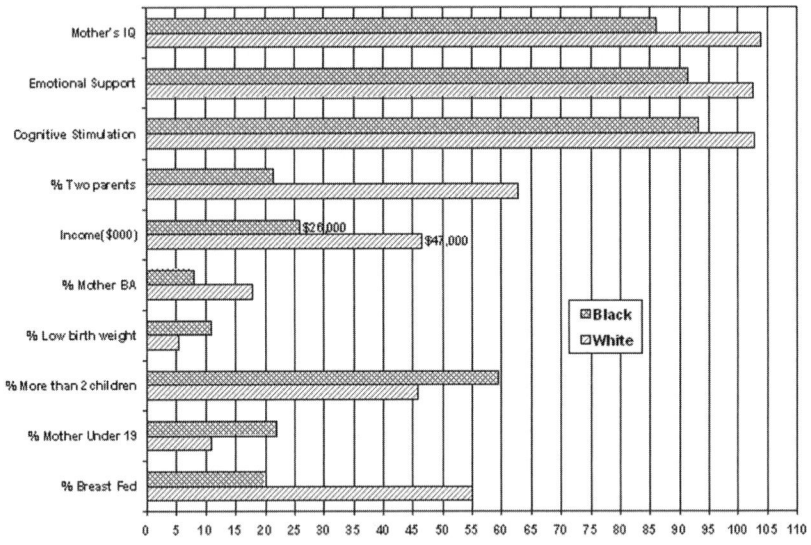

Figure 16.4 Racial differences in family risk factors. *Source:* 1996 CNLSY.

skills, we can also remove the effect of age 5 PPVT as an indicator of these idiosyncratic factors and other unmeasured family factors that operate before the start of schooling. When this is done, Figure 16.5 shows that virtually all of the test score gaps at age 11 are explained by the combination of family risk factors and age 5 verbal skills. In other words, by the end of the elementary grades virtually none of the black–white achievement gap is attributed to school factors.

This last result is very important. If virtually all of the achievement gap can be explained without reference to any school variables, then there is very little significant variation left to be explained by school policies or programs. Of course, the fact that family factors cause achievement gaps does not prove that school programs cannot overcome them. But if school programs and resources can substitute for and counter these family effects, there should be equally strong correlations showing exactly which school factors can do this job and how much they can compensate for family effects. Unfortunately, such evidence is lacking.

EFFECTS OF SCHOOL RESOURCES

This section considers the potential role of school resources in raising achievement and closing achievement gaps. By school resources I mean such factors as expenditures, class sizes, or pupil–teacher ratios, and various indicators of teacher quality such as experience, certification, education, and subject matter mastery. Specific curriculum and instructional strategies will be covered in the next

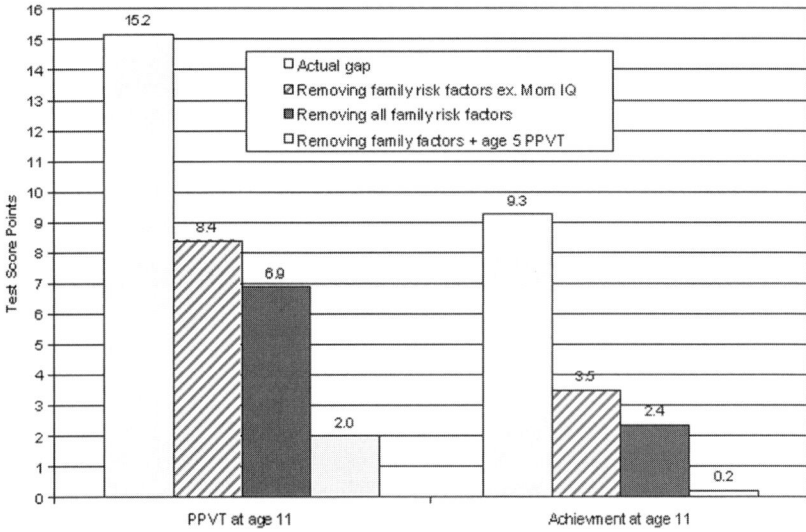

Figure 16.5 Explaining the black–white test score gap for 11-year-olds. *Source:* CNLSY.

section. There is much more systematic information for the efficacy of general resources as compared to specific curriculum and instructional strategies.

Two issues should be addressed when assessing the potential effects of school resources on the achievement gap. First, which school resources have the strongest influences on achievement? Second, what school factors show the greatest black–white differences at the present time? School resources with the greatest potential for reducing achievement gaps are those that have the strongest effects on achievement *and* that reveal large racial differences in availability.

There is still considerable debate regarding which school resources have the strongest impact on achievement. Some authors have found that none of these school resources have significant and consistent impacts on achievement (e.g., Hanushek 1996) while others have found just the opposite (Darling-Hammond 2000; Hedges and Greenwald 1996). Rather than review this extensive literature here, I will discuss some results from the 1996 NAEP data and supplement those with findings from several case studies that I have carried out in individual states or school districts. The results below are consistent with the research literature. They reveal that while most school factors have small effects on achievement, teacher quality emerges as the most important school resource for closing achievement gaps.

Figure 16.6 shows the relationships between teacher and school resource characteristics and 8th grade math achievement controlling for SES characteristics in the 1996 NAEP (individual student and teacher data). Race is included as a surrogate for unmeasured family background characteristics. The light bar is

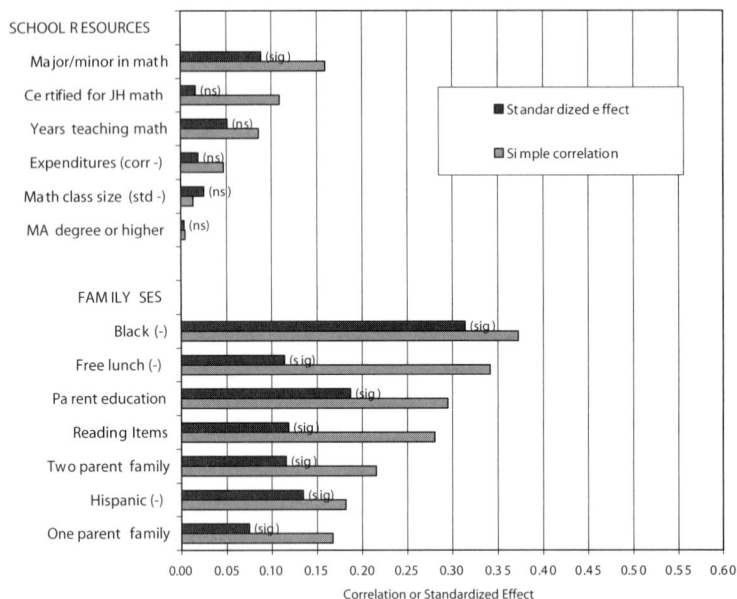

Figure 16.6 School vs. family effects on NAEP 8th grade math scores. *Source:* 1996 NAEP Individual Student Data.

the simple correlation, and the standardized regression coefficients (controlling for all SES factors) are the dark bars. Note that even the simple correlations for school resources are small compared to the correlations for SES characteristics. For example, the largest school resource correlation is only .16 for teachers with a math major/minor in college, whereas five of the SES measures have simple correlations over .2. Teacher certification has a simple correlation of only .12, and the rest of the resource correlations are less than .10. Even if we assume that the raw correlations reflect the potential effect of each school factor (an extremely generous assumption given the causal priority of SES factors), the school effects are very small compared to family factors.

After controlling for SES characteristics, only one of the school characteristics, teachers with college majors or minors in math, has a statistically significant relationship with math achievement after controlling for SES measures. This result supports the notion that teacher subject matter mastery is the most important aspect of teacher quality, especially for 8th grade math when students are beginning to study more advanced math topics like algebra. The standardized effect of .09 is quite modest, however, and lower than all of the SES factors except one parent families.

The appendix shows similar analyses of the relationship between school resources and achievement for the state of South Carolina (grades 6–8), the state of Michigan (grade 7), and New York City (grade 6). All of the analyses are carried out with school as the unit of analysis, so the aggregate correlations are generally larger than those in Figure 16.6. The South Carolina data is of particular interest because of the large number of resource measures, and New York City is interesting simply because it is the largest school district in the country.

The pattern of results is generally the same as the NAEP data: SES measures have strong relationships, many with simple correlations exceeding .5, while school resource measures generally have much smaller correlations. After controlling for SES, only one school resource measure was significant for South Carolina (principal experience, .13 SD); one was significant for Michigan (pupil–teacher ratio, .07 SD), and none was significant for New York City (two were significant but in the wrong direction).

Which school resources reveal the greatest racial disparities, and therefore might provide the most fertile ground for reducing achievement gaps? Figure 16.7 compares school resources available for black and white 8th grade students in the 1996 NAEP. There is virtually no race gap for teacher experience, class size, and hours of math instruction. There is a modest gap favoring black students in the percent of teachers with a master's degree and also instructional expenditures.

There are only two resources that show a significant race difference favoring white students, and both relate to teacher quality: teachers with a certificate for junior high math and teachers who have a college major or minor in math. While 66 percent of white students had a math teacher who had majored or minored in math, only 52 percent of black students had a similarly qualified teacher, a gap of 14 percentage points. The gap is a little smaller for certification; 75 percent of white students were taught by a certified teacher compared to 68 percent of black students. These two characteristics are highly correlated ($r = .6$), and when examining their effects on math achievement, college math appears to be more important than formal certification (as discussed below).

Since teachers' college math has the strongest effect on math achievement and also shows the largest disadvantage for black students, equalizing this resource offers an opportunity to reduce the black–white achievement gap. To illustrate, I computed the change in the gap if black and white students were equalized on the percentage having teachers with math training using the uncontrolled correlation (.16) as the true effect on achievement.[7] The effect of equalizing black and white students on this important teacher quality measure would reduce the national math gap by just 1 point, out of a total gap of about 30 points. Even if 80 percent of black students had teachers with college math, the gap would be reduced by only 2 points. This calculation illustrates how hard it is to reduce achievement gaps by improving school resources: resources have modest effects on achievement, and the existing resource differences are also modest.

These findings for teacher quality are consistent with other education research, and they also support NCLB initiatives to improve teacher quality. The absence of effects for teacher experience and degrees is also consistent with most resource

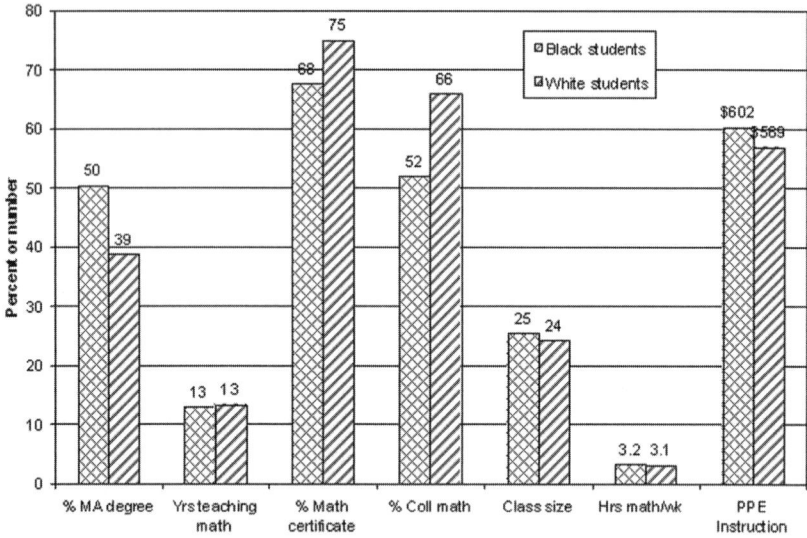

Figure 16.7 Teacher and school resource difference by race. *Source:* 1996 NAEP, Grade 8 math teachers.

studies. With respect to class size and instructional time, however, other research finds that these resources are important. These two school resources are deserving of further discussion, as is the issue of academic standards and accountability which are not examined in most resource studies.

Class Size

Because of the Tennessee Star experiment, many school reformers advocate smaller class sizes for raising minority achievement (e.g., Krueger and Whitmore, 2001). This is an especially attractive option for closing the achievement gap because states or districts can offer reduced class sizes in those schools or classes with high proportions of students below the poverty line. In fact, this practice has been followed by a number of states and school districts, including the two largest school systems in the nation, New York City and Los Angeles. [8]

With the exception of the Tennessee experiment, however, the results of class size reductions are disappointing. The largest class size initiative took place in California, where average class sizes in grades K–3 were reduced from about 30 to 20 or below (Bohrnstedt and Stecher 2002). Unfortunately, achievement gains have been minimal despite costs on the order of $1.5 billion per year.[9] Moreover, the California initiative was not destined to close the achievement gap because it was implemented across the board rather than targeting high-poverty schools. The California experience demonstrates how hard it is, politically, to adopt a popular reform only for low income or disadvantaged minority children.

Even when class size reductions are targeted for high-poverty schools, as in New York City, the results have not been successful in reducing the achievement gap. New York City has had a long-standing policy of reducing class sizes (and pupil–teacher ratios) in schools with high-poverty rates. The reductions were sizable, comparable to the reductions seen in California and the Tennessee Star experiment. Schools with high-poverty rates (as measured by free lunch) had class sizes or pupil–teacher ratios that averaged 10 students less than schools with relatively low poverty rates.

Class size reduction had an unanticipated result in New York City. It created an inverse relationship between class size and achievement, such that students in larger classes had higher achievement. Figure 16.8 shows this inverse relationship for 1998 8th grade math scores. Students in the largest classes scored 20 points higher on a standardized math test, which is nearly one standard deviation. Of course, this does not mean that small classes reduce test scores. Rather, it shows that small class size in high-poverty schools failed to raise achievement levels enough to offset the inverse relationship.

Increasing Total Instruction

Some school reformers believe that closing the achievement gap requires targeting high-poverty, predominantly minority schools and making major changes in curriculum and school climate (Thernstrom and Thernstrom 2004). This approach is embodied in the Knowledge is Power Program (KIPP), which aimed to raise black achievement by dramatically altering the school culture and increasing total instructional time by as much as 50 percent.[10]

While some KIPP schools have raised black achievement appreciably, it is hard to generalize these findings to all high-poverty or disadvantaged minority students and schools. KIPP schools require parents to be highly committed to the program, because it requires longer school days and a longer school year. Since not all parents agree with these requirements, the achievement gains of KIPP schools reflect a highly selected population of students and parents who have volunteered for the program. It is unknown whether the KIPP approach would have the same effect on achievement if it was adopted by a large school district for all of its disadvantaged minority children.

Before a KIPP-type model becomes practical for a whole state or even a whole school district, several questions must be answered. Will all disadvantaged families accept more or longer school days? Are states willing provide funds to increase instructional time for all disadvantaged students? Perhaps most important, will nondisadvantaged families want this school improvement also, once it is understood that the greater instructional time raises achievement? If so, the advantage for minority or poverty students is lost.

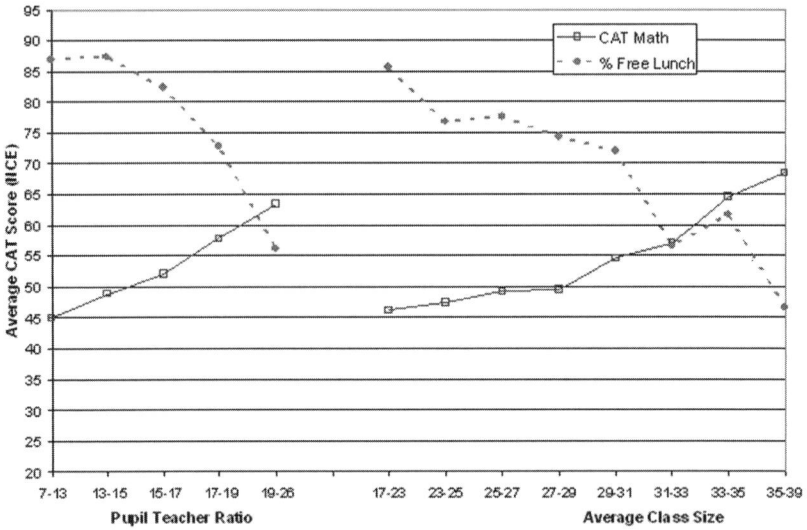

Figure 16.8 New York City math achievement by class size. *Source:* 1998 8th grade.

Standards and Accountability

Most studies of school resources do not include indicators of academic standards or accountability systems, at least at the school or school district level. A full accountability system requires setting proficiency standards for all or most grades, mandatory achievement testing, publishing test results by ethnic and poverty status, and having sanctions for schools that fail to meet standards. There is a small but growing literature on the effects of accountability on achievement, most of which are carried out using statewide achievement data. So far, this research is mixed for reducing achievement gaps.

While states with stronger accountability systems have produced some achievement gains, they have not closed the black–white achievement gap. A study by Hanushek found that white gains were larger than black gains, although he also found that Hispanics gained more white students and therefore accountability closed the white–Hispanic gap by about 2 points (Hanushek and Raymond 2003). Using a somewhat different measure of accountability and more recent data, a study by Gordon and Armor found no significant gains for whites, blacks, or Hispanics on 8th grade math between 1996 and 2003 after appropriate controls for SES (Gordon and Armor 2004).

Obviously, the standards and accountability systems required by NCLB are still under development, so it will be some years before the full impact of NCLB can be assessed. Conceptually, however, it is hard to see how NCLB by itself can close achievement gaps since it requires standards and accountability for everyone, not just minority students. Granted, states can target minority and poverty students, but it is by no means clear how academic standards themselves—if set at relatively high levels—would benefit only disadvantaged students.

Curriculum and Instructional Strategies

Some critics complain that school resource studies ignore the essence of a school's program, which is the actual curriculum and pedagogical techniques used in the classroom. While this is a fair complaint, it is not easily remedied. There are very few large-scale, systematic studies that compare different curricular and instructional strategies; most are relatively small scale studies designed to evaluate a particular classroom technique. Many of these studies have methodological problems, and even when the studies are done well, they frequently report no significant advantage compared to classrooms using conventional techniques.

This problem is well-illustrated by the What Works Clearinghouse (WWC) website, established by the U.S. Department of Education to inform states and school districts of educational programs that can improve achievement.[11] As of 2006 the only curriculum topic evaluated was middle school mathematics, and the results are not very encouraging for school districts trying to find a curriculum that will close the gaps in math achievement.

The WWC found 77 studies that evaluated 20 different middle school math curricula, but only 10 of these studies for five of the curricula met the minimum methodological requirements for establishing effectiveness.[12] Of the 10 studies judged adequate, only 2 studies found statistically significant effects on math achievement, one each for two different curricula.[13] Two small studies do not constitute a reliable basis for adopting a math curriculum that promises to close achievement gaps, particularly when eight studies found no significant impact. Some might even call this situation embarrassing, that years of educational research has produced so little evidence about the viability of alternative curricula for teaching mathematics.

Another example of the difficulty in obtaining definitive data on program effectiveness is illustrated by a recent study of the National Science Foundation's Urban Systemic Initiative (NSF USI). This program consisted of grants to high poverty urban school districts to improve the teaching of science and mathematics in urban areas; a total of 21 grants were given to large school districts. The evaluation study selected four school districts to conduct a detailed study: Chicago, Miami-Dade County, El Paso, and Memphis (Borman et al. 2005). Unfortunately, achievement data were available for only two districts, Chicago and Miami.

Through classroom observation and surveys, the study collected detailed information on more than 50 discrete measures of classroom and instructional practices, which were subsequently reduced to 17 indicators through factor analysis. Because of the relatively small numbers of teachers, most of the correlations between instructional indicators and student achievement were not statistically significant. Moreover, while the achievement correlations for some of the instructional indicators were in the expected direction, other correlations were negative and therefore not supportive of the instructional theory being tested. The authors explained some of these negative results in terms of school culture factors, whereby the teachers had not adopted the viewpoints or teaching styles recommended by the NSF program.

In summary, the situation for pedagogy is no different from that for school resources. There is simply not a solid body of evidence that validates particular curricular or instructional approaches for improving achievement and closing gaps, particularly in the time left before the NCLB deadline in 2014.

POLICY SUGGESTIONS

The fact that there are no demonstrable educational interventions for closing achievement gaps does not mean that NCLB should be abandoned. Since research has shown that standards and accountability systems can raise achievement, the policy of requiring them is clearly desirable from the standpoint of improving education for everyone. The problem is that the goals of NCLB are expressed not as improving achievement but as attaining equal proficiency for all groups within a specified time frame, and no one knows how to do that.

Perhaps the most important recommendation is that the federal government needs to take the lead in sponsoring research about how to close achievement gaps. The What Works Clearinghouse makes it clear that there is not a body of existing research that answers this question; new research has to be undertaken. Moreover, there is a unique opportunity now for using the enormous databases being created in every state to tell us which schools are and are not closing achievement gaps. Of course, additional data will have to be collected to explain why some schools are successful while others are not.

Second, the Department of Education should modify those aspects of NCLB that define progress only in terms of the goal of equal proficiency by 2014.[14] Maintaining unattainable goals can create unintended consequences. One risk is continued state opposition, requests for exceptions and waivers, and, like Utah, decisions to drop out of the program entirely. A more serious risk is that some states might keep lowering their proficiency standards until most minority and poverty students can pass. A third risk is increasing racial and economic segregation to minimize comparisons of racial groups within schools (Schwartz, Stiefel, and Chellman forthcoming).

The major purpose of NCLB can be preserved by making its main goal increasing achievement for all groups, and tying sanctions to achievement gains or growth rather than equal proficiency. A similar approach was being used by certain states prior to NCLB, such as California and Texas, and it is being advocated now by Tennessee. This approach is sometimes called a growth model or a value-added model. Indeed, the U.S. Department of Education has initiated a growth initiative which has been approved for two states, Tennessee and North Carolina (Department of Education 2006).

The descriptions of the "core principles" of these growth models emphasize that the NCLB requirement of equal proficiency by 2014 remains unchanged. Among other things, growth models simply change the way AYP is calculated. Changing the way AYP is calculated does not solve the problem I am describing, which is attainment of equal proficiency by 2014 when we have no known technology that increases minority achievement to the extent required.

I recommend that achievement still be tracked by groups within schools, but goals should be set for increasing achievement for each group relative to their baseline levels. In this way, a school would not be failing as long as achievement is increasing at some prescribed level for all of the groups in a school. This would not prevent a school or school district from implementing special programs to improve minority achievement and close the gap, but under this scenario a school would not fail simply because it cannot close achievement gaps that, at present,we do not know how to eliminate.

APPENDIX

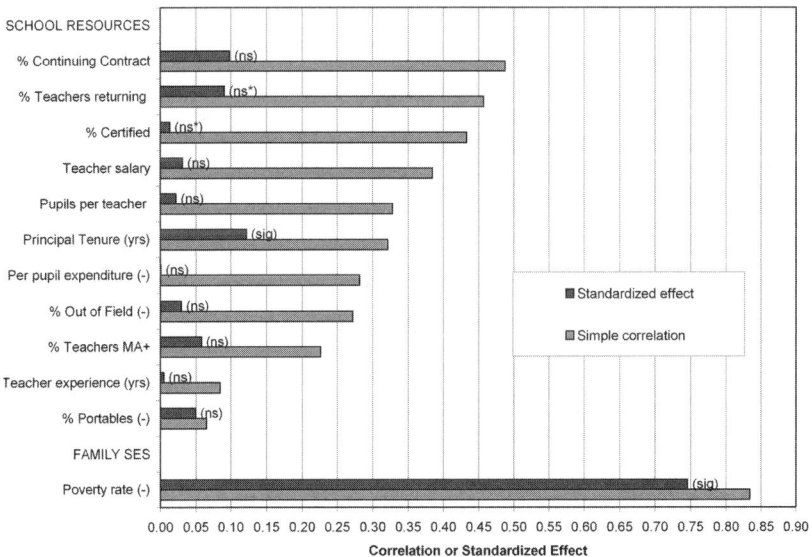

Figure 16.A1 School vs. family effects on South Carolina middle school math scores. *Source:* Average of 2001–03 state school-level data.

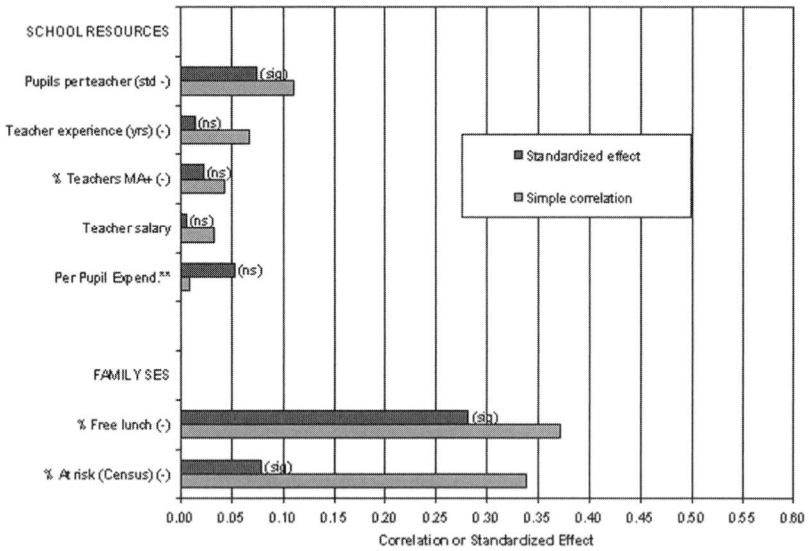

Figure 16.A2 School vs. family effects on Michigan 7th grade math scores. *Source:* 2000 state school-level data.

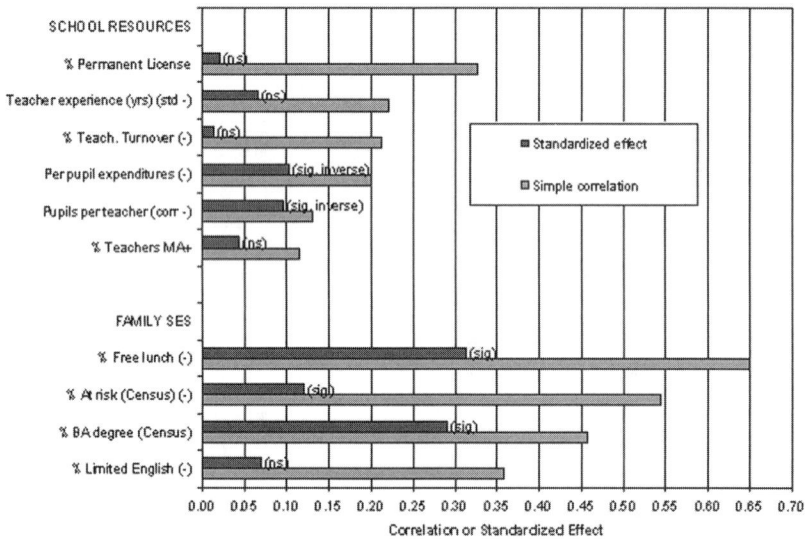

Figure 16.A3 School vs. family effects on New York City 6th grade math scores. *Source:* 1998 city school-level data.

Notes

1. This paper was delivered at the American Sociological Association, Sociology of Education Section Conference on No Child Left Behind, Philadelphia, PA, August 12, 2005
2. It is worth noting that the General Accounting Office has determined that NCLB is not an unfunded mandate.
3. National Conference of State Legislatures, "Task Force on No Child Left Behind," February 23, 2005. The report acknowledged that the constitutional issue was difficult because NCLB is not a federal mandate, only a requirement if a state wishes to keep federal funds.
4. See for example, a recent Fordham Foundation report (Finn, Petrilli, and Julian 2006).
5. The CNLSY figure is from the author's analyses (see Armor 2003); the ECLS figures are also from original analyses.
6. The ECLS shows a kindergarten reading gap that is only .5 standard deviations, which is inconsistent with the PPVT. The ECLS reading test does not measure the full range of reading skills; for example, it omits vocabulary (Rock and Stenner 2005).
7. The calculation is .16×.14=.0224 (reduction in SDs), times a math SD of 38=.85 or about 1 point.
8. Los Angeles provided smaller classes for high-poverty schools during the 1980s when the author served as a member of the LA school board.
9. Studies showed that class size reduction caused a shortage of fully credentialed teachers, so teacher quality (by this measure) also declined during the implementation period—especially in schools with high-poverty rates. So the potential benefits of class size reduction might be hampered by lower teacher quality.
10. KIPP stands for Knowledge is Power Program.
11. See http://www.whatworks.ed.gov
12. Basically, the minimum requirements were a control group of some kind (not necessarily randomized trials) and statistical procedures to adjust for any differences between the treatment and control group.
13. One was Cognitive Tutor and the other was I Can Learn.
14. Safe harbor provisions allow a group that does not make the AYP goal to be in compliance if the number of students not making proficiency is reduced by 10 percent from the prior year. This provision still requires that the group increases in achievement, albeit at a somewhat slower rate. The equal proficiency goal is not altered.

References

Armor, David J. 2003. *Maximizing intelligence*, New Brunswick, NJ: Transaction.

Bohrnstedt, George W. and Brian M. Stecher. 2002. *What We Have Learned About Class Size Reduction in California*. California Department of Education, Sacramento, California.

Borman, Kathryn M., et al. 2005. *Meaningful urban educational reform*. Albany: New York State University Press.

Darling-Hammond, Linda. 2000. Teacher quality and student achievement: A review of the state policy evidence. *Educational Policy Analysis Archives* 8 No.1 (www.epaa.asu.edu/epaa/v8n1).

Finn, Chester E., Michael J. Petrilli, and Liam Julian. 2006 *The State of State Standards 2006*. Washington, D.C.:Thomas B. Fordham Foundation,

Gordon, Bryon S. and David J. Armor. 2004. The effects of accountability systems on the achievement gap: 2000–2003. Paper presented at the 26th Annual APPAM Research Conference, Atlanta, GA, October 30.

Hanushek, Eric A. 1996. School resources and student achievement. In *Does Money Matter?* ed. Garry Burtless, 43–73. Washington D.C.: Brookings Institution Press.

———. Margaret E. Raymond. 2004. The Effect of School Accountability Systems on the Level and Distribution of Student Achievement. *Journal of the European Economic Association*, April/May 2:406-415

Hedges, Larry V., and Rob Greenwald. 1996. Have times changed? The relationship between school resources and student performance. In *Does Money Matter?* ed. Garry Burtless, 74–92. Washington D.C.: Brookings Institution Press.

Krueger, Alan B. andDiane M. Whitmore. 2001. The Effect of Attending a Small Class in the Early Grades on College-test Taking and Middle School Test Results: Evidence from Project Star. *The Economic Journal* 111:1–28.

National Education Association. 2006. Data on schools/districts not making adequate yearly progress (AYP). http://www.nea.org/esea/images/AYP-State-Lists-2005-Jan4A.pdf (revised January 19).

Rock, Donald A. and A. Jackson Stenner. 2005. Assessment Issues in the Testing of Children at School Entry. *The Future of Children* 15:35-54.

Schwartz, A. E., L. Stiefel, and C. Chellman. Forthcoming. So many children left behind: Segregation and the impact of subgroup reporting on No Child Left Behind on the racial test score gap. *Educational Policy*.

Thernstrom, Abigail and Stephan Thernstrom. 2003. *No excuses: Closing the racial gap in learning.* New York: Simon and Schuster.

U.S. Department of Education. 2006. Secretary Spelling approves Tennessee and North Carolina growth model pilots for 2005–2006. News release, May 17.

17

Symbolic Uses of NCLB

Reaffirmation of Equality of Educational Opportunity or Delegitimization of Public Schools?[1]

Mary Haywood Metz

The No Child Left Behind Act is a vast, complex piece of legislation that is having manifold, far-reaching effects. As happens with most sweeping policies (Spillane 2004), the balance of its effects in schools on children and their teachers varies as the law is locally interpreted in states, districts, schools, and classrooms. We have enough scattered systematic evidence and enough anecdotal evidence about the law's effects to suspect that some of those effects may help disadvantaged children, while many will leave their educational situation not significantly better or worse, and some of the law's effects will actively damage the quality of their education.

This paper is about the large view, the overall symbolic and institutional effects of the No Child Left Behind Act. The law has important symbolic purposes and consequences. This symbolism is not merely abstract or cultural; it has great practical importance. First, the law can be seen as a fresh attempt symbolically to balance the paradox of a fundamental American belief in offering equality of opportunity to the young through public education and a fundamental American practice of local control of schooling that creates dramatically unequal education in public schools, depending on the communities in which they are located. The political boundaries of school districts create separate regimes of schooling that draw on very unequal social, intellectual, and material resources. Such unequal provision of schooling clearly violates commonly shared American principles of equality of opportunity. It belies the powerful myth of the common school as both melting pot and provider of a fair start for all.

On the surface, NCLB is designed to reaffirm the value, and to create the reality, of public schools that provide a strong and standardized education that gives all children a firm educational foundation and an even chance. The law's insistence that all students will be proficient in reading, math, and science by 2014 makes a dramatic and symbolic statement, backed by a federal guarantee. Moreover, unlike previous symbolic laws and statements that underscored equality of educational opportunity, this law has strong enforcement mechanisms.[2]

Relying on experts in testing, however, I will argue that "adequate yearly progress toward 100 percent proficiency" is simply impossible for the majority of schools to produce in the time allowed (Goertz 2005; Kane and Staiger 2002, 2003; Linn 2003; Popham 2004). If the law is not significantly amended, eventually most public schools will fail to make AYP goals with one or more subgroups. As school after school fails, public schools as a whole will become formally labeled "in need of improvement."

This wholesale delegitimization constitutes a second symbolic thrust of the law. The current legislated path toward shaming of most, and reorganization of many, public schools will make symbolically vivid an apparent utter failure on the part of public schools, even after years of concerted federal effort to support them. Thus, rather than reaffirming and bolstering the role of public schools as providers of equal opportunity, as it appears to do, the law is on track to provide apparent evidence of the failure of public schools.

THE SYMBOLIC SIMILARITY OF SCHOOLS AS THE RESOLUTION OF A PARADOX IN PROVIDING EQUALITY OF OPPORTUNITY—1980s STYLE

In order to understand the symbolic meanings of NCLB, it is useful to explore more fully the juxtaposition of the public's genuine belief in the importance of equal educational opportunity and their attachment to deeply entrenched social structures that make such equality almost impossible to attain. In the late 1980s, I conducted a study of high schools serving homogeneous communities that differed from each other in social class. In that study, I found enormous differences in the lives of schools, their teachers, and their students that were linked to the social class of the surrounding community. This was primarily a study of teachers' work. To be very brief, I found that teachers' working goals, the way they structured a class hour, the character of their interactions with students, and the experiences that they remembered as high and low points of their careers, were significantly different, depending on the social class context in which they worked. Classroom observations showed that students' experiences in classes that bore the same course name, and often used the same textbook, were also radically different (Hemmings and Metz 1990; Metz 1990a, 1993, 1998).

I found other scholars were little interested in the questions I was asking about the lived differences I saw in schools. Researchers interested in school change spoke instead of uniformity in schools and of the consequent difficulty of getting school staffs to imagine how schooling could be "restructured" to make improvements. Puzzled at first, I soon realized that—if one focuses on the structural and technical characteristics of U.S. high schools—schools were indeed very much alike. They had similar buildings with long halls and rows of rooms of similar size isolated from one another. They had similar time schedules. At that time, teachers met each day with five groups of students of about the same size for about the same amount of time. Further, there was a widely accepted curricular scope and sequence, with common course names and a relatively small array of textbooks available for each of those courses. Schools in very different settings shared these curricular elements.

In short, there was—and still is—a common script for schooling. What others saw was that high schools all produce the same play. What I was seeing was that the production of that play in each school was radically different.

My understanding of the significance of the common script was advanced by my study of Charles Drew High School, a school deep inside an isolated and socially and economically depressed African-American portion of one of the nation's largest cities. Students struggled with the community and family issues common to impoverished areas. In some ways, the school made creative adjustments both to the demands that students' outside lives placed upon them and to their cultural style. But, despite extremely low test scores and a 50 percent dropout rate, Drew's administration insisted on a curriculum that was more demanding than the city expected. Drew's seniors read Huxley's *Brave New World* and Dante's *Inferno* in senior English and wrote papers about them, although few of them possessed the requisite comprehension and writing skills. In the same course, many struggled with the task of mastering the forms of writing business letters. Similarly, all seniors took physics, whether they had passed second year algebra or not; physics teachers tried to fill in the gaps and so did not cover the whole physics curriculum. Thus, the school required students to study high status knowledge no matter how much they were challenged by the basics (Metz 1990a, 1990b).

At Drew, following the forms of schooling used in the elite suburbs of the city gave reality to the claims of many staff that their students were as capable as students in those elite suburbs, even though Drew's students might take a little longer to master the material. Further, to follow the curriculum that appears to be common currency in the United States seemed to give the isolated students of this impoverished urban area access to the common culture, and so to rights of citizenship and personal dignity.

I wrote about the technical and structural regularities of high schools, their common script, as a drama called Real School (Metz 1990b).[3] The actors play their parts in theaters that provide different stages, props, directors, and rehearsal time.

The actors are also independent-minded: they are unpredictable as they interpret their characters, do or do not mind their cues, and may or may not even remain on stage to the end of the play. Still, despite enormous disparities in the play that is actually produced, following the script of Real School provides participation in national unity that imparts symbolic legitimacy to all concerned.

Meyer and Rowan's articles of the late 1970s (Meyer and Rowan 1977, 1978) argued a cognate point in the context of organizational change; they held that schools create externally visible, symbolic forms for purposes of winning public approval. The formal, visible organizational practices can respond easily to the winds of public opinion, but they may be quite separate from daily practice where the technical core of the organization's work proceeds in search of effectiveness in its immediate conditions. These articles became founding documents in what came to be known as the "new institutionalism" (DiMaggio and Powell 1991; Scott 2002). Ironically, the new institutionalists' observation of "loose coupling" in schools, stripped of its theoretical context, is now being widely discussed and decried among politicians and citizens active in influencing education as a simple lack of clear and strong oversight (Ingersoll 2003). It is being used as a justification for a strong tightening of hierarchical control in schools.

Oddly missing from both theoretical and practical discussions has been any acknowledgment of the larger scale political uses of this disconnect between educational form and practice. It parallels the disjunction in American society between social ideals of equality of educational opportunity and social structures that produce highly unequal educational practice. As soon as one asks the political question, the political uses of the legitimacy that inhere in the shared structures and practices of Real School become evident. *If all children have a right to attend schools that are alike in all essential respects, then all citizens are being offered an equal educational opportunity.*

Sociologists and other social scientists have long emphasized that schools not only develop the potential of individual children; they are also required to sort and label the skills and accomplishments of all the children of each generation in ways that direct different ones among them toward different kinds of work immediately after secondary school; or alternatively toward different rungs in a hierarchically sorted array of postsecondary educational opportunities (Anyon 1981; Bowles and Gintis 1976; Connell et al. 1982; Hurn 1993; Parsons 1959). Since World War II, schooling has become ever more critical to the placement of succeeding generations in the occupational world and thus in positions of stratified economic well-being, status, and power. If society is to continue as it is, some students need less than stellar school records, so that they will accept necessary but less appealing forms of work, with a sense that such work is their legitimate lot. Further, if society actually educated all children equally well, it would have no method by which to allocate new cohorts to differentially rewarded slots in higher education and the labor force. Thus members of U.S. society with even a modest degree of current privilege in the schools to which they have access have a strong incentive to believe that since schools are formally alike they produce equality of opportunity—for other people's children. Equally important, those commonalities assure students and teachers at schools such as Drew that they are legitimate participants in the larger society.

Despite these appearances, the informal differences among schools associated with social class include differences that affect the heart of the teaching and learning process. Such differences in schools help to assure differences in the accomplishments of students. They give some children an advantage and keep others out of the higher ranks of the competition.

Recently, several qualitative studies have shown how upper middle-class parents search for and select the best schools for their children through housing choices or pressure districts to move resources to their children's schools. They do so without conscious attention to how they are exploiting or even increasing inequality in the overall educational system (Brantlinger 2003; Lareau 2003; Lewis 2003). Furthermore, as other studies have shown, when changes to school enrollment boundaries are proposed, the middle-class parents in the suburbs show a keen awareness even of the difference between their schools and those in the next, slightly less affluent or less educated suburb. They strongly resist redrawing district boundaries or other changes that they fear might lower the level of privilege among their children's school peers (Mirel 1994; Wells and Crain 1997; Wells and Serna 1996). They also strongly resist state efforts to equalize funding between districts (e.g., Firestone, Goertz, and Natriello 1997).

At the same time, when such parents think about schools at the state or national level, or in the abstract, most firmly believe that our system of public schools should, and for the most part does, provide equality of opportunity for all students (Brantlinger 2003; Lewis 2003; Wells and Crain 1997; Wells and Serna 1996). According to these authors, they do not acknowledge the disparity of opportunity for others engendered by the variations in quality that they so readily perceive on behalf of their own children. This double vision should not surprise us. As both Murray Edelman (1977) and Gunnar Myrdal (1944) have shown us in different contexts, it is easy for the public to hold contradictory beliefs, bringing them to the fore as self-interest warrants.

Standardization of the formal aspects of schooling helps to create an illusion of sameness that veils the system of widely differentiated privilege in public schools. Nonetheless, the social legitimacy of schooling in the United States in the late 20th and early 21st century requires a reliable rhetorical bridge to span the gap between societal belief that the United States is an open society that provides equality of opportunity, and the reality that its public schools provide an education that varies systematically in both style and quality in ways related to the social class of the surrounding community. This rhetorical bridge requires maintenance; its braces must be updated with fresh actions. NCLB can be construed as the latest, highly visible maintenance.

NCLB AS AN INTENSIFICATION OF REAL SCHOOL

One possible reading of NCLB is that it is a reaffirmation of a national commitment to the unity, quality, and standardization expressed more diffusely in the patterns of Real School. Both can be seen as symbolic expressions of the belief and intention that U.S. schools should offer equality of opportunity. Both have just enough structural and technical effect to give them credibility but both remain far from providing equal material, social, or intellectual resources to schools in radically different, and intentionally separated, social circumstances.

That said, NCLB appears to go much further toward creating more equal conditions for children than do the informal similarities of Real School. It has provisions insisting that states upgrade the quality of teachers in all schools, especially those serving poverty areas. It requires states to develop curricular standards and to assess all children to be sure they are learning up to those standards. It monitors achievement outcomes, and supplies some funds and some required steps to support and cajole schools that are not meeting them into far reaching school improvement efforts. Thus, at first reading and in a symbolic way, NCLB reasserts the U.S. belief in equality of opportunity and also supports the provision of a single U.S. standard of educational excellence in public schools for all children. But it does so in a far more dramatic and concrete way than have previous efforts.

Several members of Congress and civic groups that advocate for poor children strongly supported the law in the hope and sincere expectation that it would go far to equalize both material and intellectual resources available to students disadvantaged by the legal and financial separation of local school districts and their segregation in terms of both social class and race. They hoped it would serve as a genuine opportunity to provide more equal opportunity and would provide strong, tangible braces for an educational bridge between children in poverty and educational opportunity, rather than a bridge supported by braces made of rituals with more symbolic than technical effectiveness (DeBray 2006).

Yet five years after its signing, instead of offering new resources for capacity building to the schools, Congress and the U.S. Department of Education have left the differences in material and social resources among the schools almost completely intact. As happens fairly frequently with federal laws, a large part of the funds that were authorized when the law was passed were never appropriated by Congress. Important among these were funds under section 1003g of the Act that were intended to provide the backbone of assistance for resources and program development in schools designated as in need of improvement

(INOI; Haycock 2005). Thus the promise of significant federal funds to help Title I schools has, in large part, not been kept, despite some increase in overall funding. In fact, many states and school districts are finding that the cost of developing, administering, scoring, and recording many more tests than before has eaten up most or all of the increase in federal funds and in some cases has required the use of state funds as well. Other funds for schools are siphoned off into transporting students from schools labeled in need of improvement to other district schools that are not so labeled and into supplemental educational services that are, at best, loosely coordinated with school programs (Burch, Donovan, and Steinberg 2006; Farkas and Dunham 2006). The provisions that require teachers to be "highly qualified" have been loosely defined, with wholesale inclusion of alternative programs (U.S. Department of Education 2003), and casually enforced (Education Trust 2003).

Unlike the standardized structures of Real School, which persist, NCLB promises to deliver not just equal provision of education, but equal *outcomes* to education. Indeed, it demands such equal outcomes by legislative fiat, even though, as enforced, it offers a bare minimum of increased resources to schools that have difficulty in creating those outcomes. Legislative fiat by itself rarely provides an effective remedy for socially and technically difficult problems. Further, the outcomes this law demands are so ambitious as to be without precedent (Linn 2003). They would be very unlikely to materialize at the level demanded and in the time allowed even if the federal government lavished financial resources and social support on the schools.

NCLB AS AN ENGINE TO DELEGITIMIZE U.S. PUBLIC SCHOOLING

Reflection on current patterns of enforcement and long-term implications of NCLB suggests that its actual symbolic effects will be precisely the opposite of what they appear to be based on its initial goals and claims. While the rhetoric framing the law and the broad sweep of its provisions point toward ensuring both equality of opportunity through the schools and up to a point even equality of outcomes, upon close inspection, NCLB is an apparatus more designed to demonstrate decisively that the nation's public schools are both *un*equal and *universally inadequate*. This symbolic impact lies not in the formal framework or language of the law, but in the predictable consequences of implementation of its detailed provisions. While the first symbolic mission of NCLB to increase equality of opportunity is officially trumpeted, its alternate symbolic message is unannounced. One knows it only by projecting the effects of the details of its provisions. As currently designed and as initially enforced, the law will result in an accumulation of data documenting persistent "need for improvement," translated by the popular press as failure, in a steadily swelling number of public schools—data that will be widely publicized and widely watched each year.

Schools will inevitably rearrange their yearly and daily practice around avoiding this label. Its initial trajectory put it on track progressively to label almost every public school in the United States as failing to educate its students to proficiency. That judgment will seem to arise "naturally" from the cumulative test score data it requires states to generate. In this way, NCLB has the potential to undercut, indeed to erase, that very faith in the equality of schooling which it is on the surface undertaking to support or restore—and to destroy faith in the quality of all public schools.

Experts in testing have pointed out that gains in scores on standardized tests of the size and speed that NCLB requires are without precedent. Nothing even close to the magnitude of steady, incremental gains in test scores across all schools of the kind demanded by the law has ever been seen in the real world (Linn 2003). The time span of 12 years to meet the goals was set without a rationale in past experience or empirical evidence. Only schools already scoring very well, with only a small distance to go, will be able to meet incremental steps for long because, for them, the gains requested are small each year. Even these schools will experience ceiling effects as they approach 100 percent proficiency.

The law requires schools to disaggregate the scores of subgroups of students who are disadvantaged. Test scores of students in the usually targeted minority racial–ethnic groups, students eligible for free or reduced price lunch, English language learners, and students in special education must each be counted separately as well as included in the schools' total scores. If students in a single subgroup do not make the cutoff, the whole school is labeled "in need of improvement" for that year. Furthermore 95 percent of the students in the school and in each subgroup must be tested or the school fails to make AYP on the basis of the proportion tested alone. Low scores in just one subgroup or failure to have 95 percent of students in that category tested can trigger not only a public "in need of improvement" label but also corrective sanctions up to and including closure and reorganization.

There are good practical reasons for breaking out scores of disadvantaged students and for requiring that 95 percent of students be tested. These measures prevent schools from hiding a variety of kinds of failures by placing students in untested categories or from neglecting disadvantaged students and then hiding their scores among the higher scores of more favored students. At the same time, breaking out these groups becomes a way of assuring that massive numbers of schools will quickly be labeled as needing improvement.

Several provisions of NCLB serve to make the negative labeling of large numbers of public schools vivid for both parents and school staffs and highly visible to the general public. First, while NCLB is building on the ESEA reauthorization of 1994, in that law only Title I schools–ones that receive federal money—were required to engage in systematic testing and report the results, not all public schools. Further, reporting under NCLB has a much higher profile. Parents must be sent individual letters about any way in which the school fails to meet testing benchmarks or if their child's teacher does not meet the formal "highly qualified" standard. NCLB requires public notification when schools do not meet AYP, so that every community and metropolitan or regional newspaper and television station carries tables noting which schools did and did not make AYP. Such tables need not note that a school failed in only one of many categories.

Even though the federal government has power over the educational policies of the states only by setting conditions for states' acceptance of federal monies, NCLB requires that *all* public schools must administer the tests to every student in the relevant grades and bear the public labels that they bring—*even if the schools are not eligible for, or do not take, Title I funds.* Schools are subject to the reach of federal regulation as long as their district or state takes any federal educational funds. On the other hand, private schools, *even when they do receive federal funds or services through Title I,* are not required to administer state tests or to report to outside audiences the results of any tests they do administer voluntarily. Private schools bear no negative labels under NCLB, whatever their quality—*even when they receive federal money or federally funded services.*

Unless private schools voluntarily provide testing data on the same tests that public school students take and voluntarily break that data down to report separately on all the same subgroups, *there will be no way to know whether they perform better, worse, or similarly to public schools.* Private schools would have no reason to report in those ways—for all the reasons that public schools have not previously done so voluntarily—with occasional exceptions for individual schools that may want to advertise that they do well with certain subgroups.[4]

Private schools will become increasingly appealing to parents simply because they are spared an array of ancillary pressures associated with the NCLB accountability system. An increasingly well-documented effect of the law is that, with such high stakes tests, public schools that are struggling to make very large increments in test scores every year on their way from current levels to 100 percent proficiency are being forced to focus their curricular and instructional efforts mostly, or even solely, on the tested subjects, and further on teaching those subjects in the style of the tests (Center on Education Policy 2006). While some states do have tests that are open-ended and call for complex thinking, these are so expensive to write, score, and report in the vast numbers required by the law that states are under extreme pressure to trade them for commercially prepared, widely used, closed-ended tests (Darling-Hammond 2004). Consequently, as public schools prepare students for the federally required tests, the content of learning both across and within subject areas is being radically narrowed in many, quite possibly in a majority, of schools. Except in the previously worst schools, the intellectual content of curricula and of children's learning may be severely compromised, not enhanced, by the law.

In short, whatever its intentions, the law will have the effect of eroding public confidence in public schools. Middle-class parents will be tempted to abandon public schools for private ones, or to flee to ever more affluent districts, where educated standars are high and the effects of the law fall more lightly on schools whose students have had advantages from birth. They will reasonably worry about the effects on their children's college admissions of coming from a "school in need of improvement." They will seek a broader curriculum than one focused around state standardized tests to ensure that their children have college level skills.

If middle-class parents abandon the public schools in the face of the law's pressures, they will then be reluctant to pay school taxes, putting further downward pressures on the funding available to schools and on the quality of programs offered to those who remain.

Capable teachers will have increasing reasons to leave public schools for private ones, and to leave public schools in poverty for more elite ones where there is at least a fighting chance to make AYP and where pressures to narrow the curriculum to test preparation are less intense. This migration also will only worsen the situation of the schools that need the most help in improving their academic performance.

Given the inevitably escalating numbers of schools in need of improvement by NCLB's criteria, popularly called failing schools, compounded with pressures likely to weaken the actual quality of the education in public schools, parents will increasingly find a system of national or state vouchers that they can use at a private school extremely appealing. Private schools will be a haven from both the label of systematic failure and the anxiety and program distortions created by the accountability system for public schools.

RESISTANCE TO NCLB AND ITS SYMBOLIC ATTACK ON PUBLIC SCHOOLS

Delegitimization of public schools may be the most fundamental and long-lasting effect of NCLB, even though this bold document has the power to create far-reaching changes in the character of schooling in the United States along several dimensions. However, such a federal education law, while having a very strong reach through its capacity to withhold badly needed funds, must itself garner some measure of assent both from practitioners and "experts" in the field and from the general public. That is, the law must itself have social legitimacy, which cannot be taken for granted.

While NCLB may have the foreseeable consequence of delegitimating the public schools; it is possible that advocates for the public schools might delegitimize the law. It now seems probable, at the least, that the scenario of broad-based delegitimization of public schools that I have just sketched will be resisted and at least partially muted. In its early years, the law had momentum as the central piece of domestic legislation from a federal administration that was enjoying nearly unprecedented freedom from criticism after the events of September 11, 2001. As legislation that passed with a clear bipartisan majority and was presented as a vehicle for high hopes for disadvantaged students, NCLB seemed to have support across the board. The U.S. Department of Education firmly enforced all of the law's conditions for testing, for measuring AYP, and for sanctions of Title I schools that did not meet states' testing benchmarks (Erpenbach, Forte-Fast, and Potts 2003) for the first two years. NCLB looked like a juggernaut rolling toward broad delegitimation of public schools.

With time, however, the Department's unyielding stance, its occasionally inflammatory denunciation of states that asked for modifications, and of other groups that offered criticisms (DeBray 2006; Sunderman 2006), the difficulty of implementing the law in educationally constructive ways, and the opprobrium the law quickly brought to public schools across the 50 states fed considerable resistance among state officials, groups of educators, and even civic groups representing the disadvantaged (e.g., Children's Defense Fund 2004). As we move toward reauthorization in 2007, the story of this law has not yet been told.

By the beginning of 2006, all but 18 states had legislation either passed or pending that in some way limited the reach of the law (Loveless 2006). The state of Connecticut is suing the federal government, claiming that testing in seven grades required under the law is both unnecessary and an unfunded mandate because it costs more than the federal funds will cover, something forbidden by the language of the law itself (Archer 2005). The legislature in Utah has passed a law mandating that the state department of education not undertake activities expected by the federal law if they conflict with Utah law. The Maryland legislature has overruled its own administrative agency which had announced the takeover of several Baltimore schools that had been listed as "in need of improvement" long enough to trigger the sanction of state takeover under the terms of NCLB.[5] The legislature has required that the local district and the individual schools be given at least an additional year for reforms they have already put in place to take effect (Honawar 2006).

Such counterpressures have clearly been noted by both state officials responsible for education in other states and by the federal Department of Education. States have been seeking, and the Department has been selectively granting, adjustments to the requirements of NCLB (Center on Education Policy 2006; Sunderman 2006). Critics find the criteria for these adjustments neither transparent nor uniform, but negotiated dependent on the relationship of each state with the Department. They believe such variability undercuts the law's credibility as a federal requirement to raise educational achievement for all students (Sunderman 2006).

Critics also charge the Department not only with treating states differently, but also with making exceptions that have differential impact with social class. Many have argued from the beginning that the fundamental design of the law has a number of features that will make it much easier for schools serving disadvantaged children to receive negative labels than for those serving the privileged (Darling-Hammond 2004; Kane and Staiger 2003; Kim and Sunderman 2005; Linn 2003; Raudenbush 2004). Now, many say, the new flexibilities that the U.S. Department of Education is offering are making the burden of stigma—and the requirement better to assist struggling students—fall even more lightly on schools that serve mostly advantaged students (Antlfinger 2006; Children's Defense Fund 2006; Kim and Sunderman 2005; Sunderman 2006) while it continues to fall heavily on schools serving disadvantaged children. Civic organizations serving the interests of such children are beginning to form alliances (Children's Defense Fund 2006) to pressure for changes in the law. These vary from suggestions for fairly minor adjustments (Haycock 2005; McClure 2005) to changes that would significantly alter the form and effects of the legislation (Children's Defense Fund 2006; Sunderman 2006).

U.S. Department of Education officials have responded to the growing activist criticism and state rebellion with a patchwork of compromises with individual states, and sometimes districts, that lower rates of schools identified for improvement in those particular localities, but they have not backed away from the fundamental principles of the law or admitted fault with any of the fundamentals that critics have most often found unrealistic (Sunderman 2006).

They seem to be hoping to weather the current storm and to gather increasing public support for the law by emphasizing its symbolically resonant mission to support higher educational goals for all students, equality of opportunity through the universal application and testing of statewide educational standards, and large scale testing to ensure that schools are accountable for results. Administration officials are likely to be helped in retaining many elements of the law through the 2007 reauthorization by a growing list of private companies and corporations that have experienced explosive growth as they provide "supplemental educational services" to students and a great variety of services to districts, such as test construction, scoring and analysis of tests, record keeping, and alignment of tests with curriculum (Burch 2006; Burch et al. 2006). These mostly for-profit private providers can expect an increasing flow of federal dollars as more and more schools and districts move from being identified as "in need of improvement" to warranting reorganization with the aid of outside entities (Burch 2006; Burch, Donovan, and Steinberg 2006). They will be further helped by some civic groups, such as the Education Trust (Haycock 2005) that believe that the principles of the law are sound and that full funding and some minor adjustments could help it to create genuinely better educational opportunities for disadvantaged students. The outcome that will emerge from the interaction of such contending forces is not yet clear.

CONCLUSION

I have argued that NCLB, at least as it is being enforced by the U.S. Department of Education, does not have the funding, the commitment, or the educational understanding and practical levers needed to be, as it claims to be, a serious federal attempt to improve the education of all children, and particularly disadvantaged children. Instead, one can reasonably see it as a gesture of allegiance to equality of opportunity. It can be understood as the latest symbolic attempt to resolve long-standing contradictions between American ideological attachment to equality of opportunity and American social, political, and educational structures that militate strongly against such equality. American society is not likely to change as a result of the gesture. We have been living with this paradox for a long time.

In another interpretation, close study of the details of NCLB reveals it to be a radical instrument, capable of creating fundamental change in American education by thoroughly discrediting public schooling. Its design, considered in relationship to what scholars and practitioners know about education, is an engine to generate data to document failure of public schools across the board and especially those that serve disadvantaged students. Private schools, whose performance is not being measured in parallel ways, will appear by default to be a preferable alternative that deserves public funding.

This second interpretation of the act is becoming increasingly visible to critics (e.g., Meier and Wood 2004.) Resistance to the law is growing in disparate quarters, including the legislatures of many states and in the work of visible nonprofit groups who advocate for the poor. At this writing, it is still too early to tell how the contending forces at work in support and opposition to various parts of the law, or to the law overall, will shape its future.

Notes

1. I have received considerable assistance in researching and writing this paper from Jennifer L. Jensen. I thank her for her insight, diligence in researching details of the law, and generous spirit.
2. See Karen, chapter 1 this volume, for a delineation of enforcement mechanisms.
3. After arriving inductively at this insight, I recognized its roots in earlier work on education (Herndon 1969; Meyer and Rowan 1978; Tyack 1974) as well as in my own earlier work (Metz 1986). My description of the common patterns of schooling and their lack of fit to the circumstances in which many students and schools found themselves—along with the ways in which the common script hid the inequality of schooling in the U.S. from public view in many social and rhetorical contexts—was expressed in my coining of the term "Real School." (Metz 1990b). I was surprised at how widely the term was taken up and used by others researchers who wrote on similar themes after me (e.g Fink 2000: Tye 2000; Tyack and Tobin 1994; Tyack and Cuban 1995).
4. Many of the architects and proponents of the law wanted it to include vouchers for private schooling. They were overruled in the interest of garnering bipartisan support for the law (DeBray 2006). In that light, the exemption of private schools that take federal money from testing, and the lack of data for systematic comparison of public and private schools is doubt-

less not an oversight.
5. When NCLB was passed, some Title I schools were already in "need for improvement" status, based on the 1994 ESEA provisions.

References

Antlfinger, C. 2006. All tested, but not all counted: No Child Left Behind allows about 2 million exemptions. *Wisconsin State Journal,* April 18:A1, A9.

Anyon, J. 1981. Social class and school knowledge. *Curriculum Inquiry* 2:3–42.

Archer, J. 2005. Connecticut files court challenge to NCLB. *Education Week,* August 31:23, 27.

Bowles, S. and H. Gintis. 1976. *Schooling in capitalist America.* New York: Basic Books.

Brantlinger, E. 2003. *Dividing classes: How the middle class negotiates and rationalizes school advantage.* New York: Routledge Falmer.

Burch, P. 2006. The new educational privatization: Educational contracting and high stakes accountability. *Teachers' College Record* 108 (12): 2611-2624

———. J. Donovan, and M. Steinberg. 2006. Markets, supplemental services, and No Child Left Behind. *Phi Delta Kappan* 129-136.

Center on Education Policy. 2006. *From the capitol to the classroom: Year 4 of the No Child Left Behind Act.* Washington, D.C.: Center on Education Policy.

Children's Defense Fund. 2004. *Joint organizational statement on no child left behind (NCLB) Act,* October 21. 2006. http://www.childrensdefense.org/education/NCLB_joint_statement.pdf (Accessed June 14, 2006)

———. 2006. *The state of America's children 2005.* Washington, D.C.: Children's Defense Fund.

Connell, R. W., D. J. Ashenden, S. Kessler, and G. W. Dowsett. 1982. *Making the difference: Schools, families, and social division.* Sydney: George Allen and Unwin.

Cuban, L. 1993. *How teachers taught: Constancy and change in American classrooms, 1890–1990.* 2nd ed. New York: Teachers College Press.

Darling-Hammond, L. 2004. From "Separate but Equal" to "No Child Left Behind": The collision of new standards and old inequalities. In *Many children left behind: How the No Child Left Behind Act is damaging our children and our schools,* ed. D. Meier and G. Wood, 3-32. Boston: Beacon Press.

DeBray, E. 2006. *Politics, ideology and education: Federal policy during the Clinton and Bush administrations.* New York: Teachers College Press.

DiMaggio, P. J., and Powell, W. W. eds. 1991. *The new institutionalism in organizational analysis.* Chicago: University of Chicago Press.

Education Trust. 2003. *In need of improvement: Ten ways the U.S. Department of Education has failed to live up to its teacher quality commitments.* http://www.edtrust.org (accessed February 2, 2005).

Erpenbach, W. J., E. Forte-Fast, and A. Potts. 2003. *Statewide educational accountability under NCLB.* Washington, D.C.: Council of Chief State School Officers.

Farkas, G. and Durham, R. 2006. The role of tutoring in standards-based reform. Paper presented at the conference, Will Standards-Based Reform in Education Help Close the Poverty Gap? Institute for Research on Poverty and Wisconsin Center for Education Research: University of Wisconsin-Madison.

Fink, D. 2000. *Good schools/real schools: why school reform doesn't last.* New York: Teachers College Press.

Firestone, W. A., M. E. Goertz, and G. Natriello.1997. *From cashbox to classroom: the struggle for fiscal reform and educational change in New Jersey.* New York: Teachers College Press.

Goertz, M. E. 2005. Implementing the No Child Left Behind Act: Challenges for the states. *Peabody Journal of Education* 80 (2):73–89.

Haycock, K. 2005. Closing the achievement gap in America's public schools: The No Child Left Behind Act http://www2.edtrust.org/EdTrust/Press+Room/Haycock+Testimony+9.29.05.htm (accessed May 14, 2006).

Hemmings, A. and M. H. Metz .1990.. "Real teaching": How high school teachers negotiate societal, local community, and student pressures when they define their work. In *Curriculum Differentiation,* ed. R. Page and L. Valli, 91-122 Albany, NY: SUNY Press.

Herndon, J. 1969. *The way it spozed to be.* New York: Bantam Books.

Honawar, V. 2006. Baltimore takeovers prevented: MD lawmakers' victory a model for NCLB foes? *Education Week* April 19:1, 25.

Hurn, C. J. 1993. *The limits and possibilities of schooling: an introduction to the sociology of education.* 3rd ed. Boston: Allyn and Bacon.

Ingersoll, R. 2003. *Who controls teachers' work? Power and accountability in America's schools.* Cambridge, MA: Harvard University Press.

Kane, T.J. and D. O. Staiger. 2002. Volatility in school test scores: Implications for test-based accountability systems. In *Brookings Papers on Educational Policy 2002*, ed. D. Ravitch, 235–84. Washington, D.C.: Brookings Institution.

———. 2003. Unintended consequences of racial subgroup rules. In *No Child Left Behind? The politics and practice of school accountability*, ed. P. Peterson and M.West, 152–76. Washington, D.C.: Brookings Institution.

Kim, J. S. and G. L. Sunderman. 2005. Measuring academic proficiency under the No Child Left Behind Act: Implications for educational equity. *Educational Researcher* 34 (8):3–13.

Kliebard, H. M. 1995. *The struggle for the American curriculum, 1853-1958.* 2nd ed. New York: Routledge.

Lareau, A. 2003. *Unequal childhoods: Class, race, and family life.* Berkeley: University of California Press.

Lewis, A. E. 2003. *Race in the schoolyard: Negotiating the color line in classrooms and communities.* New Brunswick, NJ: Rutgers University Press.

Linn, R. L. 2003. Accountability: Responsibility and reasonable expectations. *Educational Researcher* 32 (7):3–13.

Loveless, T. 2006. The peculiar politics of no child left behind. Paper presented at the "Will Standards-Based Reform in Education Help Close the Poverty Gap?" conference, University of Wisconsin, Madison WI.

McClure, P. 2005. *School improvement under no child left behind.* Washington, D.C.: The Center for American Progress.

Meier, D. and Wood, G. ed. 2004. *Many children left behind: How the No Child Left Behind Act is damaging our children and our schools.* Boston: Beacon Press.

Metz, M. H. 1986. *Different by design: The context and character of three magnet schools.* New York: Routledge.

———. 1990a. How social class differences shape teachers' work. In *The contexts of teaching in secondary schools: Teachers' realities*, ed. M. W. McLaughlin, J. E. Talbert, and N. Bascia, 40–107. New York: Teachers College Press.

———. 1990b. Real school: A universal drama amid disparate experience. In *Education politics for the new century: The twentieth anniversary yearbook of the politics of education association*, ed. D. E. Mitchell and M. E. Goertz, 75–91. Philadelphia: The Falmer Press.

———. 1993. Teachers' ultimate dependence on their students. In *Teachers' work: Individuals, colleagues and contexts*, ed. J. W. Little and M. W. McLaughlin, 269–309. New York: Teachers College Press.

——— 1998. Veiled inequalities: The hidden effects of community social class on high school teachers' perspectives and practices. Paper presented at the Annual Meetings of the American Educational Research Association, San Diego, CA.

Meyer, J. W. and B. Rowan. 1977. Institutionalized organizations: Formal structure as myth and ceremony. *American Journal of Sociology* 83:340–63.

———.1978. The structure of educational organizations. In *Environments and organizations*, ed. M. W. Meyer, 78–109. San Francisco: Jossey-Bass.

Mirel, J. 1994. School reform unplugged: The Bensenville New American School Project, 1991–93. *American Educational Research Journal* 31(3):481–518.

Myrdal, G. 1944. *An American dilemma: The Negro problem and modern democracy.* New York: Harper and Bros.

Parsons, T. 1959. The school class as a social system: Some of its functions in American society. *Harvard Educational Review* 29 (Fall):297–318.

Popham, W. J. 2004. *America's failing schools: How parents and teachers can cope with No Child Left Behind..* New York: RoutledgeFalmer.

Raudenbush, S. L. 2004. *Schooling, statistics, and poverty: Can we measure school improvement?* Princeton, NJ: Educational Testing Service.

Reese, W. J. 2005. *America's public schools: From the common school to No Child Left Behind*. Baltimore: Johns Hopkins University Press.

Scott, W. R. 2002. *Institutions and organizations*. 2nd ed. Thousand Oaks, CA: Sage.

Spillane, J. P. 2004. *Standards deviation: How schools misunderstand education policy*. Cambridge, MA: Harvard University Press.

Sunderman, G. L. 2006. *The unraveling of No Child Left Behind: How negotiated changes transform the law*. Cambridge, MA: The Civil Rights Project at Harvard University.

Tyack, D. 1974. *The one best system: A history of American education*. Cambridge, MA: Harvard University Press.

——— and L. Cuban, 1995. *Tinkering toward utopia: A century of public school reform*. Cambridge, MA: Harvard University Press.

Tyack, D. and W. Tobin. 1994. The "grammar" of schooling: Why has it been so hard to change? *American Educational Research Journal* 31(3):454–79.

Tye, B. B. 2000. *Hard truths: Uncovering the deep structure of schooling*. New York: Teachers College Press.

U.S. Department of Education, Office of Policy Planning and Innovation. 2003. *Meeting the highly qualified teachers' challenge: The Secretary's second annual report on teacher quality*. Washington, D.C.: U.S. Department of Education.

Wells, A. S. and R. L.Crain. 1997. *Stepping over the color line: African-American students in white suburban schools*. New Haven, CT: Yale University Press.

Wells, A. S. and Serna, I. 1996. The politics of culture: Understanding local political resistance to de-tracking in racially mixed schools. *Harvard Educational Review* 66 (1):93–118.

18
Conclusion
Sociological Perspectives on NCLB and Federal Involvement in Education[1]

Alan R. Sadovnik, A. Gary Dworkin, Adam Gamoran, Maureen Hallinan, and Janelle Scott

FEDERAL AND STATE EDUCATIONAL POLICY AND NCLB

A decade ago, in an analysis of Goals 2000, the sociologists contributing to *Implementing Educational Reform: Sociological Perspectives on Educational Policy* (Borman, Cookson, Sadovnik and Spade, 1996) argued that there were limits and possibilities to school-based educational reforms aimed at reducing educational inequalities based on social class, race, ethnicity, and gender. Ten years later, the sociologists contributing to this book make the same cautionary claim. Unfortunately, politicians in Washington and policymakers continue to ignore the powerful sociological dictum that schools do not operate in a vacuum and are affected by larger social, political, and economic forces.

The purpose of this book is not to add to the often rhetorical and ideological critiques of No Child Left Behind (NCLB), nor to uncritically defend the law. There has been enough of this from both sides of the political and ideological spectrum. Rather, it is to draw upon the theoretical insights and empirical findings in the sociology of education to examine the law's potential and problems and to contribute to the ongoing policy debates about reauthorization.

The chapters in this book have provided important evidence on NCLB in particular and federal involvement in education, in general. Although we support fully the law's laudable goal of eliminating the achievement gaps among different groups, these chapters provide essential cautions about the likelihood of this happening as well as pointing out significant problems with the implementation of the law. Based on the work of sociologists of education, there are a number of important conclusions:

1. A sociological analysis provides an important corrective to current policy discussions by insisting that school level policies and reforms required by NCLB must be understood in their larger societal context and in relation to external social, economic, and political factors.

2. This type of sociological analysis does not, as the Education Trust often argues, provide an excuse for failing to reduce the achievement gap (Education Trust 2005). Rather, it acknowledges 40 years of sociological research on the causes of the achievement gap demonstrating that educational inequalities are a result of both school-based and nonschool factors.

3. To ignore societal factors in policies aimed at reducing the achievement gap will inevitably limit the effectiveness of educational policies aimed primarily at the school level, as NCLB is, to adequately reduce the achievement gap.

4. Having said this, sociological research provides important evidence that school-based policies can improve schools and help reduce the achievement gap in all of the areas covered by the law under which NCLB operates. In addition, the sociological discipline provides research-based evidence for improving the implementation of NCLB and correcting some of the unintended consequences of the law.

5. Sociologists of education should continue to engage in research aimed at analyzing the various components of NCLB and that research should be used in the larger policy debates about NCLB, especially with respect to its reauthorization.

The remainder of this chapter examines the reasons for these conclusions, based both on the chapters in this book, as well as on years of sociological research.

ACCOUNTABILITY AND ASSESSMENT

From the Coleman Report (1966) to recent research by Jean Anyon (2005a, 2005b) and David Armor (chapter 16 this volume), sociologists and others (e.g., Berliner 2006; Rothstein 2004; see also Riordan, 2003; Sadovnik, Cookson and Semel, 2006), have pointed to the limited effects of schools in reducing inequality. As all these researchers point out, to ignore factors external to schools is to deny reality. Berliner calls poverty "the 600-pound gorilla" on the back of school reform. Rothstein documents the powerful effects of poverty on the learning of poor children and the positive effects that could be garnered by improvements in health care, including dental and eye care, housing and environmental reforms, including increases in affordable housing and removal of lead paint from apartments in cities. Anyon analyzes the deleterious effects of federal and state housing and wage policies, as well as the negative effects of the free market on the poor. Armor reminds us that cognitive inequality among children is evident even before they begin school, and that it is tied to family risk factors such as income, cognitive stimulation, and health. To ignore what Berliner and Biddle (1996) concluded 10 years ago—that when U.S. achievement scores are disaggregated by socioeconomic factors the major crisis in achievement is a crisis for low-income children, children of color, and children whose first language is not English, not of all children—is to ignore these data. Although NCLB recognizes these achievement gaps as the central policy problem, NCLB in large measure ignores the important conclusions of sociologists of education that to reduce these gaps requires reducing poverty, as well as improving the schools that poor children attend. Neither is sufficient on its own, but both are necessary if all students are to meet the high performance demands of modern society. Importantly, the federal government is in a unique role to help on both fronts through policies on reducing poverty as well as education reform.

In light of the importance of family conditions to children's school success, enhancing parent involvement in schooling is an important policy issue. Yet as Epstein and Sheldon (chapters 13 and 14 this volume) argue, NCLB provisions on connecting school districts, schools, and families must be more effectively implemented. Other sociologists of education, especially Annette Lareau (1989, 2002, 2003) have provided compelling evidence that social class differences in the relationship between families and schools must be understood in order to develop meaningful policies.

Since the work of Ronald Edmonds (1979, 1982) on effective schools for low-income children, effective school researchers have analyzed the characteristics of such schools in hopes of replicating them. In addition, research on the effects of comprehensive school reform, urban systemic reform, and other school based policies have demonstrated that schools and teachers do make a difference in the lives of poor children and children of color (G. Borman et al. 2003; K. M. Borman et al. 2004; Darling-Hammond 1996a, 1996b, 1997; O'Day 2002). NCLB's curriculum and teaching components are based on the belief that successful programs can be replicated and that there are no excuses for failing to do so (Thernstrom and Thernstrom 2003). However, as Brint and Teele (chapter 7, this volume), Talbert and McLaughlin (chapter 9, this volume), and Ingersoll (chapter 8, this volume) point out, there are significant problems with current policy and the need to learn from the lessons of sociological research to replicate successes. For example, putting a qualified teacher in every classroom takes more than the law provides; it takes fundamental changes in school climate and culture in order to ensure that qualified teachers stay, especially in schools with low-income children. Helping teachers effectively teach low-income children will require sustained professional development and the development of profession communities of teachers within schools as argued by Talbert and McLaughlin (chapter 9, this volume).

The most controversial aspect of NCLB has been its testing and accountability requirements. Researchers have pointed out how these requirements negatively affect schools with large concentrations of low-income children and children of color and how overreliance on standardized tests often results in the narrowing of curriculum and teaching to the test (Firestone, Schorr, and Monfils 2004; Kim and Sunderman 2005). Swanson (chapter 3, this volume), Booher-Jennings and Beveridge (chapter 4, this volume), Weitz White and Rosenbaum (chapter 5, this volume), and Dworkin and Lorence (chapter 12, this volume), make valuable contributions to understanding the problems with current implementation and the need for changes in the reauthorization. Among these, including growth and value-added models and expanding the types of assessments included should be examined for reauthorization. Educational historian Diane Ravitch (2000), who has called for a federal, rather than state assessment and accountability regime, points to the problems with "state rights" based accountability systems, including the large differences in curriculum and testing systems that make national comparisons impossible, except through NAEP (which is not used for NCLB accountability). Although there may be sound reasons for such a national system, similar to the ones used in most other countries, they are not without problems—see Walford (1999) for a discussion of the United Kingdom. In addition, given the historical commitment to local control of public schools in the United States, the lack of a federal constitutional provision, and the likely large scale political opposition to a national curriculum and testing system, it is unlikely that this could be enacted in the reauthorization.

The school choice component of NCLB is likely to emerge as a controversial aspect of the reauthorization. It is well established that President Bush wanted a voucher component similar to the Florida voucher system in the 2001 law, one where low-income children in schools in need of improvement would have the option of transferring to private schools by means of federal tuition vouchers. Although the Democrats, with the assistance of the National Education Association (NEA) and the American Federation of Teachers (AFT) blocked this provision, the emergence of the District of Columbia voucher policy and the recent U.S. Department of Education proposal to Congress for a national voucher program, suggest that the Bush administration may try to include a private school voucher option as part of its reauthorization proposal. Lauen (chapter 10, this volume) and Useem (chapter 15, this volume) provide important evidence for this upcoming debate. Although many critics of NCLB have argued that the law's real intent has been the destruction of public education and the privatization of schooling (e.g., Metz, chapter 17, this volume), this book suggests that although some supporters of the law may have this intent, others such as the Education Trust are strong supporters of public schools. The evidence on the effects of existing voucher programs in Milwaukee, Cleveland, and Florida (Van Dunk and Dickman 2003; Witte 2000) and recent research on the differences between public, private, and charter schools (Lubienski and Lubienski 2006) suggests that private school vouchers are not magic bullets for low-income students. However, given the lack of student level longitudinal data on achievement differences among public, charter, and private schools, better research is needed before a private school voucher policy is considered. Rather, given the research evidence in this volume and elsewhere on effective practices for low-income students and students of color, it makes sense to find ways in the reauthorization to ensure such practices are replicated in public schools, including charter schools, and that federal funds are available for research and implementation of best practices.

With respect to interdistrict public school choice programs, Lauen points out that such programs have not been adequately utilized to provide transfer options for children in schools in need of improvement. Given the lack of capacity within low-income rural and urban districts, interdistrict choice options might be strengthened, perhaps through innovative funding and assessment mechanisms to make it attractive for districts to accept low-income students from neighboring districts without being punished by AYP requirements. That is, districts that accept low-income students from neighboring districts must be given adequate time to help them improve without these students threatening their own AYP status. However, given the unintended consequences of the Michigan interdistrict choice program (Arsen, Plank, and Sykes 1999), we need better evidence on the type of programs that will work. It would make sense to encourage states to implement trial programs with a strong evaluation component built in to assess success.

The chapters in this book provide an important tool for policymakers as they think about the reauthorization of NCLB. The Forum on Educational Accountability, a group of 80 national education and civic associations, issued a joint statement on changes needed in the act to make it fair and effective (2006, 1). They state:

> ...Among these concerns are: over-emphasizing standardized testing, narrowing curriculum and instruction to focus on test preparation rather than richer academic learning; over-identifying schools in need of improvement; using sanctions that do not help improve schools; inappropriately excluding low-scoring children to boost test results; and inadequate funding.

The statement goes on to support a number of changes in the areas of progress measurement, assessments, building capacity, sanctions, and funding that they argue would make the law fairer and more realistic to implement. Included in their list are more realistic proficiency targets, the use of growth and value-added models, the use of more comprehensive assessment systems that do not rely exclusively on standardized tests, the building of local capacity to improve schools, the development of more realistic time lines before sanctions are used, the need to fund a significant portion of state and districts costs of implementation, and the need to fully fund Title I to ensure that all poor children are served (2006, 2–3). Many of the authors in this book have recommended similar changes. In addition, based on the research of O'Day (chapter 2, this volume), Ingersoll (chapter 8, this volume), and Talbert and McLaughlin (chapter 9, this volume), the government should provide incentives for the further development of teaching as a profession.

More specifically, the authors raise a number of questions about current NCLB policies and make specific recommendations for reauthorization.

Accountability and Assessment

- Testing of students should be only part of the assessment process, given that the more indicators, including portfolios, that schools have about a student's performance the greater the likelihood that a true estimate of the student's knowledge will be assessed.
- The development of fair, reliable, and valid tests takes considerable time. Under pressure from NCLB many states that have not previously relied on a standardized test have been forced either to adopt an off-the-shelf, norm-referenced test or quickly to construct a criterion-referenced one.
- Establish more realistic standards for campus standardized test passage rates that account for the array of disabilities students may bring to school. Recognize that 100 percent passage rates, even with consideration of 95 percent testing rates may be unreasonable for some school populations and that the goal may not be attainable in the short period allowed under the law.
- Since the United States is a mobile society in which citizens can become actors in communities other than the ones in which they were born and educated as children, it is reasonable to develop a national curriculum and appropriate tests of that curriculum. Of course, the curricula can be augmented by local issues, but the goal will be to have a common core of knowledge shared by all students.
- Reliance on value-added models to assess schools that consider school, student, and neighborhood effects on student achievement so that children with disparate achievement levels can be compared and schools with greater numbers of disadvantaged students will be assessed more equitably.
- NCLB is too quick to punish low-performing schools by taking away some

of their Title I funding, notifying parents that they have the opportunity to transfer their children to another school, and by threats of closure. Struggling schools should receive more resources to improve student achievement.

- Support schools and school districts in the collection and maintenance of accurate student records so that graduation, completion, and dropout data have a more reasonable chance of being accurate. Reward schools for verifiably improved "stay-in-school" programs, rather than punishing schools for their dropout rates.

- Some states encourage their schools to use the results from individual test item objectives to locate student weakness and improve curricula to mitigate those weaknesses. This practice should be done more widely, but not to the exclusion of nontested curricula.

- Provide in-service training of school administrators and teachers to help them to understand that teaching a broad curriculum actually expands the student's knowledge base and improves test performance. Encourage scholars from many disciplines to aid in the development of curricula in science, social studies, art, music, even physical education that can benefit a student's breadth of perspective and facilitate overall achievement.

- Reward schools that engage in inclusive practices in which all children are provided with enrichment and educational services. Do not engage in educational triage activities that deny challenging curricula to students who are likely to pass the test and diminish the educational opportunities for course selections by students whose test performance is most problematic.

- Focus on developing an accountability system that relies on the professional development of school staff and encourages their input and buy-in, rather than one that only imposes rules externally.

TEACHING AND TEACHER QUALITY

Brint and Teele's analysis of teachers' attitudes toward NCLB and the behavioral changes they need to make to comply with the legislation reveals widespread dissatisfaction with several aspects of the law (chapter 7 this volume). Many teachers are concerned about pressure to teach to the test and about scripted teaching. They believe that these pedagogical strategies restrict the breadth of curricular instruction and limit teachers' educational goals. They also dislike the fact that the additional time they must devote to core subjects assessed by NCLB limits instruction in other subject areas. A majority of teachers are not convinced that NCLB teacher requirements improve the quality of instruction to any great extent.

Taking these concerns seriously should lead to a number of changes in NCLB. First, the legislation should broaden the assessment tools used to measure student progress. Scores on standardized tests provide only a narrow window into student learning. Academic progress is measured more accurately by longitudinal data showing change in students' test scores over time and by tests that place more emphasis on higher order thinking skills as opposed to rote learning. A stronger emphasis on professional development would promote the enhancement of teacher quality by complimenting academic credentials with teaching skills.

A recent comprehensive national study of NCLB conducted by the Center for Education Policy (2006) reveals that 88 percent of the districts studied expect to meet the highly qualified teacher regulation by the end of 2006. One reason for this seemingly positive finding is that many states have made it easy for teachers to achieve highly qualified status. The NCLB HOUSSE option gives the states authority to set standards for certification. Many states have set low standards for passing certification examinations and for ways to gain credit for professional development. A reauthorized NCLB should eliminate the HOUSSE option, require states to set high standards for passing competency tests, and define more rigorously what professional activities count as professional development.

At the same time, NCLB needs to better address the problem of out-of-field teaching. Simply raising requirements to make the designation of highly qualified teachers more meaningful is not sufficient. As Ingersoll points out (chapter 8 this volume), one way of addressing the problem is by providing training programs that would show principals how they can reduce out-of-field training through organizational and administrative decisions. In addition, NCLB should set up mechanisms to recruit teachers to teach in underserved areas, such as math and science, as well as special education. Entry incentives, salary bonuses, and fast-track routes to advancement provide attractive benefits and enticements for teachers to remain in teaching.

In the present culture of NCLB, primary emphasis is placed on academic credentials and less attention is paid to teacher professional development. Yet, Title II of NCLB makes approximately $3 billion available to improve student performance by raising teacher quality. Devoting these resources to the professional development of teachers should play a significant role in raising teacher quality and improving student achievement.

Borko (2004) claims in her AERA presidential address that the professional development of teachers is seriously inadequate. Talbert and McLaughlin (chapter 9 this volume) join her in forcefully arguing for better professional training for teachers. They recommend teacher learning communities as an effective and powerful method of helping teachers work together to promote student learning. Yet, it is unclear whether NCLB would fund schools to establish teacher learning communities or other recognized models of professional development. At present, NCLB regulations indicate that states may receive funds for developing and utilizing proven, innovative strategies to deliver intensive professional development programs. A reauthorized NCLB should make clear the kinds of professional development programs that are eligible for funding and whether programs like teacher learning communities qualify for support.

Moreover, considerable flexibility and scope are needed in endorsing professional development programs. Since teaching is situationally determined, some programs are better suited for one school setting than for another. NCLB should support strong, conceptually grounded professional development programs that are backed by rigorous research and that promise significant improvements in student learning.

In reauthorizing NCLB, lawmakers need to address the weaknesses and limitations in the present legislation. The first step in making NCLB more effective is to provide a strong conceptual framework to support its requirements. If the law were firmly grounded in social science theory and empirical research, its priorities would likely shift in a direction that is more consistent with teachers' insights and instructional experience. If lawmakers were to take into account the influence of the demographic characteristics of students, teachers, and schools on student achievement, the reauthorized legislation would be more equitable. If the unrealistic goals of the present law requiring full compliance in a short space of time were replaced by more reasonable ones, teachers would find compliance less stressful and alienating. A reauthorized NCLB that takes into account what has been learned since the inception of the law in 2001 would improve teacher attitudes toward the legislation, increase their willingness to comply, and ultimately lead to significant improvement in student achievement.

SCHOOL CHOICE AND PARENTAL INVOLVEMENT

The authors imply a number of issues for the future implementation of the NCLB school choice and parental involvement provisions. First, they demonstrate the need for more mixed-method study where quantitative and qualitative methods can complement one another to paint a more complete picture. Mixed-method approaches would be especially helpful in ascertaining the number of school districts that have implemented parental involvement programs while also examining the nature and quality of the programs developed. This is an area in which the choice and involvement provisions intersect, and where more information is needed regarding the quality of information district leaders provide to parents about their school transfer options. Such study could also inform our understanding of how districts and schools not already inclined to parental involvement develop will and capacity. In the area of school achievement and school choice, mixed-method study could also pinpoint the bureaucratic, curricular, organizational, and institutional forms that help to support schools that are higher achieving. The findings from such research could help to inform policy debates about the role of suburban schools and the ways in which their boundaries facilitate the spatial isolation of many urban schools and districts. A question to be debated is whether these school systems might be opened up to urban students instead of or in addition to privatized solutions such as vouchers or private management of public schools.

This leads to a second issue: the nature and quality of options available for parents. In 2006, the options were intradistrict public choice, supplemental educational services, charter schools, limited private school vouchers, and private management of public schools. Judging the success of these from an achievement metric alone, none of these have proved to be clear successes, and all the data on them are contested. While more research is needed, and while performance on standardized achievement tests is just one measure of student learning and school quality, under NCLB and state standards-based accountability reforms, a finding that cuts across nearly all the research is that market based choice reforms (vouchers, charters, privately managed schools), as a whole have failed to outperform public schools. In those cases where some choice forms do better than some public schools, more research is needed about what makes these schools remarkable—what resources, curriculum, and student populations are behind the schoolhouse doors? While just 2 percent of eligible students availed themselves of transfers under NCLB, 20 percent of those eligible utilized supplemental educational service tutors (Center on Education Policy 2006). More information about the quality of these providers as well as the effects they are having on student achievement is in order. Research that helps parents, school leaders, and teachers understand these issues can help facilitate meaningful choice, parental involvement, and a reduction of achievement gaps through better schooling for more students. The chapters in this section call for close attention to the conflicting reports of achievement data between private, charter, and traditional public schools, and suggest that a reliance on more radical choice and privatization measures beyond the current public school transfer options are premature solutions that should be delayed until there is more evidence to support their adoption.

Next, research on choice and family involvement can benefit from multiple paradigms. The authors provide original empirical study framed by sociological analysis. Such analysis helps to shift the dominant paradigm for examining choice policies. Especially since the mid-1980s, economists of education have largely defined and framed the parameters of school choice policy, research, and evaluation. The policy debates, research methods, analysis, and implementation recommendations have tended to emphasize rational choice models and randomized studies to determine whether school choice results in greater educational efficiency. Sociologists of education in comparison have tended to focus on issues of stratification and equity within and across institutions under existing and theoretical school choice programs. Also of interest are the ways in which school choice programs interact with varying levels of social privilege amongst parents who choose alternative educational settings and parents who stay in traditional public schools. The point is not to disparage one approach, but rather to encourage the ways in which multiple disciplinary frames can produce a more complete picture and help us understand the choice process and choice outcomes more holistically.

Finally, the chapters suggest that NCLB policy needs to attend better to local context. Preexisting institutional, racial, social, political, economic conditions can lead to success or struggle. Districts with experience and support for developing family partnerships are implementing the family involvement requirements under NCLB. Yet data about the lack of transfers for eligible students indicate, in part, that parents are not as informed as they could or should be about their options. Districts need help meeting the school transfer requirements of NCLB; especially those serving racially isolated schools and students where the majority of schools are in need of AYP in any given year. Many are already financially strained, and do not have the organizational capacity to implement the choice provisions. NCLB holds that lack of space is not an excuse for implementing the transfer provisions, and that Local Education Authorities (LEAs) should establish partnerships with receiving ones or set up trailers on the facilities of higher performing schools. This places the onus on local districts, rather than state governments to equalize capacity across districts. It seems clear that for many overburdened districts, mandates will not simply make them know how to do better for their students. This is not to excuse LEAs that have willfully neglected their most needy schools and students, but rather to encourage a policy approach that will support local officials to provide better opportunities to their students.

The NCLB mandates for school districts and LEAs to develop school choice and the family involvement programs are likely here to stay. In order for the choice and family involvement NCLB provisions to meet the needs of parents and students who have been the least well served by public institutions, the legislation could be strengthened to provide more support to districts and schools to implement them. Though they engage slightly different aspects of choice and family involvement, the chapters in this section point to important indicators of successful implementation of the provisions. These include: existing expertise and capacity, local context, and historical precedent. Ultimately, each chapter calls for more and better data to gauge the implementation with more accuracy, a critical examination of local context, a renewed public debate about what the nation wants its public schools to look like, and the role of the state realizing the public will.

REDUCTION OF ACHIEVEMENT GAPS

We began this book with the overall question as to whether NCLB will significantly reduce, if not eliminate, the achievement gap by 2013–14. Based on the chapters, we conclude that it *is* possible to raise achievement and reduce gaps, and that standards-based reform can be part of the solution, but only if more time is allowed for new programs to take effect. One response to the timing problem would be to simply slow down the rate of increase at which schools are required to bring increasing numbers of students to proficiency; in other words, to push the time frame beyond 2014. However, this approach would not avoid the problem that a school that contributes to student learning may nonetheless be judged ineffective because of a low starting point, whereas a school that contributes little may be judged effective because of a high starting point. A better approach, as noted by Armor (chapter 16, this volume), is to bring schools' "value added" into the accountability system; that is, to consider the extent to which schools contribute to growth in achievement for an individual student from one year to the next.

The value-added approach, however, has its own limitations. In particular, crediting schools with high value added when absolute achievement is low risks never reaching proficiency for the most disadvantaged students. Consequently, a more realistic NCLB would take into account both value added and absolute levels of achievement. The Milwaukee Public Schools has recently embarked on a reporting system that has these features (Borsuk 2006). In Milwaukee's approach, schools are sorted into four quadrants: those with high achievement and high value added, those that are low on both measures, and those that are high on one and low on the other. Adopting this system on a statewide basis would allow states to target sanctions against schools that are low on *both* measures, rather than those that are low only on absolute measures. Schools that are high on value added but low on absolute levels of achievement would be encouraged rather than stigmatized, and might be eligible for special resources, such as incentives to maintain a stable teaching force. By noting their low average scores, however, an approach that combines value added and absolute targets makes it clear that closing the proficiency gap is the ultimate goal.

A value-added approach would also respond to Metz's concern that NCLB is a weapon used to attack public schools, because it would allow the public to see that public schools *can* be effective, even those with highly disadvantaged populations. Instead of disparaging all schools with low-test scores, it would hold up for sanction only those schools that have both low scores *and* fail to contribute to student learning, relative to their starting points. Moreover, it would target resources more effectively than the current system. In particular, students would not be encouraged to transfer out of schools where test scores are low unless their schools also fail to raise achievement as much as other schools might.

Are the operators of NCLB conspiring to undermine public education? We have no doubt that some of its framers had exactly this goal in mind. Their aim would have been to establish a voucher system, as the followers of Milton Friedman (2002) have long advocated, so that all schools would compete with one another for students in a fully privatized system. But we are equally convinced that NCLB had strong supporters among its architects who intended nothing of the sort. Indeed, many advocates of NCLB are firmly aligned with preserving public education; that was the basis for the extraordinary bipartisan coalition that made it possible to pass the NCLB law. Our sense is that public education interests in this country are strong enough that NCLB will collapse long before public education does.

Our expectation, however, is that neither public education nor NCLB-like requirements will meet their demise any time soon. On the contrary, we suspect that NCLB's emphasis on accountability through testing is here to stay. As currently written, long-term success in its stated mission is impossible, even if the latent aims of some of its advocates may not come to pass to the degree that Metz has warned. Yet if NCLB is respecified so that it focuses on growth as well as on absolute targets, it may be possible to raise achievement and reduce gaps in the long run.

A few years ago, Gamoran (2001) predicted that the black–white gaps in achievement and attainment would be nearly gone by the end of the 21st century. It is too soon to judge whether progress toward this goal is occurring, but new evidence is available that is worth considering. On the one hand, after a decade of regressing or, at best, no change, national achievement testing suggests that the gap may be slowly narrowing once again (Olson 2005). On the other hand, recent research has undercut the claim that a virtuous cycle of intergenerational transmission of gains will inevitably reduce the gaps (Long, Kelly, and Gamoran 2006). Although black–white gaps narrowed substantially in many areas, analysis of attainment trends across the 20th century suggests that the gains did not reflect improvements in family background of blacks. Consequently, the prospects for further narrowing the gap during the 21st century may depend more heavily on specific programs and policies than Gamoran had allowed. Whether standards-based reform will contribute positively to the closing of gaps depends on whether it is implemented realistically instead of outlandishly, whether resources are allocated strategically instead of perversely, and whether research provides better answers to questions about how to improve achievement for disadvantaged children.

CONCLUSION

We agree with the Forum's statement that,

> …[we] are committed to the No Child Left Behind Act's objectives of strong academic achievement for all children and closing the achievement gap. We believe that the federal government has a critical role to play in attaining these goals. We endorse the use of an accountability system that helps ensure that all children, including children of color, from low-income

families, with disabilities, and of limited English proficiency, are prepared to be successful, participating members of our democracy.

Although we believe achievement gaps can be reduced, the chapters in this book caution us that the types of changes recommended by the Forum will nonetheless not be sufficient to reduce, let alone eliminate the achievement gap. Useem's analysis of educational reform in Philadelphia suggests that NCLB has provided the impetus for systemic changes in the school system that show promise. Although we believe that the school-based reforms related to NCLB have the potential to reduce the achievement gaps, we return to our first point above. Without simultaneous efforts to reduce the pernicious effects of poverty on low-income children, "the 600 pound gorilla" will continue to prevent school based reforms from fully eliminating these gaps. Just as educational inequalities are caused by both factors inside and outside of schools, their solutions must be aimed both inside and outside the schoolhouse door

Note

1. The recommendations sections of this chapter are written by Dworkin (accountability and assessment), Hallinan (teachers and teacher quality), Scott (parental involvement and school choice) and the reduction of the achievement gaps (Gamoran). The other sections are written by Sadovnik.

References

Anyon, J. 2005a. *Radical possibilities: Public policy, urban education and a new social move*ment. New York: Routledge.
———. 2005b. What "counts" as educational policy? Notes toward a new paradigm. *Harvard Educational Review* 75 (1):65–88.
Arsen, D., D. Plank, and Sykes, G. 1999. *School choice in Michigan: The rules matter.* Ann Arbor, MI: Educational Policy Center. http://www.epc.msu.edu/Publications/RULES/SUMMARY. PDF (accessed August 10, 2006).
Berliner, D. 2006. Our impoverished view of educational reform. *Teachers College Record* 108 (6):949–95.
——— and Biddle, B. 1996. *The manufactured crisis.* New York: Longman.
Borko, Hilda. 2004. Professional development and teacher learning: Mapping the terrain. Presidential address delivered at annual meetings of the American Educational Research Association, San Diego, California, April.
Borman, G., G. Hewes, L. Overman, and S. Brown. 2003. Comprehensive school reform and student achievement: A meta-analysis. *Review of Educational Research* 73 (2):125–230.
Borman, K. M., P. W. Cookson, Jr., A. R. Sadovnik, and J. Z. Spade.1996. *Implementing educational reform: Sociological perspectives on educational policy.* Westport, CT.: Ablex.
Borman, K. M., G. Kersaint, T. Boydston, R. Lee, B. Cotner, K. Uekawa, G. Baber, J. Kromrey, and W. Katzenmeyer. 2004. *Meaningful urban education reform: Confronting the learning crises in mathematics and science.* Albany: SUNY Press.
Borsuk, A.. 2006.. MPS puts new focus on progress: "Value-added" data combines with test scores to rate schools' achievement. *Milwaukee Journal Sentinel,* January 11.
Center for Education Policy. 2006. *From the capital to the classroom: Year 4 of the No Child Left Behind Act,* March. Washington, D.C.: Center for Education Policy.
Coleman, James S., Ernest Q. Campbell, Carol F. Hobson, James M. McPartland, Alexander M.

Mood, Frederic D. Weinfeld, and Robert L. York. 1966. *Equality of educational opportunity.* Washington, D.C.: U.S. Government Printing Office.

Edmonds, R. (1979). Effective schools for the urban poor. *Educational Leadership* 37:15–27.

———.1982. Programs of school improvement: An overview. *Educational Leadership* 40:4–11.

Education Trust. 2005. *ESEA: Myths versus realities.* Washington D.C.: Education Trust.

Firestone, W. A., R. Y. Schorr, and L. A. Monfils. 2004. The ambiguity of teaching to the test: Standards, assessment, and educational reform.

Forum on Educational Accountability 2006. *Joint statement on No Child Left Behind.* Washington D.C.: National School Boards Association http://www.nsba (accessed July 11, 2006).

Friedman, M. 2002. *Capitalism and freedom.* 40th anniversary ed. Chicago: University of Chicago Press.

Gamoran, A. 2001. American schooling and education inequality: A forecast for the 21st Century. Extra issue, *Sociology of Education* 74:135–53.

Kim. J. S. and G. L. Sunderman. 2005. Measuring academic proficiency under the No Child Left Behind Act: Implications for educational equity. *Educational Researcher.* 34 (8): 3–13.

Lareau, A. 1989. *Home advantage: Social class and parental intervention in elementary education.* New York: Falmer Press.

———.2002. Invisible inequality: Social class and childrearing in black families and white families. *American Sociological Review* 67 (5):747–76.

———.2003. *Unequal childhood: Class, race and family life.* Los Angeles: University of California Press.

Long, D. A., S. Kelly, and A. Gamoran. 2006. *Whither the virtuous cycle? Past and future trends in black-white inequality in educational attainment.* Madison, WI: Wisconsin Center for Education Research.

Lubienski, C. and S. T. Lubienski. 2006. *Charter, private, and public schools and academic achievement: New evidence from NAEP mathematics data.* New York: National Center for the Study of Privatization in Education.

O'Day, J. A. 2002. Complexity, accountability, and school improvement. *Harvard Educational Review.* 72 (3):293–329.

Olson, L. 2005. NAEP gains are elusive in key areas: Friends and foes question NCLB law's effectiveness. *Education Week* October 26:1, 22–23.

Ravitch, D. (2000). *Left back: A century of failed school reforms.* New York: Simon & Schuster.

Riordan, C. 2003. *Equality and achievement: An introduction to the sociology of education,* 2nd ed. Boston: Allyn and Bacon.

Rothstein, R. 2004. *Class and schools: Using social, economic, and educational reform to close the black-white achievement gap.* New York: Teachers College Press.

Sadovnik, A. R., P. W. Cookson, and S. F. Semel. 2006. *Exploring education: An introduction to the foundations of education,* 3rd ed. Boston: Allyn and Bacon.

Thernstrom, A. and Thernstrom, S. (2003). *No excuses: Closing the racial gap in learning.* New York: Simon and Schuster.

Van Dunk, E. and E. Dickman. 2003. *School choice and the question of accountability.* New Haven, CT: Yale University Press.

Walford, G. 2001. Educational reform and sociology in England and Wales. In *Sociology and education: An encyclopedia,* ed. D. Levinson, P. W. Cookson, and A. R. Sadovnik, 211–20. New York: Routledge/Falmer.

Witte, J. F. (2000). *The market approach to education.* Princeton, NJ: Princeton University Press.

Contributors

David J. Armor is Professor of Public Policy at George Mason University. He has conducted research and written widely in the fields of education and education reform, school desegregation and related civil rights issues, and military manpower. He has consulted on and testified as an expert witness in more than 40 school desegregation and educational adequacy cases. In 1999 he was appointed to the National Academy of Science Committee on Military Recruiting. He is currently studying the effects of family vs. schools on academic achievement, supported by grants from various organizations.

Andrew A. Beveridge is Professor of Sociology at Queens College and the Graduate School and University of CUNY and chairs the Queens College, Sociology Department. He has published numerous articles and reports, as well as books. Since 1993, he has been a consultant to the New York Times, which has published many news reports and maps based upon his analysis of the Census data. He writes the demographic topic column for the Gotham Gazette, an online publication of the Citizens Union.

George W. Bohrnstedt is Senior Vice President for Research at AIR where he is involved in the development of new programs of research for the organization and brings a deep interest in education policy issues. Formerly, he was the Principal Investigator of the Bill and Melinda Gates Foundation-funded evaluation of their initiative to create small, personalized high schools and the Coprincipal Investigator of the evaluation of California's K–3 Class Size reduction program, prior to which he was the Principal Investigator of the evaluation of the College Board's Equity 2000 initiative. Dr. Bohrnstedt has served as coeditor of the American Sociological Association's yearbook, *Sociological Methodology* and also has been editor and coeditor of *Sociological Methods and Research* and *Social Psychology Quarterly.*

Jennifer Booher-Jennings is a doctoral candidate in Sociology at Columbia University. Her research focuses on the unintended consequences of accountability systems and the extent to which they reproduce inequality. Her publications include "Rationing Education in an Era of Accountability," in *Phi Delta Kappan* (2006*) and* "Below the Bubble: 'Educational Triage' and the Texas Accountability System," in *American Educational Research Journal* (2005).

Kathryn M. Borman is Professor of Anthropology and is affiliated with the Alliance for Applied Research in Education and Anthropology in the Department of Anthropology at the University of South Florida. She served as Principal Investigator of the NSF Project, Assessing the Impact of the National Science Foundation Urban Systemic Initiative, in which researchers assessed the systemic educational reform model in four cities. This study resulted in the authored SUNY Press book, *Meaningful Urban Education Reform: Confronting the Learning Crisis in Mathematics and Science in 2005.* Dr. Borman has authored or edited more than 20 books, book chapters, and series in areas involving educational policy and reform.

Steven Brint is Professor of Sociology and Education at the University of California, Riverside. He is the author of *The Diverted Dream* (with Jerome Karabel), *In an Age of Experts*, and *Schools and Societies*. He is also the editor of *The Future of the City of Intellect*. His research has won awards from the American Educational Research Association, the American Sociological Association, and the Council of Colleges and Universities. He is currently at work on a book about institutional change in American research universities.

A. Gary Dworkin is Professor of Sociology, cofounder of the Sociology of Education Research Group (SERG) at the University of Houston, and Editor of "The New Inequality Series" at SUNY Press. His publications include works on teacher burnout and student dropout behavior, minority–majority relations, and racial and ethnic stereotyping, gender roles, and the impact of accountability systems on student learning outcomes (coauthored with SERG colleagues and published by the Brookings Institution). He has recently published an essay on accountability and high-stakes testing under *No Child Left Behind* (*Sociology of Education* 2005). Dworkin and Lawrence J. Saha are coauthors of *The International Handbook on Research on Teachers and Teaching* (Springer, forthcoming).

Joyce L. Epstein is Director of the Center on School, Family, and Community Partnerships and the National Network of Partnership Schools (NNPS), Principal Research Scientist, and Research Professor of Sociology at Johns Hopkins University. She has over 100 publications on the nature and effects of school, family, and community connections. Recent books include: *School, Family, and Community Partnerships: Your Handbook for Action, Second Edition* (Corwin

Press, 2002) and *School, Family, and Community Partnerships: Preparing Educators and Improving Schools* (Westview Press, 2001). She is a recipient of the 2005 American Orthopsychiatric Association's Blanche F. Ittleson Award for scholarship and service to strengthen school and family connections. In all of her work, she is interested in the connections of research, policy, and practice.

Adam Gamoran is Professor of Sociology and Educational Policy Studies and Director of the Wisconsin Center for Education Research at the University of Wisconsin-Madison. His research has focused on educational inequality, school organization, and school reform, and he has published widely on these topics in the leading sociology and education journals. He has also coedited three books and is the lead author of *Transforming Teaching in Math and Science: How Schools and Districts Can Support Change* (Teachers College Press, 2003). Gamoran has been a visiting professor at the University of Edinburgh and at Tel Aviv University. A member of the National Academy of Education, he has served on a variety of national panels including the Board on International Comparative Studies of Education, and he currently serves on the National Research Council's Board on Science Education. His current studies include a large, school-based randomized trial in Los Angeles, designed to test the impact on elementary science achievement of an intensive teacher development program for inquiry-based science instruction.

Maureen Hallinan is the White Chair in Sociology and Director of the Center for Research on Educational Opportunity at the University of Notre Dame. Her research interests include the effects of school and classroom organization on student cognitive and social development. She is currently examining best practices in public and private schools. Her latest edited volume is *School Sector and Student Outcomes* (2006), and she is the editor of the *Handbook of Sociology of* Education (2000).

Richard M. Ingersoll, a former high school teacher is currently Professor of Education and Sociology at the University of Pennsylvania. Professor Ingersoll's research is concerned with the management and organization of elementary and secondary schools and the character and problems of the teaching occupation. Since the mid-1990s Dr. Ingersoll has done extensive research on the problems of teacher shortages and underqualified teachers. His research on these issues has been widely reported in the media and featured in numerous major education reports. Dr. Ingersoll has been invited to present his research to numerous federal, state, and local legislators and policymakers. In 2004 he received the Outstanding Writing Award from the American Association of Colleges for Teacher Education for his book, *Who Controls Teachers' Work? Power and Accountability in America's Schools* (Harvard University Press).

David Karen is Professor of Sociology at Bryn Mawr College. He has written extensively on differential access to higher education. An elected school board member in the Upper Merion Area School District, he deals regularly with NCLB stipulations issued from the U.S.and Pennsylvania Departments of Education. Professor Karen is currently doing research and writing in the fields of sociology of education and sociology of sport. Among his publications are "Toward a Political-Organizational Model of Gate-Keeping: The Case of Elite Colleges," *Sociology of Education* 63:227–40; "Achievement and Ascription in Admission to an Elite College: A Political-Organizational Analysis," *Sociological Forum* 6:349–80; "Politics of Race, Class, and Gender: Access to Higher Education in the United States, 1960–1986," *American Journal of Education* 99:208–37; "Changes in Access to Higher Education in the United States: 1980–1992," *Sociology of Education* 75:191–210.

Douglas Lee Lauen is an Assistant Professor of Public Policy at University of North Carolina, Chapel Hill who specializes in educational policy, research methods, and urban school reform. His doctoral dissertation examined the causes and consequences of school choice in Chicago.

Kerstin Carlson Le Floch is a Principal Research Analyst with the American Institutes for Research (AIR) who specializes in studies of accountability and school improvement. Since 2004, her work has focused almost exclusively on the implementation of the core components of No Child Left Behind. At present, Dr. Le Floch directs the Study of State Implementation of Accountability and Teacher Quality under NCLB (SSI-NCLB) and is Deputy Director on the National Longitudinal Study of No Child Left Behind (NLS-NCLB), both for the U.S. Department of Education.

Jon Lorence is Associate Professor of Sociology at the University of Houston and a cofounder of the Sociology or Education Research Group (SERG) at the University of Houston. He is interested in educational issues pertaining to the impact of grade retention on student academic achievement, determinants of teacher effectiveness, and the evaluation of education programs. His recent articles have appeared in *Review of Policy Research* and *International Education Journal.*

Milbrey W. McLaughlin is the David Jacks Professor of Education and Public Policy and Codirector of the Center for Research on the Context of Teaching at Stanford University. She is the author or coauthor of books, articles, and chapters on education policy issues, contexts for teaching and learning, productive environments for youth, and community-based organizations. Her recent books include: *Building School-Based Teacher Learning Communities* (with Joan Talbert) (Teachers College Press, 2006); *School Districts and Instructional Renewal* (with Amy Hightower, Michael Knapp, and Julie Marsh) (Teachers College Press, 2002); *Communities of Practice and the Work of High School Teaching* (with Joan Talbert)

(University of Chicago Press, 2001); *Community Counts: How Youth Organizations Matter For Youth Development* (Public Education Fund Network, 2000).

Mary Haywood Metz is Professor of Educational Policy Studies at the University of Wisconsin in Madison. The author of *Classrooms and Corridors: The Crisis of Authority in Desegregated Secondary Schools* (University of California Press, 1978) and *Different by Design: The Context and Character of Three Magnet Schools* (Teachers College Press, 2003), she is a sociologist who uses qualitative methods to study classrooms, schools, and school districts. Her current work concerns the use of both "old" and "new" institutional theory together with qualitative studies from diverse disciplines to develop better models of school organization. She is also involved in a project of tracing the multiple paths through which community social class affects the internal life and work of schools.

Roslyn Arlin Mickelson is Professor of Sociology at the University of North Carolina, Charlotte. Among her many publications are *Children on the Streets in the Americas: Globalization, Poverty, and Education in the US, Brazil, and Cuba* (2000); "Gender, Bourdieu, and the Anomaly of Women's Achievement Redux," Sociology of Education (2003); "What Constitutes Racial Discrimination in Education? A Social Science Perspective," *Teachers College Record* (2003); and "Subverting Swann: First- and Second- Generation Segregation in Charlotte, North Carolina," *American Educational Research Journal* (2001).

Jennifer A. O'Day is a Managing Research Scientist and policy analyst in the Education Program of the American Institutes for Research. Dr. O'Day has carried out research and written extensively in the areas of systemic standards-based reform, educational equity, and capacity building strategies. Much of Dr. O'Day's recent research has centered on accountability policies and school improvement efforts, particularly in high poverty, low-performing schools. In this vein, Dr. O'Day has served as Principal Investigator/Project Director for a series of national, state, and district studies, covering such topics as Title I accountability under both IASA and NCLB, the implementation and effects of California's Public School Accountability Act of 1999, and district interventions in low performing schools in Chicago and San Diego. Dr. O'Day is currently leading a four-year investigation of the effects of site-based leadership and professional learning opportunities on instructional practices and student achievement in San Diego City Schools.

James E. Rosenbaum is Professor of Sociology, Education, and Social Policy at Northwestern University. He has advised the Chicago public schools and the Chicago mayor's office on educational issues. His books include *Crossing the Class and Color Lines* (University of Chicago Press, 2000) and *Beyond College for All* (Russell Sage Foundation, 2001), which was awarded the Waller Prize in Sociology of Education, *After Admission: From College Access to College Success,* a study of community colleges (2006). He has also studied the Gautreaux housing mobility program. His research has been published in sociology and policy journals, and has been reported in the *New York Times*, the *Washington Post*, the *Wall Street Journal, Fortune Magazine, Chronicle of Higher Education,* and *Sixty Minutes.*

Alan R. Sadovnik is Professor of Education, Sociology, and Public Affairs at Rutgers University, Newark, New Jersey. He is the author of *Equity and Excellence in Higher Education* (1995); coauthor of *Exploring Education: An Introduction to the Foundations of Education* (1994, 2001, 2006); editor of *Knowledge and Pedagogy: The Sociology of Basil Bernstein* (1995) and *Sociology of Education: A Critical Reader (2007)*; and coeditor of *Exploring Society* (1987), *International Handbook of Educational Reform* (1992), *Implementing Educational Reform: Sociological Perspectives on Educational Reform* (1995), *"Schools of Tomorrow," Schools of Today: What Happened to Progressive Education* (1999, 2005), *Sociology and Education: An Encyclopedia* (2002); and *Founding Mothers and Others: Women Educational Leaders During the Progressive Era* (2002).

Janelle Scott is an Assistant Professor at New York University's Steinhardt School of Education in the Department of Administration, Leadership, and Technology. A former urban elementary school teacher, Scott earned a PhD in Education Policy from the University of California, Los Angeles, Graduate School of Education and Information Studies. Scott studies the politics of urban education with an emphasis on issues of race, class, and equity. Research areas include charter schools, educational privatization, and the impact of school choice reforms on high poverty communities of color. She is the editor of *School Choice and Student Diversity: What the Evidence Says* (Teachers College Press, 2005).

Steven B. Sheldon is an Associate Research Scientist with the Center on School, Family, and Community Partnerships at Johns Hopkins University. He studies the development of family and community involvement programs in school, and the impact of these programs on student outcomes. He also conducts research into the influences on parental involvement including parental beliefs, parents' social relationships, and school outreach. Currently, Dr. Sheldon is working on a project collecting data from parents and students to study the effects of parents' social networks on their involvement in their children's education, as well as the effects of parent involvement on student achievement and attitudes toward school.

Stephanie Southworth is a doctoral candidate in educational and public policy at the University of North Carolina, Charlotte. She is the coauthor (2005) of "When Opting-Out is Not a Choice; Implications for NCLB from Charlotte, North Carolina," *Equity & Excellence in Education* 38:1–15.

Christopher B. Swanson is the Director of the Research Center for Editorial Projects in Education Inc. He was formerly a researcher at the Urban Institute, where he authored numerous reports on statewide and national graduation rates.

Joan E. Talbert is Senior Research Scholar and Codirector of the Center for Research on the Context of Teaching (CRC, founded in 1987) in Stanford University's School of Education. She has a PhD in Sociology from the University of Washington and conducts research on teacher professional communities and careers, school organization and change, embedded contexts of teaching, and district system reform. Her recent books and articles include *Building School-based Teacher Learning Communities in Schools: Professional Strategies to Improve Student Achievement,* (with Milbrey W. McLaughlin: Teachers College Press, 2006*)*; *Professional Communities and the Work of High School Teaching* (with Milbrey W. McLaughlin; University of Chicago Press, 2001); "Conceptions of evidence use in school districts: Mapping the terrain" (with C. E. Coburn in *American Journal of Education,* 2006); "Professionalism and politics in high school teaching reform" (*Journal of Educational Change,* 2003); and "Reforming Districts" (with M. McLaughlin), *Center for the Study of Teaching and Policy,* 2003.

Sue Teele is the Director of Education Extension at University of California, Riverside. She administers a minimum of 800 courses annually to over 10,000 educators per year. She has created a spatial inventory entitled *The Teele Inventory for Multiple Intelligence* (TIMI), which is used in over 10,000 locations and in thirty-five countries. This inventory can be used with children as young as two years of age to gain an understanding of how they learn. She has written five books, the last three are *The Multiple Intelligences School: A Place For All Students to Succeed, Rainbows of Intelligences: Exploring How Students Learn* (Corwin, 2000) and *Overcoming Barricades to Reading: A Multiple Intelligence Approach* (Corwin, 2004).

Elizabeth Useem is a Senior Research Consultant to Research for Action, a non-profit education research firm located in Philadelphia where she is one of the principal researchers on a multi-year project, Learning from Philadelphia's School Reform. From 1993 to 2004, she was Director of Research and Evaluation at the Philadelphia Education Fund where she conducted studies in teacher quality and supply, comprehensive secondary school reform, and teacher professional development. Prior to coming to PEF, she was Director of Teacher Education at Bryn Mawr College and Haverford College. She spent 21 years as a faculty member in the Sociology Departments of Boston State College and the University of Massachusetts at Boston. Her doctorate is from the Harvard Graduate School of Education.

Katie Weitz White is a doctoral student in the Human Development and Social Policy program at Northwestern University. After graduating from Carleton College with a degree in political science, she taught in Chicago area schools for five years. Katie earned her Master of Arts degree from Northwestern and a Master of Education degree from DePaul University. Currently, she is on leave and working with the Sherwood Foundation to improve Omaha Public Schools.

Index

lack of progress in Philadelphia school
reform, 309
Enrollment data, as basis of graduation rate
reporting, 57
Entrenched interests, opposition to reform
implementation, 204
Epstein, Joyce L., 376–377
Equal proficiency
vs. achievement growth as goal, 324, 338
difficulty of accelerating for minority
children, 325
lack of knowledge on attaining for all
groups, 323, 339
Equality of educational opportunity
NCLB as reaffirmation of, 343–344
stratification and, 203–205
symbolic similarity of schools and, 344–348
Equality of outcomes, NCLB promises of, 349
Equity Plan, in CMS schools, 231
Equity Plus II schools, 231, 236
Ethnographic methods, in Chicago study, 100
Evidence-based practice, 26
Exceptions. *See also* Exemptions
district requests for, 17
Exemplary schools, 89, 90, 259
exemption from Texas accountability
standards, 245
risk of benefits loss from accepting low-
achieving students, 245
in Texas Accountability System, 250, 251
Exemptions
district requests for, 17
in Houston Independent School District
(HISD), 77–78
incentive systems and gaming strategies, 78–79
likely outcome of extending, 79
strategic use in Houston, 81
study data and methods, 79–80
study discussion and implications, 90–92
study results, 80–90
Expectancy perception, 124
Expectancy theory, 124
Experienced teachers
criticism of NCLB by, 137–138, 142
demonstration of content knowledge by,
121–122
likelihood of out-of-field teaching by, 166
and out-of-field teaching, 163
practice of rewarding with preferred class
assignments, 183
role in teacher learning communities, 185
External control, 35

ambiguous gains by Philadelphia schools
under, 309, 312
influence over internal operations, 27
top-down, 39

F
Facilitators
district leaders as, 274
for professional change, 190, 197–198
role in teacher learning community
development, 187–191
Failing students, dispersion throughout all
Texas schools, 262
Familial factors
as cause of achievement gap, 323, 327–330
and cognitive inequality, 361
effect on age 5 PPVT, 329
effects on Michigan math scores, 340
effects on South Carolina math scores, 339
influence on cognitive skills, 326–327
racial differences in, 330
role in achievement gap, 9
Familial involvement. *See* Parental
involvement
Familial partnerships. *See also* Parental
involvement
schools' progress on, 274
Family Choice Plan, 230–231
achievement and concentrated poverty with,
233
over- and underutilization of school
facilities with, 233–235
parents' failure to use choice options,
235–237
termination of, 237
Family structure, effects on achievement gap,
328, 329
Federal control, 11
and achievement gap reduction, 295
expansion into teacher quality, 6
Illinois state law limitations on, 219
and inability to ensure uniform interstate
standards, 222
incursion into local educational policy, 204
limitations on forcing compliance, 219–220,
221–222
perception as intrusion, 25
and possible withdrawal of Utah, 325
relative newness of, 14
Federal educational policy, xi, 4, 11, 359–360
Federal funds, insufficiency for testing
activities, 349

Social inequalities
  ESEA promise to redress, 2
  role in achievement gap, 9
Social norms
  challenges for school culture change,
    185–186
  resources for cultural change, 197–198
  and teacher learning communities, 195
Social promotion
  termination in CPS, 213
  termination in Texas, 252
Social studies, curtailment in accountability
    culture, 106
Social systems, districts as, 3
Socioeconomic status (SES), 37
  association with perceived rewards in
    Chicago example, 99
  as determinant of student performance, 3
  and reduced association between race/
    ethnicity and test scores, 19
  relationship to achievement gap, 333
  relative unimportance with teacher learning
    communities, 180
  and response at school level, 36
  vs. role of other family factors in
    achievement gap, 328
  of schools vs. individual students, 233
Sociology
  potential contributions to NCLB debate,
    xi, 2–4
  tendency to ignore potential contributions
    of, 13
South Carolina
  poor graduation rate standing, 55
  resource measures and achievement gap,
    333
  school vs. family effects on middle school
    math scores, 339
South Shore High School, 214
Southern California
  study data and methods, 133–135
  study results, 135–145
  teacher comments on NCLB, 6, 131–133
Southworth, Stephanie, 380
Special education students
  classifying students as, 78
  disaggregation of test scores in HISD study,
    86
  disproportionate representation in Chicago
    schools, 214
  exempted vs. imputed pass rates in HISD, 89
  exemptions for, 77

in HISD, 80
increased classification since accountability,
  102
likelihood of taking high-stakes test, 81
subgroups among, 84
and teacher shortages in Philadelphia, 308
unintended long-term cost consequences,
  111
Specialist teachers. See also Out-of-field
    teaching
  effects on achievement gap, 332
  refocusing on tested subjects only, 108
Specificity, 38, 42
Spheres of influence, spheres of overlapping,
  282
Staffing practices, 177
  and teacher quality, 158
  and teacher unions, 158–159
  trade-offs in, 174
Standardized tests, 36
  centrality of, 146–147
  complaints about excessive, 324–325
  costs of administering and recording, 349
  demands for quicker processing of, 210
  negative effect on teacher learning
    communities, 189
  in Philadelphia school reform, 309
  reliance on, 35
  testing schedules, 221
  in Texas Accountability System, 249
  tying to receipt of federal funds, 16
  unprecedented demand for gains in, 350
Standards-based reform, 2
  with Goals 2000, 15
  inability to benefit disadvantaged students
    only, 337
  questionable effects on closure of
    achievement gap, 336–337
Stanford Achievement Test, 86, 92
  as low-stakes alternative test, 80
  relationship with TAKS test-taking, 82
State autonomy, 117–118
  in defining accountable students, 79, 362
  effects on pass rates with, 91
  gaming strategies and, 82–90
  in graduation rate determination, 54, 56
  and tinkering with AYP definitions, 127
State AYP results, 69–70
  selected results for alternative simulations,
    71
  in simulated model system, 72–74
  three-state comparisons, 73–74